# FROM PARNELL TO

# From
# Parnell to Paisley

## Constitutional and Revolutionary
## Politics in Modern Ireland

*Edited by*

CAOIMHE NIC DHÁIBHÉID
COLIN REID

*To Granny Scott,*
*With much love,*

*Colin*      *Caoimhe*

26. V. 2010

IRISH ACADEMIC PRESS
DUBLIN • PORTLAND, OR

*First published in 2010 by Irish Academic Press*

| | |
|---|---|
| 2 Brookside | 920 NE 58th Avenue, Suite 300 |
| Dundrum Road | Portland, Oregon, |
| Dublin 14, Ireland | 97213-3786, USA |

This edition © 2010 Irish Academic Press
Individual Chapters © Contributors

**www.iap.ie**

British Library Cataloguing in Publication Data
An entry can be found on request

978 0 7165 3061 9 (cloth)
978 0 7165 3062 6 (paper)

Library of Congress Cataloging-in-Publication Data
An entry can be found on request

Printed by Good News Digital Books, Ongar, Essex

# Contents

# Acknowledgements

This book began as a conference of the same title, held at the Institute of Irish Studies, Queen's University Belfast, in September 2008. For support in organising the conference, we wish to thank the Irish Studies International Research Initiative and the School of Politics, International Studies and Philosophy, Queen's University Belfast. We would like to record our appreciation to all those who participated in the conference. We are extremely grateful for the advice of Roy Foster, Matt Kelly, Peter Leppard, Ian McBride, James McConnel and Mike Wheatley. The forbearance and support of Lisa Hyde at Irish Academic Press has been immense throughout. We are most especially grateful for the advice, encouragement and friendship of Richard English, without whom none of this would have been possible.

Caoimhe Nic Dháibhéid and Colin Reid
March 2010

# Contributors

JOHN BORGONOVO is an American based at University College Cork, where he recently completed his doctoral dissertation entitled 'Evolution of a Revolution: Cork City, 1916–18'. He is the author of *Spies, Informers, and the Anti-Sinn Féin Society: The Intelligence War in Cork City 1920–1921* (Irish Academic Press, 2007), and edited *Florence and Josephine O'Donoghue's War of Independence* (Irish Academic Press, 2006).

FRANCES FLANAGAN is a DPhil candidate and senior scholar at Hertford College, Oxford, and she is working on the thesis 'Your Dream not Mine: Nationalist Disillusionment and the Memory of Revolution in the Irish Free State'. She holds a BA and an LLB from the University of Western Australia, and her research interests include the uses of memory and history in Ireland, political violence, transitional justice and the relationship between nationalism and law in Ireland and Australia.

JAMES GREER is completing a PhD in the School of Politics, International Studies and Philosophy at Queen's University Belfast. His doctoral research is concerned with the development of Ulster unionism from the civil rights crisis of the 1960s through to the early stages of the Troubles, with particular concentration on the exploration of local variations. His wider areas of interest include British government policy towards Ireland, devolution and identity in Britain, and the interaction between popular culture and the Northern Irish conflict.

STEPHEN KELLY is a final-year PhD candidate at University College Dublin. He also holds a BA and MA from UCD. His doctoral thesis is entitled 'Fianna Fáil and the Ulster Question, 1938–1966', and his research interests include nineteenth- and twentieth-century Irish history, with an emphasis on British–Irish and north–south relations.

MICHAEL KEYES completed his PhD, 'Money and Nationalist Politics in Nineteenth-Century Ireland: From O'Connell to Parnell', as a Government of Ireland Scholar at NUI Maynooth, and is currently combining research with the delivery of a course in modern Irish history at NUI Maynooth.

SHAUN McDAID completed an MA in the History of International Relations at University College Dublin in 2004, and recently finished a PhD in Modern History at Queen's University Belfast. His thesis examined British–Irish relations from 1972 to 1975. He has published a book chapter on Ulster unionism in the 1970s, and forthcoming publications include an article on the Irish Labour Party in *Irish Political Studies*. He is primarily interested in twentieth-century British and Irish political and diplomatic history.

CAOIMHE NIC DHÁIBHÉID is a post-doctoral research fellow at the Institute of Irish Studies, Queen's University Belfast. Her doctoral thesis examined the republican career of Seán MacBride, and she is preparing a monograph on the same topic for publication in 2011.

MARGARET O'CALLAGHAN teaches in the School of Politics, Philosophy and International Studies at Queen's University of Belfast. Her publications include *British High Politics and a Nationalist Ireland: Criminality, Land and the Law under Forster and Balfour* (Cork, 1994) and recent articles on the politics of Irish history-writing, Roger Casement and the British empire, and Richard Pigott and the fringe-Fenian press. She is also co-editor of *1916 in 1966: Commemorating the Easter Rising* (Dublin, 2007).

SIMON PRINCE is a research fellow at Queen's University Belfast. He was both an undergraduate and a postgraduate at St John's College, Cambridge, before taking up a junior research fellowship at Lady Margaret Hall, Oxford. He is the author of *Northern Ireland's '68: Civil Rights, Global Revolt and the Origins of the Troubles* (Irish Academic Press, 2007) as well as numerous articles on Northern Ireland and the Sixties.

COLIN REID is an Irish Research Council for the Humanities and Social Sciences post-doctoral fellow at NUI Maynooth. He was previously the Irish Government Senior Scholar at Hertford College, Oxford. His first monograph, a biography of Stephen Gwynn, is forthcoming.

ANDREW SANDERS is Professor of History at Seattle University. A PhD graduate of Queen's University Belfast, he has written on several aspects of Northern Irish politics and history and his first book, *Inside the IRA: Splits and Splinter Groups*, is forthcoming with Edinburgh University Press.

# Foreword

## RICHARD ENGLISH

Revolutionary and constitutional politics in modern Ireland have very often been considered, but the great strength of this compelling book is to address each tradition – the violent and the parliamentary – with sustained, simultaneous consideration also of the other. In doing, so the editors have put together an excellent team of younger scholars, whose powerful chapters suggest that the study of modern Ireland is in talented hands.

Central to the book's implied argument is the complex, fluid relationship between these two persistent approaches towards the pursuit of political change. As the editors rightly say in their thoughtful Introduction, 'neither constitutional nor revolutionary methods can always be considered in isolation'. So the eleven case studies in the book respond to the challenge of understanding the interactions and tensions and mutual influences and surprises involved in the revolutionary and the constitutional in modern Ireland.

Much of it involves local or individual analysis. James Greer's valuable local study of Ian Paisley's politics plausibly presents the famous preacher as having embodied a more malleable, even pragmatic, politics than some still assume to have been the case. Frances Flanagan offers a compelling chapter on P .S. O'Hegarty's shift from pre-revolutionary optimism to after-the-event disillusionment. Drawing on research from her illuminating Oxford DPhil thesis, she reinforces here a frequent Irish story of global resonance: the tendency of revolutionary violence to change the world but not as its agents intended or anticipated.

The individual is helpfully central too in Shaun McDaid's impressive interrogation of the able but awkward David Thornley, and his scrutiny of the striking evolution of Thornley's own attitudes towards political violence in Ireland. Likewise, Stephen Kelly's reassessment of the pragmatic Sean Lemass in relation to the North, Margaret O'Callaghan's literarily-inclined, fascinating depiction of Tom Kettle, and John Borgonovo's exploration of the 1918 General Election in Cork, all demonstrate the value of the closely-focused chapter-length study.

Some chapters opt for a wider-angled lens. Colin Reid's careful reflection on the Irish Party's relationship with the Irish Volunteers during 1913-16 suggests that the Party's demise originated significantly in its own risky war-time strategic choices; Michael Keyes considers funding and finance in the Parnellite story; Simon Prince's stringent research on non-violence in the civil rights era presents ultimately gloomy findings about the attempts of various wings of Irish nationalism to break away from futility; Caoimhe Nic Dháibhéid's valuable study of Fianna Fáil's attitude towards the IRA during the Second World War details an important phase in that party's shift from revolutionary instinct to governmental responsibility; and Andrew Sanders's fresh and internationally-contextualized examination of Sinn Féin's transition towards parliamentary rather than more conspiratorial forms of assembly reflects the vital reality that it was only once the Provisionals had shifted away from armed struggle that their political party became the dominant voice of nationalism in the North (a corrective to the still persistent popular notion that Northern Irish politics embody the victory of the violent or the extreme).

This book emerged from a thoughtfully-constructed and very successful conference held at Queen's University, Belfast, late in 2008, and it shows just what can be done when very talented young scholars innovatively address subjects of enduring, enigmatic importance by means of high-quality research, argument and writing. *From Parnell to Paisley* represents a major contribution to the understanding of modern Irish history, and as such it deserves to be very widely read.

Richard English
Belfast, March 2010

# Introduction:
# The Constitutional and
# Revolutionary Histories
# of Modern Ireland

CAOIMHE NIC DHÁIBHÉID and COLIN REID

In 1910, Frank Hugh O'Donnell, nationalist maverick and contro-versialist, published his monomaniacal *A History of the Irish Parliamentary Party*. O'Donnell stressed his own importance in formulating the 'New Departure', the agreement between constitutional and revolutionary Irish nationalism that defined the early years of Charles Stewart Parnell's leadership of the Irish Party. In 1877, O'Donnell, then an Irish Party lieutenant, sat across the negotiating table from a Fenian delegation, of whom he asked, 'You wish to know, gentlemen, how an insurrectionary party and a constitutional but masculine policy can co-operate? The simplest thing in the world.'[1] O'Donnell, however, rapidly became disillusioned by the Parnellite revolution, which linked land agitation to the constitutional struggle for Home Rule; his self-serving *History* laments the downfall of Isaac Butt and the earlier, more inclusive nationalist campaign. O'Donnell's opposition to Parnellism, though, had little to do with the violent tendencies of Fenianism; he relished retelling the tale of the coming together of what he called 'the voice and sword'.[2] The voice and the sword are the themes of this book: the blurring of the constitutional and the revolutionary, as described by O'Donnell, has been a frequent occurrence through modern Irish history.

No fixed definitions can be positioned in any discussion of 'constitutional' and 'revolutionary' impulses in the history of Irish political

culture. Constitutional methods can be interpreted as operating primarily within the boundaries of parliamentary structures. This implies
a general acceptance of the state apparatus, even if this is being fer-
vently opposed. Thus the Nationalist Party after partition sporadically
took their seats in the Northern Irish Parliament, opposing the unionist state, and the entire basis on which it was constructed, from within.
Similarly, Fianna Fáil accepted the oath and entered Dáil Éireann
in 1927, implicitly recognising the state structures while working to
entirely reconfigure them. The suitability of the term 'revolution' in
modern Ireland has attracted significant historiographical attention,
particularly in relation to what has come to be known as the 'Irish
Revolution', *circa* 1916–23.[3] This is a considerable grey area; for
example, civil disobedience may be a non-violent act, but it is revolutionary in its intent. For the purposes of this book, though, the terms
of reference of the term 'revolutionary' are understood to encompass
all forms of violent and/or radical political activity. 'Revolutionary',
therefore, should not merely be conceived of in terms of the overthrow
of an *ancien régime*, nor should it necessarily imply a commitment to
a transformation of existing social structures. Rather, the peculiarly
Irish interpretations of the dictums of revolution often merely signify
the indiscriminate and unflinching use of extreme violence for political ends. Ireland has a long and ignoble tradition of political violence,
and it is in this sense that the use of 'revolutionary' is intended.

As the chapters of this book demonstrate, however, neither constitutional nor revolutionary methods can always be considered in isolation.
One of the most striking features of modern Irish history is the extent
to which constitutional and revolutionary manifestations have
appeared as two sides of the same coin. Indeed, one has blurred into
the other, often with emphatically successful results. When Danny
Morrison uttered one of the most famous dictums during the recent
Northern Troubles – 'with a ballot paper in this hand, and an Armalite
in this hand, we [will] take power in Ireland' – he memorably
verbalised a dramatically altered Provisional republicanism; but this
was nothing new within the longer span of Irish history. The Home
Rule crisis of 1912–14 and the growth of private paramilitary forces
attached to constitutional political parties is an earlier example of the
blurring of the 'voice and sword'.

This blurring, moreover, does not merely apply to constitutional
parties with violent appendages; questions of civil disobedience and
other extraparliamentary methods also occupy a median position
between the constitutional and the revolutionary axes in Irish history.

The political campaigns for Catholic emancipation and repeal led by Daniel O'Connell were ostensibly peaceable but were conducted through parliamentary and extra-parliamentary channels. This latter strain carried a deliberately threatening charge; the monster meetings that defined the O'Connellite enterprise were characterised by bellicose language and peaceful dispersal of the vast assemblies. The implication that the crowds could be turned to non-peaceful activities, should O'Connell so wish, was not lost on the British authorities. A further example of the obscured boundaries between constitutional and revolutionary modes of action came later in the nineteenth century, with the activities of the Land League. Here agrarian radicalism was overtly politicised by its twinning with the national question under the leadership of Charles Stewart Parnell. The Land League mobilised Irish peasantry into a centralised campaign of civil disobedience; the darker, violent side of land agitation persisted, however, with the continuing spectre of agrarian crime.[4] Of course, the most powerful example of civil disobedience in modern Ireland is the civil rights campaign of the 1960s in the North. An apparently non-violent mass mobilisation confronted the Unionist establishment in a campaign for justice in housing allocation, reform of the local election franchise and fair employment practices. Here, too, the shadow of violence lay heavily across the wider movement; the idealistic spirit of '68, as Simon Prince outlines in this volume, unleashed forces that were beyond the control of its leaders. While constitutional movements can at times act as safety-valves at revolutionary moments, it is not always clear if the fluid boundaries that have existed between parliamentary and violent methods can necessarily be controlled or kept in check by constitutional parties. Recent work by Timothy Bowman, for example, has demonstrated that Sir Edward Carson and the Ulster Unionist leadership did not exert complete control over the Ulster Volunteer Force on the eve of the Great War.[5]

This last point leads us to consider the constitutional and revolutionary traditions within unionism in Ireland. In its most basic form, unionism stands for the maintenance of the union between Britain and Ireland (later Northern Ireland). Unionism, therefore, is more concerned with a remembered utopian past than with an imagined utopian future.[6] Unlike nationalism, unionism has not expressed a desire for an alternative political constitutional reality; that it does not imply any reimagining of existing political structures should not, however, preclude a consideration of its militant aspects. In fact, the determination to preserve or recreate the idealised previous political

structures goes some way to explain the belligerence of hard-line unionism. As hinted at above, the UVF during the third Home Rule crisis
offers a case in point. Unionist opposition to Home Rule – a programme for limited self-government in Ireland – was fierce and took
many forms. The most prominent of these was the fusion of constitutional and revolutionary methods with the establishment of the Ulster
Volunteer Force under the control of the Ulster Unionist Party leadership. The Unionist Party deployed the voice and the sword in their
struggle against Home Rule – and by implication against the British
government that passed the Home Rule legislation. Unionism, therefore, set itself in violent opposition to the state in order to maintain the
existing constitutional arrangements.[7] The UVF was the ultimate
political show, the vehicle to bring militant loyalists more directly
under the control of Carson, who could then deploy the *threat* of force
to gain political leverage.[8] Taken on these terms, it was a remarkably
successful approach: clearly Ulster could not be coerced into a Home
Rule settlement. But the logic of politicised private armies could
equally have ushered in a sectarian conflict of immense proportions in
Ireland; indeed, the consequences of the dangerous precedent set by
the UVF can be traced throughout the violence that engulfed Ireland
over the subsequent decade. Carson was interested in channelling the
rhetoric of threat, but this ignored realities on the ground: hardliners
within the UVF were clearly ready to fight.[9]

How has the threat and/or the use of violence been justified? Here,
notions of legitimacy are entangled with political morality as well as
political expediency. Daniel O'Connell presented himself as the moderate leader representing the most militant nationalist opinion in Ireland. It was in the British government's interest to do business with
him, he argued, rather than face the alternative.[10] This was a political
argument that combined moral force with self-interest. Parnell was
skilled in utilising this trick, too, and such rhetoric can be found in the
political discourse of contemporary Northern Ireland. Sinn Féin justi-
fications for IRA violence during the recent Troubles tended overwhelmingly to be centred on the rhetoric of war, granting a
Clausewitzean legitimacy to campaigns of assassination and terror.
Gerry Adams's response to the IRA's murder of Lord Mountbatten, an
elderly female relative and two teenage boys in Sligo Bay in 1979 is a
case in point: 'What the IRA did to him is what Mountbatten had been
doing all his life to other people; and with his war record, I don't think
he could have objected to dying in what was clearly a war situation.'[11]
Conversely, the manipulation of violent connections has been used to

a strikingly effective extent by Provisional Sinn Féin during the protracted negotiations leading to the Belfast and St Andrew's Agreements, particularly in relation to the issue of decommissioning of IRA weaponry. The leadership of Sinn Féin exploited the implicit threat of the IRA retaining arms in order to extract further concessions from the British government. Of course, there were a number of other factors impeding progress on the decommissioning issue, particularly relating to the need to appease hardliners within the republican movement and 'selling' the decommissioning process to the support base. Just as the decommissioning issue needed to be 'sold' to the IRA rank and file, so too has the entire meaning of the armed struggle been skilfully manipulated in the era of the peace process. Adams, again, has been adept at reshaping the recent republican past into a teleological march towards the Good Friday Agreement, even if the provisions therein fall decidedly short of republican core principles. During his speech at the Sinn Féin Ard-Fheis in 2007, he ascribed the success of his party to

> the courage and resilience of thousands of people who have given the best years of their lives to the republican cause ... our struggle is rooted in their sacrifice. But these heroes were always about the future. The great advances of our time are built on their efforts.[12]

While the functional, political fruits of violence may for some excuse, justify or even recommend its use,[13] the human cost, for victims and the bereaved as well as for wider society, carries a terrible legacy.

The proponents of political violence in Ireland have frequently claimed popular sanction for their actions. The War of Independence of 1919–21, for instance, was book-ended by elections in 1918 and 1921, and the results of these two elections have been interpreted by republicans as giving anticipatory and retrospective legitimacy to violent opposition to the British state in Ireland. Discussion of the legacy of Sinn Féin's massive electoral victory in 1918 is fraught with moral ambiguities. Sinn Féin won 73 from a total of 105 seats; but what, exactly, did this mandate entail? Paul Bew has asked a number of penetrating questions of the superficially clear-cut 1918 results – was this a vote for a 32-county Irish republic? Did this imply coercion of Ulster? Was this a vote for a republic at all? Was this a mandate for violence?[14] Answers to these questions are not straightforward, and have enormous implications for interpreting the subsequent War of Independence. The legitimacy of the IRA's armed campaign against the British state in Ireland, according to republicans such as the gunman *par excellence* Dan Breen, came

from the 1918 election.[15] Senior republicans, however, such as P.S.
O'Hegarty (whose retrospective analysis of the War of Independence
is discussed in this book by Frances Flanagan), later queried whether
the vote in 1918 had actually endorsed the subsequent violent campaign: it was 'questionable whether the Irish people, when they voted
Sinn Féin, knew they were voting for war; it is questionable whether,
if they did, they would have so voted.'[16] Sinn Féin again dominated
the 1921 poll, which returned the much revered Second Dáil. The Second Dáil has occupied a sanctified place in republican conceptions of
legitimacy: the later twentieth-century incarnations of the IRA trace
their lineages to the last surviving members of the 1921 assembly, the
final parliament in Ireland before the hated Anglo-Irish Treaty.[17] The
democratic basis of this supposed legitimacy can, however, be queried.
The 1921 elections, officially the first to the two institutions – north
and south – established under the Government of Ireland Act, were
not contested outside of Northern Ireland. Sinn Féin won 124 unopposed seats in the south. Not a vote was cast; hardly a 'referendum for
[the party's] own policy', as Alan O'Day has argued.[18] Claims of democratic or constitutional endorsements of violent or revolutionary programmes are, as we have seen, inherently problematic.

That said, constitutional expressions of revolutionary positions have
been one of the defining characteristics of Irish political culture. Fenian
ideology in the nineteenth century was hostile to parliamentary politics,
but Isaac Butt's Home Rule initiative of the 1870s was the subject of a
three-year trial for constitutionalism by the IRB.[19] For some Fenians, this
went beyond three years. James McConnel has delineated the presence
of a number of ex-Fenians within the Edwardian Irish Parliamentary
Party. This, he argues, does not signify a renewal of the 'New Departure'
entente; rather, the 'aging band of ex-rebels' served more as a living
link to the purity of revolution.[20] Both of the two main southern Irish
political parties, Fianna Fáil and Fine Gael, were born from revolution, and many within the parties' membership had blood-stained
hands. Such a taint should not altogether be seen as a hindrance to
electoral prowess; rather, a good fighting record was often viewed as
an essential contribution to political advancement. For instance,
Éamon de Valera's early political success (for Sinn Féin) in large part
rested on his command of Boland's Mills during the Easter Rising,
while Seán Lemass, de Valera's successor as leader of Fianna Fáil, was
very likely to have been one of the young IRA gunmen who took part
in the systematic assassination of British agents on 'Bloody Sunday' in
November 1920. The two men, however, adopted drastically different

approaches to their war record. Lemass never publicly admitted his involvement in the events of Bloody Sunday, which is perhaps indicative of a certain ambivalence, or regret, towards the violence that engulfed Ireland in the early 1920s. In contrast, the early election literature of de Valera emphasised his military prowess.[21] While such a divergence is partly driven by the periodisation of the two men's leadership – de Valera in the turbulence of revolution and its aftermath; Lemass in the more sober post-war era – it is equally ascribable to a fundamental difference in the two men's political temperaments and visions. In fact, Lemass's leadership of the Fianna Fáil party can be read as an attempt to undo de Valera's Ireland on a number of fronts. One such example can be found in this volume, where Stephen Kelly explores the changing tone of political language towards Northern Ireland that took place during Lemass's stewardship. While de Valera and his followers in what would become Fianna Fáil had a relatively long period of transition to acceptance of the constitutional norms of the new Irish Free State during their years in the political wilderness following the civil war, the pro-treaty side, in contrast, had to effect an abrupt turnaround from gunmen to statesmen – not that they did not have gunmen aplenty in their ranks. Yet the success of Cumann na nGaedheal, the Irish Free State's first governing party, lies in the fluidity of this transition: the revolution, imperfect and incomplete, was nevertheless consolidated constitutionally.[22]

For both parties, however, this constitutional consolidation did not entirely efface the inherent problems of a violent state formation. The difficulty of commemorating the state's insurgent past has produced, as David Fitzpatrick has asserted, 'a chronicle of embarrassment'.[23] The nature of Irish political culture is such that the imperative of commemoration is deeply inscribed both north and south of the border: more often than not, commemorations are utilised for contemporary political purposes. The centenary and bicentenary commemorations of the 1798 rebellion offer a striking case in point. The 1898 commemorations served as a rallying point for various shades of 'advanced' nationalism amidst the demoralising aftermath of the Parnell split.[24] In contrast, the legacy of 1798 in 1998 was officially manipulated to boost the peace process in Northern Ireland, with the sectarian tensions of eighteenth-century Ireland played down and the 'cross-community' appeal of the United Irishmen emphasised. As Roy Foster mordantly observed, it was a case of 'don't talk about the war'.[25] The most famous relic of the 1798 rebellion is, of course, Wolfe Tone, whose grave in Bodenstown, county Kildare, has been the site of republican pilgrimage since the 1840s. As the nationalist movement splintered in the wake of the Treaty split, and increasingly fragmented through the remainder of the twentieth century, so the number of rival Bodenstown ceremonies multiplied. Since the formation of independent Ireland, Tone's sleep has been disturbed by various parties seeking to appropriate his legacy. These have included, but are not limited to, Cumann na nGaedheal, Sinn Féin, Fianna Fáil, Provisional Sinn Féin, Republican Sinn Féin, the Irish Republican Socialist Party and the Workers' Party. Given Tone's express intention to 'unite Catholic, Protestant and Dissenter under the common name of Irishman', the competing ceremonies carry an ironic force which apparently eludes their devotees. Taking into account, however, that the senior Democratic Unionist Party politician, Nelson McCausland, has recently stressed that the project of the United Irishmen was for closer union with Great Britain, to the extent that most became unionists after 1800, one wonders whether a DUP delegation might tread the same path to Bodenstown in the future – thus incongruously fulfilling Tone's 'unionist' vision for Ireland.[26]

As the example of Tone illustrates, the revolutionary dead occupy a sacred space in Irish political culture. Writing of the 'great show of pomp' at the funeral of Fenian John O'Leary, James Joyce struck an ambivalent tone: 'the Irish, even when they break the hearts of those who sacrificed their lives for their country, never fail to show a great reverence for the dead'.[27] Nowhere is this reverence more visible than in the case of the Easter Rising of 1916. The Rising is the self-proclaimed foundation stone of the southern state, the memory of which has become an intrinsic component of Irish life, through the countless railway stations, streets and bridges named after the dead. Indeed the construction of the Ballymun Towers in the 1960s took this tendency to a new high, with the seven high-rises named after the seven signatories of the Proclamation of the Irish Republic (six of the towers have since been demolished; it is a delicious irony that the last one standing is named after the sickly, consumptive Joseph Mary Plunkett). Much of the commemorative zeal surrounding the 1916 Rising occurred around its fiftieth anniversary; Conor Cruise O'Brien forcefully connected the state-sponsored activities and official exhortations to 'recapture the spirit of 1916' with the recurrence of violence in the north from 1969 onwards.[28] As with remembering 1798, the historical legacy of 1916 can at times be problematic. When conflict engulfed Northern Ireland in the late 1960s, the celebration of insurgency became somewhat embarrassing for the Dublin government, prompting the abandonment of official 1916 commemorative parades in 1971. The constitutional southern government found it difficult to celebrate its foundational revolutionary moment when the values which underpinned that moment were perceived to be fomenting violent revolution across the border. It is no coincidence that the resurrection of the military parade on Easter Sunday came as recently as 2006, with the peace process embedded. It was not for entirely altruistic motives that the Fianna Fáil-led government sponsored this revival; rather, it was to reassert their republican credentials against the rise of Sinn Féin in the south. At times, then, commemoration of the past can be understood in relation to the present; the past is explicitly enlisted in the service of the present.

If the logic of Irish nationalist culture, as the writer Francis Hackett observed in 1920, means that 'the history of Irish freedom now dates from 1916', the dictums of this revolutionary year zero necessarily exclude the constitutionalist thread of much of the Irish political tradition.[29] As David Fitzpatrick has pointed out, in the first decades of independence, 'no government cared to claim the inheritance of the Repeal or Home Rule movements'.[30] The grand statues of Daniel O'Connell and Charles Stewart Parnell that stand in the centre of Dublin were erected by popular subscription *before* independence; the legacies of O'Connell, Butt, Parnell and Redmond have largely been ignored by their revolutionary successors. Echoing Hackett, as far as public consciousness is concerned in the Republic of Ireland, independence was born from a seven-day armed rebellion; the long nineteenth-century constitutional struggle for self-government, which attracted the support of the vast majority of Irish people, has been discredited. John Redmond's reputation, in particular, has suffered: it was his misfortune to be leader of Irish nationalism at the time of the Great War and the Easter Rising. It was only in the 1990s, with the publication of Paul Bew's *Ideology and the Irish Question*, that the Redmondite strategy was rehabilitated in a scholarly manner. On becoming Taoiseach in 1994, the Fine Gael leader John Bruton incurred the wrath of Fianna Fáil by replacing the portrait of Patrick Pearse over his desk with one of Redmond. His successor in office, Fianna Fáil's Bertie Ahern, ostentatiously reversed Bruton's gesture, suggesting that Redmond's portrait had no place in the highest office of the Republic of Ireland.[31] In a state born of violence, remembering both its constitutional and revolutionary pasts raises difficult questions about political legitimacy and historical legacies.

This book offers eleven case studies of the revolutionary and constitutional political traditions in Ireland. With the time span book-ended by Parnell and Paisley, each chapter offers an insight into the difficulties, paradoxes and continuities of revolutionary and constitutional politics. Michael Keyes delves into the financing of Parnellism, revealing the importance of money in guiding political strategy in the context of the 'New Departure'. The murky world of political funding has been underexplored in the historiography of nineteenth-century Ireland; Keyes offers a much needed corrective to this oversight, highlighting Parnellism's transnational make-up and the implications of American money in the shaping of Irish nationalism's ideological and strategic positioning. With the blessing of the Fenians, Parnellism combined constitutional struggle with agrarian agitation, radically departing from Isaac Butt's purely parliamentary strategy of the 1870s. The legacy of this transition continued to reverberate in the Edwardian Irish Party, under the leadership of John Redmond. Colin Reid sketches a focal point of the Home Rule crisis of 1912–14, the foundation and evolution of the Irish Volunteers. Formed independently of the Irish Party, the Volunteers altered the tone of the Ulster crisis, representing a potential vehicle of civil war and bloodshed. As Reid shows, the Irish Party's belated appropriation of the private army was beset with problems: Redmond was not able to use the Volunteers to gain political leverage, while the Edwardian 'cult of the gun' ultimately served to undermine his leadership of nationalist Ireland.

The Redmondite tradition of constitutional nationalism – one that envisaged a self-governing Ireland at the heart of the British empire – was the great loser of the revolution of 1916 to 1923. In her chapter, Margaret O'Callaghan examines the prehistory of this defeat through a biographical lens, taking as a subject the nationalist politician, economist and cultural activist, Tom Kettle. Kettle offers a Redmondite twist on the 'cult of the gun' epitomised by the Volunteers: like Redmond, Kettle fundamentally believed in the righteousness of the Great War and the cleansing effect that blood spilt on the killing fields of Europe could have on Irish politics. Ultimately, though, the blood spilt on the streets of Dublin was to become more important in state formation and political success. The Irish Party, tired and discredited in Ireland, was destroyed in the 1918 general election by Sinn Féin, which represented a more militant, anti-imperial nationalism. John Borgonovo charts the contest between the Irish Party and Sinn Féin on a micro level in his chapter on the 1918 election in Cork City. This adds local colour to the national question, illuminating the ambiguities of the Sinn Féin position; the party knew what it was against, but not always what it was for. Borgonovo presents a snapshot of the constitutional struggle for the hearts and minds of Irish nationalism in the capital of what was to become the most violent county during the War of Independence of 1919–21: a form of revolutionary constitutionalism won the day in Cork City in 1918, and the moderate programme of the Irish Party was repudiated.

The revolution of 1916–23, like all constitutional upheavals, brought its own disputed legacies and historic residues. Frances Flanagan grapples with the memory of the revolution through the political writings of P.S. O'Hegarty, historian, cultural activist and IRB man. O'Hegarty's writings offer an idealistic critique of the realities of the Irish revolution, stressing the negative effects of the dilution of his brand of Edwardian Fenianism and the inherent dangers of a political insurrection by more than a select few. Flanagan's chapter probes his political thought, placing key texts such as *The Victory of Sinn Féin* into their intellectual context, and offers an insight into the memory of a discontented revolutionary. Discontented, but passive, revolutionaries are one thing; Caoimhe Nic Dháibhéid explores the persistence of revolutionary mindsets and violence in the constitutionally oriented Irish Free State, specifically during the external and internal crises precipitated by the Second World War. The determination of a formerly revolutionary party, Fianna Fáil, to face down the threat posed by violent republicanism from 1939 to 1945, enlisting extraordinary legal manoeuvres in pursuit of the overriding goal of safeguarding Irish sovereignty, illustrates the contradictions and inconsistencies inherent in Irish political culture when confronted with the vestiges of radical republicanism. Stephen Kelly probes the sensitivities of the politics of language in 1960s Ireland, when Taoiseach Seán Lemass attempted to unshackle southern discourse from the tired sabre rattling of anti-partitionism. In instigating a significant shift in terminology from the 'Six Counties' to 'Northern Ireland', and in instituting an explicit de facto recognition of the North as a separate political entity, Lemass aimed to thaw the long-frozen north–south relations. It took an impeccably revolutionary figure, with an unimpeachable pedigree, to effect this transition, particularly within the traditionally irredentist Fianna Fáil party.

The emergence of the Troubles in Northern Ireland from the late 1960s reignited the revolutionary tradition and left constitutional politics foundering. The adoption of a 'third road' approach characterised the early years of the civil rights movement; as Simon Prince outlines, explicit inspiration was drawn from international precedents and especially the use of non-violent direct action. But the limitations of this approach within the boundaries of national politics in Northern Ireland proved insurmountable. The upheavals of Northern Ireland's '68 revitalised nationalist politics, both of a constitutional and a revolutionary hue; not the anticipated result of the activists. The subsequent thirty years of violence, as well as extracting a dreadful human toll, caused significant ideological difficulties for political parties north and south. In his chapter, Shaun McDaid paints an illuminating portrait of one southern intellectual burned by the revolutionary North: the Irish Labour politician and Trinity historian David Thornley. McDaid examines the difficulties the Labour Party encountered in responding to the Northern crisis. Although alone among the main southern parties in that they did not spring from the revolutionary tradition, the Irish Labour Party did suffer from the challenges posed to southern political culture by the Provisional IRA. Thornley, in particular, offers a case study of the pro-Provisional wing within the Labour Party; as McDaid demonstrates, this wing was by no means dominant, and variety of opinion on the Northern question within the party was extremely wide.

The shift from the politics of revolution to constitutional methods during the 1980s is the theme of Andrew Sanders's chapter. Sanders charts the rise of a viable political programme within the Provisional movement following the hunger strikes. The electoral successes that Sinn Féin enjoyed demonstrated the Provisionals' ideological malleability: the abandonment of abstention represented a compromise of a revolutionary ideal in pursuit of practical political gains. The American response to the Northern Irish Troubles played a significant role in shaping Provisional strategy. The importance of the dollar, echoing Keyes's chapter on Parnellism, is emphasised by Sanders.

The final chapter of this book, by James Greer, switches attention to unionism in Northern Ireland, and charts the emergence and evolution of Paisleyism within its heartland of North Antrim. Underlining the value of the local study in understanding the nuances of national politics, Greer presents Ian Paisley as a radical alternative to established unionism. In fact, Paisleyism became the first widespread challenge to UUP hegemony from within the unionist bloc, combining the rural, the local, the urban, the secular and the fundamentalist. Paisley flirted with militant loyalism, but largely followed the constitutional path; the picture Greer paints is one of a political opportunist who combined firebrand fundamentalism – religious and political – with a certain flexibility, thus enabling his brand of unionism to shift from a minority protest position to a hegemonic force in North Antrim.

Ultimately, as the contributions to this book make clear, the demarcations between the constitutional and the revolutionary in modern Ireland are far from fixed. The degenerating force of violence remains a corrosive presence within the Irish body politic: while the northern state attempts to recover from the bloodshed of the last forty years, the southern state continues to grapple with the inherent stresses of a democratic, constitutional republic born of violent revolution. Although it has been stated that 'violence was the only way of securing a hearing for moderation',[32] the bitterness and divisiveness of Ireland's troubled legacies is a sobering reminder of the inherent dangers of confusing constitutional structures with revolutionary mentalities.

## NOTES

1. F.H. O'Donnell, *A History of the Irish Parliamentary Party*, 2 vols (London: Longman's, Green, 1910), vol. i, p.273.
2. Ibid., p.270.
3. For an introduction to this discussion, see Charles Townshend, 'Historiography: Telling the Irish Revolution' in Joost Augusteijn (ed.), *The Irish Revolution, 1913–1923* (Basingstoke: Palgrave, 2002), pp.1–16.
4. Philip Bull, *Land, Politics and Nationalism: A Study of the Irish Land Question* (Dublin: Gill & Macmillan, 1997).
5. Timothy Bowman, *Carson's Army: The Ulster Volunteer Force, 1910–1922* (Manchester: Manchester University Press, 2007), pp.77–8.
6. Ian McBride, *The Siege of Derry in Ulster Protestant Mythology* (Dublin: Four Courts Press, 1997); Alvin Jackson, 'Unionist Myths, 1912–1985', *Past and Present*, vol. 136 (August 1992), pp.164–85.
7. David W. Miller, *Queen's Rebels: Ulster Loyalism in Historical Perspective* (Dublin: Gill & Macmillan, 1978).
8. Alvin Jackson, *Sir Edward Carson* (Dundalk: Dundalgan Press, 1993), p.36.
9. Bowman, *Carson's Army*, p.94.
10. Maurice Goldring, *Pleasant the Scholar's Life: Irish Intellectuals and the Construction of the Nation State* (London: Serif, 1993), p.138.
11. Adams, quoted in *Time Magazine*, 14 November 1979.
12. Gerry Adams, speech to Sinn Féin Ard-Fheis, 3 March 2007, www.cain.ulst.ac.uk, accessed 25 January 2010.
13. David Miller, 'The Use and Abuse of Political Violence', *Political Studies*, vol. 32 (1984), p.402.
14. Paul Bew, *Ireland: The Politics of Enmity, 1789–2006* (Oxford: Oxford University Press, 2007), pp.390–2.
15. Dan Breen, *My Fight for Irish Freedom* (Dublin: Talbot Press, 1924), p.52.
16. P.S. O'Hegarty, *The Victory of Sinn Féin: How it Won it, and How it Used it* (Dublin: Talbot Press, 1924), p.38.
17. Richard English, *Armed Struggle: The History of the IRA* (London: Pan Books, 2004; first published 2003), p.214.
18. Alan O'Day, *Irish Home Rule, 1867–1921* (Manchester: Manchester University Press, 1998), pp.299–300.
19. David Thornley, *Isaac Butt and Home Rule* (London: MacGibbon & Kee, 1964), p.161.
20. James McConnel, '"Fenians at Westminster": The Edwardian Irish Parliamentary Party and the Legacy of the New Departure', *Irish Historical Studies*, vol. 34, no. 133 (2004), pp.42–64.
21. Anne Dolan, 'Killing and Bloody Sunday, November 1920', *Historical Journal*, vol. 49 no. 3 (2006), pp.789–810; Michael Laffan, *The Resurrection of Ireland: The Sinn Féin Party, 1916–1923* (Cambridge: Cambridge University Press, 2005; first published 1999), pp.108–12.

22. John M. Regan, *The Irish Counter-Revolution, 1921–1936: Treatyite Politics and Settlement in Independent Ireland* (Dublin: Gill & Macmillan, 1999).
23. David Fitzpatrick, 'Commemoration in the Irish Free State: A Chronicle of Embarrassment' in Ian McBride (ed.), *History and Memory in Modern Ireland* (Cambridge: Cambridge University Press, 2001), pp.184–203.
24. Senia Pašeta, '1798 in 1898: The Politics of Commemoration', *Irish Review*, no. 22 (1998), pp.46–53.
25. R.F. Foster, 'Remembering 1798' in *The Irish Story: Telling Tales and Making it up in Ireland* (London: Allen Lane, 2001), p.226.
26. Nelson McCausland's blog, 'The Minister's Pen', www.theministerspen.blogspot.com/2009/11/andrews-and-drennan.html, accessed 26 January 2010.
27. James Joyce, 'Fenianism: The Last Fenian' in *Occasional, Critical and Political Writing* (Oxford: Oxford University Press, 2000), pp.140–1.
28. Conor Cruise O'Brien, *States of Ireland* (London: Hutchinson, 1972), pp.150–1. For a wider consideration of the fiftieth anniversary of 1916, see Mary E. Daly and Margaret O'Callaghan (eds), *1916 in 1966: Commemorating the Easter Rising* (Dublin: Royal Irish Academy, 2007).
29. Francis Hackett, *Ireland: A Study in Nationalism*, fourth edition (New York: B.W. Huebsch, 1920; first published 1918), p.376.
30. Fitzpatrick, 'Commemoration in the Irish Free State', p.189.
31. Bew, *Politics of Enmity*, p.548.
32. William O'Brien, quoted in Conor Cruise O'Brien, *Parnell and his Party* (Oxford: Oxford University Press, 1957), p.69.

# CHAPTER ONE

# Parnellism:
# The Role of Funding in the Journey from the Semi-Revolutionary to the Purely Constitutional

## MICHAEL KEYES

At first glance, nineteenth-century Irish nationalism appears to have held a duality of expression, existing in both constitutional and revolutionary forms. One can point to the constitutional nationalism of O'Connell giving way to the revolutionary nationalism of Young Ireland, but it is important to remember that in this and subsequent shifts in nationalist expression, the dividing lines between the constitutional and the revolutionary were not always very distinct. Under the influence of O'Connell, Irish nationalism became broadly Catholic and firmly constitutional. O'Connell set his face against physical force in favour of moral force in his campaigns for emancipation, reform and repeal, but even here the lines between the purely constitutional and the revolutionary were blurred. O'Connell's mass movements of the 1820s and 1840s set out to win concessions by confronting the British government with a massive and controlled popular force; but there was also a veiled threat of civil disorder if the demands of that popular force were not met. From the ranks of the Repeal movement grew Young Ireland's more revolutionary brand of nationalism, which blossomed before the botched rebellion of 1848, sowing the seeds that would grow into the Tenant Right movement that supported the constitutionalism of the Independent Irish Party of the 1850s. The revolutionary tradition of 1848 also re-emerged in the shape of the Irish Republican Brother-hood. Fenianism in its purely revolutionary incarnation was defeated in 1867, but from the plight of its prisoners and the death of its martyrs sprung the Amnesty Association and the cross-fertilisation continued in the shape of Isaac Butt's Home Government Association, which managed for a time to accommodate all shades of nationalist sentiment: Catholic and Protestant, constitutional and Fenian. Butt's genteel constitutionalism harked back to the petitioning of the pre-O'Connell Catholic Committee; just as O'Connell had defied the cautious approach of the Catholic Committee, in the 1870s another ambitious young politician was to challenge Butt's polite petitioning with an impatient agitation. Charles Stewart Parnell was to the Irish Home Rule League what O'Connell was to the Catholic Committee – a wind of change – but in Parnell's case, the contemporaneous incarnation of revolutionary nationalism had found a leader in John Devoy, whose reasoned pragmatism brought him close enough to the constitutional movement to make a highly improbable alliance possible.

The 'New Departure' was essentially a plan by American Fenians to manipulate parliamentary nationalism and to exploit Parnell's political profile to boost their own organisation. Instead, they unwittingly provided Parnell with the means to develop a political movement that dwarfed and overtook their own. The American dollars to which Parnell gained access as a result of the New Departure were to become the engine of Parnellism: firstly as the Land League's war chest, and later to sustain a highly organised and successful parliamentary party.

The political events that unfolded in the years following the New Departure can only be fully grasped via an understanding of the motivational effects of money: funding heavily influenced political dynamics and the responses of key individuals. The flow of money must be followed from its origins in Irish America, where John Devoy's re-formed Fenian grouping, Clan na Gael, backed the New Departure, in the hope of fomenting insurrection in Ireland, by funding elements within the country that would stoke popular grievance. Parnell was to be their agent, rural distress became the grievance, and the Land League became the vehicle for the project.

The Land War of 1879–81 must, then, be considered in the light of this conscious determination to manipulate the difficulties of the Irish tenant farmer, using American money to achieve an outcome beyond the stated aims of the organisation being funded. Parnell used the American money as the 'sinews of war' for the Land League. That said, it was used strategically: not to win the Land War, nor to foment revolution, but to turn localised agrarian unrest into a broad popular movement. The twists and turns of this movement can be directly linked to the ebb and flow of American funding. Policy shifts that were designed to widen the appeal of the movement can be seen to involve the substitution of cash for genuine resolve and sacrifice on the part of the tenants. It can be argued that it was the guiding hand of Parnell that determined the direction of the movement, but it can be shown that money from abroad was the principal tool in this endeavour. This money created the illusion of unity and solidarity among Irish tenants, and it would be the limitations of the funding that would determine the tipping point when compromise became inevitable and Parnell retreated from the semi-revolutionary Land League.

The Land War was a resounding victory for Parnell. Constitutional nationalism had won out over revolutionary nationalism, and had done so using its own money. There was even a surplus, which Parnell would use for the next phase of his political plan: to fashion a model political party. American money was key to Parnell's success, and it continued to be critical to his plans as he progressed along the path of constitutional politics. It will be argued in this chapter that Parnell's dependence on revolutionary funding to progress a purely constitutional agenda was bound to compromise his plans. Try as he might to turn his back on the semi-revolutionary, it continued to complicate his political plans. Competition for funds, between constitutional and more revolutionary elements, contributed to the ultimate divisions that split the movement.

### AMERICAN DOLLARS TRANSFORM THE LAND LEAGUE INTO A NATIONAL MOVEMENT

Parnell once confided to his brother that politics was 'the only thing that ever made him any money'.[1] However, it was not for want of trying. In business, he was a risk-taker who embarked on a variety of unsuccessful ventures. His mining schemes, in particular, lost money and nearly caused him to lose his estate, Avondale; but one speculative venture he engaged in did pay dividends. The New Departure, like his business ventures, was a risky proposition. In business parlance, it appeared that in return for a capital investment, American Fenians were to take a shareholding in Parnell's parliamentary operation. Parnell saw in it the promise of American funds to assist in his efforts to take control of the Home Rule League. It was, of course, something of a Faustian pact, and Parnell quickly found himself leading a land war in the company of some strange bedfellows.

Parnell's political ambitions were at odds with those of Devoy, Michael Davitt and John Dillon. He was not a land agitator; he was a constitutional parliamentary politician whose priorities lay in building a strong Home Rule party in Westminster. His adoption of the cause of 'the Land for the people' has to be seen as a cynical political move to provide him with a springboard from which to launch a national political movement. It was a radical and risky strategy. Parnell used American money to replace Buttism with Parnellism, but in the process he was accused of polarising opinion and alienating Protestant support for Home Rule. Parnell's fellow obstructionist and later bitter critic, Frank Hugh O'Donnell, claimed 'that nothing is more certain than the fact that it has been the American money which destroyed the Home Rule of Isaac Butt'.[2] The sense of unease among the landed class that greeted Parnell's shift to the left was even reflected in the popular literature of the day. Bemoaning the radicalisation of the Home Rule movement, one of the characters in Anthony Trollope's novel *The Landleaguers* declared: 'the latter-day Home-Rulers, of whom I speak, brought their politics, their aspirations, and their money from New York'.[3] Parnell did, however, run the risk of ceding control to his new-found allies. The alliance of constitutional and revolutionary politics was an uneasy one, and from the outset his attempts to divert funds to aid his own parliamentary project were frustrated. Although Parnell was president of the Land League, he wielded very little power in the organisation in its early stages,[4] and he was not going to receive much support from his Land League colleagues in his efforts to build a strong parliamentary party.

Two of the decisions taken by the Land League at its founding conference on 21 October 1879 made this point abundantly clear. It was resolved '[t]hat the president of this League, Mr Parnell, be requested to proceed to America for the purpose of obtaining assistance from our exiled countrymen and other sympathisers for the objects for which this appeal is issued.' However, this resolution was immediately followed by one stating '[t]hat none of the funds of this League shall be used for the purchase of any landlord's interest in the land or for the furthering of the interests of any parliamentary candidate.'[5] According to Michael Davitt, this second resolution was influenced by American opinion: the more revolutionary the platform, the greater the support in America.[6] So it was that on 21 December 1879, when Parnell set sail for America, he was on his way to raise huge sums of money; none of it, however, for the purpose which he would have chosen.

One detects a certain uneasiness, an ambiguity as to who is using whom; but despite the strictures placed on the eventual use of the funds, Parnell threw himself into the fundraising with gusto. He tailored his message to his American audience in order to maximise the money raised, and he made statements on American platforms that he would not have made at home. Talk of severing the last link with Britain may have outraged British opinion, but in America it had the effect of boosting the flow of donations.[7] Parnell also defied his Clan na Gael hosts by insisting on collecting money for relief of distress as well as for purely political purposes. Using references to 'terrible famines sweeping across the face of our island',[8] he was able to play on the natural concerns of audiences who had been directly affected or whose lives had been shaped by the great tragedy of the 1840s. A purely political appeal would not have had the same effect on the purse strings, and by combining the plaintive appeal for aid with an allied request for the means to challenge the causes of the distress, Parnell managed to maximise the overall take from his tour. Between 14 January 1880 and 30 June 1880, £66,217 was received from America, of which £56,350 was specifically designated for the relief of distress, with the remaining £9,867 for the use of the Land League.[9]

When Parnell returned from America to fight the 1880 general election, his frustration continued. The Land League's antipathy towards parliamentary politics meant that only £2,000 was advanced to Parnell to fight the election, showing that the constitutional was still very much subservient to the semi-revolutionary.[10] Parnell knew the value of the money raised in America, however, and he understood that indirect benefits would accrue to him when that money was spent in Ireland. According to Davitt, the administration of the relief funds was used successfully to develop the organisation of the League and to involve the clergy in its activities.

> The distribution of relief and of seed potatoes in the most distressed districts gave the organisation a growing prestige, especially among the clergy ... Where no League organisation existed the parish priest, or curate, was made the medium for the distribution of grants, the result being, in most instances of this kind, the formation of a branch of the movement.[11]

The distribution of the money by the League added to its popularity and to Parnell's; just as O'Connell had bound the priests into his organisation by getting them to collect money, Parnell achieved the same result by getting them to distribute money.

The operation of the Land War was in itself an exercise in the subversion of funds subscribed for a semi-revolutionary movement, instead using those funds to reorientate and deradicalise that movement. Parnell used the American money to turn localised agrarian unrest into a broad popular movement. The Land League moved from its western radical agrarian base into Munster and Leinster, cultivating the same political constituency that had sustained O'Connell – the Catholic middle class – and it was money that facilitated this shift from radicalism to safer conservative ground.

The policy adopted by the League to appeal to these more substantial grazier farmers of Munster and Leinster involved using the American money to minimise the sacrifice required of farmers who, with bigger holdings, had more to gain in terms of rent reductions but also had more to lose should they be evicted. The policy was referred to as 'rent at the point of a bayonet', a term that resonates with images of resolute resistance. In truth this term was something of a sham, to use the word Anna Parnell was later to apply to the Land War in general.[12] The new policy asked only that farmers delay paying their rent rather than refuse to pay. When the legal process ran its course and eviction loomed, the farmer could then pay the rent 'at the point of a bayonet' and the League would pay the legal costs incurred. The Land League found it easier to secure the support of the bigger farmers for this almost painless form of resistance. It was, of course, expensive, and could not have been sustained without the generosity of Irish America.

At the other end of the spectrum, money was also the key to bringing poorer tenants along with the movement. Most of the evicted tenants financially supported by the League had not been evicted because they supported League principles, but because they were unable to pay their rent. Anna Parnell maintained that when the Ladies' Land League took over operations in October 1881, all the applications for relief came from what were termed 'poverty cases', and she found no cases where the eviction was due to Land League policy.[13] It was through this benevolent expenditure that the League maintained its support among the poorer tenants, while attracting the support of the stronger farmers by covering their costs and averting eviction. Land League resources were now divided between two very different types of expenditure; as long as it had the resources to keep up the payments, it was possible to gloss over the great differences between the two categories of beneficiaries.

The levels of expenditure, however, could not be sustained. By June 1881 the League was devouring resources at the rate of £2,700 a month;[14] against that, contributions to the Land League from the tenantry could be as low as £163 a month.[15] Correspondence between the League and its branches gives the impression of something akin to a highly organised insurance company paying out on claims, except that the premiums of the beneficiaries could in no way fund the constant payouts. With next to nothing being contributed by the branches, there was an almost complete dependence on external funding, and there seemed to be an impression that America would provide an inexhaustible flow of money. Patrick Egan complained to the *Irish World* that 'one of the bishops a while ago stated that there was £300,000 in the fund and the clergy seem to act as if these exaggerated statements were true'.[16] Of course, it suited the League to encourage the belief that tenants could, and would, be supported. John Dillon spoke of 'a considerable organisation' in America that would supply evicted tenants with a 'steady income'.[17] Certainly, the American organisation did provide approximately 90 per cent of the £261,000 received in total by the League, and without it there could have been no Land War. The League would not have been able to substitute cash for genuine resolve and sacrifice on the part of the tenants in order to widen the appeal of the movement; but such was the model the Land League had created, that the more successful it became, the more funding it required.[18]

### INCREASING COSTS PRECIPITATE A RETREAT TO CONSTITUTIONAL POLITICS

When demand inevitably outstripped supply, the League tried to cut costs. It replaced 'rent at the point of a bayonet' with the policy of 'letting the farms go'. Rather than paying the tenant's costs and staving off eviction, the League now expected the tenant to resist, up to and including eviction. Tim Healy pointed out that the League could no longer afford to pay out cash to what were, in effect, charity cases.[19] The new policy had the distinct disadvantage of demanding real sacrifice from the tenants and many, particularly the stronger farmers in Munster, were loath to give up their farms, while the smaller tenants in the west were disgruntled as a result of the League's increasing reluctance to assist evicted tenants on the grounds that their eviction was due to arrears. The need to conserve funds strained support for the League within its two distinct tenant groupings.

The American money had allowed for rapid and painless growth, but for this very reason an organisation that had favoured real resistance now had a soft underbelly, which was open to compromise. If the agitation was wavering before the passing of the 1881 Land Act, then its passing signalled a headlong rush to benefit from its concessions. The semblance of unity and solidarity among the tenantry was now shattered, and the reaction to the Land Act put the unity of the entire movement at risk. Parnell played a masterful political game in these difficult circumstances. He had to promote concession while appearing belligerent, and he did this to such good effect that he managed to hold the movement together. The real force of the Land League agitation was spent by the middle of 1881, but in order to cover his retreat to constitutional politics, Parnell continued to fan the dying embers of the agitation for a further year. Having convinced the doubters to accept the Land Act 'on approval', he then proceeded with a series of belligerent speeches to deflect attention from the compromise. The fact that the speeches led to his imprisonment only added to the effect Parnell sought to achieve, and thus secured for him martyrdom status, which appealed very much to his American supporters.[20]

The next move was cynicism itself. The 'no rent manifesto' issued from Kilmainham Jail by Parnell and his Land League colleagues called on their now disunited and leaderless foot soldiers to embark on a course that, even when the agitation was at its peak, the organisation had not dared to suggest. The no rent manifesto can be described as a call to arms issued by a retreating general, and Anna Parnell, writing in 1907, summed it up very well: 'Ostensibly a measure of retaliation for the practical suppression of the Land League; in reality it was the only cover under which they could withdraw from the impossible position they had created for themselves, and at the same time keep up some semblance of a continuous policy.'[21] Applying the law of diminishing returns, Parnell had realised that he had proceeded as far as this expensive model of political agitation could permit. Turning back to constitutional politics, he used the Ladies' Land League to ensure that the retreat did not become a collapse.

It proved to be an effective but expensive withdrawal, for under the Ladies' Land League the expenditure continued to increase. In just over eight months, between December 1881 and September 1882, the Ladies' Land League spent £69,372 5s 10d, while the Land League, over its almost two years of operation, had expended no more than £71,256 19s 4d.[22] At an average of £2,000 per week, the Ladies' Land League had almost quadrupled expenditure. Apart from the fact that such levels of expenditure could not be sustained, in Parnell's eyes this was now money wasted. The agitation and the American funds had served their purpose, and it was time to suspend the former in order to preserve what remained of the latter. Soon the ladies found their requests for advances from Patrick Egan, Land League treasurer, being ignored. They were, according to Anna Parnell, 'to make the bricks, but henceforth to make them without straw'.[23]

Having forced the Ladies' Land League out of existence by starving them of funds, Parnell placed the £31,900 that remained of the League's funds in a Paris bank under his own personal control. In the same month, October 1882, he replaced the Land League with the Irish National League, retaining the benefits of the old organisation while carefully ensuring that the new organisation was bound to, and controlled by, the parliamentary party. The new League would not be autonomous, nor would it be agrarian. The programme approved at its foundation conference placed 'national self-government' as its first objective, with 'land-law reform' relegated to second place.[24] The transformation was now complete. Parnell had extinguished the semi-revolutionary and replaced it with an entirely constitutional movement, the organisation and funding of which were under his control.

## PARNELL STRUGGLES TO FIND A DEPENDABLE STREAM OF FUNDING

Try as Parnell might to put the agitation behind him, it continued to hamper his progress long after the seemingly decisive victory of parliamentary politics in October 1882. The problems revolved around funding. Parnell had secured what remained of the Land League money, and when he dissolved the Ladies Land League, he seemed to have stopped the leeching of resources to the land agitation. However, after October 1882 there were still 470 evicted families: the collateral damage from the land war, who remained in need of assistance. A special fund, the Mansion House Evicted Tenants' Fund, was set up to provide for them, but it failed to attract adequate support. In the early months of 1883, the fund was issuing grants to evicted tenants at a rate five times greater than it was receiving contributions. The Irish National League was therefore forced to provide for the tenants from its own hopelessly inadequate resources.[25] Members of the Irish National League were required to pay an annual subscription that 'shall be at a rate of 1s for every £5 valuation, and in no case shall it be less than 1s or more than £1'. Of this, 'the treasurer of each branch shall forward 75 per cent of all subscriptions received' to head office.[26] However, no more than had been the case with the Land League, the new organisation never showed any signs of delivering significant funds to head office. On 17 January 1883, three months after its establishment, the League's treasurer, Alfred Webb, reported that receipts amounted to £1,723 8s 11d, but it was noted 'that 343 country branches had been formed to date but only 200 have complied with the fundamental rule of the League, namely to send up 75 per cent of the money received to the central committee'.[27]

Parnell was now faced with three interlinked funding-related problems. Firstly, the Irish National League carried on the Land League tradition of failing to generate adequate funding to sustain itself from within its own membership. Secondly, what little money the League did generate was being swallowed up by the demands of the evicted tenants. Finally, and most critically, was his almost total dependence on American funding, the providers of which were not keen to follow his lead into constitutional politics. Having provided almost £250,000 to the various Land League funds between 1879 and 1882, American support dropped to a mere £3,322 in 1883.[28] The rapid shift to the right during 1882 had alienated much of the American support, but in early 1883 Parnell attempted to put the American organisation on a sound footing by replacing the American Land League with the Irish National League of America. If he had hoped to produce in America an organisation that mirrored the disciplined and docile League he had created in Ireland, he was to be sorely disappointed. Parnell's ability to shape the destiny of such an organisation in America had always been extremely limited, but he may have held out hope that he could re-assert some degree of control. He had planned to go there in person to launch the new League; unfortunately for Parnell, the League in America came to be dominated by the 'triangle' – three members of Clan na Gael led by Alexander O'Sullivan. When an unseemly squabble erupted between the opposing O'Sullivan and Devoy camps at a meeting held to plan for Parnell's visit, it proved too much for the Irish leader and he cancelled his trip.[29]

With O'Sullivan as its president, Parnell could not count on support from the American League for his constitutional aims, and the chasm between the two wings of the organisation on either side of the Atlantic now seemed as great politically as it was geographically. As leader of the parliamentary party, Parnell could not appear to be too closely linked to Americans accused of supporting the dynamite campaign in Britain. Indeed, American support and funding would remain conspicuous by its absence. In the first six months of its existence, the National League received a mere £937 from America, or less than £40 per week. This compared to £2,297 or just under £100 per week from the Irish branches, and a very respectable £1,050, or an average of £40 per week, from Australia and New Zealand.[30] All in all, however, less than £200 per week was not the level of funding that would drive a burgeoning political movement. While Parnell had successfully used American money to gain control of the movement in Ireland, and to guide it into constitutional politics, he had failed to gain control over the source of his funding.

Parnell needed to establish an alternative stream of funding in order to sustain his parliamentary party, and he needed to ring-fence it from the persistent demands of the evicted tenants. His instincts in early 1883 were to look beyond the League to the individual constituencies, suggesting that local subventions might be raised to cover the parliamentary expenses of an Irish Party MP. He cited Queen's County and other constituencies where something of this nature had been undertaken. He stressed the need for such support, saying that otherwise 'I certainly should not continue to ask members to place themselves in a false position of undertaking duties which they are not financially able to carry out, and I should be obliged to consider on my own part whether I could persevere with the thankless task of endeavouring to keep together an independent Irish party.'[31] A number of constituencies took up the idea, but the results were disappointing. Queen's County only managed to raise half of the £1,000 they had hoped for, but the notion of paying MPs had begun to take hold.[32] At a public meeting held in Limerick on 13 May, the Reverend D. Humphries said it was 'essential to strengthen Mr Parnell's hand by giving him supporters he could rely on and that until the country paid its representatives they could not expect good men to sacrifice their time and means in Parliament'.[33]

The disappointing results from the constituency-based initiative pointed to the need for a more dependable system for supporting MPs. Through 1883 and 1884, Parnell did manage to strengthen his parliamentary party by winning a series of by-elections, but this was done on a very tight budget. In March 1885 he set up the Irish Parliamentary Fund to raise funds for purely parliamentary purposes. Initially the fund was operated under the auspices of the National League, but in November 1885 Parnell placed the money under his own direct control, safe from the evicted tenants. It was thereafter completely independent of the National League, and for the first time Parnell had a source of political funding that was sacrosanct.

With the general election looming, an appeal for funds was issued to America. If Parnell were to maximise his party's potential to win seats in the election, he would need American money to boost the parliamentary fund. He seems to have succeeded in bringing the American leadership around to the idea that Home Rule was achievable; when Patrick Egan relayed his appeal to the branches of the Irish National League of America in June 1885, it had the effect of breaching the funding log jam. Irish American money began to flow in from late 1885. The Parliamentary Fund provided funds for most of the eighty contested seats, and while the amount contributed to the cost of winning an individual seat was relatively modest, ranging from £100 in West Wicklow to £325 in Mid-Tyrone, cumulatively the cost of the general election, according to the accounts of the Parliamentary Fund, came to a hefty £14,610.[34] If one takes the period from the launch of the Parliamentary Fund in Ireland in March 1885 to the end of the year, a time frame that includes the general election, the total receipts were £19,415, of which only £415 came from Ireland. Approximately £1,000 came from Australia and the balance came from America.[35] It can be said, therefore, that the 1885 election, resulting in an unprecedented eighty-six seats for the Irish Party, was funded more or less exclusively by American money.

The prospect of Home Rule had united the vast majority of the Irish electorate behind Parnell. Irish America, despite its internal divisions and more radical leanings, had also been won over to Parnell's aggressive constitutional approach. If Irish America's conversion to constitutional politics were to be measured in monetary terms, then the conclusion would have to be that it was complete. In the four-month period between May and August 1886, America provided the Parliamentary Fund with an incredible £66,152. The conversion was, however, short-lived, and when the Tories won the July 1886 election and Home Rule was shelved, Parnell once again lost the support of Irish America. At the Irish National League of America convention in Chicago in August 1886, the moderate Devoy camp failed to unseat the 'triangle'-backed Patrick Egan. The funding, like the monsoon rains, was gone again as quickly as it had come, but not before Parnell had salted away another £52,293 in a second Paris account.

The existence of the Parisian reserve fund was immediately significant: Parnell stood at the head of a political machine, the Irish Parliamentary Party, with eighty-six MPs, approximately half of whom he was providing with a salary of £200 a year. It was a political model that delivered a tightly-disciplined political party, but at a cost; and it was castigated by Parnell's opponents. Frank Hugh O'Donnell denounced 'the dishonourable hiring or rewarding of indigent followers at the hands of a dominant colleague', saying that by means of it, a dominant clique 'could manufacture and maintain a poor-box majority out of the pauper tail of the party, and in the name of discipline fasten the yoke of foreign finance upon the honest section of the representation'.[36] In all, the cost of running Parnell's 'poor-box majority' ran close to £30,000 per annum in the years between 1886 and 1890. In that same period the annual income of the Parliamentary Fund dropped to £10,763 in 1887, £9,377 in 1888, and £6,213 in 1889. In order to maintain the party, Parnell was forced to draw on the Paris funds to the tune of £34,500 over the four years.[37] Meanwhile, the land question again took centre stage in Ireland, and once more Parnell struggled to preserve funds for constitutional politics against competing demands from the semi-revolutionary land agitation.

### THE 'PLAN OF CAMPAIGN' GENERATES COMPETITION FOR RESOURCES AND DIVISION

For four years Parnell had striven to turn the organisation away from campaigns that won favour in one quarter but alienated others. The measure of his achievement in this regard was the fact that he oversaw a movement that drew its funding from American Fenians, while simultaneously being the official representative in Westminster of the Catholic Church in Ireland. A return to any form of land war would inevitably upset this precarious equilibrium, and, on a more basic level, such a direction would inevitably consume his new-found financial reserves. With this in mind, Parnell issued an appeal to the League in America for subscriptions in support of an anti-eviction fund, but the American response was slow in coming. The National League of America sent no remittance to Ireland until 20 December 1886, when £5,000 was dispatched.[38]

Parnell seems to have accepted that the land question could not be ignored, but he did everything in his power to curtail the extent of the agitation and its expense, particularly in the light of the poor response from America. The 'Plan of Campaign', published on 23 October 1886, was ostensibly self-funding, the idea being that tenants would pool their rent in a fund that would be administered locally, usually by the Catholic clergy, for the benefit of the tenants in their struggle with their landlords.[39] This aspect of the plan worked well in its first year, but Parnell pointed out a flaw in its operation to William O'Brien in December 1886. 'What will you do for money?' he asked O'Brien; 'You will never succeed in collecting your rents a second year.' O'Brien seems to have conceded this point, but added optimistically that if the landlords engaged in wholesale evictions, America would come to their aid with funds.[40]

Parnell was right and O'Brien was wrong: receipts from the tenants tailed off in the early months of 1887 and America failed to take up the slack. The £5,000 received from America in December 1886 did not herald a flood of funding for the plan, and it was more than six months before a further remittance of £5,000 was received from the National League of America.[41] America did not appear to be prepared to bankroll the second phase of the Land War with the same level of enthusiasm it had shown during 1880–2; worse, the money now being directed towards the anti-eviction fund was money that would otherwise have gone to the parliamentary party. In the twelve months from the launch of the 'Plan of Campaign', the parliamentary fund received a mere £34 from America.[42] Not only had the political focus been diverted from the parliamentary party, so had its life blood: the American money.

By December 1887 the plan was in financial difficulties. John Dillon vented his frustration to Tim Harrington over what he perceived as Parnell's neglect of the plan:

> He plainly means to boycott us till the opening of parliament at all events ... but it is an extraordinary line of policy to go off without a word – and most of all without, so far as I know, making any arrangement to secure that we shall not be stranded for money ... It will be simply monstrous if we run short of money in a crisis like this.[43]

Dillon's comments betray a naivety born out of the 'money no object' approach to the land agitation in the early days of the Land League. He clearly assumed that Parnell had access to ample means to assist the plan, and his comments betray no awareness of any reason why Parnell might be disinclined to support the agitation. He did not seem to grasp that the purely constitutional political model Parnell had worked to achieve was being threatened by the resurgence of the semi-revolutionary land war. It ran counter to Parnell's political priority of winning over liberal public opinion in Britain, and in purely material terms it presented a real and present danger to the operation of his parliamentary organisation, with its competing demands for scarce financial resources.

In 1888 the plan's financial problems continued to deepen. O'Brien grimly informed Dillon: '[t]he expenses are swelling frightfully ... if our great list goes on swelling there will be a collapse unless you or I get off on a begging mission'.[44] In June 1888 grants to evicted tenants were running at £750 a month, but by October this had increased to £1,261 a month. Dillon estimated that this would mean 'an expenditure of £20,000 a year – all items included'.[45] Only a week later, though, he had raised the estimate, noting in his diary: '[i]t will take at least £25,000 to run our movement to this time next year'.[46] Even this turned out to be an underestimation of the actual expense. Dillon's own figures for 1889 show that £30,780 was spent, of which more than £26,000 was in support of evicted tenants, with grants averaging close to £2,000 per month.[47]

On 14 January 1889, John Dillon wrote in desperation to Parnell, telling him: 'I find that £10,000 to be the very smallest sum with which I can hope to carry on the movement till it may reasonably be expected that money will begin to come in from Australia – as a result of my tour.' In his reply, Parnell said that he hoped 'to be able to scrape together £10,000 for you'; he made it quite clear, however, that he was not prepared to touch his reserves, reminding Dillon 'that I do not feel justified in selling any more bonds'.[48]

In July 1889 the Tenants' Defence League was inaugurated with a view to raising money to match the £30,000 Dillon was expected to raise in Australia, but Parnell's refusal to promote the initiative caused further bitterness between him and the campaigners.[49] O'Brien told Dillon, '[t]hings have reached a crisis between Parnell and myself', explaining that '[h]aving started the new Tenants' Defence League, with the assurance that it would be used in support of the Plan, [Parnell] now flatly refuses to take any steps to put life in it'. In an attempt to 'force him out of a most cruel and infatuated policy of veiled hostility', O'Brien confided in Dillon that he planned to allow his upcoming prosecution to go undefended, calculating that with his being sent to jail, '[t]he result will be that Parnell and the rest will be coerced into activity and that the result will be a big fund which cannot possibly be used for any purpose except the support of the Campaigners'.[50] O'Brien's plan seems to have worked and the parliamentary party got behind the League, which was launched while O'Brien was in prison. When the fund closed on 25 May 1890, an impressive £61,000 had been raised.

Any hopes of solvency for the plan were shattered, however, by the attempt to recreate the town of Tipperary, populated by the tenants evicted from the original town, an initiative supported by the 'Plan of Campaign'. In 1889 the agitation had cost over £30,000, but 'New Tipperary' more than doubled those costs in 1890. Meanwhile

Irish-American politics continued its internecine squabbling and became less and less effective as a source of support. In over three years, from August 1886 to the end of 1889, the Irish National League of America contributed only £21,400 to the plan, and only £7,700 was sent to the Parliamentary Fund.[51]

Competition for resources created tensions and divisions between Parnell and the leaders of the plan. Parnell failed to limit the extent of the agitation, which suggests that he had not fully completed his mission of shifting the movement from the semi-revolutionary to the purely constitutional. He also failed to communicate to his lieutenants the precarious nature of the finances, having failed to dispel the notion that the Paris funds were some inexhaustible war chest. Parnell therefore gave the impression that he was unwilling to assist the 'Plan of Campaign', when he might have been able to prove that he was in fact unable to do so. Parnell's brusque treatment of Dillon and O'Brien made him enemies where he ought to have had friends, while the competing demands for funds set the Irish leader at loggerheads with the plan and its supporters. Even if he was not in a position to be more supportive, had he been more communicative Parnell might have found himself in a much stronger position later, when his leadership was challenged in 1890.

It might be said that American funding made Parnell's achievements possible, and that the lack of it had much to do with his downfall. It had been the prospect of the American funding that led Parnell into an alliance with revolutionary nationalists, and it was that same funding that enabled him to steer the semi-revolutionary land war into the broader and calmer waters of constitutional nationalism. From October 1882, this funding was devoted to the construction and maintenance of a political machine designed to win Home Rule for Ireland. But having come close to achieving its objective, limitations in the design of Parnell's political model began to emerge. His overdependence on a particular source of funding, the ebbs and flows of which he was unable to control, left him exposed when the money dried up in 1886. He had also failed to fully decommission the vehicle that had launched his constitutional project, and when that resurgent semi-revolutionary agitation began to compete for the reduced funds, it fuelled divisions within the movement that would eventually bring Parnell down.

NOTES

1. J.H. Parnell, *C.S. Parnell: A Memoir* (London: Constable, 1916), p.228.
2. F.H. O'Donnell, *A History of the Irish Parliamentary Party*, 2 vols (London: Longman's, Green, 1910), vol. i, p.v.
3. Anthony Trollope, *The Landleaguers*, 3 vols (London: Chatto & Windus, 1883), vol. iii, p.161.
4. Paul Bew, *Land and the National Question in Ireland, 1858–1882* (Dublin: Gill & Macmillan, 1978), p.99.
5. *Freeman's Journal*, 22 October 1879.
6. Michael Davitt, *The Fall of Feudalism in Ireland* (London: Harper & Bros, 1904), p.173.
7. F.S.L. Lyons, *Charles Stewart Parnell* (London: Collins, 1977), pp.111–12.
8. From Parnell's address to the American House of Representatives, ibid., p.198.
9. Special Commission Act 1888; reprint of the shorthand notes of the speeches, proceedings and evidence taken before the commissioners appointed under the above named Act (London, 1890), (hereafter cited as Special Comm. Proc.), vi, p.343.
10. Special Comm. Proc., vii, p.27.
11. Davitt, *Fall of Feudalism*, p.211.
12. See Anna Parnell, *The Tale of a Great Sham* (Dublin: Arlen House, 1986).
13. Ibid., p.91.
14. *Freeman's Journal*, 22 June 1881.
15. *Freeman's Journal*, 16 September 1881.
16. *Irish World*, 13 May 1882.
17. *Freeman's Journal*, 21 July 1880.
18. Special Comm. Proc., vi, p.343; Davitt, *Fall of Feudalism*, p.173.
19. *Freeman's Journal*, 30 March 1881.
20. Bew, *Land and the National Question*, p.196.
21. Parnell, *Tale of a Great Sham*, p.104.
22. Special Comm. Proc., vi, p.343.
23. Parnell, *Tale of a Great Sham*, p.153.
24. *Freeman's Journal*, 18 October 1882.
25. *Freeman's Journal*, February–May 1883.
26. Police reports 1848–1921, Irish National League proceedings 1883–90, carton 6, Irish National League, Rules for Branches, National Archives of Ireland (NAI).
27. *Freeman's Journal*, 21 February 1883.
28. Police reports 1848–1921, Irish National League proceedings 1883–90, carton 6, Receipts and Expenditure of Irish National League, NAI.
29. *New York Herald*, 19 March 1883; Irish Parliamentary Party minute book 1880–5, Dillon Papers, Trinity College Dublin (TCD), MS 9233.
30. Special Comm. Proc., vi, p.326.
31. *United Ireland*, 10 February 1883.
32. Lyons, *Parnell*, p.254.
33. *Freeman's Journal*, 14 May 1883.
34. Irish Parliamentary Fund, cash book, 21 November 1885–22 March 1886, J.F.X. O'Brien Papers, National Library of Ireland (NLI), MS 9229.
35. Receipts and expenditure of the Parliamentary Fund, J.F.X. O'Brien Papers, National Library of Ireland (NLI), MS 9229.
36. F.H. O'Donnell, *How Home Rule was Wrecked* (Dublin: Mecredy & Kyle, 1895), p.9.
37. Irish parliamentary fund ledger, J.F.X. O'Brien Papers, NLI, MS 9227; Parliamentary Fund balance sheet, J.F.X. O'Brien Papers, NLI, MS 13461.
38. Rev. C. O'Reilly's statement of Irish National League of America funds for period 24/08/1886–31/12/1889, J.F.X. O'Brien Papers, NLI, MS 13461.
39. *United Ireland*, 23 October 1886.
40. Lyons, *Parnell*, p.377.
41. Rev. C. O'Reilly's statement of Irish National League of America funds for period 24/08/1886–31/12/1889, J.F.X. O'Brien Papers, NLI, MS 13461.
42. Irish Parliamentary Fund ledger, J.F.X. O'Brien Papers, NLI, MS 9227.
43. Sally Warwick-Haller, *William O'Brien and the Irish Land War* (Dublin: Irish Academic Press, 1990), pp.102–3; John Dillon to T. Harrington, 12 December 1887, 26 January 1888, Dillon Papers, TCD, MS 6732a.

44. O'Brien to Dillon, 13 September 1888, Dillon Papers, TCD, MS 6737.
45. John Dillon's journal, 28 October 1888, Dillon Papers, TCD, MS 6559.
46. Ibid., 5 November 1888.
47. Expenses of the land war 1889, Dillon Papers, TCD, MS 6820.
48. Parnell to Dillon, 26 January 1889, Dillon Papers, TCD, MS 6745.
49. O'Brien to Dillon, 14 July 1889, Dillon Papers, TCD, MS 6737.
50. O'Brien to Dillon, 14 August 1889, Dillon Papers, TCD, MS 6737.
51. Rev. C. O'Reilly's statement of Irish National League of America funds for period 24/08/1886–31/12/1889, J.F.X. O'Brien papers, NLI, MS 13461.

# CHAPTER TWO

# The Irish Party and the Volunteers: Politics and the Home Rule Army, 1913–1916

## COLIN REID

The formation of rival armed groups, the Ulster Volunteer Force (UVF) and the Irish Volunteers, in 1913 radically altered the dynamics of politics in Ireland and Britain. The constitutional struggle over the third Home Rule bill, which was introduced in 1912, now expanded to encompass dangerous extra-parliamentary methods. Both sets of Volunteers contained the inherent contradictions and ambiguities that inevitably follow the fusion of constitutional and unconstitutional political struggle: after 1913 the gun and the threat of force became provocative weapons in the arguments for and against Irish self-government. Volunteering represented a mass mobilisation on a scale not seen since the days of the Land League, as politics opened up to include the drilling fields of Ireland as well as the secluded walls of Westminster. As the world went to war in August 1914, the gun was firmly embedded in the mindset of unionist and nationalist Ireland: the mentalities of the Ulster crisis years made paramilitarism an acceptable, and perhaps even a desirable, moral force within Irish society.[1]

The year 1913 witnessed an astonishing rise of militarism throughout Ireland. The UVF was founded in January; the socialist militia, the Irish Citizen Army, was established on 19 November to protect workers engaged in the escalating labour disputes in Dublin of that year. One week later saw the creation of the Irish Volunteers. Against the backdrop of the rise of these private armies – unionist, socialist and nationalist – was the terror campaign of militant suffragettes, who violently targeted political opponents, including individual Irish Party members. Numerous elements of Irish society were thus permeated by competing ideologies that stressed the political and moral virtues of militarism. Both the Ulster and Irish Volunteers expanded rapidly, with the growth of the private armies intimately tied up with the turbulent political events between the introduction of the Home Rule bill in 1912 and the outbreak of the First World War. The formation of the UVF represented the flowering of Ulster resistance against Home Rule, the menacing proof that the case put by Sir Edward Carson and other unionist leaders was more than mere bluster. Crucially, the UVF was intimately tied to the Ulster Unionist Party. It is clear that unionism was preparing to arm itself to combat the Home Rule threat as early as 1910; the formation of the UVF in January 1913 was overseen by the Unionist leaders, who were eager to control their mass following and instil discipline in the ranks during an incredibly contentious period in British and Irish politics.[2] The Ulster unionist leadership's primary aim was to smash the Home Rule bill, or at least its application to Ulster, using parliamentary methods: the threat of force, represented by the UVF, was a calculated – if exceedingly dangerous – move to strengthen the unionist negotiating hand.[3] 'Carsonism', however, became an inspiration (ironic or otherwise) for many nationalists, such as Patrick Pearse, Sir Roger Casement and Bulmer Hobson, who favoured the establishment of a pro-Home Rule version of the UVF. Hobson later asserted that it was Ulster militarism which shook the Irish people out of their lethargy, while also paralysing the British administration in Ireland: quite an achievement for a unionist force.[4]

The Irish Party, under the leadership of John Redmond, and Irish Volunteers did not enjoy anything like the symmetrical relationship of their Ulster rivals. The Irish Volunteers were established without the sanction of the party; the party only formally involved itself with the Volunteers once it became a mass movement. The impact of the Irish Party on the Volunteers – and vice versa – remains cloudy in the historiography of Edwardian Ireland. Despite the historically-minded rhetoric that accompanied the formation of the Volunteers, which linked the movement with its 1782 counterpart, the modern variation of the citizen-soldier was, as Matthew Kelly has argued, a genuinely new departure in Irish life.[5] This 'new departure' had huge implications for the Irish Party and the Home Rule project. The Volunteer movements founded in 1913 were harbingers of the violence of the 1919–23 period; they also offer a unique Edwardian twist on the ideals of the citizen-soldier and national militia, so beloved by the Young Ireland generation of the 1840s.[6] The aim of this chapter is to explore the Irish Party– Irish Volunteer connection between 1913 and the Easter Rising of 1916. It will examine the origins of the Volunteer movement within the context of the Home Rule crisis, the response of the nationalist political establishment to this new threat to their hegemony, the impact of the Great War on the fragile bonds holding together the disparate forces within the wider Volunteer movement, and, finally, the decline and destruction of the Redmondite National Volunteers.

## THE ORIGINS OF THE IRISH VOLUNTEERS

The Irish Volunteers were officially established on 25 November 1913 at a massively oversubscribed meeting at the Rotunda Rink in Dublin. The spark of creation came not from the Irish Party, but from an assortment of nationalist figures from outside its ranks. These included Gaelic League enthusiasts, Sinn Féiners, O'Brienites, supporters of the Irish Party and members of the underground Irish Republican Brotherhood (IRB), hinting at the fractured nature of nationalism in Ireland in 1913.[7] While its membership was diverse, the first committee of the Irish Volunteers was heavily weighted with IRB men. These included five of the seven future signatories of the 1916 Proclamation of the Irish Republic, with only the socialist, James Connolly, and the old-school Fenian, Tom Clarke, missing. The IRB was a driving force behind the Volunteers, keenly manipulating the ideal of the citizen-solider; this is not to say, however, that the leaders of the Volunteers were merely a band of separatists intent on stoking revolution at the first opportunity. The choice of Eoin MacNeill as the Volunteers' figurehead was a deliberate sop to the forces of moderation: MacNeill was a respected scholar, Gaelic Leaguer and, politically, a supporter of the Irish Party and Home Rule. Unlike the top tier of the UVF, the leadership of the Irish Volunteers, centred on MacNeill, was not comprised of military men: Colonel Maurice Moore, who was appointed inspector general of the Volunteers early in 1914, was the only member of the provisional committee with actual military experience.[8] Instead, a cluster of politico-cultural figures of differing political outlooks was placed at the top of a rather unclear leadership structure. Volunteering was a deeply multifaceted phenomenon, organisationally and in mindset, and was not solely the domain of Irish revolutionaries.

The complexity of Volunteering was reflected in the new movement's first manifesto, a document that is as fascinating for its omissions as for its content. It stressed both the danger posed to Ireland from the Tory-inspired 'menace of armed violence' and the need for Irishmen to form a citizen army, '[i]n the name of National Unity, of National Dignity, of National and Individual Liberty, of Manly Citizenship'.[9] The manifesto's emphasis was on the indelible rights and duties of Irishmen, rather than assaulting the Ulster unionist position; it was left to Patrick Pearse to inform the Volunteers' inaugural meeting that their movement was *not* being founded to combat the UVF.[10] Also missing from the manifesto were any references to the Irish Party or the political campaign for Home Rule. It was envisaged, however, that the Volunteers would maintain its organisation and form a 'prominent element in the national life under a National Government', despite the fact the Home Rule legislation prohibited the raising of an Irish army. At the inception of the nationalist army, MacNeill was privately adamant that the Volunteers should do nothing that harmed Redmond's standing in either Ireland or Britain, but he feared Irish Party control over the new force.[11] Whatever the motives of individual leaders across the political spectrum of Volunteering, they did not wish to become merely a cog in the constitutional wheel spun by Redmond and the Irish Party, a fate which befell other nationalist groupings in past years, such as the United Irish League (UIL) and the Ancient Order of Hibernians (AOH).

The existence of a 'Home Rule army' inferred to most that the enemies of nationalist Ireland were British Conservatism and Ulster unionism; but the raising of a citizen army also implied a critique of Redmond's leadership of nationalist Ireland and the resolve of British Liberalism, as well as the entire constitutional process.[12] In all this, there was vagueness in purpose: as David Fitzpatrick has noted, the hopes and ambitions of the Volunteers were as hazy as they were great.[13] The Volunteers were all things to their members, and provided a particular Irish perspective to the wave of martial enthusiasm sweeping Europe, before the horrors of the First World War destroyed the romance of violence. For Joseph Plunkett, writing in the first edition of the *Irish Volunteer*, the new organisation's official journal, Ireland's citizen-soldiers represented the means to 'reassume our manhood' and 'once again voice our claim to stand among the nations of the world in the full tradition of the Christian civilisation'. For Colonel Maurice Moore, writing in the same volume, the Volunteers 'do not desire to imitate the boastings of Sir Edward Carson; they wish only to ensure that the rights and liberties, gained through years of labour and self-denial by their parliamentary representatives, shall not be bartered away by English party managers'.[14] On the one hand, therefore, the Volunteers were a spiritual movement, romantically destined to ignite Ireland's soul and enable Irishmen to reach the truest expression of nationality; on the other, they were a political army that would fight, if necessary, for Home Rule, while ostensibly declaring themselves 'apolitical'. The movement was, in fact, both: there is an important overlap between the discourse of Volunteering and the language revival of the late nineteenth and early twentieth centuries.

The Irish Volunteers was an organisation not unlike the Gaelic League in many ways. The Gaelic League was founded in the late nineteenth century to preserve, protect and promote the Irish language: the survival of the 'old tongue' was intimately bound up, in the discourse of the Irish revival, with notions of renewed nationality and civilisation. The League spearheaded the cultural nationalist programme of nation-building. It was apolitical, in a formal sense, but its agenda unrepentantly championed Irish-Ireland ideology, as it sought to construct a nationally mature people to operate the institutions of self-government. The League represented the educational wing of Irish-Ireland, just as the Gaelic Athletic Association carried the mantle of 'native' sport: in this context, the Volunteers can be seen as another offshoot of the early twentieth-century politico-cultural philosophy of Irish self-improvement and activism. Furthermore, many Volunteer leaders were senior figures within the Gaelic League; Eoin MacNeill's legendary article, 'The North Began', which issued the first public call for a nationalist version of the UVF, was originally published in the Gaelic League's newspaper, *An Claidheamh Soluis*. The Gaelic League was captured by political extremists during the Great War, but before this occurred there was a blurring of the ideals of the Volunteers and the revival of the Irish tongue. The League's president, Douglas Hyde, praised the Volunteers at a public meeting in July 1914, claiming that the private army was endeavouring to 'resuscitate the nation upon Irish lines'.[15] For Peter Macken, writing in the Volunteers' official organ, the link was more overt: 'The Gaelic League taught us to distinguish between Nationality and Party Politics'; now 'it is the mission of the Volunteer movement to train us to distinguish between Party Politics and Patriotism'.[16]

The Volunteers, like the Gaelic League, emerged and developed under men without solid links to the Irish Party. Likewise, the Volunteers cast themselves not as an alternative to the Irish Party, but as a necessary supplement in the process of nation- and state-building in Ireland. The party, though, was unwilling to share this responsibility with any organisation it could not control, Gaelic League, Volunteers or otherwise. Hence, Irish politics in the post-Parnellite period can be read as a clash between the realism of political nationalism and the idealism of cultural nationalism, with each wing mistrustful of the others' motives. This hostility was generally hidden from public view, and only occasionally came to the fore. Under John Redmond's leadership, the Irish Party unsubtly pushed a neutral line on most issues not related to Home Rule, for the sake of wider nationalist unity. The Irish language and class politics were two such potentially divisive issues: the efforts by the party hierarchy to remain aloof from the heated debates over compulsory Irish in the National University of Ireland in 1909 and the worker–capitalist clash during the Dublin lock-out of 1913 must be seen in this light.[17] The rise of the Volunteers at the end of 1913 posed obvious problems to the Irish Party, and initially it adopted the same coldly detached approach as it had done in the past.

## POLITICAL PARTIES AND PRIVATE ARMIES

The Irish Party was the most dominant component of Irish nationalist life, and at the end of 1913 it stood on the threshold of winning the holy grail of Home Rule. The birth of the Volunteers, wholly outside of its control, was thus an undesirable distraction at a time when the party was attempting to convince British opinion of Ireland's suitability for self-government. Redmond and the leadership of the Irish Party were convinced that unionist militancy was a bluff, one which threatened to make Carson a prisoner of his own rhetoric; the creation of a nationalist rival to the UVF somewhat undermined this notion. While public attacks on the Volunteers by Irish Party MPs were uncommon (with the exceptions of Richard Hazleton, MP for North Galway, and Thomas Lundon, MP for Limerick East), proclamations of support were even rarer, with only J.P. Farrell, MP for North Longford, willing to identify with the new organisation.[18] The party's triumvirate – Redmond, Dillon and Joseph Devlin – were justifiably alarmed at the rise of a military body dedicated to obtaining arms at such a contentious time in Anglo-Irish relations.[19] But the fears of the constitutionalist hierarchy might have been out of step with grassroots opinion, which was much more sympathetic to the logic of a nationalist Volunteer force to counterbalance the threat posed to Home Rule from the UVF. In March 1914, with the Irish Volunteers well established with twenty-five branches and 14,000 members, the party was forced to issue a blunt rebuke to Joseph Devlin's Ancient Order of Hibernians in Belfast, warning them that they were forbidden to drill with the Volunteers under pain of exclusion. In the same month, the Monaghan executive of the United Irish League, the local organisation of the Irish Party, heard a heated argument before a resolution against drilling was defeated by a large majority.[20] Despite the lack of party sanction, AOH and UIL members were prevalent in a number of Volunteer branches across provincial Ireland.[21] It was a confusing picture: the party enjoyed no official links to the Volunteers, while individual UIL and AOH men were active at the grassroots of both organisations. As the inspector general of the Royal Irish Constabulary (RIC) reported in April 1914, '[t]he official approval of the Nationalist Party is still withheld from the [Volunteer] movement, but apparently general sympathy is with it'.[22]

The Volunteer movement mushroomed in response to external events in the first half of 1914, such as the Curragh 'incident', which demonstrated that the British Army could not be relied upon to enforce Home Rule in Ulster, and the success of the UVF in landing guns in Larne, county Antrim. A number of new recruits rallied to the cause: the police believed that the Volunteers were 25,000 strong at the beginning of May 1914.[23] This increase was partnered by a weekly newspaper established in February 1914, the *Irish Volunteer*, which was printed out of the offices of the strongly Sinn Féinish local, the *Enniscorthy Echo*.[24] The *Irish Volunteer* ran articles, all with a nationalistic bent, on military tactics and weaponry. These occasionally verged on the amusing, such as the first-aid section, which informed readers that snake bites received on the field of battle should be treated immediately with brandy.[25] Where, exactly, Irish Volunteers might be under threat from snakes was not identified; but such writings serve to highlight the confused ambitions inherent within the Volunteering psyche.

The continuing growth of the Volunteers outside the sphere of parliamentary influence posed a grave threat to Irish Party hegemony over nationalist Ireland, while undermining Redmond's efforts to reach an accommodation with Ulster. The inspector general of the RIC highlighted the grim logic of the growth of Volunteering in the wake of the Larne gunrunning: 'Each county will soon have a trained army far outnumbering the police, and those who control the Volunteers will be in a position to dictate to what extent the law of the land may be carried into effect.'[26] The leadership of the Irish Party realised this too. Dillon, who became a convert to Volunteering in the aftermath of the Curragh 'incident', wrote to his friend, the English radical Wilfred Blunt, expressing the need for responsible hands at the top of the Home Rule

army, without which, he argued, the army risked repeating the 'disas-
ters of 1798'.[27] By the time Blunt read Dillon's words, in May 1914,
they had become official Irish Party policy. In the wake of the expansion of Volunteering, MacNeill, along with Colonel Maurice Moore
and Roger Casement, became sympathetic to the idea of co-opting Irish
Party representatives on to the army's provisional committee; negotiations between the three Volunteer leaders and the Irish Party hierarchy opened in early May.[28] Crucially, these were conducted without
the consent of the IRB-heavy provisional committee, who were left in
the dark by MacNeill, a negotiating tactic of which Redmond was un-
aware. The two sides, however, swiftly became locked in a *dialogue
des sourds*, with MacNeill unwilling to surrender control of the Volunteers to 'persons acting merely in the capacity of custodians on behalf of another interest'.[29] Redmond, conversely, refused to back down
from his national right, as he saw it, to control the Home Rule army.
The negotiations broke down amidst what MacNeill painfully described as a 'poison of suspicion',[30] with Redmond threatening to establish a rival armed force if he could not secure ample representation
for his interests on the Volunteers' provisional committee.[31] During
the negotiations, Redmond authorised Hibernians to join local companies of the Volunteers: this signalled in advance his ruthless determination to take control of the nationalist militia. In mid-May the
northern nationalist daily the *Irish News* reported that the AOH was
actively embracing Volunteering throughout the country.[32] The question was finally forced by Redmond the following month, when he issued a public ultimatum to the provisional committee: accept twenty-five
party nominees on the Volunteer executive, or face the divisive possibility of a new Irish Party-sponsored Volunteer movement.[33] While the
provisional committee, threatened with losing control of the Volunteers,
initially defied Redmond's declaration, it soon backed down, with
Hobson particularly alert to the very real threat of a damaging split.[34]
D.P. Moran, the maverick editor of the *Leader*, a journal that was un-
afraid to issue attacks on the Irish Party, contributed a cautious reading of the situation: until Home Rule was granted, 'the effective and
concrete expression of Irish national will is the Home Rule Party'. Redmond, as leader of that party, was thus the only man who could 'receive the salute of the Irish Volunteers'.[35] The logic of this stance was
accepted by the Volunteers' executive, but at a price. Accepting Redmond's invitation to join the provisional committee, John McCaffery
warned that the Irish leader had not 'heard the last of an attempt to turn
the Volunteers from support of the Party and the immediate objects

before us'.[36] Many of the Volunteers' most influential elements be-grudged the heavy-handed nature of the Redmondite takeover: this smouldering resentment pre-empted the bitter split within the move-ment during the opening stages of the First World War.

With explicit support at last emanating from the Irish Party, nationalists flocked to the Volunteers at a hurried rate. Just nine days after Redmond's proclamation, the *Freeman's Journal* reported that the Volunteers were receiving two thousand recruits per day.[37] With the weight of the parliamentary party behind it, the Volunteer move-ment would claim in excess of 160,000 members by July 1914, with an astonishing 51,700 men joining its ranks in June alone.[38] But the Irish Party–Volunteer connection was as politically precarious as it was organisationally chaotic. Once the Irish Party achieved control, the re-alisation that it did not know what to do with the Volunteers swiftly set in; the constitutional leadership did not possess the enthusiasm, expertise or disposition to direct a private army. One example of this was the arming of the Volunteers. Before the Redmondite takeover, popular enthusiasm for Volunteering was on the rise, but weapons were few and far between. In a cabinet paper penned by the Irish chief secretary, Augustine Birrell, in April 1914, the Irish Volunteers were described unkindly but accurately as consisting of 'somewhat ragged regiments, ill-equipped as yet and not particularly disciplined'.[39] Despite the obsession with rifles – as articulated constantly in the Irish Volunteers' journal – there were conspicuously few within the move-ment. At the end of July, the Irish Volunteers ran their biggest haul of guns into Howth, county Dublin. One month later, however, police intelligence highlighted the fundamental problem facing the Home Rule army: it was estimated that the Volunteers' share of rifles was in-sufficient to arm even 1 per cent of its number.[40]

Under the Union, Ireland had traditionally suffered tougher gun con-trol restrictions than the rest of Great Britain.[41] These were relaxed in 1906, but fearful of the rise of public militias through 1913, the gov-ernment took steps to tighten the rules again: a proclamation forbid-ding the importation of guns into Ireland was issued at the end of the year, to the wrath of nationalist observers.[42] With the arms proclamation in place, the inspector general of the Volunteers, Colonel Maurice Moore, spelt out to Roger Casement the dangers of a rising tide of popular civic soldiery:

> The success of the Ulster Volunteers has led some of us to suppose that rebellion can be successful: but Ulster is armed and we are

not: but much more important is the fact that the army won't fight against Ulster, but will readily shoot us: and the tories will readily arrest the leaders and hang them too. We could not stand a week.[43]

If the Volunteers hoped that their 'new understanding' with the Irish Party would yield movement on the prohibition of gun importation, they were soon disappointed. The official Redmondite line was broadcast by P.J. Brady, MP for St. Stephen's Green in Dublin, who in July 1914 told a Volunteer meeting that the Irish Party were 'not going to turn out the Government and lose Home Rule, if the proclamation is not withdrawn'.[44] The Irish Party had its own priorities, which were not necessarily directly shared by the Volunteers. 'I do not know how nationhood is achieved except by armed men', an increasingly disillusioned Patrick Pearse told an Emmet commemoration in New York in March 1914;[45] the Irish Party leadership begged to differ.

While the Volunteers became ostensibly more 'representative' of Irish opinion after the Redmondite takeover, the movement was hampered by internal suspicions. There was fierce competition between the Fenian and parliamentary factions for the scant resources within the Volunteers. The IRB was determined to resist passing control of the movement to the Irish Party, while the party was equally eager to flex its muscle to its advantage. Hobson later gleefully recorded that Redmondite control was 'completely illusory': the work of the Volunteers was carried on by the original founders, he argued, who crucially managed to retain what little funds there were within the movement.[46] But this was mirrored by party figures protecting their own interests over those of the wider Volunteer movement. Colonel Maurice Moore later recorded that Redmond improperly entrusted J.D. Nugent, a Dublin MP and leading Hibernian, with a number of recently won rifles, rather than presenting them to the Provisional Committee for distribution.[47] Hobson also claimed that Redmond had raised £6,000 while fundraising on behalf of the Volunteers in the US, but none of the money ever found its way into the movement's exchequer.[48] Quite apart from internal espionage and deceit, the Redmondite-sanctioned Volunteers were struck with organisational paralysis. Flooding the Volunteers' executive body with party representatives did not make for an effective leadership structure. Joseph Devlin informed Colonel Moore of the discomfort he felt in attending executive meetings of fifty men, crammed into a small room, on a hot summer's day. Even after a smaller standing committee was appointed, Moore lamented that the continual bickering therein merely proved that these men were not fit to lead a military force.[49]

This tension led Patrick Pearse to issue a desperate appeal to Irish America for material support, behind Redmond's back. Writing to Joseph McGarrity and John Devoy, leading figures in the Irish-America network, Pearse claimed to speak for nine dissenters – most likely all IRB men – on the provisional committee who opposed what they saw as the Irish Party's negative influence on the Volunteers. He urgently requested arms and ammunition to be sent to them, and not to Redmond and the provisional committee. Pearse's case was a compelling one: he accused the Irish Party of attempting to place guns in the hands only of their own followers, at the expense of the wider Volunteer movement. The most damning allegation was that Redmond was seeking to divert Volunteer resources to the north, in a bid to arm Joseph Devlin's AOH. The Ulster melting-pot was tense: the dynamics of Belfast in particular led Colonel Maurice Moore to label the city the 'most dangerous place in Ireland' in mid-July.[50] In this context, it is perhaps understandable that Devlin and the northern leadership of the Volunteers wished to see their followers armed for reasons of self-defence; but Pearse was aware of the probable fall-out of such an action. He feared that if Home Rule was forced through Westminster, then the Irish Volunteers might be called on to enforce it in Ulster, which could only lead to the eventual 'dismemberment of Ireland'.[51] One Belfast Volunteer officer later recalled that his rank and file 'were enthusiastic about the idea of fighting against Carson's Ulster Volunteers'.[52] Even if this reminiscence was exaggerated, the potential of a sectarian bloodbath was very real. Captain George Berkeley, the chief commanding officer of the Irish Volunteers in Belfast, offered his men to General Nevil Macready, the head of the British Army in Belfast, in the event of trouble breaking out (quite a significant gesture in itself): Berkeley stressed that the city was 'in a state of some tension', with 'reports of a proposed attack on the Catholic district'.[53] The rank and file in Belfast were warned by Devlin to brace themselves for the worst, following the collapse of the Buckingham Palace conference, which represented the last attempt to reach a compromise between Ulster unionism and Irish nationalism before the outbreak of the First World War. The breakdown of the talks 'and the nature of the general situation', cautioned Devlin, made it imperative that nationalists in Ulster 'should be prepared for whatever emergency should arise'. It was clear that Devlin was referring to a potential attack from the UVF: 'if we are attacked', he proclaimed, 'we will defend ourselves'.[54]

## THE IMPACT OF WAR

Only the outbreak of war in Europe halted the slide towards absolute chaos in Ireland. Constitutional politics had failed to resolve the Ulster crisis between 1912 and 1914; it took an international calamity to stem the rising tide of militarism and the potential consequences of the existence of duelling private armies. Where this left the Irish Party in August 1914 is a moot point. The party was unsuccessful in its bid to secure Home Rule on its own peaceful terms; its parliamentary strategy was rocked by the militancy of Ulster resistance to Irish self-government. The establishment and evolution of the Irish Volunteers was also a manifestation of constitutional nationalism's failures.[55] But by sponsoring Volunteering only from May 1914, the party suffered the worst of both worlds: Redmond did not enjoy the same status within the Irish Volunteers as Carson did within the UVF; and Redmond was not able to secure the same political benefits with his army as Carson had secured with his. The Redmondite takeover rendered the Volunteers' executive committee impotent and prone to damaging factionalism. The crux of the problem was the Irish Party's hesitancy in dealing with the Volunteers, which granted the army room to expand and develop its own sense of identity (or identities). The problems of this approach were amplified by the alienating heavy-handed annexation in June 1914. 'Wisdom is easy after the event,' the former Redmondite MP, Stephen Gwynn, lamented in 1919, 'and few would dispute now that the constitutional party ought either to have dissociated itself completely from the appeal to force, or to have launched and controlled it from the outset.'[56] As it was, with war sweeping across Europe in the summer of 1914, the Irish Party was nominally in control of the Volunteers without providing any clear sense of direction. Even as Redmond prepared to offer the Volunteers for the British war effort, police intelligence in Ireland was reporting that the Home Rule army were 'still unorganised and without responsible leadership'.[57]

It was the Irish Party's backing for the British war effort that finally broke the fragile governing body of the Volunteers. In September, after the Home Rule bill had been placed into the statute book, Redmond enthusiastically declared at Woodenbridge, county Wexford, that Irishmen should fight for Britain 'wherever the firing-line extends'.[58] MacNeill and the IRB element on the provisional committee deemed this a violation of the Volunteers' original manifesto, forcing a split in the movement. The vast bulk of the Volunteers, numbering some 170,000, followed Redmond and the Irish Party; a small minority, around

10,000, adopted the dissident MacNeillite line. Among those in the leadership of the smaller wing were many of the original founders who had felt aggrieved at the Irish Party's graceless appropriation of their movement. Organisationally and ideologically, the split actually benefited the two wings, permitting each to assume its own separate identity. The majority, who were renamed the National Volunteers, was large enough not to miss the dissidents; the minority, who retained the name Irish Volunteers, was able to regroup and reorganise on a much more manageable scale, without the interference of the constitutional nationalist movement.

The shift from 'Irish' to 'National' in the labelling of the Redmondite Volunteers was profound. It represented a formal move from the core, if vague, elements of the first Volunteer manifesto – unity, liberty, dignity – to sectional party politics. The National Volunteers became another component of the Irish Party's organisational network, much like the UIL or the AOH. This was the very fate that Volunteer leaders such as Roger Casement and MacNeill had strenuously wished to avoid. Casement was adamant at the founding of the Irish Volunteers in November 1913 that local branches of the new movement should not be formed 'with sectarian or party aims':[59] in other words, UIL and AOH agencies in any area should not be permitted to join en masse as separate battalions. During the Volunteers' first few months of existence, Casement was also an advocate for clarifying some confusion that hung over their official label. 'Please always bear in mind,' he scolded Colonel Maurice Moore, 'the correct title IRISH Volunteers not NATIONAL or NATIONALIST Volunteers (the latter wholly damnable).'[60] Casement's correction might sound pedantic, but it in fact touched on the very ethos of the citizen-soldier in the early twentieth century. The Irish Volunteers frequently claimed the legacy of their eighteenth-century namesakes: the spirit of 1782 in particular, when the Dungannon convention of the Volunteers called for the legislative independence of Ireland, was often cited in contemporary propaganda. This reading of history was straightforward: the Volunteer movement of the 1780s represented a high point of patriotism, a military as well as cultural expression of Ireland's independence, and as such, was to be enthusiastically emulated. Following the Volunteer split, however, it became more problematic for the National Volunteers to appropriate this historical identity, and the great legitimacy it conferred on a psychological level. Tied to the Redmondite machine, representing party politics more than the mystical expressions of nation-building of old, the National Volunteers could not claim, as

Irish Volunteer propaganda put it, to defend Irish men and women of all religions and political beliefs.[61] That it can hardly be said that the minority Irish Volunteers represented all aspects of the 'nation' was irrelevant: they were not tarnished, as they saw it, by constitutional politics.

Several months into the split of 1914, the Irish Volunteer's official journal carried an article entitled 'A Few Words to the Honest Men of Mr Redmond's Volunteers'. The author of the article, who identified himself only as 'A Fenian', made a devastating point: 'Mr Redmond and the Party profess to decry "physical force". What are the Irish Volunteers of all shades but physical force parties?'[62] This issue remained clouded throughout the war: what was the point of the National Volunteers? Were they a paramilitary wing (albeit a poorly equipped one) of the Irish Party, a private army under the control of constitutional nationalism? Were they now, after Redmond's Woodenbridge speech, stumbling into the strange territory of becoming part of the British Army? And if the National Volunteers were the Home Rule army under the Home Rule leadership, what were the Irish Volunteers? Slimmed down to a manageable level, which the IRB could more fully infiltrate, the Irish Volunteers doggedly retained their idealism. At the end of 1914, the movement's journal proclaimed: 'Ireland's best security for Home Rule is the Irish Volunteers who have not accepted Party control.'[63] The central thought underpinning this rationale was that an independent militia was still fundamentally required in the struggle for a full measure of Irish self-government, as the constitutional politics represented by the Irish Party and the Westminster system more generally could yet fail. In this context, the Irish Volunteers represented an alternative vessel of nationalist sentiment, which stood to flourish if the Irish Party miscalculated with its wartime strategies. 'A political party is a means to an end,' trumpeted the *Irish Volunteer* in March 1915, 'and the public mind is well able to realise that the end must not be made subordinate to the means.'[64] There was still space within civic society for the anti-Redmondite Volunteers, then, who cast themselves as the guardians of Ireland's *national* rights, as opposed to mere political rights.

The role of the National Volunteers, on the other hand, is more difficult to probe. Despite the great numbers who followed Redmond in September 1914, the organisation became moribund at a rapid rate. There are several explanations for this. Although a mighty force on paper, the reality on the ground was somewhat different. Many of the National Volunteers' leaders and drill sergeants, such as Captain George Berkeley in Belfast, left for the battlefields of Europe as soon as the war broke out, thereby weakening the force at home. The Volunteers had long been an organisational shambles, particularly after the massive growth that followed the Irish Party's sanction. But the unique circumstances of war, with the sudden departure of what Dillon described as 'all the good men',[65] drained the National Volunteers of purpose, and its organisation crumbled under the strain. Structural chaos was linked to the ideological confusion that blighted Irish nationalism during the war, sapping the life force of the National Volunteers. Despite the euphoria of Redmond's Woodenbridge declaration, the majority of Irish Party MPs did not encourage enlistment to the British Army.[66] Rather, the Irish Party endured a hazier relationship with the war effort, with the Redmondite leadership articulating the defence of the British empire while the grassroots looked on somewhat diffidently. The psychological switch imposed by the Redmondite wartime strategy on Irish nationalism – playing a full role within the British Army and supporting the imperial war machine – represented a fundamental paradigm shift, and arguably it came too soon and too quickly for it to be successfully accomplished. D.P. Moran's *Leader* captured the essence of this mood in contemporary Ireland. 'We think the Irish Party are asking the Irish people more than the Irish people will agree to give,' Moran dolefully argued, 'if we had it [self-government] for twenty or even ten years, periods that might be expected to see the fruits of Home Rule realised, it would probably be reasonable if we were expected in a crisis to take up an extra special load of the British Empire's burden.'[67] The Irish Party's approach, then, made reciprocal gestures from Britain imperative, so nationalist leaders could show their base what Ireland was gaining in return for its sacrifices. But the record of British concessions to Ireland during the war was notably poor, which did much to undermine Redmond and the Irish Party at home. Lord Kitchener, the Secretary of State for War, rejected arming and regularising the National Volunteers for home service; when an Irish Division was belatedly established within the British Army, with the express intention of attracting recruits from the Volunteers, it was in reality Irish only in name. The authorities constantly rejected the mainly symbolic requests from Redmond for Irish badges, uniforms and regalia, undermining nationalist confidence in the course that the Irish Party had plotted for Ireland. The failure of British political and military leaders to recognise the Volunteers as a free-standing brigade within the army, in particular, was retrospectively highlighted as being fatal to the wartime Redmondite project by senior constitutional nationalists Stephen Gwynn and John Horgan.[68]

THE NATIONAL VOLUNTEERS: DECLINE AND DESTRUCTION

The lack of sympathy from the British war leaders to the peculiarities of the Irish situation certainly damaged Redmond's standing. But where did it leave the National Volunteers? The National Volunteers remained in a limbo state, neither a meaningful Irish force nor a genuine unit within the British Army. One of Redmond's great ambitions for the National Volunteers was to see them transformed into a distinct territorial force for home service, equipped and trained by the British. Despite courting sympathy with members of the government and the civil service, the plan was rejected by the War Office, thereby dealing an enormous blow to the Irish leader.[69] In reality, though, the party's starting point for such a scheme was not promising. During the same month that Redmond made his Woodenbridge pledge, police intelligence reported that the Irish leader's militia was 'not even formed into definite units ... It is a strong Force on paper, but otherwise, without officers, and untrained, is little better than a huge mob'.[70] In this context, the apparent intransigence of the War Office becomes more understandable. With the hopes of an Irish Territorial Force dashed, the prospect of a short war also looked decidedly shaky: the high death toll in Europe and rumours of conscription from the autumn of 1914 chipped away at nationalist Ireland's initial enthusiasm for Redmond's stirring words of action. All this impacted negatively on the National Volunteers. According to police intelligence, at the end of December 1914 the National Volunteers boasted 156,750 members; by November 1915 the same source strikingly reported that the 'National Volunteer Force is practically dead'.[71]

The sudden decline of such a large organisation offers a snapshot into the ideological confusion that dogged constitutional nationalism during the war and was symptomatic of the Irish Party's own electoral obliteration, which followed in 1918. The fate of the National Volunteers was telling, illuminating the gulf that quickly opened up between Redmond's imperially minded rhetoric and the mood on the ground in Ireland. No issue crystallised the differences within Ireland during the war as much as recruitment, which split the wider nationalist movement across a range of axes. Only a minority of Irish Party MPs, such as Stephen Gwynn, Hugh Law and William O'Malley, actively participated in recruiting rallies across the country, arguing that Ireland's moral duty was to fight alongside Britain in the war. But not all who followed Redmond after the Volunteer split were inclined to wholeheartedly agree. One week after the Woodenbridge declaration,

Colonel Maurice Moore, who became the Inspector General of the National Volunteers, chastised Joseph Devlin on the issue of mixing politics and Volunteering, issuing the Belfast MP with a message for his leader: 'Mr Redmond ought not to make a speech about recruiting at a Volunteer inspection,' argued Moore pointedly, 'he ought not to tell Volunteers to enlist more than any other Irishmen.'[72]

Moore's point begs an obvious, but thorny, question: if they were not meant as recruits to the war effort, what were the National Volunteers for? This is a question riddled with complexities. While the Irish Party pushed for Territorial status for the National Volunteers, popular enthusiasm for militarism within the force was ebbing away at an alarming rate. Following Redmond's Woodenbridge declaration, and the first public airings of the possibilities of conscription, a sense of dread that Volunteering would increase the chances of being called up for military service crippled the National Volunteers.[73] Reporting on the mood of the country in October 1914, RIC intelligence noted that no significant National Volunteer drills had been held during the month: the conclusion was that 'general apathy seems to have set in'.[74] Many local branches simply ceased to meet, fearing that turning out in National Volunteer colours implied an intention to serve in Europe. The result was a rapid decay of the organisation. While on paper the National Volunteers could boast a membership of some 100,000 on the eve of the Easter Rising, many of these men had long since left the ranks. As early as December 1914, a major Irish Party recruitment drive at Tuam, county Galway, found the senior MPs, Redmond, Gwynn, Hazleton, O'Malley and Cosgrave, addressing 2,000 people. Four hundred were members of the National Volunteers, but the force in the area supposedly numbered 5,000.[75] By February 1916, only some 19,000 National Volunteers had enlisted in the British Army; the vast bulk of Irish recruits were actually unconnected with any private militia, nationalist or unionist.[76] Following the split of September 1914, the *Irish Volunteer* attacked the Redmondite strategy: 'Not a single man worthy of the name of Irishman', it proclaimed, 'will join the army of England.'[77] Given that fewer than 10 per cent of the National Volunteers enlisted for service, it appears that many within the organisation, for one reason or another, agreed with the dissident analysis. The vast majority of Volunteers sided with Redmond, but enthusiasm for Volunteering did not automatically equate to military commitment.[78]

A notable and underexamined aspect of the politics of the National Volunteers is their official newspaper, a reading of which confirms the sense of ideological disorientation that coupled its organisational decline. The *National Volunteer*, as it was called, was launched in October 1914 as a counter to the now dissident-run *Irish Volunteer*. The paper was published out of the offices of the *Freeman's Journal* weekly until Easter 1916.[79] The first issue proudly bore the motto, 'Defence not defiance', sending a clear message to its audiences that this militia group did not represent the impenitent Fenianism of old. But a reading of the *National Volunteer* does not make clear what it did represent. The journal frequently published articles professing the moral repugnancy of the German and Austro-Hungarian empires, while refusing to salute any aspect of the British empire. Germany was described as 'a robber amongst the nations', 'a depredator' and 'an oppressor'.[80] The positive pro-British imperial sentiment of Redmond was largely missing from its pages, though, and the *National Volunteer* even occasionally degenerated into a classic anti-British mode. 'The Union is dead', bragged an editorial column from March 1915, '[t]he long night of slavery is all but ended.'[81] This stance was at quite a distance from Redmond's willingness, in the words of Stephen Gwynn, 'to take part in any demonstration which implied that Nationalist Ireland under its new legal status accepted its lot in the British Empire fully and without reserve'.[82] Like the movement from which it took its name, the *National Volunteer* endured an ambiguous relationship with the British Army, standing aloof from concerns over the low levels of recruitment from nationalist Ireland. This remained the case even when conscription, the issue which more than any other sapped the constitutional movement, became a very real possibility in 1915. Conscription and its potential application in Ireland was resolutely opposed by all elements of constitutional nationalism throughout the war, yet the only realistic alternative of voluntary recruiting, which could have combatted the threat of compulsory service, was advocated by a mere handful of Redmondite MPs.[83] This dilemma was replicated in the pages of the *National Volunteer*, with the journal unwilling to position itself as a recruiting sergeant for the British forces and instead asking nationalists to place their trust in the Irish Party to defeat conscription in Westminster.[84] In November 1915, however, the Irish undersecretary, Matthew Nathan, held an interview with John Dillon, informing the Irish second-in-command of his general impression that 'the Sinn Fein and Irish Volunteer Party [were] gaining in strength and that the Parliamentary and National Volunteer Party were losing'.[85] One month before this meeting, police intelligence reported that while nationalist MPs fiercely condemned conscription, 'the Irish Volunteers are better organised to resist it'.[86] This was a devastating indictment of the decline of the constitutional movement during the war.

From the outbreak of the war to the Easter Rising, the decline of the National Volunteers was mirrored somewhat by the growth of the Irish Volunteers. This is not to imply a simple numerical equation – those men who left the National Volunteers did not flock to the rival organisation. But what is clear from police reports is that while the structures of the National Volunteers (loose as they were to begin with) disintegrated, the small bands of units that made up the Irish Volunteers became more active. The whereabouts of guns became a major headache for the party and the government, as the rival Volunteer forces benefited materially from the lax structures of the National Volunteers. In February 1915, Nathan informed Redmond of his doubts that rifles being shipped into Ireland for the National Volunteers were reaching 'proper hands': 'It is believed that they are sold to Volunteers in the Provinces without any very strict enquiry with regard to the persons to whom the sale is made.'[87] In August, a hundred rifles belonging to the National Volunteers were stolen; Redmond strongly believed that these had been taken by the Irish Citizen Army.[88] This was symptomatic of an apathy that paralysed the National Volunteers from within. 'The extreme section,' announced an intelligence report twelve months before the Easter Rising, 'are far more active at present than the more constitutional societies.'[89] There is an odd paradox here, for the Irish Party won all five of the contested by-elections in Ireland between the outbreak of war and the Rising, while its grassroots structures rotted away.[90] But this, perhaps, is more indicative of a failure of a national alternative to the Irish Party to appear, a process that changed with dramatic results following the rebirth of Sinn Féin in 1917. The striking decline of the National Volunteers and the UIL, coupled with low levels of recruitment from formal Home Rule circles, serves as a reminder of the failure of the Redmondite project before the Rising.

Nineteen-sixteen was a dark year for constitutional nationalism in Ireland. The Rising gave focus to anti-Redmond discontent, while the failure to deliver an immediate enactment of Home Rule in its aftermath was retrospectively lamented by one senior Irish Party lieutenant as the crucial turning point in the party's destiny, making the march towards electoral obliteration more certain.[91] While the Easter rebellion was undoubtedly a watershed moment, the seeds of the Irish Party's destruction were planted in its wartime strategies, which were heavily dependent on the successful delivery of a number of variables – the length of the war, British policies in Ireland and a reciprocal gesture from Ulster unionism – all of which were outside of its control. None of these were forthcoming; Redmond gained nothing materially for promoting Irish involvement in the war. 'There is only one way of winning Irish legislative freedom', a *National Volunteer* editorial claimed in January 1916, 'though nominally there are two – the constitutional and revolutionary ... Home Rule is our goal, and constitutional methods the only way'.[92] The Rising violently destroyed this belief. The events of Easter 1916 stunned what remained of the National Volunteers. There was initially little sympathy for the rebels' stand, but the mood among Redmondite Volunteers altered rapidly following the executions of the Rising's leaders and the heavy military presence that remained in Ireland in the aftermath of Easter week.[93] While the force was largely moribund by the time Pearse read aloud the Proclamation of the Irish Republic, there was an incredible sense of detachment within surviving branches. For instance, after issuing a resolution condemning the Rising, the ruling committee of the National Volunteers in Belfast moved the agenda towards its three most pressing concerns: organising a garden party, a regimental dance, and a picnic party.[94] Conspicuous by its absence was any hint of a military parade or drill.

Just before the Irish Party initiated its takeover of the Irish Volunteers at the height of the Ulster crisis, John Dillon warned that the militia, without 'reliable control', was 'playing with fire'.[95] In reality, it was the Irish Party who was playing with fire after gaining control of the Volunteers – a paramilitary force it could not adequately lead in an age when Home Rule's fate hinged on the success of constitutional action. The First World War may have provided the backdrop for the immediate defusing of the Ulster crisis, but this was won at the price of destroying the Home Rule movement. It took the international crisis to bring all the ideological contradictions of the Irish Party–National Volunteer connection to the surface. The vast majority of Volunteers followed Redmond at the outbreak of war, but only a small minority were willing to serve in the British Army. As late as the eve of the Easter rebellion, government sources were still being informed that the National Volunteers were 'untrained, unorganised, and practically unarmed' – at least where they existed.[96] Nevertheless, Irish Party morale, badly wounded by the Rising and its aftermath, was further dented by the National Volunteers' formal and symbolic break with Redmond in 1917, which thereby paved the way for reunification with the Irish Volunteers.[97] With the close of the war came the end of the Irish Party, while Volunteering moved on to a new and decidedly more aggressive phase of action.

## NOTES

I wish to acknowledge the assistance of the Irish Research Council for the Humanities and Social Sciences.

1. Peter Hart, *The IRA at War, 1916–1923* (Oxford: Oxford University Press, 2003), p.107.
2. Tim Bowman, *Carson's Army: The Ulster Volunteer Force, 1910–22* (Manchester: Manchester University Press, 2007), pp.18, 77.
3. Alvin Jackson, *Sir Edward Carson* (Dundalk: Dundalgan Press, 1993), pp.36–7.
4. Bulmer Hobson, *Ireland Yesterday and Tomorrow* (Tralee: Anvil Books, 1968), p.43.
5. Matthew Kelly, 'The Irish Volunteers: A Machiavellian Moment?' in D. George Boyce and Alan O'Day (eds), *The Ulster Crisis 1885–1921* (Basingstoke: Palgrave Macmillan, 2006), p.64. This notion is amplified further in Kelly's *The Fenian Ideal and Irish Nationalism, 1882–1916* (Woodbridge: Boydell Press, 2006), pp.179–236.
6. David Dwan, *The Great Community: Culture and Nationalism in Ireland* (Dublin: Field Day Press, 2008), pp.68–72.
7. Patrick Maume, *The Long Gestation: Irish Nationalist Life, 1891–1918* (Dublin: Gill & Macmillan, 1999), p.141.
8. Bulmer Hobson, *A Short History of the Irish Volunteers* (Dublin: Candle Press, 1918), p.172. Previously, Moore had served with the British Army.
9. F.X. Martin (ed.), *The Irish Volunteers 1913–1915: Recollections and Documents* (Dublin: James Duffy & Co., 1963), pp.98–101.
10. *Freeman's Journal*, 26 November 1913.
11. Eoin MacNeill to Roger Casement, 25 and 27 November 1913, Roger Casement Additional Papers, National Library of Ireland (NLI), MS 36, 203/2.
12. Kelly, *Fenian Ideal*, p.207.
13. David Fitzpatrick, *Politics and Irish Life 1913–1921: Provincial Experience of War and Revolution* (Dublin: Gill & Macmillan, 1977).
14. *Irish Volunteer*, 7 February 1914.
15. *Freeman's Journal*, 13 July 1913.
16. *Irish Volunteer*, 14 February 1914.
17. For these, see Maume, *Long Gestation*, pp.98–9, and James McConnel, 'The Irish Parliamentary Party, Industrial Relations and the 1913 Dublin Lockout', *Saothar*, no. 28 (2003), pp.25–36, respectively.
18. Michael Wheatley, *Nationalism and the Irish Party: Provincial Ireland 1910–1916* (Oxford: Oxford University Press, 2005), p.182.
19. J.J. Horgan, *Parnell to Pearse: Some Recollections and Reflections* (Dublin: Browne & Nolan, 1948), p.229.
20. Inspector General (IG) report, March 1914, The National Archives, London (TNA), CO 904/92/416 and 423.
21. Wheatley, *Nationalism and the Irish Party*, pp.185–6.
22. IG report, April 1914, TNA, CO 904/93/19.
23. IG report, May 1914, TNA, CO 904/93/233.
24. C.J. Irvine to Eoin MacNeill, 5 December 1914, Eoin MacNeill Papers, University College Dublin Archives (UCDA), LA1/H/1(15).
25. *Irish Volunteer*, 7 March 1914.
26. IG report, May 1914, TNA, CO 904/93/235.
27. Wilfrid Scawen Blunt, *My Diaries: Being a Personal Narrative of Events, 1888–1914*, 2 vols (London: Martin Secker, 1920), vol. ii, p.444.
28. Michael Tierney, *Eoin MacNeill: Scholar and Man of Action*, ed. F.X. Martin (Oxford: Oxford University Press, 1980), pp.130–1.
29. MacNeill to John Redmond, 2 June 1914, John Redmond Papers, NLI, MS 15, 204.
30. MacNeill to Stephen Gwynn, 22 May 1914, John Redmond Papers, NLI, MS 15, 204.
31. Redmond to MacNeill, 13 May 1914, John Redmond Papers, NLI, MS 15, 204.
32. *Irish News*, 19 May 1914.
33. *Freeman's Journal*, 10 June 1914.
34. Hobson, *Short History*, p.123; Marnie Hay, *Bulmer Hobson and the Nationalist Movement in Twentieth-Century Ireland* (Manchester: Manchester University Press, 2009), p.134.
35. *Leader*, 20 June 1914.

36. McCaffery to Redmond, 22 June 1914, John Redmond Papers, NLI, MS 15,257/3.
37. *Freeman's Journal*, 19 June 1914.
38. IG report, June 1914, TNA, CO 904/93/495; July 1914, TNA, CO 904/94/14.
39. Paper circulated to the Cabinet by A.B., 2 April 1914, Birrell Papers, Bodleian Library, Oxford (Bod.), MS Eng. c. 7035/312
40. IG report, August 1914, TNA, CO 904/94/220.
41. For a history of gun control in the United Kingdom, see Joyce Lee Malcolm, *Guns and Violence: The English Experience* (Cambridge, MA: Harvard University Press, 2002).
42. The proclamation is printed in full in F.X. Martin (ed.), *The Howth Gun-Running and the Kilcoole Gun-Running 1914: Recollections and Documents* (Dublin: Browne & Nolan, 1964), pp.3–4.
43. Maurice Moore to Casement, 8 April [1914], Roger Casement Additional Papers, NLI, MS 36, 203/3.
44. *Irish Volunteer*, 18 July 1914.
45. Patrick Pearse, *The Collected Works of Pádraic H. Pearse: Political Writings and Speeches* (Dublin: Phoenix Publishing Co., 1924), p.75.
46. Hobson, *Ireland Yesterday and Tomorrow*, p.51.
47. Colonel Maurice Moore, 'Account of the Irish Volunteers 1914', Maurice Moore Papers, NLI, MS 8489(5), p.291.
48. Hobson, *Short History of the Irish Volunteers*, p.134.
49. Moore, 'Account of the Irish Volunteers 1914', Maurice Moore Papers, NLI, MS 8489(5), p.242.
50. Maurice Moore to Captain George Berkeley, 13 July 1914, George Berkeley Papers, Cork City and County Archives (CCCA), PR12/55.
51. Pearse to Joseph McGarrity, 17 July 1914, in Séamas Ó Buachalla (ed.), *The Letters of P.H. Pearse* (Gerrards Cross: Colin Smythe, 1980), pp.318–21.
52. Quoted in A.C. Hepburn, *Catholic Belfast and Nationalist Ireland in the Era of Joe Devlin, 1871–1934* (Oxford: Oxford University Press, 2008), p.162.
53. George Berkeley to Nevil Macready, 24 July 1914, George Berkeley Papers, CCCA, PR12/93.
54. *Irish News*, 27 July 1914.
55. Kelly, *Fenian Ideal*, p.207.
56. Stephen Gwynn, *John Redmond's Last Years* (London: Edward Arnold, 1919), p.92.
57. IG report, August 1914, NA, CO 904/94/215.
58. The text of this important speech can be found in Denis Gwynn, *The Life of John Redmond* (London: George G. Harrap & Co., 1932), pp.391–2.
59. Casement to MacNeill, 24 November 1913, Roger Casement Additional Papers, NLI, MS 36, 203/2.
60. Casement to Moore, 2 June 1914, Maurice Moore Papers, NLI, MS 10, 561(3).
61. Hobson, *Short History of the Irish Volunteers*, p.41.
62. *Irish Volunteer*, 14 November 1914.
63. *Irish Volunteer*, 26 December 1914.
64. *Irish Volunteer*, 20 March 1915.
65. Interview with John Dillon, 27 November 1914, Sir Matthew Nathan Papers, Bod., MS 467 fo.36.
66. James McConnel, 'Recruiting Sergeants for John Bull? Irish Nationalist MPs and Enlistment During the Early Months of the Great War', *War in History*, vol. 14, no. 4 (2007), p.419.
67. *Leader*, 3 October 1914.
68. Gwynn, *Redmond's Last Years*, p.153; Horgan, *Parnell to Pearse*, p.262.
69. See the reports of various meetings between the Irish Party leadership and the Under-Secretary for Ireland, Sir Matthew Nathan, dated 25 January, 4 February and 20 February 1914, for the party's enthusiasm for the National Volunteers to be given the same status – if not the contentious name – of the British Territorial Forces. Matthew Nathan Papers, Bod., MS 467, fos. 111, 133 and 155.
70. IG report, September 1914, TNA, CO 904/94/407.
71. IG reports of December 1914, TNA, CO 904/95/436 and November 1915, TNA, CO 904/98/363.
72. Moore to Devlin, 28 September 1914, Maurice Moore Papers, NLI, MS 10, 561(8).
73. Wheatley, *Nationalism and the Irish Party*, p.214.
74. IG report, October 1914, TNA, CO 904/95/21.

75. IG report, December 1914, TNA, CO 904/95/436.
76. IG report, February 1916, TNA, CO 904/99/226. See David Fitzpatrick, 'The Logic of Collective Sacrifice: Ireland and the British Army, 1914–1918', *Historical Journal*, vol. 38, no. 4 (1995), pp.1017–30 for the complexities of Irish recruiting to the British Army.
77. *Irish Volunteer*, 3 October 1914.
78. Charles Townshend, *Easter 1916: The Irish Rebellion* (London: Allen Lane, 2005), p.44.
79. Records of the National Committee, National Volunteers, 2 March 1915, Maurice Moore Papers, NLI, MS 9239.
80. *National Volunteer*, 31 October 1914.
81. *National Volunteer*, 13 March 1915.
82. Gwynn, *Redmond's Last Years*, p.182. This view, however, should be tempered with reference to Wheatley, *Nationalism and the Irish Party*, p.265: Redmond's imperial nationalism was 'substantially different from that of the mass of his followers'.
83. Kelly, *Fenian Ideal*, p.244; McConnel, 'Recruiting Sergeants for John Bull?', pp.408–28.
84. *National Volunteer*, 15 January 1916.
85. Memorandum of interview with John Dillon, 12 November 1915, Augustine Birrell Papers, Bod., MS Eng. c. 7033.
86. IG report, October 1915, TNA, CO 904/98/185.
87. Nathan to Redmond, 7 February 1915, Matthew Nathan Papers, Bod., MS 462, fo.470.
88. Memorandum of interview with Redmond and Devlin, 21 August 1915, Matthew Nathan papers, Bod., MS 468, fo.243.
89. IG report, April 1915, TNA, CO 904/96/602.
90. Paul Bew, *John Redmond* (Dundalk: Dundalgan Press, 1996), pp.38–9.
91. Gwynn, *Redmond's Last Years*, p.239.
92. *National Volunteer*, 8 January 1916.
93. IG report, April–May 1916, TNA, CO 904/99/632.
94. Belfast Committee, National Volunteers, minute book, 26 April, 4 May, 11 May and 26 May 1916, UCDA P81.
95. Blunt, *My Diaries*, vol. ii, p.444.
96. Untitled and unsigned, statistics relating to the Volunteer forces in Ireland, 17 April 1916, H. H. Asquith Papers, Bod., MS Asquith 44/18.
97. Maume, *Long Gestation*, p.200.

# CHAPTER THREE

# Political Formations in Pre-First World War Ireland: The Politics of the Lost Generation and the Cult of Tom Kettle[1]

## MARGARET O'CALLAGHAN

The most successful Irish novel of 2005 was Sebastian Barry's *A Long Long Way*.[2] Winning numerous awards, it was celebrated in 2007 as the selected title of Dublin City Council's 'One City; One Book' Initiative, with sentences from its pages appearing at Dart stations and in other surprising venues. Centred on the fictional character of Willy Dunne, a young Dubliner who joined the Royal Dublin Fusiliers, its hero dies at Guinchy in France on 9 September 1916. This was the date of Tom Kettle's death, and he died at Guinchy.

It is difficult not to see the figure of Kettle lying like a palimpsest behind the book. For in recent years, Tom Kettle has become a figure representative of the generation 'forgotten' in a twentieth-century Ireland that ignored the sacrifice of Irishmen, many of them former Irish Volunteers and Irish nationalists, who died with other British troops, many of them Irish or Ulster unionists, in the trenches of the First World War. The *Irish Times* search engine for the online newspaper reveals over a hundred mentions of Kettle over the past decades; yet on every occasion on which he is introduced, he is cited as 'forgotten' or written out of history. The writing out of the war itself has been addressed in the context of revised apprehensions of Northern Ireland, and a series of recent titles analyse aspects of the Irish experience of the First World

War.[3] These works may be seen as part of a wider politics of commemorations and their political meanings within modern Ireland.[4]

This chapter attempts to look at Kettle's formation in the context of his own time and to place his choices in the context of his own generation; in doing so, it also reflects on the contemporaneous and subsequent cult of the lost parliamentary party generation, and its complex relation with the cult of the Rising. Kettle, here, is crucial because he appeared to straddle in his person and style the old and the new politics in the decade and a half before his death.

Tom Kettle was born in 1880, into the same generational cohort as James Joyce.[5] Their contemporaries were the generation who after 1891 engaged in what William Butler Yeats claimed was the moulding of modern Ireland.[6] After the fall of Parnell, the divided Irish Parliamentary Party continued to dominate Irish electoral politics, but it remained riven by divisions between Redmondites (incorporating Dillonites), Healyites and O'Brienites, maverick agrarian radicals and others. Complex political realignments of an unpredictable nature took place, as landlords who desired to be bought out of their estates met with certain leaders of the old land movement to bring about a series of parliamentary acts culminating in Wyndham's of 1903 and Birrell's of 1909. Through these acts, most of the land of Ireland changed hands; the revolution in ownership followed over two decades of complex battling.[7]

Agrarian politics remained alive in many localities,[8] but the old revolutionary leaders of the high days of the Home Rule and Land and National League campaigns of the 1880s became increasingly successful at the political arts of gaining advantage for their supporters, while Home Rule itself was resolutely stymied. 'Home Rule Comes of Age', James Joyce wrote mordantly in a Triestine newspaper in 1907 – the twenty-first anniversary of the first (failed) Home Rule bill.[9] Residues of the rhetoric of the Land War remained the discourse of nationalist party politics, despite changes in the landscape of alliances and divisions.[10] Official Conservative Unionist policy to 'kill Home Rule by kindness'[11] was briefly seen to promote a form of devolution under the Chief Secretaryship of George Wyndham; rapidly repudiated by all parties, it led to Wyndham's resignation in 1905. Unionist bodies such as the Irish Landowners' Convention, the Irish Unionist Alliance and others fought a sturdy propaganda battle before a London metropolitan and provincial British audience to stiffen the back of Tory resistance to Home Rule and to demonstrate the dangers and terrors Home Rule would hold for Irish unionists, for Britain and for the empire.[12]

The Conservative Party moved irrevocably against Irish Home Rule in 1886, and once they consolidated this choice to their own satisfaction through the 'Parnellism and Crime' Commission of 1887–9, the Home Rule cause was entirely dependent on Liberal promotion. Had the Liberals been proactive in this endeavour, the veto of the House of Lords – which defeated Gladstone's second Home Rule bill of 1893 after it had successfully passed the House of Commons – would have prevented success; as it was, they avoided the issue.[13] The Irish Party was therefore in a political bind. They could not proceed towards Home Rule without the Liberals; but, until the budget crisis of 1909, they had no significant leverage over the Liberal Party. They had leverage over both the Tory and Liberal parties for specific measures of 'amelioration', however, and in many ways it was through the Irish Party's exploitation of these practical possibilities that the years 1898 to 1912 were a period of steady improvement in a variety of social areas in Ireland.

## THE CHANGING LANGUAGES OF POLITICS

The apocalyptic nature of Home Rule rhetoric of the 1880s, and the image of Parnell as a prophet leading his people to within sight of the Promised Land, gave way to a political language of expectation after Parnell's cataclysmic fall. This context of expectation in a younger generation provided a range of discussions and debates, through fringe nationalist publications, about what the New Ireland, the post-Home Rule Ireland, might be. This world is partly explored in Louis Paul-Dubois's work, translated into English and introduced by Tom Kettle as *Contemporary Ireland* in 1908.[14] The fringe theatres of cultural production ignored the apparent political impossibility of an imminent Home Rule Ireland, and extended this unreality to an articulated contempt for Irish Party politicians.[15]

The debate, or series of debates, about what a Home Rule Ireland would resemble was conducted in pamphlets, novels, literary manifestoes, in cultural and literary groups and clubs, and in the mainstream and fringe nationalist press.[16] Fringe journalists, and apparently marginal literary figures, established a new language of cultural politics in the years 1891 to 1916. The exception to this largely internal debate was Yeats's desire culturally to create an appetite in literary London for a canon of new Irish literature that he wanted to bring into existence, which crucially required an external as well as an internal appreciation of the literary antecedents with which he wished it to be furnished.

Even Joyce explained Ireland to an external audience through his political writings published in the *Piccolo della Sera* in Trieste.[17]

The cultural capital of all nationalist groupings was to some extent a shared one. They all drew on the nineteenth-century Irish written nationalist and separatist tradition; evoked memories of 1798, 1848, Fenianism and the Manchester Martyrs; and shared a Land War-generated language and iconography of grabbers and emergency men, the evicted tenant's hut, the smashed house by the roadside, and the famine ship. As Kettle's later volume on Irish oratory shows, he was firmly attached to the nineteenth-century Irish rhetorical tradition.[18]

This is the context of the political formation of Tom Kettle as that unusual phenomenon: an Irish Catholic liberal. Kettle was a young adult in what was called the Royal University or University College, Dublin in the years from 1898 to 1902. His contemporaries were Arthur Clery, Constantine Curran, William Dawson, Francis and Hanna Sheehy-Skeffington, Frank Cruise O'Brien, James Joyce, Oliver St John Gogarty and Hugh Kennedy. The Boer War and nationalist opposition to it, together with the centenary celebrations of the 1798 Rebellion in 1898, encouraged new and often separatist nationalist groupings to set new political agendas through a host of publications. In the *Shan Van Vocht*, their Belfast journal, Alice Milligan and Ethna Carbery produced and published heroic tales looking back to the United Irishmen of 1798, patriotic ballads and historical reconstructions glorifying the past shared agendas of Catholic, Protestant and Dissenter, and celebrations of the unity and purity of pre-Christian Ireland. They tried through commemoration to create a new radical separatist politics. The Belfast circle around Francis Bigger's house *Ard-Righ* on the Antrim Road took the fieldwork of the Ulster Archaeological Society and formed an advanced nationalist nexus. Arthur Griffith took over the *Shan Van Vocht* subscription list when he set up his own papers, the *United Irishman* and later *Sinn Féin*, through which he elevated Thomas Davis and the Young Ireland generation as prophets of a new nationalism. Douglas Hyde and Eoin MacNeill built on Hyde's seminal 1893 text, 'The Necessity for De-Anglicising Ireland', to propose through the Gaelic League a radical reconstruction of the demands that free nationhood would place upon a people. The Irish people themselves, according to this interpretation, betrayed their language, and it was up to them (albeit those of a different generation) to recreate it in the present. D.P. Moran, through his highly successful newspaper the *Leader*, ostensibly attacked aspects of the social class to which he belonged – the Catholic middle class – in a radical attempt to advance Catholic power, break

Protestant ascendancy in business, and set the Irish economic and cultural agenda by the standards of his worldview.[19]

Kettle in his twenties was a highly intelligent if somewhat unworldly Catholic liberal. This liberalism derived from his own particular intellectual formation; it derived, too, from the history and positions of those who became his friends and by extension from some of his in-laws, the Sheehys.[20] The most important figure for understanding Kettle is his exceptional and powerful father, Andrew Kettle. From the late 1860s, through his association with Isaac Butt, Andy Kettle's name was well known in political life in Ireland. His own background was interesting, though his social status is hard to gauge with precision. Eventually farming on a grand scale, he began as a tenant farmer of thirty acres in north county Dublin. By the 1880s he was a figure of some economic weight. He married into the McCourt family for what he himself described as 'agricultural produce factors'. The Kettles had close associations with the old Catholic family of Drynam House, the Russell Cruises. Tom Kettle was brought up in the family home, Mill-view in Malahide. The main family farming was done at Artane, Kilmore and Newtown, where they grew barley for the Guinness brewery. North county Dublin farming was atypical by Irish standards, though not necessarily by Leinster or North Leinster standards. It was tillage, not grazing; labour intensive, and employed labourers on a scale that was almost industrial.

Andy Kettle had a powerful sense of his own family history, and an even more powerful sense of north Dublin as a place and of his position within it. Born in 1833 at Drynam near Swords, he evoked in his memoirs 'the hill of Feltrim with its holy well, windmill, lime kiln and rabbit warren', and also the ruin of a mansion where it was said 'the king', James II, stopped when running from the Boyne.[21] His mother was an O'Kavanagh, and her mother was an O'Brien who was a 'folk medicalist' with considerable reputation. Kettle senior writes at length about her role in 1798. He claimed that as a young attractive woman, she was messenger and buyer for her family's carmenstage (a staging-post for coach drivers) at Turvey, and so 'she armed the men of north Dublin with guns and pikes'. Her husband was arrested with a man named Coughlan; they escaped hanging.[22] The Kettles at this point in history were of a substantial Irish Catholic class, with self-proclaimed assured roots in the history and landscape of North Dublin.

Andy Kettle had a relationship of easy intimacy with Parnell, for whom he had an unshakeable regard, which was reciprocated. Throughout Parnell's career Kettle was a guide, a mentor, and sometimes a steadying influence. More radical than the Fenians at times – he proposed withdrawing from Westminster in the early 1880s – he was an early advocate of peasant proprietorship and architect of aspects of the Land War, a conservative if benevolent employer, and a figure of considerable political range. At the end of Parnell's career, Kettle was one of the few who, despite his devout Catholicism, stood by Parnell with, since it was necessary, the hillside men – who were scarcely to his liking. He did so anyway. As a man of sixty, he stood on a Parnellite platform in the final brutal Carlow by-election after the split. The Kettle attitude to John Redmond was framed by Redmond's singular attachment to Parnell and willingness to support him in 1891. The Kettles and the Redmonds were Parnellites when the Liberal Party, the Catholic Church, most of the respectable classes, and Tim Healy, John Dillon, William O'Brien and Michael Davitt had denounced him. Tom Kettle was a youth of eleven at the time of the Parnell split: it had a decisive influence on him, coming as he did from such a political family. Parnell haunted the imagination of nationalist Ireland for decades, but particularly haunted Tom Kettle's personal formation.

In the *Leader*, D.P. Moran, himself a product of Castleknock College, castigated the alumni of other 'good' Irish schools as West British, anglicised, shoneens or Castle Catholics.[23] These lines were not initially deployed about Tom Kettle's Clongowes Wood Jesuit education, when he began to acquire a public profile in the early 1900s; in due course, however, they were so deployed. Ironically, at least some of Kettle's schooling had been with the Christian Brothers in North Richmond Street; the emerging Catholic elite did not see the somewhat plebeian brothers as desirable educators for their own sons. Kettle had been with Arthur Clery, Constantine Curran, and Oliver St John Gogarty at what was still sometimes known as the Catholic University, before it was fully formalised as University College Dublin in the Liberal chief secretary Augustine Birrell's University Act of 1908.[24]

Catholic university education had been a burning political question for most of the late nineteenth century, and Tom Kettle and his circle of friends and acquaintances were a generation expected to form the elite of a Home Rule Ireland, although educated in what was effectively a college funded on a shoestring on revenue brought in by Royal University teaching fellowship monies.[25]

Kettle's education was not dissimilar to that depicted by Joyce in *A*

*Portrait of the Artist as a Young Man*. Their shared university circle is also depicted there and in *Dubliners*, which Joyce completed in 1907. Gabriel Conroy in 'The Dead' may have something of Kettle to him. Kettle's first full biographer, J.B. Lyons, has documented many of his political responses during these years.[26] It is perhaps crucial to contrast his choices with those of his contemporaries. He was academically brilliant, handsome, a superb speaker, had a gift for friendship, and was great company. He was also highly strung, was affected by the death of his brother in May 1903, was deeply religious and wracked by doubts about the purpose of existence. He was also the younger son of a formidable father who was nearly 50 years old when he was born. In a letter to his sister, Kettle wrote:

> [i]t seems to me that in our family more than any other I know there is an almost complete absence of that close and confidential intercourse which makes some homes so delightful ... It was in order to bring into ours a little sprightliness and good fellowship that I wanted Charlie and the youngsters to learn music and dancing and other sociable accomplishments.[27]

Kettle had been brought up on narratives of the battles of the Land War; his ears had echoed with its rhetoric. But the language of the oppressed tenant, which incorporated everyone from the five-acre tenant to the substantial, almost gentry farmers of his own family, must have rung slightly hollow as the Kettles consolidated their financial and social position as Irish Party insiders. By the early 1900s the party was reunited as the United Irish League and remained wedded to the Liberal alliance, albeit with complaints and caveats. During the following decade certain challenges to that alliance were presented, but all of these were ultimately defeated by Redmond and the party leadership. Joyce flew by the nets of nation, family and duty to establish himself as a free man and a writer abroad, or, as he immodestly and presciently put it, 'to forge in the smithy of my soul the uncreated conscience of my race'.[28] Joyce's father's life had been a chronicle of downward social mobility. Kettle's family were anything but downwardly mobile socially, and serious expectations of continued upward mobility framed Kettles' life from his college years. When the brilliant linguist fell apart after his brother's death, just before what should have been his finals, it was assumed that he would spend a period of time in Germany and Austria and then come home.[29] Kettle dropped out before his finals, perhaps under the pressure of familial expectation, and graduated later in 'mental and moral sciences' or philosophy, not with the languages and literature degree on which he had originally embarked. Though he spoke in the college's Literary and Historical Society, though his early journalistic writings were literary and historical, he began a pattern of not playing to his strengths, a pattern confirmed much later when he became Professor of National Economics at University College Dublin. He then joked to Padraic Colum that he would 'write an essay on the outline of an introduction to a preface to the study of national economics'.[30]

## KETTLE AND POLITICS

Apart from Richard Hazleton and Stephen Gwynn, both winners of by-elections in 1906, the Irish Party had not had a new MP of substance and youth since Joe Devlin, in the embrace of the Ancient Order of Hibernians, entered the Commons in 1904. For Redmond, a brilliant, articulate, personable individual like Kettle was potentially attractive, even if Kettle's French and German political and philosophical interests were irrelevant. The fringe and not-so-fringe nationalist papers, attempting to set an anti-parliamentary party agenda and what Patrick Maume calls the mosquito press, presented Kettle as 'a place-seeker' currying favour with the corrupt and ancient parliamentarians. But Kettle himself had a career as a part of that fringe press, through the *Nationist*, which he edited, and also through the range of journals in both Dublin and London in which he published. It appears that the *Nationist* had been designed as an attempt to create a rival to D.P. Moran's *Leader*. Perhaps Kettle's most significant essay was his review of Arthur Griffith's new book *The Resurrection of Hungary: A Parallel for Ireland* in the *New Ireland Review* of February 1905.[31] Kettle referred to 'the Extreme Right of Nationalism, the Separatists', and spoke of their response to a political stasis: 'The imagination of a people is tidal and periodic; and the debacle of '93 was succeeded, as by a natural law, by the dreariness of retreating waves.'[32] For him, though, the separatists were to be commended for their energy: 'Through their journal *United Irishman* and through their various societies they have been doing excellent work in promoting language, literature and industries, and still more brilliant work in keeping alive the idea of absolute independence.' What they lacked, he claimed, until this pamphlet of Griffith's, was a policy to replace parliamentarianism: 'It may be that appeal to arms has been advocated, but that is not a policy. A policy is something that we can put in force at once; and, as things stand, the doctrine of physical force is no more than a piece of *blague*, and not very amusing *blague* at that.' If Griffith advocates a new policy on the Hungarian model, then perhaps he should return to a slightly earlier position when

> there was hinted a readiness to treat the so-called 'Constitution-alists' with the same wise tolerance that Kossuth's party exercised towards that great constitutionalist Deak. Nor does it seem wildly unreasonable that such relations should exist between two parties which are certainly going the same road if they are not ostensibly going the same length of it.

For Kettle, the constitutional and 'separatist' wings existed in a symbiotic relation:

> For ten years, then, both sections of Nationalism have been, in relation to their central object, futile and fruitless; the one having a political ideal, but no policy; the other a policy indeed and an indeterminate ideal, but insufficient enthusiasm and driving force to make it work. Such a condition of things is so unnatural that it cannot be permanent. A political revival and reunion there must be; a dissipation of that crude unbelief which has been mistaken by some for common-sense politics, and a fusion of all Nationalist groups unless the country is to perish of its own ill-temper. This feeling is beginning to take captive a larger and larger number of people in Ireland. They want a movement that will march, that will justify enthusiasm and their desire for it will soon be so great as to incapacitate them from quarrelling with those who are their natural allies. They want a movement that will knit together in a national synthesis the ideas rediscovered and revitalised in the last ten years: and if the 'Hungarian Policy', the policy, that is, of withdrawal from Westminster, is capable of doing this it certainly comes in its hour.

His objections to Griffith's policy are serious, but not insurmountable; his main point is that though *The Resurrection of Hungary* is beautifully written, the plan is ill thought-out, insufficiently developed, and the parallel ignores the very considerable differences between Hungary's relation to Austria and its Empire and Ireland's to Great Britain. Kettle's belief that Home Rule was imminent also tended to reduce the impact of Griffith's arguments:

> To abandon the old methods at the precise moment when they may begin to bear fruit is a project that can hardly be seriously

proposed ... it is certainly the largest idea contributed to Irish politics for a generation ... this pamphlet will have justified its existence if only it leads up to a working alliance between the two sections of Nationalism, now standing deplorably apart.[33]

In the following year, Kettle took issue with Francis Sheehy-Skeffington's characterisation of Ireland as subject to clericalism. Here again, he pursues a middle path, but one that inclines to a sympathetic understanding of the new status quo. He also retains the old Irish Party reluctance to concede to accusations of church influence.

> The chief complaint I have to make against Mr Sheehy-Skeffington is this; he totally ignores the new forces in Ireland. If there is one thing [on] which everyone who walks through the country with open eyes and ears is agreed, is that the whole fabric of Irish opinion is in process of reconstruction. It is a matter not so much of this or that concrete event as of a change of psychological climate. We have had a quarter of a century of Intermediate Education, and practically the same of the Royal University; and defective as both undeniably are you cannot put books into the hands and ideas into the heads of your children for twenty-seven years and fail to sweep away certain cobwebs. There is one virtue, at all events, that has been developed by our machinery of instruction, and that is freedom of mind. Anybody who knows Dublin, for instance, knows that there is no human problem from the striping [*sic*] of a Connaught ranch to the perilous novels of Fogazzaro, from the proper method of teaching Irish to the latest movement in French verse, but has entered and exercised the minds of some group or other ... Up to the present its characteristic creation has been the Gaelic League; although that organisation, with its miraculous avoidance of the root issues, political and philosophical, by no means expresses the full tide of new ideas.[34]

In 1906 Kettle was elected as MP for East Tyrone; despite representing a northern constituency, he never took unionist opposition to Home Rule seriously. It may be that his later writings, particularly after 1915, about the war forging new bonds between Irish nationalists and unionists were influenced by this period from 1906 to 1910, and by his friendship with Joe Devlin. Forced immediately after election by Redmond into a fundraising tour of the United States as United Irish League (UIL) representative, Kettle was persecuted and maligned by

John O'Callaghan, the tour organiser, who proclaimed Kettle and Hazelton to be young snobs. As J.B. Lyons documents clearly, the American Irish nationalist touring scene was a web of tensions, vested interests and rival cabals. It was almost impossible for young and inexperienced men such as Kettle and Hazelton not to make mistakes. It seems, perhaps, that Kettle was too handsome, too groomed and too socially polished, witty and urbane for O'Callaghan's liking.[35] Kettle also had a wounding tongue. He was further attacked by the veteran Fenian John Devoy, who was sponsoring Bulmer Hobson on a US tour that was organised in opposition to the 'clapped out' policies of the parliamentary party representatives at the time.

Kettle performed brilliantly on the Westminster stage. He was assiduous as the Irish Party finance spokesman, producing a book on Home Rule finance some years later.[36] He did a variety of tasks well, but his earlier fluid position on Sinn Féin and other new formations hardened as he was unremittingly attacked. The main point that Arthur Griffith, Bulmer Hobson, the Dungannon Clubs and the Belfast republican circle around *Ard-Rìgh* wished to make, was that the Irish Parliamentary Party were has-beens, ancient, dilapidated figures who had done their job in the 1880s, but who were now superannuated old men. Kettle was a prime target because he was none of these things. He does not seem to have had the most robust of constitutions for the receipt of such attacks. Kettle had published the work of Bulmer Hobson in the *Nationist* when he edited it with Francis Sheehy-Skeffington in 1906. He had found many of Sinn Féin's ideas interesting. His early position was that they were all working together for the same goal of a Home Rule Ireland. Everything that he wrote and published, certainly up to 1910, suggested that he supported the most expansive form of Home Rule attainable. He crossed into the circle of Hobson and Roger Casement through a warm acquaintance with Alice Stopford Green, who can be regarded as an historian to what was to become the revolutionary generation. Kettle was sympathetic to the aims of the Gaelic League; he did not make much progress in learning Irish, but he was scarcely worse in this respect than D.P. Moran and many others. As it became apparent that his gestures of friendship towards more radical nationalists were not reciprocated, so he hardened his position and used his considerable wit and verbal ingenuity to wound.

Kettle proclaimed himself to be a European.[37] This was a standard Irish nationalist trope for which there was both Irish Republican Brotherhood (IRB) and Catholic precedent: it permitted escape from unionist accusations of Irish provincialism. In Kettle's case it did, however, reflect real intellectual and sentimental ties. During the early years of the Irish Volunteers, he particularly targeted for attack those he saw as late converts to the cause of Irish nationality. He displayed singular viciousness in his later attacks on Roger Casement when the Irish Party annexed the Volunteers, and later during Casement's disastrous foray in Germany. Kettle's published writings, in association with his speeches and public addresses, are intellectually revealing in analysing his position on 'the national question', and here Casement may provide a key and a contrast.

Time after time in his speeches, Kettle referred back to the glory days of the 1880s and to his father's role as Parnell's man. In class terms, the Kettles had been styled as a nationalist dynasty by the Land War and by association with Parnell. The Young Ireland Branch (YIB) of the UIL, which was founded in 1904, had partly represented Kettle's desire to break with the narrowness of his past. He had further embarked on a new politics with his own generation through the Literary and Historical Society and through the *cui bono* dining club. But while Kettle edited and published the *Nationist*, Redmond had already, through Kettle's father, offered him a reasonably safe party seat at Westminster. Kettle's new beginnings were stymied or closed off by his family, by the Catholic Church and by the parliamentary party.[38]

Kettle met, through the Literary and Historical Society, in which he was a leading light, all of the politically, socially and intellectually active public personalities of his time. He enjoyed good relations with Patrick Pearse,[39] had limited sympathy for Yeats, against whose *Countess Cathleen* he had protested in 1899, and formed a close friendship with Joe Devlin. At this time, Roger Casement, Bulmer Hobson and Douglas Hyde sought to construct new cultural, intellectual and economic models of what it meant to be Irish; but Kettle was secure in his sense of his Irishness, and thought 'going on about it' unnecessary and superfluous. He taunted Sinn Féiners and advanced separatists with accusations that they had done nothing in the 1880s when Land Leaguers had taken the plank bed and others had taken more, a taunt that was to torment and torture him after 1916. For Kettle was, in a European sense, a liberal: a liberal who was represented by his contemporaries as not understanding class,[40] the role of class in politics, and where he was seen to stand in the class hierarchy. He saw himself as enlightened and above class, but this is not how others saw him. Tom Garvin's study of the social background of those who became revolutionaries in Ireland in this period emphasises their social class and their rejection of the previous generation, particularly of their fathers.[41]

Kettle liked London, just as he liked Dublin. He was convivial, congenial. In Dublin, he liked the Bailey and other establishments around Grafton Street, as did Griffith and others. But revolutionaries tend to be puritans and Kettle was labelled a boozer, which he clearly sometimes was. It is difficult not to believe, reading letters from his future wife Mary Sheehy, that he may well have traded one controlling family context for another. He had had doubts about marriage, but had pressed on nonetheless. Kettle was friendly with relatively young political and cultural nationalists such as Stephen Gwynn and Robert Lynd. His friendship with Joe Devlin[42] appears from one late letter to have been close, but the Kettle archive in UCD reflects only his early college friendships and reveals little about his friendships with Joseph Hone or Lynd, or with his London circle. Though we know that he was a member of the Ancient Order of Hibernians, as was common among members of the Irish Party, particularly in the north in these years, there is little in his record to give us any insight into what, if anything, that meant to him. His earlier friendship with the Sheehy-Skeffingtons, though strengthened by marriage to Mary Sheehy, does not appear to have remained close.

All of his early college and *Nationist* friendships seem attenuated after he became an MP. Those who remained behind in the Young Ireland Branch – the new hope to unite the parliamentary party with the broader cultural agendas of the new generation, which Kettle had played a key role in setting up in 1904 – became increasingly critical of the parliamentary party and of Kettle himself. They saw him as having betrayed them for party loyalism; a fact made all the more bitter because he had been a friend. William Sears, of the advanced nationalist *Enniscorthy Echo*, wrote to Sheehy-Skeffington after the disastrous 1909 UIL convention, which effectively killed the YIBs:

> The same crowds that cheered Mr Devlin and Mr Dillon at the Convention last week would do the same next week and every other week for the rest of their lives ... I know the country delegate well ... He wants to be bossed and bulldozed. He wants a Devlin and he has the right man in Joe. The young men in the country are different. They are thinking for themselves, they read the *Irish Nation*[43] every week and *Sinn Féin*. They look down with contempt on the UIL, the Party and the *Freeman*. Are you not on the wrong side? Come over to us?[44]

A series of challenges to the Redmondite hegemony were mounted from 1906 onwards, but all failed. The revolt in 1907 on the so-called

Council bill led to the departure of William Sears, William Ganly (the former UIL party boss in Granard and president of the North Longford UIL),[45] Sir Thomas Esmonde and James O'Meara.[46] Richard Hazleton was ground down by 'bankruptcy arising out of an electoral dispute with Tim Healy'.[47] The February 1908 by-election in Leitrim, in which former Irish Party MP C.J. Dolan stood for Sinn Féin, represented the high-water mark of party rebellion. The so-called Baton Convention of 1909 indicated Redmondite and Devlinite unwillingness to tolerate any deviation from the party line. This style of leadership anticipated the authoritarian manner in which the party took over the Volunteers in 1914. In all of these instances, Kettle's formerly independent voice was suppressed or muffled. It was difficult for him to retain good relations with his former circle, who represented him as cowed by parliamentary conformity. On the other hand, London, Fleet Street and the House of Commons opened up a new world to this convivial, amusing, intellectually curious and engaging man. In the Commons, he spoke on the Irish university question and on finance, but the main focus of his interests seems to have been Egypt and the rights of subject peoples.

He was widely read and highly cultivated. His translation of Paul-Dubois' book on Ireland was driven by a desire to introduce an outsider's perspective to an Irish audience. He was 30 years of age when his parliamentary career was suddenly ended, perhaps due to financial pressure or frustration at his circumscribed role, and he became a professor of economics in the new National University; in the same year he married Mary Sheehy, whom he had known for a decade. He was a qualified barrister, though he rarely practised. It is difficult not to see the university choice as evidence yet again of family control, a desire to pull Kettle back from London, and an example of Andy Kettle's determination to steer his sons into safe and prestigious positions in an emerging new Ireland.[48] The prize of a professorship, in a new university, in a subject he would not have chosen, with hardly any students, and without a generational cohort in place seems threadbare and depressing. Marriage may have been a reason for the decision not to commute to London; but with London removed, Kettle lived in the full glare of Dublin.

## KETTLE AND THE GREAT WAR

Tom Kettle was an Irish liberal, a European liberal. But he was also a liberal in a British tradition. He thought Nietzsche a genius, but detested him for his attacks on Christianity.[49] This was later to turn into a vigorously espoused loathing of what he and others called *Prussianism*. But like many educated men of his generation in Britain before 1914, his Germanism was a given; a given that understood human progress and the civilising and improving of society as a manifestation of the infusing of Christian morality with idealist philosophy. His Europeanism was essentially bound up with his Catholicism – European civilisation was for him essentially Catholic civilisation – and much of his Catholicism runs in tandem with that of Hillaire Belloc and G.K. Chesterton. As his article 'The Soldier Priests of France' demonstrates, he shared Belloc and Chesterton's sense of modern France as essentially the creation of the Revolution, heroically manifest in the citizens-in-arms whose republicanism had finally been reconciled with the ancient Catholic traditions of France by the war. It is also notable that Kettle's dispatches on German atrocities in Belgium in 1914 were published in the *Daily News*, the pre-eminent journalistic voice of British liberalism, financed by the chocolate manufacturing, non-conformist and pacifist Cadbury family, who provided Chesterton with one of his main sources of income as a journalist.

At the outbreak of war, Kettle was buying arms for Redmond and the Irish Volunteers in Belgium. Redmond had taken over MacNeill, Moore and Casement's Volunteers, in the language of the Irish prime minister-in-waiting. Redmond's Volunteers were to be the army of an almost emergent Home Rule Ireland. This rhetoric, developed as part of the process of bringing the very considerable Volunteer movement under Redmond's control, was a language that those who supported the war in 1914 utilised again and again.[50] It was Ireland fighting alongside Britain, not for Britain; on the right side, with Britain.

In 1914 Tom Kettle claimed that what Germany then represented was what Britain represented at the time of the Boer War, when he passionately opposed Britain's position. Kettle's sense of the dark side of Germany, epitomised as Prussian militarism made manifest in the destruction of Catholic Louvain, was represented by him as analogous to the Cromwellian desecrations in Ireland of another age. This, to him, was barbarism, and Ireland had to stand against it. In *Battle Songs for the Irish Brigade*, put together with Stephen Gwynn, he tried to refashion Irish nationalist martial tradition for the purpose of defending European civilisation. In 1914 this had an appeal for some young nationalist Irish males.[51]

In the autumn of 1914 Kettle was in Newry and countless other locations all over the country militantly recruiting for the war. Accompanied by a Belgian priest, he made comparisons between Catholic

Ireland and Catholic Belgium, the sack of Drogheda by the Cromwellians and the sack of Louvain by the Germans. But enlisting Irish historical memory and cultural capital in the cause of the war in Europe was potentially a strained lineage. Most of the songs of the Irish Brigade (which was never formed by the British Army in any case) were evocations of Fontenoy and other staple Wild Goose engagements on which the Irish had usually been found on the anti-British side.[52]

For Kettle in 1914, the matter of Home Rule was effectively resolved. The pressing matter was barbarism in Europe. But the history of the dealings of the Irish nationalist leadership with the British Army indicate that Redmond was not a man with the powers of a prime minister-in-waiting, nor were those Irish nationalists who enlisted in an Irish brigade on a footing with the Ulster Volunteers. The strains present throughout the ongoing years of the war, in the attempt to create a new beginning for Ireland and Britain through their shared crusade, were never entirely absent, as Redmond's frustrated attempts to get more recognition for the Irish position within the army demonstrated. Recruiting died off in 1915, and Kettle was driven to propose conscription for a righteous cause.[53] But the strains of 1915 were as nothing compared to the impact of the Easter Rising on many Irish nationalists within the British Army. As initial irritation with the rebels turned to a questioning of the actions of the military on the streets of Dublin, the new dispensation of a partnership in morality between Britain and Ireland came increasingly under strain.

Cologne Cathedral and the Catholic university of Louvain were Kettle's Europe. He thought that Home Rule was as good as won in 1914, and that a shared crusade would consolidate links between a Home Rule Ireland and Britain. The sheer hell of the war, the continuation of politics throughout it, and the Rising of 1916 confounded his liberal vision but emphasised what was for him the stark nature of the choice between barbarism and civilisation. His own comment about being remembered in the uniform of a British officer may be apocryphal, but it shows that the meaning of a British uniform in Irish history was to become again in predominant representation analogous to that of 'the captain of the yoes'. This was a terrible legacy for nationalists who had fought and died for a Home Rule Ireland in the most barbarous war of modern memory. In 1927 Dublin Corporation proposed to take over Merrion Square as a memorial to those Irish who had fought and died in the First World War,[54] but they were not honourably mentioned again until Seán Lemass, in a speech at the King's

Inns in 1966, recognised their honourable fight as Irish nationalists. Maurice Moynihan echoed these words, remembering the death of his own brother at the penultimate moment of that war.[55]

Asked in the United States during his 1906 tour how 'dear old Ireland' stood, Kettle had replied: 'Ireland doesn't stand. She moves on.' It was his tragedy to live in a time of great upheaval, a war that went on longer than any could have imagined, and an Irish revolutionary set that figuratively shoved his words down his throat. In the manifesto of the National Volunteers in November 1914, Kettle had written of 'the histrionics of Sinn Féin humbugs, whose posturing as so many Robert Emmets and Wolfe Tones when such posturing may be indulged in with safety even by salaried servants of the British.'[56] Days before his death he wrote to Robert Lynd: '[t]he Skeffington case oppresses me with horror'.[57] He wrote home a week before his death:

> We are moving up tonight into the Battle of the Somme. The bombardment, destruction and bloodshed are beyond all imagination, nor did I ever think that the valour of simple men could be quite as beautiful as that of my Dublin Fusiliers. I have had two chances of leaving them – one on sick leave and one to take a staff job. I have chosen to stay with my comrades.

Kettle was too familially and intellectually steeped in an Irish nationalist tradition not to realise the implications of the Rising of 1916. Conor Cruise O'Brien, Kettle's wife's nephew, always claimed that family lore had it that Kettle said the Rising in Dublin in 1916 placed him in an impossible position. Emmet Dalton, who was later with Michael Collins at the time of his death, was with Kettle at Guinchy. Kettle's talent, his wit and his sensitivity live on in the poem that he wrote for his daughter Elizabeth Dorothy or Betty, several days before his death, a death which perhaps he did not fear.

> To my darling Betty
> The gift of God
>
> In wiser days my darling rosebud, blown
> To beauty proud as was your mother's prime,
> In that desired, delayed, incredible time,
> You'll ask why I abandoned you, my own,
> And the dear heart that was your baby throne
> To dice with death. And oh! They'll give you rhyme
> And reason; some will call the thing sublime
> And some decry it in a knowing tone

> So here, while the mad guns curse overhead,
> And tired men sigh with mud for couch and floor,
> Know that we fools, now with the foolish dead,
> Died not for flag, nor King, nor Emperor,[58]
> But for a dream, born in a herdsman's shed,
> And for the secret Scripture of the poor.[59]

On Kettle's death Dublin City Council passed a motion: 'Ireland has paid another toll in this terrible war by losing one of her most brilliant young intellects. Tom Kettle gave his life for a cause that to him meant Truth and Justice and Humanity, and no greater tribute can be laid on any man's grave.'[60] The complex allusiveness of the meaning of 'the secret scripture of the poor', and the conflicting versions of his reaction to the Rising circulating then and later from contemporaries, left a space for a variety of interpretations of his death and of how it framed the life that had preceded it. One of his oldest friends, Arthur Clery, wrote three years afterwards:

> The last time I met Kettle was a few weeks after Easter 1916, He was driving in military uniform on a car with his little daughter, and stopped to speak to me. I congratulated him on the preface to *Irish Orators*. But his whole conversation was of MacDonagh and the others who had been put to death in Low Week, of the fortitude they had shown. He felt very bitterly, and he spoke of their fate with that wistfulness which Mr Lynd also noticed. I think there must have been a time in his life when he looked forward to die as they had died. He died in a different way and for a different cause. But the idea of final self-sacrifice was as much a haunting desire with him as it was with Patrick Pearse.[61]

William Fallon, a friend and contemporary, said in a lecture in the 1930s that Kettle had stated on Easter Tuesday that '[t]he circumstances of this rebellion are so peculiar that one does not know which side one ought to join'. Sheehy-Skeffington's death in Portobello Barracks led Kettle to write: '[t]his brave and honourable man died to the rattle of musketry, his name will be recalled to the ruffle of drums'.[62] Denis Gwynn, in a 1966 lecture in UCD, claimed that Kettle had said of the leaders of the Rising that they had 'spoiled his dream of a free united people in a free Europe'.[63]

Mary Sheehy Kettle wished to scotch the notion that her husband had sought death in the trenches. Politically, his legacy was contested from the moment of his death. Through his range and connections,

his fame and brilliance, he knew everyone of significance in nationalist Ireland in the years between 1898 and 1914. He knew all of the positions, and had been intimately acquainted with all of the options.
The almost unbelievable peculiarity of the fact that Home Rule became imminent and finally due to pass in the year that the First World
War broke out meant that Kettle, like so many of his generation, operated in a terrain without maps. The war had its own dynamic and
swept the certainties of the years that preceded it away; Kettle was one
of many victims of this extraordinary shift.

NOTES

1. This chapter draws upon the recorded proceedings of a public meeting in the Chamber of
   the old House of Lords in College Green, Dublin on 7 September 2006, commemorating the
   life of Tom Kettle, who was killed at Guinchy in France on the same day one hundred years
   earlier. The talks on Kettle were given by: Conor Cruise O'Brien, Frank Callanan, Brendan
   Walsh, Patrick Maume and the present author. The proceedings were published as Gerald
   Barry (ed.), *Remembering Tom Kettle 1880–1916* (Dublin: privately printed, 2009).
2. Sebastian Barry, *A Long Long Way* (London: Faber, 2005).
3. Adrian Gregory and Senia Paseta (eds), *Ireland and the Great War* (Manchester: Manchester
   University Press, 2002); Nuala C. Johnson, *Ireland, the Great War and the Geography of Re-
   membrance* (Cambridge: Cambridge University Press, 2003); Keith Jeffery, *Ireland and the
   Great War* (Cambridge: Cambridge University Press, 2002); John Horne (ed.), *Our War: Ireland and the Great War* (Dublin: Royal Irish Academy and RTÉ, Thomas Davis Lectures,
   2008). The last collection was launched by RTÉ through a series of public lectures and debates in Dublin and Belfast.
4. Mary Daly and Margaret O'Callaghan, *1916 in 1966: Commemorating the Easter Rising*
   (Dublin: Royal Irish Academy, 2007).
5. Joyce once described Kettle as his best friend in Dublin. Letter from James Joyce to Nora Bar-
   nacle, 5 September 1909, reprinted in Richard Ellman (ed.), *Selected Letters of James Joyce*
   (London: Faber & Faber, 1975), p.168.
6. R.F. Foster, *W.B. Yeats: A Life*, vol. ii, *The Arch-Poet* (Oxford: Oxford University Press, 2003).
7. For the propaganda wars around Land War of the 1880s, see Margaret O'Callaghan, *British
   High Politics and a Nationalist Ireland: Criminality, Land and the Law under Forster and
   Balfour* (Cork: Cork University Press, 1994).
8. On the politics of the post-Parnellite factions, see Paul Bew, *Conflict and Conciliation in Ireland, 1890–1910: Parnellites and Radical Agrarians* (Oxford: Oxford University Press, 1987);
   Frank Callanan, *The Parnell Split* (Cork: Cork University Press, 1992), pp.175–7; and Patrick
   Maume, *The Long Gestation: Irish Nationalist Life, 1891–1918* (Dublin: Gill & Macmillan,
   1999).
9. 'Home Rule Comes of Age' in Kevin Barry (ed.), *James Joyce: Occasional, Critical and Political Writing* (Oxford: Oxford University Press, 2000), pp.142–4.
10. See Michael Wheatley, *Nationalism and the Irish Party: Provincial Ireland, 1910–1916* (Ox-
    ford: Oxford University Press, 2005) for a study of the complex actualities of the Irish Party
    at a local level.
11. Andrew Gailey, *Ireland and the Death of Kindness: The Experience of Constructive Unionism,
    1890–1905* (Cork: Cork University Press, 1987).
12. Patrick Buckland, *Irish Unionism 1885–1923* (Belfast: HMSO, 1923).
13, Gladstone presented Home Rule as a crusade; his successors saw it as a burden. A strong
    Liberal imperialist element within the Liberal Party wanted to dump it altogether. This
    retrospectively fuels the insistence of the Parnell myth that Liberals are not to be trusted. I
    am grateful to Patrick Maume for this point.
14. Louis Paul-Dubois, *Contemporary Ireland*, with an introduction by T.M. Kettle (Dublin:
    Maunsel & Co., 1908). It appears that Kettle translated the text. Paul-Dubois, an academic
    sociologist, was a son-in-law of Hippolyte Taine and a member of the important intellectual

cohort around Ferdinand Brunetière and the *Revue des Deux Mondes*. Some of Kettle's more tendentious views on the correct function of literature, to provide moral uplift, were derived from the post-Comtean positivist position of Brunetière. See Mary Sheehy to Tom Kettle, 7 November 1908, LA/34/6(6), T.M. Kettle Papers, University College Dublin Archives (UCDA).

15. For the reading of educated young men in rural Ireland in these years, see the author's introduction in Deirdre McMahon (ed.), *The Moynihan Brothers in Peace and War, 1909–1918: Their New Ireland* (Dublin: Irish Academic Press, 2004). They read Griffith's papers, Ryan's *Irish Nation and Peasant* and D.P. Moran's *Leader*, and many of them also read a wide spectrum of the London press, particularly the writings of G.K. Chesterton and Hillaire Belloc in *New Age*. See, too, Virginia E. Glandon, *Arthur Griffith and the Advanced Nationalist Press in Ireland, 1900–22* (New York: Peter Lang, 1985).

16. This world is depicted by James Stephens in his article 'Arthur Griffith, President of Dáil Éireann' in *Review of Reviews* (March 1922), pp.210–17.

17. Barry (ed), *Joyce: Occasional, Critical and Political Writings*, pp.217–88.

18. In his introduction to his *Irish Orators and Oratory with an introduction by T.M. Kettle* (Dublin: Talbot Press, 1916), Kettle repeats a story he has been told by an acquaintance who heard it from an old man who had been present, a story of 'how the Liberator was able to transmit his speech to the utmost fringes of great gatherings, like those of Tara or Mullaghmast' (p.xii). He also reveals his romance of political leadership in quoting lines from Lionel Johnson, close friend of and influence on the young W.B. Yeats, the Catholic symbolist and youthful hero of Kettle's. Kettle claims Lionel Johnson insisted that the opening words of one of the last speeches of Parnell were: 'Once again I am come to cast myself into the deep sea of the love of my people' (Kettle, *Irish Orators*, p.xix).

19. On Moran see Patrick Maume, *D.P. Moran* (Dundalk: Dundalgan Press, 1995).

20. For an account of the family of David Sheehy, the Irish parliamentary party MP, see Conor Cruise O'Brien, *States of Ireland* (London: Hutchinson, 1972). Cruise O'Brien was Sheehy's grandson. His daughters Mary, Hannah and Kathleen married respectively Tom Kettle, Frank Sheehy-Skeffington and Frank Cruise O'Brien. See, too, Diarmuid Whelan, *Conor Cruise O'Brien: Violent Notions* (Dublin: Irish Academic Press, 2009), pp.3–16.

21. Laurence J. Kettle (ed.), *The Material for Victory: Being the Memoirs of Andrew J. Kettle, Right-Hand Man to Charles S. Parnell* (Dublin: C.J. Fallon, 1958), p.1. This sense of Viking descent, of Fingal and North County Dublin as a place with a special identity, is hard to recapture now that it has been absorbed into the city.

22. Ibid., pp.2–3.

23. One of Moran's projects was to Gaelicise the elite Catholic colleges and by extension the upwardly mobile Catholic middle class. Margaret O'Callaghan, 'David Patrick Moran and the Irish Colonial Condition, 1891–1921' in D. George Boyce, Robert Eccleshall and Vincent Geoghegan (eds), *Political Thought in Ireland Since the Seventeenth Century* (London: Routledge, 1993), pp.146–60.

24. J.B. Lyons, *The Enigma of Tom Kettle: Irish Patriot, Essayist, Poet, British Soldier 1880–1916* (Dublin: Glendale Press, 1983); Senia Pašeta, *Thomas Kettle* (Dublin: University College Dublin Press, 2008).

25. See Tom Dunne (ed.), *The National University of Ireland: Centenary Essays* (Dublin: University College Dublin Press, 2008), and Donal McCartney (ed.), *UCD: A National Idea. The History of University College, Dublin* (Dublin: Gill & Macmillan, 1999).

26. Lyons, *Kettle*, p.80.

27. Quoted ibid., p.39.

28. James Joyce, *A Portrait of the Artist as a Young Man* (Ware: Wordsworth Editions, 1992; first published 1916), p.196.

29. For a brilliant analysis of Kettle's formation as a European intellectual and Irish Catholic nationalist, see Richard S. Sutherland, 'The life and times of Tom Kettle', Trinity College Dublin, Ph.D. thesis, 1980.

30. Quoted by Brendan Walsh in Barry (ed.), *Remembering Kettle*, p.7.

31. 'Would the Hungarian Policy Work?', *New Ireland Review* (February 1905), pp 320–28. The *New Ireland Review* was the important 'in-house' intellectual journal of the Royal University/University College Dublin. It can be seen as a forerunner of the Jesuit periodical *Studies*. This article is based on a talk that Kettle gave to the Literary and Historical Society, to which Griffith had been invited. See James Meenan (ed.), *A Centenary History of the Liter-*

*ary and Historical Society of University College Dublin 1855–1955* (Dublin: A. & A. Farmar, 2005; originally published 1955), p.58. See essays by Kettle's contemporaries William Dawson, Felix Hackett, Eugene Sheehy, Patrick Little and W. G. Fallon, pp.35–92.

32. 'Would the Hungarian Policy Work?', *New Ireland Review* (February 1905), p.321.

33. Ibid., p.328.

34. 'Religion and Politics in Ireland', *Independent Review* (October–December 1906).

35. John O'Callaghan, former Land Leaguer, *Irish Independent* correspondent in the United States in the 1890s and right-hand man to Redmond in the States until his death in 1913.

36. T.M. Kettle, *Home Rule Finance: An Experiment in Justice* (Dublin: Maunsel & Co., 1911).

37. This attachment pervades all of his writings, particularly the essays in *The Day's Burden: Studies, Literary and Political and Miscellaneous Essays* (Dublin: Browne & Nolan, 1937).

38. On the initial closeness and later estrangement between members of the Young Ireland Branch and the party, see A.C. Hepburn, *Catholic Belfast and Nationalist Ireland in the Era of Joe Devlin, 1871–1934* (Oxford: Oxford University Press, 2008), pp.102–5.

39. Pearse's *Barr Buadh* letters can be seen as the voice of the new generation rebuking the old, but Kettle and Pearse were effectively of the same generation.

40. As John O'Leary had been represented by land agitators in the 1880s. In fact, contrary to this stereotype, Kettle in fact supported cattle driving on occasion in these years, which was certainly not the behaviour of someone locked into his own class position.

41. Tom Garvin, *Nationalist Revolutionaries in Ireland, 1858–1928* (Oxford: Oxford University Press, 1987).

42. See again Hepburn's brilliant study, *Catholic Belfast*.

43. Run by W.P. Ryan and Bulmer Hobson.

44. Hepburn, *Catholic Belfast*, p.104. The original members of the Young Ireland Branch were Kettle, Sheehy-Skeffington, Francis Cruise O'Brien, W.G. Fallon, Thomas Dillon (later professor of chemistry at UCG), Rory O'Connor (executed by the Free State cabinet in 1922) and others.

45. On Ganly, see Wheatley, *Nationalism and the Irish Party*, p.39.

46. See James Quinn and James McGuire (eds), *A Dictionary of Irish Biography from the Earliest Times to 2002*, 9 vols (Cambridge: Cambridge University Press, 2009), vol. vii, p.687. He was elected for Kilkenny South in 1900, becoming the youngest Irish Party MP. In 1903 he seconded William Redmond's bill to have St Patrick's Day declared a national holiday. He resigned his seat and left the Irish Party in protest at the limited provisions of the Irish Council Bill, and later that year he joined Sinn Féin.

47. Hepburn, *Catholic Belfast*, p.105.

48. See the career of Laurence Kettle, trained in Germany as an electrical engineer and designer, as promoted through Dublin municipal politics. There were persistent complaints in the fringe nationalist press of the advantages that his father's former colleagues gave to his career.

49. Kettle wrote the introduction to Joseph Hone's translation of Daniel Halévy's *Life of Frederich Nietzsche* (Dublin: Maunsel & Co., 1911). Hone, a friend of Kettle and of Stephen Gwynn, later became the first official biographer of W.B. Yeats, for whom he had worked as a secretary. He wrote, under the pseudomym Nicholas Marlowe and with Warre Bradley Wells, *A History of the Irish Rebellion of 1916* (Dublin: Maunsel & Co., 1916).

50. See D.R. O'Connor Lysaght, 'The Rhetoric of Redmondism, 1914–16', *History Ireland*, vol. 11, no. 1 (spring 2003), pp.44–9.

51˙.See McMahon (ed.), *Moynihan Brothers*.

52. See martial poems in William Dawson (ed.), *Poems and Parodies by T.M. Kettle* (Dublin: Maunsel & Co., 1916).

53. For this, see Pašeta, *Kettle*.

54. This did not happen. The First World War memorial was erected at Islandbridge, and Archbishop Byrne bought Merrion Square to construct a cathedral on its site. Kevin O'Higgins made a speech refusing Merrion Square for memorial purposes. His own brother had died in the war.

55. See McMahon, *Moynihan Brothers*, pp.ix–x for an insight into how Maurice Moynihan wished his brother's death to be remembered.

56. Lyons, *Kettle*, pp.269–70.

57. He refers here to the death of his old friend and brother-in-law, Francis Sheehy-Skeffington, the feminist, pacifist and sometime nationalist who had died at the hands of the British offi-

cer Bowen-Colthurs, having been taken into custody while trying to prevent looting or un-rest during the 1916 Rising. On 29 June 1915 Skeffington, rather shockingly, had written of Kettle in his diary: 'a bullet in the front would be the best end for him'. Quoted from Skeff-ington's diary in Pašeta, *Kettle*, p.90. The long letter home is quoted by Robert Lynd in his preface to *T.M. Kettle, An Irishman's Calendar: A Quotation from the Works of T.M. Kettle for Every Day of the Year Composed by his Wife* (Dublin: privately published, 1938).

58. This may echo 'Neither King nor Kaiser but Ireland', as suggested by Conor Cruise O'Brien in Barry (ed.), *Remembering Kettle*, p.7.

59. Interestingly 'The Secret Scripture' was the title of Sebastian Barry's next book, the story of another lost Ireland.

60. Motion proposed by Councillor J.S. Kelly, Minutes of Dublin City Council, 1916, Dublin City Archives, p.414.

61. Arthur Clery, *Dublin Essays* (Dublin: Maunsel & Co., 1919), p.14.

62. Callanan in Barry (ed.), *Remembering Kettle*, p.11.

63. Ibid.

CHAPTER FOUR

# Throwing Discretion to the Wind: The 1918 General Election in Cork City

JOHN BORGONOVO

She [Ireland] has thrown discretion to the wind, and at a very
critical moment has trusted her affairs to men of little experience.
(*Cork Examiner*, 30 December 1918)

In the last months of the First World War it became increasingly clear
that British prime minister David Lloyd George intended to call a
general election shortly after the armistice. In Cork City's two-seat
constituency, the timing of the campaign generated optimism among
republicans, fear in Redmondites, and confusion among unionists and
Labour. Cork was one of the few areas in Ireland where the Irish Party
faced strong organisational resistance prior to the Easter Rising.
William O'Brien's All-for-Ireland League (AFIL) held nine of ten seats
in County Cork after 1910, and controlled both the Cork Corporation
and Cork County Council until 1914.[1] The AFIL's rivalry with the Irish
Party was intense and frequently bloody in Cork City, producing violent clashes during election campaigns. Competition among the AFIL
and the Irish Party also divided the Cork Labour Party, which split into
two separate trades councils affiliated to each party, though these re-
unified in late 1916. The Cork Labour Party had only elected a single
member of the Corporation in 1914, though a number of union leaders were elected under the auspices of the AFIL and Irish Party organisations. The AFIL had secured a narrow majority in Cork through the
support of trade unionists, separatists and followers of William

O'Brien, along with tactical voting by the city's unionist minority. However, the Irish Party had been in the ascendancy since the Home Rule crisis of 1913, and remained the most dominant nationalist bloc until the end of the war.

## THE OPPONENTS

Despite its ascendency, however, the Irish Party in County Cork, as across the country, was declining rapidly during 1918. Yet the organisational atrophy attributed to it in this period was not apparent in Cork City.[2] The Redmondites retained political patronage networks in the local government, enjoyed the support of the commercial elite, and controlled two of the city's three daily newspapers (the third was unionist). Though weaker than in 1914, the city's Redmondite political machine remained tight, well financed and battle-hardened from a decade of intense competition with the AFIL. The Irish Party retained enough organisational strength to win a campaign, assuming it could find support among voters.

Facing the Redmondites was Cork's neophyte Sinn Féin organisation composed of twelve branches and 5,000 members.[3] The organisation was supported by 2,000 Irish Volunteers in sixteen city companies, along with an estimated 500 members of Cumann na mBan, in fourteen branches. The Irish Party failed to contest any County Cork constituencies outside the city, enabling republicans to direct resources to the city contest (the Royal Irish Constabulary [RIC] County Inspector believed that Sinn Féin would have won any of the non-contested seats by a margin of four to one).[4] But despite its strength, Sinn Féin was less than two years old and possessed little institutional knowledge of electioneering.

## PREPARING THE REGISTER

The revision (or update) of the electoral register required early political mobilisation, which was especially vital in 1918. The Representation of the People Act (passed earlier in the year) expanded the franchise to all males over the age of 21 and to women over 30.[5] Both parties had to painstakingly review the rolls to ensure the registration of their supporters, including new voters. Sinn Féin began its update in March 1918,[6] and the Irish Party followed suit in July, indicating the activation of its Cork election machine.[7] Both sides had their work cut out, as the new franchise rules tripled the Cork City electorate from 12,298 voters to 45,017.[8]

Rate collectors distributed voting claim forms to new voters during April 1918, at the height of the Conscription Crisis.[9] According to Sinn Féin's director of elections, Redmondite rate collectors 'dropped hints that the claim forms, when filled up would be likely to be utilised for the enforcement of conscription', resulting in thousands of voters leaving their forms blank.[10] As the registration deadline approached, the Crown Clerk only issued blank voter registration forms to individuals appearing in person at City Hall, except military commanders, whose servicemen voters presumably would not be supporting Sinn Féin.[11] Fortunately for Sinn Féin, a republican clerk in City Hall stole thousands of blank registration forms, which were distributed during Sinn Féin canvasses.[12]

Additional vote suppression was apparent during the Revision Court hearings, which allowed the public to challenge individual voter registrations. Sinn Féin and the Irish Party representatives objected to scores of voters, requiring their attendance to prove eligibility.[13] Though few registrations were overturned, some voters had been registered without their knowledge, indicating preparations for polling-day impersonation. The exasperated Crown Clerk condemned 'the philanthropist who is going around putting in claims on the part of people who don't exist or are children'.[14] Evidence indicates the involvement of both Sinn Féin and the Irish Party in the fraud, along with individual unionists and police constables.[15] In Cork, no party was above electoral chicanery.[16]

THE INCUMBENTS

The two parliamentary incumbents, the AFIL's William O'Brien and Maurice Healy, did not seek re-election. Though the dominant city party in 1910, the AFIL steadily ceded ground to the Redmondites, losing its majorities on the Cork Corporation and County Council in 1914. O'Brien and Healy's enthusiasm for the First World War further undercut the party, which wound down at the end of 1916 after a by-election loss to the Irish Party in Bantry. In early 1918, O'Brien graciously, if reluctantly, passed the baton to Sinn Féin,[17] telling former protégé Frank Gallagher, '[t]he Sinn Féiners have saved the country from partition, conscription, and parliamentary corruption, and they were the only force in Ireland who could have done it.'[18] O'Brien and his fellow AFIL MPs were prepared to resign in early 1918, but waited until the franchise expansion, to maximise the damage to the Irish Party.[19] This reflected a belief that many new voters would support the

Republicans, echoed by Cork's Irish Party leader J.J. Horgan. 'The Register has increased from 18,000 to 45,000,' he warned, 'and it is full of irresponsible young males and females.'[20]

In late October, William O'Brien announced his retirement, endorsed Sinn Féin and published his new pamphlet, *The Downfall of Parliamentarianism.*[21] J.J. Horgan informed John Dillon that the AFIL rank and file had already gone over to the Republicans, and 'O'Brien will strain every nerve to get all his poisoned followers to vote S.F.'[22] The Cork All-for-Ireland Club applauded O'Brien's decision to allow 'the younger minds to work out the realisation of Ireland as a nation', and offered a traditional AFIL farewell: 'We pray God may spare you to see the serpent of Molly Maguirism finally crushed.'[23] Tim Healy tried to cheer up his brother Maurice about the demise of the AFIL. 'In the end they have come round to our opinions, and I don't care by what road or reasoning!'[24] Maurice Healy announced his withdrawal a month later, denouncing the 'treason' of the Irish Party, but failing to endorse Sinn Féin.[25] 'I can see no grounds for believing that unconstitutional methods are likely to bring better results,' he wrote, 'nor is it obvious to me how this poor country, no matter how grossly provoked, can at this juncture benefit from turbulence, disorder, and abortive rebellion.'[26]


## NOMINATING CANDIDATES

All the city parties had difficulty selecting their standard-bearers. Despite the presence of a few high-profile Redmondite defectors, Sinn Féin in Cork sought a complete electoral departure, looking within its separatist community for nominees. The easiest choice was J.J. Walsh, who received a death sentence for his participation in the Easter Rising.[27] Walsh was a national leader of the Gaelic Athletic Association (GAA) and the president of its Cork County Board. He co-founded the Irish Volunteers in 1914, and already held office as a town councillor. A proponent of physical force, he exploited his multiple jail terms, appearing at a Cork demonstration in his old prison uniform.[28]

A second Sinn Féin candidate proved more difficult to secure. Sinn Féin initially approached Cork's Irish Transport and General Workers' Union (ITGWU) organiser, Cathal O'Shannon. The socialist O'Shannon ticked a number of boxes for Sinn Féin. He was a member of the Irish Republican Brotherhood (IRB), the Gaelic League, and (until recently) the Cork City Sinn Féin Executive and the Sinn Féin National Executive.[29] O'Shannon also served on the Irish Trades Union Congress and Labour Party executive (hereafter the Irish Labour Party), and led 7,000 ITGWU members in Cork.[30] However, he refused to stand for Sinn Féin, citing his primary allegiance to the Irish Labour Party, whose election stance was still undetermined. He assured republicans, 'holding all the views I do, my best service to the national cause is in Labour rather than as a Sinn Féin MP'.[31]

In his stead, the Cork Sinn Féin executive chose Liam de Róiste for the second city seat. A commercial teacher employed by the County Technical Education Committee, de Róiste was a safe choice. He was a national leader of the Gaelic League, a prewar Sinn Féin pioneer and the secretary of the Cork Industrial Development Association. De Róiste faced some opposition from the ITGWU, as they regarded him as a 'Griffithite' and probable opponent of socialism.[32] Republican trade unionists also feared de Róiste would be challenged by an 'old labour' craft union leader, who could unify the city's constitutionalists into a single anti-Sinn Féin block. Though the *Cork Examiner* encouraged a labour candidacy,[33] 'old labour' could only launch a campaign with the full support of the Cork Labour Party, whose rank and file largely supported Sinn Féin.[34] After weeks of internal debate, Cork Labour deferred its decision to the Irish Labour Party Annual Congress, which chose to abstain from the election. By delaying its decision, the labour movement missed an opportunity to leverage its electoral abstention, rejecting seats offered by Sinn Féin and receiving nothing in return.[35]

The Irish Party faced even deeper divisions prior to the election. Recognising likely defeat and the implications of the post-war peace conference, Cork Redmondites sought to arrange an electoral pact with Sinn Féin. Catholic bishop Daniel Cohalan floated the idea, calling for national unity prior to the Paris Peace Conference, which was supported by the *Cork Examiner* days later.[36] The bishop approached Liam de Róiste about a pact, explaining that city Redmondites desired to avoid a contest in order that they could 'approach the Peace Conference with one vote'.[37] Sinn Féin and the Irish Party would divvy up the seats, with all candidates agreeing to a number of terms: temporary abstention from Westminster; support for an appeal for Irish self-determination at the Paris Peace Conference; and, if that was rejected, a referendum to decide whether to resume their seats in London. The republicans demurred, with de Róiste telling Bishop Cohalan that the pact smacked of the very 'bossism' and 'machine methods' Sinn Féin sought to destroy.[38] Regardless, on 10 November the Cork United Irish League (UIL) executive – the party's constituency organisation – called on John Dillon to secure an agreement with Sinn Féin along the terms outlined by Cohalan.[39]

Cork UIL activist Henry Donegan reported that the Cork pact enjoyed little support beyond the city's three senior party leaders, Coroners J.J. Horgan, William Murphy and James McCabe, who pushed it through the city executive.[40] Regardless, John Dillon promptly dismissed the Cork compromise, claiming Sinn Féin had rejected his overtures, 'with insult and abuse'.[41] Without a pact, J.J. Horgan believed they had no 'earthly chance of winning in Cork',[42] and he, Murphy and McCabe urged Cork's UIL executive to withdraw from the election. When they were outvoted, the three coroners resigned from the party.[43] During these weeks, city Redmondites could not persuade anyone to stand.[44] As republican Margaret O'Leary wrote:

> The Irish Party found great difficulty in finding candidates. George Crosby was asked to stand and refused – so was T.C. Butterfield – so was J.J. Horgan – so was Sir Henry O'Shea – so was Coroner Murphy – so was [Coroner] McCabe – so was Jerh Lucy [Chairman, Southern Ireland Cattle Trade Association], who said he couldn't really speak for the Cattle Trade Association as ¾ of its members were Sinn Féiners ...[45]

After three successive evening meetings, the UIL executive finally convinced high sheriff Willie O'Connor and town councillor Richard Tilson to stand.[46] Unfortunately, these candidates withdrew the following week, when O'Connor found out his High Sheriff office prohibited attendance in Westminster. The Irish Party was forced back to the drawing board.[47] 'The actions of the Dillonite supporters have been amusing, in fact grotesque,' laughed Liam de Róiste.[48]

The Cork Redmondites found two replacement candidates, Maurice Talbot-Crosbie and Richard O'Sullivan, both apparently selected to appeal to the city's ex-serviceman population. Talbot-Crosbie owned a large asphalt company in Cork and was the son of a prominent Home Rule landlord in Kerry. In 1914 he commanded the city's Irish Volunteers and the National Volunteers, before joining the British Army and seeing action in France and Palestine, where he was wounded multiple times. Talbot-Crosbie's running mate was Cork native Lieutenant Richard O'Sullivan, a London-based barrister and journalist, returned from British Army service in Flanders.[49] Having lived abroad for almost a decade, O'Sullivan was relatively unknown in Cork City.[50] Imprisoned Republican leader Tadg Barry was delighted. 'I laughed when I read of Talbot Crosbie turning up ... he is as big an ass as ever … What are all the Mollie TCs [Town Councillors] and coroners doing. Have they deserted?'[51] The selection of two such unlikely candidates reflected disarray in the Irish Party prior to the election.

Cork unionists also suffered from internal discord. In prior elections, unionists endorsed the AFIL rather than run their own slate, and in 1918 they could not agree whether to vote tactically for the Irish Party or to put up unionist candidates.[52] The militant *Cork Constitution* argued against a unionist contest: 'The view of the immense majority of the better classes in Cork seems to be that under the present circumstances it is a waste of prestige and money to bring a unionist into the field at all.'[53] The *Cork Examiner* noted division between hardline unionists, who opposed any change to the Act of Union, and moderates, willing to consider Home Rule. The moderate faction included 158 'citizens, merchants, and traders of the City of Cork', who had recently called for an acceptance of the Irish Convention's Home Rule settlement.[54]

Left to their own devices, militant unionists proposed Daniel Williams and Thomas Farrington.[55] Williams was a marginalised town councillor, noted for his vocal loyalty to the king and recent endorsement of conscription in Ireland.[56] Farrington was a chemical engineer and a minor figure in the conservative Cork Ratepayers' Association.[57] Many unionists reluctantly supported their campaign,[58] but numerous leading merchants ignored the candidacy, and Church of Ireland clergy did not participate.[59] Unionists were a traditional swing vote in Cork, and it was unclear if they would support the Irish Party, even in a contest with Sinn Féin. The Cork UIL appealed for unionist votes, first by nominating Protestant Home Ruler Henry Tilson, and (after his withdrawal), another Protestant, Talbot-Crosbie. Despite this outreach, the candidacy of Williams and Farrington split the Protestant vote.

There was little sectarianism during the campaign, with Sinn Féin largely refraining from using anti-Protestant language against Talbot-Crosbie or the unionist candidates. The city's Catholic clergy essentially sat out the election, with few priests attending the Irish Party and Sinn Féin campaign launch meetings. Though the bishop was 'glad that the old party is ended', he refused to endorse Sinn Féin, largely on pragmatic lines.[60] Cohalan reflected clerical ambivalence towards the election in Cork. Scarred by the violent O'Brienite–Redmond rivalry of recent years, clerics stayed onside and waited for the people to make their decision.

## TALKING REPUBLICANISM

Sinn Féin launched its campaign at Cork City Hall on 18 November. Speakers placed the election in the context of free speech, democracy and the popular upheaval sweeping Europe. Professor Alfred O'Rahilly heralded 'a wave of democracy in the world, and it could not be sunk with cruisers in the Irish Sea'.[61] Candidate Liam de Róiste claimed republicans wanted 'to assert the right of public meeting in the country to assert the right of free speech in the country, and also to assert the right of individual liberty in the country'. But J.J. Walsh's speech caused the greatest sensation within the republican leadership. Like de Róiste, Walsh made ill-defined allusions to securing 'sovereign independence', but he failed to use the term 'Irish Republic' and downplayed physical-force resistance. Writing privately, Liam de Róiste claimed that prior to the City Hall rally, certain Sinn Féin leaders asked Walsh 'not to talk "wildly" as he sometimes does'.[62]

The issue erupted at the ensuing meeting of the Cork City Sinn Féin Election Committee. Walsh 'asked permission to talk "republicanism"', explaining his pre-rally instructions.[63] This prompted a heated debate between those wanting Sinn Féin candidates to clearly articulate a republican position and others preferring to obfuscate the issue in order to avoid alienating moderate voters. Representing the Irish Volunteers, Florrie O'Donoghue disliked this 'general tendency to slur over the suggestion of J.J. Walsh to keep the Republican programme well in the foreground'.[64] Having lost the meeting, Liam de Róiste added fuel to the fire by remarking, 'what we wanted to do now was to win the election, to get votes: not lay down principles'.[65] He privately mused about his opponents: '[h]ow queer some of us are and how clung to words'. Florrie O'Donoghue urged the Volunteers to stand over the republican position: 'It must not be confused by any talk of influencing timid and doubtful voters, or anything else. The issue must be kept clear and definite.'[66]

The fight continued at the committee's next meeting, when Seán O'Hegarty (acting commander of the Volunteers) threatened to boycott the election if the candidates failed to publicly enunciate a republican position. According to Liam de Róiste, '[h]e [O'Hegarty] raised the question again of the words "Irish Republic" in his own truculent fashion ... We were dishonest if we did not say the words "Irish Republic"'. De Róiste refused to share his election address with the committee, insisting, 'I will put the issue of the election in my own way, and will not be dictated to about it.'[67] The impasse was resolved when Sinn

Féin platform speakers explicitly called for a Republic, which apparently satisfied the Irish Volunteers enough to resume their participation in the campaign.[68]

The controversy revealed differing separatist concepts of mandates and parties. Physical-force militants advocated the clearest approach to the Cork electorate, while moderates proposed a less open and honest campaign strategy. This reflected the hardliners' almost millennial approach to electoral politics. Tom Garvin has cited parallels throughout Europe of young people tempered by the Great War, rejecting seemingly old, corrupt societies.[69] Cork republicans expressed similar attitudes that were anti-political rather than anti-democratic, while they also reacted against long-time demagoguery from the local UIL and AFIL political machines. Speaking of 'political tricks', Tomás Mac-Curtain warned, 'once the bad influence gets hold it eats its way to the core to our entire destruction'.[70] Éamon de Valera told a Cork audience in 1917 that 'Sinn Féin was out to purify politics', while republican labour leader John Good (National Union of Railwaymen) claimed that 'Sinn Féin was not a political party but a national party.'[71] To many republicans, Sinn Féin expressed nationality and transcended personal and political pettiness. There was an inherent tension when putting such high-minded ideals into practice, as seen by the response of Liam de Róiste, who resented subordinating himself to the collective will of the city's republican leadership.

## SWING VOTES: SERVICEMEN, LABOUR AND WOMEN

Both parties targeted the 5,500 Cork residents serving as soldiers and sailors overseas, who could cast their ballots by mail. The Irish Party aggressively pursued these votes by nominating two ex-soldiers as candidates. Advertisements exhorted: 'Vote for the men who fought in the war.'[72] Speaking to ex-servicemen, Major Talbot-Crosbie exclaimed that '[t]hey as soldiers, absolutely denied the Sinn Féiners had got a monopoly on patriotism, and that they alone represented Ireland'. The Redmondites secured the endorsement of the Cork branch of the Demobilised and Discharged Soldiers and Sailors Federation (DDSSF), a lobbying group whose 600 members were considered to be 'one of the strongest organised bodies of voters in the city at the present'.[73] DDSSF leaders spoke on Irish Party campaign platforms and members marched en masse to meetings.[74] 'The soul of Ireland was in Flanders where Irish National soldiers fought in the name of Ireland a nation,' remarked DDSSF branch chairman Maurice Donovan. 'They certainly did not fight for an Irish American Republic under the tyrannical leadership of a hybrid Portugee.'[75]

Surprisingly, the Irish Party largely refrained from attacking Sinn Féin's anti-war stance. The *Cork Examiner* publisher George Crosbie reflected the sentiment by remarking that '[t]here had been, God knows, enough of war in the world'. Again, the lack of engagement on the most compelling issue of the day illustrates the altered political landscape in 1918. Sinn Féin speakers, on the other hand, celebrated their opposition to the war. 'Had it ever dawned on the Parliamentarians,' asked J.J. Walsh, 'that by the sacrifice of 60,000 of their Gaelic brothers in the damnable war just terminated, more suffering had been caused to the Irish race in four years than twenty rebellions for the freedom of Ireland.' 'Were it not for British Imperialism,' offered Cumann na mBann leader Annie Scott, 'the women of Ireland would not be today mourning the loss of husbands, sons, and brothers lost in the war.' J.J. Walsh memorably told a Blackpool meeting that '[t]he Irish people were not in the sense alleged Pro-German, but if the devil himself and all the devils in hell were up against the British Government, the Irish people would be pro devil and pro hell (cheers).'[76]

Sinn Féin's anti-war rhetoric did not extend to hostility towards ex-servicemen. Cork republicans lobbied for ex-serviceman votes, revealing a more subtle approach than is often appreciated.[77] Denouncing Talbot-Crosbie and O'Sullivan as 'sham soldiers', Sinn Féin's Denis Tobin claimed that '[e]very soldier he knew was a Sinn Féiner'. John Good told a rally: 'They had been told ... that they were out to penalise the soldiers and sailors, and the relatives of those who fell in the war – the Irish Republic was out to see that every man, woman, and child earning their living in Ireland would get the same chance and the same rights.' At a large Sinn Féin meeting, ex-sailor Patrick Healy denounced job discrimination against ex-servicemen. Professor Alfred O'Rahilly followed him, explaining, '[w]hether it be a sailor or soldier or even a policeman, his vote was welcome provided he believed in Ireland's claim to nationhood'. At its final rally of the campaign, Sinn Féin invited disabled soldier E. Walsh to speak before a gathering of 10,000. Calling for independence, Walsh asked voters to join the struggle, quoting a wounded comrade from France: 'They were called broken men now, but though broken in limb they were not broken in spirit.'[78]

Besides the votes of ex-servicemen, both sides aggressively pursued working-class voters, many of whom would be casting ballots for the first time. The Irish Party ran essentially on an economic platform, arguing that Sinn Féin's abstention from Westminster would damage local

commercial development and employment opportunities. The Redmondites also emphasised the protection of government pensions and
the need for government-financed housing assistance, which appealed to
voters living in the city's numerous slums. Despite this effort, the Cork
Labour Party remained aloof from the Redmondites, with union leaders
failing to appear on an Irish Party platform during the campaign.

Sinn Féin believed Irish independence would end British economic
exploitation, thereby generating jobs and industrial development in
Cork. Organised labour played a prominent role in the Sinn Féin campaign, with union leaders speaking at fifteen of eighteen election meetings.[79] John Good of the National Union of Railwaymen promised a
'worker's republic', and claimed that 'Labour and Sinn Féin were one
in the same thing.'[80] He subsequently asserted that Sinn Féin would
'make short work of autocracy, vested interests, and industrial and
commercial thieves'.[81] Liam de Róiste vowed, '[t]he day had come
when the working classes would have the power in the government of
the country'.[82]

A final swing vote was women, first-time voters who comprised
one-third of the electorate. On this ground the Irish Party was found
wanting, with election reports indicating no outreach to female voters.
This contrasts sharply with Sinn Féin, which aggressively sought
women's support, primarily through the work of Cumann na mBan. It
started registering female voters in June 1918, with its leader declaring that 'women will be the deciding vote at the next election'.[83] Sinn
Féin also held a women's election meeting addressed by de Róiste and
female republicans, including suffragist Marie Lynch, and Annie Scott
and Mary MacSwiney of Cumann na mBan.[84] Rather than promising
gender equality, Sinn Féin candidates focused on what they considered
to be 'women's issues', such as improved pay for teachers and better
housing and working conditions. Women played a prominent role in
the republican campaign, as canvassers, poll watchers and collectors
of the Sinn Féin election fund. On polling day, Cumann na mBan even
offered child-minding duties to enable women supporters to get to the
polls. It would be surprising if this activity did not translate into a significant advantage with women voters.

PLATFORMS

Considering the implications of the 1918 election, much was left unsaid
by both campaigns. The Irish Party rarely mentioned republican involvement in the anti-government street riots and arms raids experienced

during the previous two years. Though the Irish Volunteers were a constant presence in the Sinn Féin campaign, Redmondites failed to question physical-force republicanism. This omission is even more remarkable considering that a few weeks before polling day, armed Irish Volunteers broke one of their officers out of Cork Gaol after he shot a policeman. Redmondites did vaguely warn that Sinn Féin represented 'chaos',[85] claiming the Irish Party stood for 'moderation and reason, when striving against passion and prejudice'.[86] However, their muted approach failed to raise voter anxiety about a Sinn Féin victory, which was probably their only chance for victory. This likely reflected recognition of the public's profound anti-government sentiments in the wake of the anti-conscription campaign.

Irish Party officials often used violent language against the British administration. After the military authorities banned the annual Manchester Martyrs commemoration, Talbot-Crosbie warned that 'the feelings of the people revolted at such a miserable and wretched sight'.[87] Councillor William Hart argued that Irish Party MPs in Westminster were 'the only weapon to fight Imperialism', while councillor John Horgan claimed Dublin Castle was 'doing everything in their power to destroy the Constitutional movement'.[88] Candidate Richard O'Sullivan told an audience that 'they would go to Parliament to demand the rights of Ireland, and if they were denied them there would be war'.

The Irish Party primarily argued that abstention from Westminster would leave nationalists without representation in an unsympathetic parliament. To the *Cork Examiner*, 'the only voices that will have authority to speak for Ireland in the House of Commons are those of Sir Edward Carson and his followers'. Major Talbot-Crosbie agreed that the south of Ireland 'would therefore be in the extraordinary position of merely having to take the crumbs that fell to them by the grace of Ulster'. The Redmondites repeatedly emphasised the necessity of parliamentary representation to defend the city's railways, shipping, and industrial concerns. Election literature asked voters to support the candidates 'who will protect your interests during demobilisation and reconstruction'.[89]

Predating the Anglo-Irish Treaty of 1921, the Irish Party demanded Dominion Home Rule in 1918, rather than the limited measure of Home Rule which was on the 1914 statute-book.[90] Before resigning from the party, coroner William Murphy urged the Irish Party 'to adopt as its battle cry "Colonial Home Rule"',[91] telling John Dillon that 'the national demand should be as wide as possible, and it must be so if it is to receive wide support from our people'.[92] George Crosbie instructed voters that 'there was nothing left to them now but to demand Colonial Home Rule'.[93] Richard O'Sullivan vowed to work for 'full Colonial Home Rule with Irish control of the Customs and Excise', and added that if the public demanded independence, 'then he would take his mandate from the people and reiterate their demand'.[94] Campaign advertisements promised 'Colonial Home Rule' along the basis of the Irish Convention proposal,[95] which was ridiculed by Sinn Féin. Liam de Róiste wanted to know how the Redmondites could secure Dominion status, 'if for over forty years the whole Irish Party could not get Home Rule with partition thrown in'. Asking his supporters if they wanted Home Rule, J.J. Walsh thundered, '[t]hey did not and he said to hell with it'.[96]

Sinn Féin framed the election debate as a referendum on Irish independence prior to the Paris Peace Conference, within the context of an outbreak of democracy across Europe. Liam de Róiste explained to voters: 'The people who had not yet won the war were the people who had not overthrown their militarists, Imperialists, and autocrats ... They were trying to put Ireland in the forefront of the fight for democracy and nationality.' 'A greater result of the war from their own standpoint,' thought J.J. Walsh, 'was the awakening of the small nations, including Ireland, that they, like the empires, were entitled to a separate existence.' Despite earlier platform division, Sinn Féin speakers repeatedly called for sovereign independence in the form of an Irish Republic.[97] De Róiste frequently utilised Britain's wartime rhetoric against the Irish Party. 'These two gallant men joined the army to gain independence for Belgium, Serbia, and Poland, and what objection had they to Ireland getting the same independence.'[98] He emphasised that Sinn Féin wanted the same 'sovereign independence' as other small European nations, and that they 'press for representation at the Peace Conference, as a right'.[99]

Though republicans clearly explained their appeal to the Paris Peace Conference, they failed to explain their Plan B. Speakers outlined tax boycotts and the establishment of Dáil Éireann, but downplayed physical-force alternatives. Campaign chairman Denis Tobin claimed that 'they were all pacifists,' while J.J. Walsh told supporters that '[p]hysical force had no particular fascination for him nor for most of the people who thought with him.'[100] Republican speakers did not advocate a violent overthrow of the British administration, or suggest physical resistance to a potential government repression of Dáil Éireann. At the same time, the Irish Volunteers were very much in the forefront of the election, acting as stewards and canvassers and frequently marching en masse to meetings. Both candidates encouraged young men to join the Volunteers, and Cork Brigade commander Tomás MacCurtain addressed four election meetings. The Irish Party never exploited the tension between the two wings of republicanism, allowing Sinn Féin to effectively have its cake and eat it. The Irish Party also failed to force the republicans into engaging on the subject of Ulster and partition, though the Redmondites showed little appetite to put their own feelings on the subject before the electorate.

ORGANISATION

Cork republicans created a superior campaign organisation, which operated independently of Dublin. Months before the election, Sinn Féin had completed the painstaking update of the electoral registry, vital given the massive expansion of the franchise. Republicans also made vigorous house-to-house canvases for votes, utilising Sinn Féin's great numeric advantage in enthusiastic election workers. With Sinn Féin clubs, Cumann na mBan branches, and Irish Volunteers companies organised geographically, republicans were perfectly positioned for localised get-out-the-vote efforts.

Since all three Cork newspapers were decidedly anti-republican, Sinn Féin in the city produced its own election literature and posters. The printing costs were covered by an election fund of £1,600, raised almost entirely through small donations (the largest individual contribution was £26).[101] During the campaign Sinn Féin held meetings in every part of the Cork City constituency, which were characterised by their orderliness and attention to detail. Volunteers typically acted as stewards, while Cumann na mBan members took voter details or donations. Election-day preparations were run with a military-like precision. Three hundred Irish Volunteers from County Cork were drafted into the city as 'peace patrols', freeing the city Volunteers for canvassing and poll-tallying duties.[102] Cumann na mBan members monitored polling places, canvassed and provided thousands of meals for election workers across the city. Automobiles ferried workers and voters across town, and the *Constitution* noted an unusually large number of 'old and decrepit' residents at the polls, which indicated an effort to get them there.[103] At the close of the polls, shifts of Irish Volunteers guarded the ballot boxes for twelve days until the votes were counted. Overall, Sinn Féin displayed strong and thorough organisation, which was all the more impressive considering its electoral inexperience.

While the Irish Party was ultimately out-organised, its political machine was not inactive. In August 1918 Irish Party activists attended all the sittings of the Revision Court, challenging scores of Sinn Féin voters. During the race, UIL organising committees met virtually every night and undertook a vigorous canvas. On polling day Redmondite election workers were stationed outside every polling place, and twenty supporters monitored the ensuing ballot count. Normally, this level of organisation was sufficient to secure victory. The Irish Party also enjoyed an institutional advantage in its administration of the election machinery. Redmondite officials registered voters, ran polling booths and counted the votes, making each part of the process vulnerable to abuse. Cork republicans overcame their disadvantage by attending the Registry Court, observing polling places, guarding the ballot boxes and monitoring the vote count.

Evidence indicates that both sides engaged in voting fraud. Redmondites were accused of suppressing republican votes and adding phantom soldier voters to the registry.[104] UIL election manager Henry Donegan, in turn, complained of a registry 'hopelessly stuffed with bogus names'.[105] Activists from each party registered voters without their knowledge, indicating preparations for polling-day impersonation. Newspapers reported the detection of impersonators at various polling places, such as an old lady wearing fashionable and 'dainty shoes', who beneath a shawl was found to be 'a rather good looking young girl'.[106] When Liam de Róiste and his family arrived to cast their ballots, he discovered that his elderly mother-in-law had been personated. De Róiste claimed the Irish Party personated throughout the morning, but Sinn Féin did so in the afternoon: 'I am sorry to say ... It is looked upon in the light of a good joke.'[107] Unfortunately, it is impossible to quantify and identify the various election frauds perpetrated during the contest. However, it is safe to say that the voting irregularities were not exceptional by the standards of the day, that both parties employed these tactics, and that no irregularities can explain Sinn Féin's substantial victory margin.

Perhaps the most surprising aspect of the 1918 contest in Cork was its lack of violence. With only three minor faction fights in four weeks, the campaign compared very favourably with recent elections, which usually produced nightly clashes. Volunteer stewards and 'peace patrols' seem to have kept republican supporters in check. Tension remained, as Henry Donegan informed John Dillon: 'intimidation by Sinn Féin made it almost criminal for us to bring rival crowds into conflict'.[108] The UIL preferred to hold its meetings in the safety of its Ancient Order of Hibernians (AOH) hall, and took steps to discourage mob violence, which was a departure from prior campaigns against the AFIL.[109]

Polling day was largely incident-free, and its peaceful tenor was recognised across Cork's political spectrum. The *Cork Examiner* described the contest as 'the most quiet, orderly, interesting, and momentous in Cork during a century'.[110] Irish Party candidate Richard O'Sullivan claimed that '[i]t had been fought with good sense, good humour, and it was an example to their own country and to other countries also'. Unionist Dan Williams remarked that '[h]e would like to refer to the way in which the peace of the city had been kept during the elections, and great credit was due to the leaders of the two parties concerned'. Redmondite High Sheriff Willie O'Connor added that he 'was glad to say that not a single regrettable scene occurred in connection with the whole election'.[111]

POLLING

The final results showed an unquestioned Sinn Féin triumph. Just under 31,000 ballots were cast, representing 69 per cent of registered voters, with turn-out lowered by poor returns from soldiers still at the front, who only cast 27 per cent of their ballots. Sinn Féin dominated the returns, with J.J. Walsh securing 67 per cent of votes cast (20,801) and Liam de Róiste 66 per cent (20,506). The Irish Party's Talbot-Crosbie received 24 per cent (7,480) and Richard O'Sullivan 23 per cent (7,162), with the two Unionists winning 8 per cent and 7 per cent respectively (2,519; 2,254). Compared with 1910, the Irish Party increased its tally by almost 3,000 votes, indicating that it had retained its base but failed to make meaningful headway with new voters, who represented nearly three-quarters of the electorate.

Republicans greeted the Cork returns with parades, fireworks and burning tar barrels. Capuchin monks wired Liam de Róiste: 'Congrats to you from all of us. The country is splendid and Cork superb.' Writing to the jailed Tadg Barry, J.J. Walsh harboured no illusions as to the difficult path ahead: 'Get a few cells ready for the new MPs, it seems the date of our departure is already fixed.' Cork's AOH looked for a bright side to its comprehensive defeat. 'The City showed fight and although it had to give way, it took its beating manfully.' A headline in the unionist *Cork Constitution* newspaper summed up the campaign's implications: 'The Irish Party "A Thing of the Past".'[112]

In 1918 Cork voters did not provide a mandate for the violent IRA campaign of 1920–1. However, they did strongly reject both continued citizenship within the United Kingdom and Dominion Home Rule within the British empire. By voting for Sinn Féin in such overwhelming

numbers, Cork City clearly expressed a desire for full and sovereign independence, in the form of an Irish Republic.

## NOTES

1. Patrick Maume, *The Long Gestation: Irish Nationalist Life 1891–1918* (Dublin: Gill &
   Macmillan, 1999), pp.103–12, 144–56.
2. For example, see Tom Garvin, *The Evolution of Nationalist Politics* (Dublin: Gill & Macmillan 1981), p.99.
3. *Cork Examiner*, 12 April 1918; British Army Southern District Intelligence Report for April
   1918, British in Ireland series (microfilm), University College Cork (UCC), CO 904/157.
4. Royal Irish Constabulary (RIC), 1918, Intelligence Notes, The National Archives, London
   (TNA), CO 903/19, part IV.
5. See James McConnel, 'The Franchise Factor in the Defeat of the Irish Parliamentary Party,
   1885–1918', *Historical Journal*, vol. 47, no. 2 (June 2004), pp.355–77; and Brian Farrell,
   *The Founding of Dáil Éireann* (Dublin: University College Dublin Press, 1971), pp.45–50.
6. *Cork Examiner*, 11 June 1918; De Róiste diary, 29 June 1918, Cork City and County
   Archives (CCCA); meeting minutes of Cumman na mBan Cork District Council for 3 March
   1918 and 5 May 1918, Cork Public Museum, 2007–38–21.
7. *Cork Examiner*, 1 July 1918.
8. *Cork Examiner*, 2 October 1918; *Cork Constitution*, 16 November 1918.
9. Poor Law Guardians (PLG), clerk's memo, 16 April 1918; PLG, Clerk to Rate Collectors, 27
   April 1918, 29 April 1918; PLG, Clerk to Crown Clerk Henry Wright, 24 April 1918, 1
   May 1918, 9 May 1918 and 12 May 1918; PLG, clerk's letter book. CCCA, BG/69/B9.
10. Denis Tobin to the Dáil Éireann Department of Home Affairs, 7 October 1921, National
    Archives of Ireland (NAI), DE 10–6.
11. PLG, Clerk to Officer Commanding Naval Station Queenstown, 24 June 1918; PLG, Clerk
    to Henry Wright, 27 June 1918. CCCA, BG/69/B9.
12. Tobin to the Dáil Éireann Department of Home Affairs, 7 October 1921, NAI, DE 10–6.
13. *Cork Constitution*, 3, 8, 9, 10, 12, 13, 14, 17 and 22 August 1918.
14. *Cork Constitution*, 17 August 1918.
15. *Cork Constitution*, 1 and 19 August 1918.
16. *Cork Constitution*, 3 and 14 August 1918.
17. See Tim Healy, *Letters and Leaders of My Day*, 2 vols (London: Thornton Butterworth,
    1928), vol. ii, p.59; 'An All for Ireland Memento', pamphlet, Christmas 1918, University
    College Dublin Archives (UCDA), P150/628.
18. William O'Brien to Frank Gallagher, 3 January 1918, William O'Brien Papers, UCC,
    UC/UOB/PP/AS/161.
19. Tim Healy to Maurice Healy, 15 October 1918, Bureau of Military History, Irish Military
    Archives, Cathal Brugha Barracks, Dublin, CD 21-1.
20. J.J. Horgan to Miss O'Brien, 18 November 1918, Trinity College Dublin (TCD), 6772/273.
21. *Cork Constitution*, 17 October, 19 November and 2 December 1918; *Cork Examiner*,
    31 October 1918. See also William O'Brien, *The Irish Revolution and How it Came About*
    (London: George Allen & Unwin, 1923), p.385.
22. J.J. Horgan to John Dillon, 19 June 1918, TCD, 6772/270; J.J. Horgan to Miss O'Brien, 18
    November 1918, TCD, 6772/273.
23. Cork All-For-Ireland Club to O'Brien, 26 November 1918, UCC, UC/UOB/PP/AS/169.
24. Tim Healy to Maurice Healy, 21 May 1918, Bureau of Military History, Irish Military
    Archives, Cathal Brugha Barracks, Dublin, CD-21.
25. *Cork Examiner*, 21 November 1918; *Cork Constitution*, 21 and 23 November 1918; De
    Róiste Diary, 15 November 1918, CCCA.
26. 'All for Ireland Memento'; *Cork Constitution*, 25 November 1918; *Irish Independent*, 25
    November 1918.
27. Arthur Norway to the Under-Secretary, Dublin Castle, 12 November 1914, 'Sinn Féin and
    Republican Suspects 1899–1921, Dublin Castle Special Branch Files', Eneclann Ltd CD,
    Dublin, 2006, CO 904/212/351; John Power, *A Story of Champions* (Cork: Lee Press, 1941),
    pp.93–6; J.J. Walsh, *Recollections of a Rebel* (Tralee: Kerryman Press, 1944); *Evening Echo*,
    4 November 1954. Bureau of Military History [copies in NAI], witness statement (WS) 91,
    J.J. Walsh; WS 89, Michael O'Cuill; WS 77, Harry Lorton.

28. *Cork Examiner*, 7 April 1918.
29. Tomás MacCurtain diary (transcribed), 21–22 July 1916, Cork Public Museum, L1966-145-2; MacCurtain notes, 19 December, 28 December 1917, Cork Public Museum, L1966-141; Bureau of Military History, WS 153, Eamon Dore; O'Shannon draft memoir, undated, Irish Labour History Museum, Dublin, 93-12-12 (iii).
30. *Cork Examiner*, 8 August and 11 October 1918; *Voice of Labour*, 2 March and 17 August 1918.
31. Cathal O'Shannon to Liam de Róiste, 21 August 1918, CCCA, F15; De Róiste diary, 5 and 6 September 1918, CCCA.
32. De Róiste diary, 10 September 1918, CCCA; *Cork Examiner*, 5 February 1918.
33. *Cork Examiner*, 6 November 1918.
34. De Róiste diary, 10 September 1918, CCCA. See also ITGWU's secretary William O'Brien's diary, 8 September 1918, National Library of Ireland (NLI), MS 15,705; *Voice of Labour*, 28 September 1918; *Cork Examiner*, 27 September 1918.
35. De Róiste diary, 28 September, 22 and 25 October 1918, CCCA; Cork Coopers' Society meeting minutes, 9 October 1918, CCCA, U218A/7.
36. *Cork Examiner*, 22 and 30 October 1918.
37. De Róiste diary, 5 November 1918, CCCA.
38. Ibid.
39. *Cork Examiner*, 11 November 1918.
40. Henry Donegan to John Dillon, 3 January 1919, TCD, 6775/87/1878.
41. John Dillon to J.J. Horgan, (Secretary, Cork City UIL Executive), 11 November 1918, NLI, MS 18,271.
42. John Dillon to J.J. Horgan, 20 November 1918, NLI, MS 18,271; Horgan to Miss O'Brien, 18 November 1918, TCD, 6772/273.
43. Henry Donegan to John Dillon, 3 January 1919, TCD, 6775/87/1878; De Róiste diary, 1 December 1918, CCCA. See also the *Cork Examiner*, 21 November 1918 and 1 February 1919.
44. See the *Cork Examiner*, 1, 10, 11, 16, 18, 20, 21, 22 and 23 November 1918.
45. M. O'Leary to Considine O'Donovan, 2 December 1918, Postal Censorship reports, British in Ireland Series, UCC, CO 904/164.
46. *Cork Examiner*, 20–23 November 1918.
47. *Cork Examiner*, 2 December 1918; W.F. O'Connor to Lord-Lieutenant, 23 November 1918, 29 November 1918; J.J. Taylor to W.F. O'Connor, 25 November 1918, NAI, CSORP 1918/2791.
48. De Róiste diary, 1 December 1918, CCCA.
49. *Cork Examiner*, 2 December 1918; Gerry White and Brendan O'Shea, *'Baptised in Blood': The Formation of the Cork Brigade of the Irish Volunteers, 1913–1916* (Cork: Mercier Press, 2005), p.34.
50. He recently challenged Éamon de Valera to a public debate. See the *Southern Star*, 19 January 1918. He also wrote a letter to the *Cork Examiner*, 16 August 1917.
51. Tadg Barry to Seán Courtney, 8 December 1918, Bureau of Military History, CD 75-3-4.
52. *Cork Examiner*, 15, 19, 20, 23, 28 and 30 November 1918.
53. *Cork Constitution*, 2 December 1918.
54. *Cork Examiner*, 2 November and 6 December 1918.
55. *Cork Constitution*, 5 December 1918.
56. *Cork Constitution*, 23 June 1917, 12 April and 16 November 1918.
57. *Cork Constitution*, 1 August 1918.
58. *Cork Constitution*, 3, 4 and 13 December 1918.
59. *Cork Constitution*, 19 June 1919.
60. Bishop Cohalan to Liam de Róiste, 30 November 1918, CCCA, U 271/F21.
61. *Cork Examiner*, 19 November 1918.
62. De Róiste diary, 2 December 1918, CCCA.
63. Ibid.
64. Florrie O'Donoghue to 'Seán', undated, NLI, MS 31,172.
65. De Róiste diary, 2 December 1918, CCCA.
66. O'Donoghue to 'Seán', NLI, MS 31,172.
67. De Róiste diary, 2 December 1918, CCCA; Seán Scanlan to Liam de Róiste, 28 November 1918, CCCA, C215.
68. For examples, see the *Cork Constitution*, 2 and 4 December 1918; *Cork Examiner* 3, 6 and 7 December 1918.

69. Tom Garvin, *Nationalist Revolutionaries in Ireland, 1858–1928* (Oxford: Oxford University Press, 1987), pp.118–19.
70. Tomás MacCurtain, 'Davis, Lalor, and Sinn Féin', lecture, *c*. January 1919, Cork Public Museum, L1945-245-4,.
71. *Cork Examiner*, 10 December 1917, 6 December 1918.
72. *Cork Examiner*, 13 December 1918.
73. *Cork Constitution*, 5 December 1917, 21 November and 7 December 1918.
74. *Cork Constitution*, 9, 10 and 13 December 1918; *Cork Examiner*, 25 November and 3, 7, 12 and 13 December 1918.
75. *Cork Examiner*, 3 December 1918.
76. *Cork Constitution*, 7 December 1918; *Cork Examiner*, 19 November, 3, 11 and 12 December 1918.
77. For example, see John Ellis, 'The Degenerate and the Martyr: Nationalist Propaganda and the Contestation of Irishness, 1914–1918', *Eire Ireland*, vol. 35 (2000/1), pp.11–18.
78. *Cork Examiner*, 2, 6, 9 and 14 December 1918.
79. Good spoke at rallies on 19 and 25 November, and on 2, 4, 6 and 9 December 1918; Eamon O'Mahoney, president of the Cork Trades Council, spoke on 2 December (at three separate meetings) and on 4, 5 and 14 December; Michael Lynch of the Cobh Trades Council spoke on 2, 5 and 11 December; Tom Donovan, Cork ITGWU secretary, spoke on 2 December.
80. *Cork Examiner*, 19 November, 4 December 1918.
81. *Cork Examiner*, 13 December 1918.
82. *Cork Examiner*, 19 November 1918
83. Cumann na mBan CDC meeting minutes, 2 June 1918.
84. *Cork Examiner*, 12 December 1918
85. *Cork Examiner*, 3 and 9 December 1918.
86. *Cork Examiner*, 21 November 1918.
87. *Cork Examiner*, 25 November and 9 December 1918.
88. Ibid. Councillor John Horgan should not be confused with Coroner J.J. Horgan.
89. *Cork Examiner*, 25 November, 2 and 13 December 1918.
90. *Cork Examiner*, 6 December 1918.
91. William Murphy to John Dillon, 10 August 1918, TCD, 6775/87/1775.
92. William Murphy to John Dillon, 20 September 1918, TCD, 6775/87/1776.
93. *Cork Constitution*, 6 December 1918.
94. *Cork Examiner*, 6 December 1918.
95. *Cork Examiner*, 13 December 1918.
96. *Cork Examiner*, 3 December 1918.
97. *Cork Constitution*, 4 December 1918; *Cork Examiner*, 19 and 25 November, 6, 9 and 14 December 1918.
98. *Cork Examiner*, 6 December 1918.
99. *Cork Examiner*, 15 October 1918.
100. *Cork Examiner*, 19 November, 4 December 1918.
101. Sinn Féin Election Fund Treasurer's Report, CCCA.
102. *Cork Examiner*, 16 December 1918.
103. *Cork Constitution*, 16 December 1918.
104. *Cork Constitution*, 1, 3, 10, 13, 14 and 17 August 1918.
105. Henry Donegan to John Dillon, 3 January 1919, TCD, 6775/87/1878.
106. *Cork Examiner*, 16 December 1918.
107. De Róiste diary, 15 December 1918, CCCA.
108. *Cork Constitution*, 25 November 1918; Henry Donegan to John Dillon, 3 January 1919, TCD, 6775/87/1878.
109. For outdoor UIL meetings, see *Cork Examiner*, 7, 9 and 11 December 1918.
110. *Cork Examiner*, 11 December 1918. See also the *Cork Examiner*, 6 and 30 December 1918.
111. *Cork Constitution*, 30 December 1918.
112. Father Augustine telegram to Liam de Róiste, 2 January 1919, CCCA, U271/C12; J.J. Walsh to Tadg Barry, 7 January 1919, Postal Censorship Reports, British in Ireland series, UCC, CO 904/164; Report of the AOH County Cork Convention, 2 February 1919, CCCA, U389a/25; *Cork Constitution*, 30 December 1918.

# CHAPTER FIVE

# The Disappointed Revolutionary: P.S. O'Hegarty and the Ambiguous Victory of Sinn Féin

## FRANCES FLANAGAN

The experience of constitutional nationalists who were marginalised by the Irish revolution has been a subject that has attracted increasing attention from historians in recent years. Senia Pašeta, for example, has traced the expectations and disappointments of the generation who anticipated acquiring power through the granting of Home Rule,[1] and Paul Bew has evoked the reactions of moderates such as Joe Devlin, John Dillon and Stephen Gwynn, who recoiled against the coercion of the north and the use of violence in the years from 1916 to 1921.[2] The critical evaluations of the revolution that came from within the revolutionary movement itself have been less studied. A small number of advanced nationalists published critical reflections on the revolutionary period in the 1920s and early 1930s that probed the brutal and often indiscriminate nature of nationalist violence, the physical and psychological costs associated with guerrilla warfare, and questioned the political gains that had been achieved. These were revolutionaries who had been avid members of the pre-Rising Gaelic intelligentsia and did not get the revolution they expected. This chapter explores the criticisms of revolution pressed by one such revolutionary, P.S. O'Hegarty, who, unusually for the period, criticised Ireland's revolution from a nationalist standpoint without masking his arguments behind the veil of fiction or pseudonymity.[3] This chapter explores the nature of O'Hegarty's critique in his 1924 book,

*The Victory of Sinn Féin*, and places it in the context of his pre-1916 expectations of the course that political separatism would take.

### 'THE MOST COURAGEOUS ACT OF O'HEGARTY'S LIFE': *THE VICTORY OF SINN FÉIN* (1924)

As a guide to O'Hegarty's verdict on the revolution, the title *The Victory of Sinn Féin* was spectacularly misleading. The book was no chronicle of an uncomplicated 'victory', but was rather a composite of two ostensibly antithetical verdicts on the revolution. One was a conventional nationalist celebration of the struggle, a story of triumph in which Ireland mounted an historic challenge to the empire by launching a skilful and defensive war that brought England to her knees. This struggle had been heroic, apparently hopeless, and waged with the support of the entire Irish people.[4] Conversely, the dominant and more forcefully articulated analytic strand was a severe indictment of the politics of force. According to this argument, the revolution had done no less than bring about a general moral collapse in Ireland, transforming it into a 'physical slaughter-house' characterised by 'contempt for life, for decency, for charity and tolerance'.[5] The civilian population had been terrorised by both sides, not only by the Black and Tans. The decision to wage a guerrilla war was not a necessary act of national defence for which Britain must wholly bear responsibility. Rather, it was nationalists who had adopted the 'guerrilla-war-ambush-and-shooting-of-civilians policy', who taught 'young people to rely on the gun and to disregard everything else', and who 'helped to swell the blood river by the elimination of the Dublin G-men, the shooting of spies, and the general suppression of civil authority by the gun'.[6] Nor could partition be entirely blamed on Britain. The policy of Ulster Boycott, O'Hegarty argued, established 'spiritual and voluntary partition' before physical partition had been imposed, creating a 'hatred of the North' in the south that had made Protestant Home Rulers in the north ashamed of their principles, turned 'apathetic Protestant Unionists into bitter partisans' and given 'the irresponsibles in the South their first taste of loot and destruction'.[7]

O'Hegarty refused to sentimentalise or celebrate the martial comradeship of revolution. At a time when revolutionary histories on both sides of the Treaty divide were very often little more than compilations of daring rescue and heroic escape stories, O'Hegarty argued that 'the strain of revolution on military men was slight', since, apart from the times when they were engaged in operations, Volunteers spent most of their hours hidden in secure places or wandering around free. The ordinary civilian, by contrast, was 'searched regularly in the streets, never knew when he might run into a Volunteer's bomb or an "Auxy's" revolver; ... had to stand behind his desk or counter although five minutes before there had been an ambush outside his window'.[8] The Irish people were not only victims, according to O'Hegarty, but also accomplices in their own moral degeneration. Having voted for Sinn Féin, they had failed to understand what Sinn Féin had actually meant, and had in the course of revolution turned themselves into a terrorised and degraded mob.

> When it was open to any Volunteer Commandant to order the shooting of any civilian, and to cover himself with the laconic legend 'Spy' on the dead man's breast, personal security vanished and no man's life was safe ... With the vanishing of reason and principle and morality we became a mob, and a mob we remained.[9]

O'Hegarty saw no evidence of the Irish people recovering from this 'mob status', and bemoaned, in tones worthy of the *Catholic Bulletin*, the 'waves of loot and materialism' that dominated the Free State, the 'grave increase in sexual immorality, and a general abandonment to levity and dissipation' evident in the 'unruly and ungainly' postures of jazz dancing that had 'swept Ireland like a prairie fire'.[10] For him, the revolution was a kind of schism in Irish history, a catalyst for moral degeneration which was an enduring, if not permanent, blight on the nation's history.

The book was highly controversial when it was published in 1924. Four thousand copies were initially printed and sold quickly,[11] and an advertisement in the newspaper *Honesty* described the book as 'the Most Discussed Book in Ireland', having been both 'highly praised' and 'wholly condemned'.[12] The internal inconsistency of the argument in the book was noted by several reviewers. The *Nation* called O'Hegarty an abstemious man who had written a 'drunken book',[13] and D.P. Moran described *The Victory* as a 'muddle of contradictions'.[14] Several readers wondered why, if O'Hegarty had believed that the War of Independence constituted a 'complete moral collapse', he had not protested at the time.[15] George Russell, writing under the pseudonym 'Y.O.', vigorously endorsed *The Victory* in the *Irish Statesman*, describing it as the most courageous act of O'Hegarty's life and a book that few others would have had the moral or physical bravery to write.[16] The danger that O'Hegarty's critique of the revolution would

be read as straightforward anti-nationalism was realised in at least one
reaction to *The Victory*, that of the judge and unionist James O'Connor in his *History of Ireland* (1925). O'Connor dramatically misap-
propriated O'Hegarty's analysis, selectively quoting him and cynically
reframing his statements to make *The Victory* look as if it were evidence for Irish incapacity for self-government.[17] O'Hegarty's statements endorsing the revolution (which leavened his critique in *The
Victory*) were all omitted, while his observations about the negative
impact of the war on civilians were aligned side by side with quotes
from Dan Breen's racy account of revolutionary ambushes and escapes,
*My Fight for Irish Freedom*, which O'Connor set up as exemplifying the
moral degeneration in Irish society that O'Hegarty perceived.[18] The
effect was to shift the meaning of O'Hegarty's analysis from an argument about the moral effect of guerrilla warfare to an almost racial
suggestion that the Irish were inherently predisposed to chaos and violence.

### A SCHOLAR OF REVOLUTION, 1902–1916

How and why did O'Hegarty come to fashion this courageous, if eccentric, critique of the revolution? It might be tempting to imagine
that his condemnation of the Anglo-Irish war was the product of a
principled objection to the use of political violence. Writing from a
distance of thirty years in *A History of Ireland Under the Union* (1952),
O'Hegarty gave an account of the revolution that suggested as much.
This book, which was a standard text in Irish schools for fifteen years,[19]
contained none of the critical analysis of revolution that distinguished
*The Victory*. National 'emergence' was euphemised as an organic, tranquil and painless process, a '<u>general, formidable, and heroic</u> attack on
the attackers',[20] untroubled by the counternarrative of 'moral collapse'
or civilian casualties. The IRA were depicted as having been supremely
fair and morally superior combatants, who shot only individuals 'doing
political work' and 'made clear that no policeman who confined himself to police duties had anything to fear'.[21] *A History of Ireland Under
the Union* also presented an emphatically non-violent account of the
origins of the War of Independence, with its roots placed firmly in a
Sinn Féin movement that 'did not contemplate an insurrection, a guerrilla war, or anything in the nature of violence', but was, rather, strictly
concerned with passive resistance.[22] O'Hegarty's grandson, Cian
Ó hÉigheartaigh, characterised P.S.'s attitude to violence in similarly
pacifist terms, describing him as a man who 'mistrusted the increasing

emphasis on force' during the period.[23] An examination of O'Hegarty's pre-revolutionary beliefs suggest that O'Hegarty's 1924 critique of the revolution had a different explanation.

Patrick Sarsfield O'Hegarty was born in Carrignavar, county Cork in 1879, to a Fenian father, John Hegarty, and from his early twenties he became intensely involved in Irish separatist circles in London. He lived an exemplary revolutionary lifestyle. He worked as a clerk at a post office, and would compress a day's worth of work into three hours and then stay up until one or two in the morning in order to keep up with a hectic schedule of reading, writing and attendance at meetings of the Gaelic League, Cumann na nGaedheal, the London Dungannon Club, the Irish Republican Brotherhood (IRB) (he served on the Supreme Council representing the south-east of England from 1908 to 1914), the Gaelic Athletic Association (GAA) and Sinn Féin.[24] O'Hegarty mentored the young Michael Collins in London and smoothed his passage up the ranks of the IRB and the GAA.[25] He was a teetotaller and an autodidact, and he and his wife, Wilhelmina Dill Smith, learned and spoke Irish to their children at home.[26] A preoccupation with Irish history, so common among revolutionary elites, ran to an obsessive extreme in O'Hegarty's case. He was a rapacious collector of books, particularly works of Irish history, literature and politics, and by the end of his life had amassed a world-class collection of over 25,000 items. His rented flat in London was meticulously stacked with books (friends wondered why his landlady never complained), and his bibliophilia eventually necessitated him getting the pockets of his jackets customised by a tailor to contain the ever-present volumes he transported about on his bicycle.[27] In only one substantive respect did O'Hegarty depart from the normative profile of an Irish revolutionary, and that was in his lack of religious belief. Although his published writings struck all the notes of moralism and anti-modern piety typical of many separatists of the time, O'Hegarty had been an agnostic from his schooldays.

Desmond Ryan memorably recalled O'Hegarty in these London years as a frenetic polemicist, a man who 'announces a new series of a hundred articles on history or books or his pet, physical force, and in the correspondence columns angry controversialists howl questions and challenges at P.S. O'H "Sarsfield", "Lucan", "Landen", and the whole half-dozen P.S. O'Hegartys'.[28] The array of monikers that O'Hegarty adopted all came from the Jacobite military commander after whom he was named – the Earl of Lucan, Patrick Sarsfield, who led the second flight of the Wild Geese and was killed at the battle of Landen in 1693 – and they were a fitting choice for a writer keen to incite revolutionary war against the English oppressor. The young O'Hegarty was consumed with the project of insisting that passive resistance to England had to be backed by force to be effective.[29] In 1907 he wrote that he looked forward to one day seeing 'the blessed glimmer of guns and bayonets',[30] and in 1912 he implored readers to 'stand for digging up the hatchet and sharpening it, for wild politics, and for dying for Ireland'.[31] In the same year he joined Patrick Pearse and Eoin MacNeill in their praise of the arming of Ulster.[32] His advocacy of violence also extended to the suffrage movement. Irish history had lessons for the cause of women's suffrage, in O'Hegarty's view, namely that 'reason', 'patience' and all the other apologies for action were futile.[33]

The 'lessons of Irish history' were indeed a matter in which O'Hegarty regarded himself expert. From his earliest published writings in Bulmer Hobson's *Republic* in 1906, O'Hegarty self-consciously fashioned himself as an exponent and protector of orthodox separatist principles, which he distilled from a highly teleological reading of the Irish past. There were, in O'Hegarty's view, a variety of 'near misses' in Irish history in which deviation from a 'policy of fight' had cost the nation freedom, and he drew the lesson that it was essential for the nationalist movement to embrace a policy of 'no compromise' in order to avoid these mistakes in the future.

> Had Emmet gone straight to the Castle instead of worrying about Kilwarden, had the young men prevailed and Mitchel been rescued, had the IRB Supreme Council put up the barricades in Dublin when the *Irish People* was suppressed and the staff arrested, had Parnell stuck to the No Rent Manifesto, to take the more modern instances, then the policy of fight would have succeeded fully, but the policy of diplomacy stepped in under one pretext or another and the result was partial failure.[34]

O'Hegarty pressed this doctrine of 'no compromise' emphatically and consistently in the majority of his publications and correspondence until 1914. He argued with the pacifist Robert Lynd in favour of physical force in the pages of *Sinn Féin* in 1909, a dispute which resulted in him being hauled before the secretary of the department on accusations of disloyalty.[35]

O'Hegarty was a harsh judge of his separatist colleagues as well. He took on the role of policing other nationalists whom he believed to have succumbed to the corrosive temptations of compromise. His foremost opponent in this regard was his mentor Arthur Griffith, whose pursuit of the Hungarian dual monarchy model for Ireland and pragmatic co-operation with parliamentary nationalists grated on O'Hegarty as insufficiently separatist.[36] Griffith was as avid a disciple of the Young Irelanders as O'Hegarty, and published several edited editions of Mitchel, Davis and Lalor's work.[37] However, O'Hegarty, like Bulmer Hobson, regarded himself as the more faithful disciple.[38] In 1907 O'Hegarty wrote that he found himself 'differing more and more from Mr Griffith's increasing tendency to slur over, in the goal of a complete unity of the nation, essential political axioms, and to follow the line of least resistance on all fighting questions; but I write also with a recognition of the greatness of his work'.[39] In 1909 his tone in private correspondence was exasperated. Griffith had, O'Hegarty believed,

> watered-down everything as low as he possibly can. In Thursday's issue he proposes an alliance with the Tories! And the only definite idea in the paper seems to be conciliate the unionists at all hazards. I believe in conciliating them but not at the expense of lowering our own practice or profession of nationalism.[40]

He eventually split with Griffith in 1910 over the perceived compromises of the *Sinn Féin* newspaper. Hobson and O'Hegarty established *Irish Freedom* in 1910,[41] a newspaper that, in Matthew Kelly's estimation, was the most sustained promotion of the Fenian ideal since the turn of the century, if not the 1860s.[42] Any hint of the desirability of linking separatism with social reform in Ireland was dropped (O'Hegarty had flirted with socialism in 1907),[43] and O'Hegarty's rhetoric about physical force became more extreme as the possibility of Home Rule approached.

O'Hegarty's hyper-vigilance against compromise was perhaps a function of the fact that he expected 'uncontaminated' separatism to deliver a very great deal. O'Hegarty's early separatism contained a distinctly utopian strain. It was an instinct that, he imagined, had the power to grip individuals and dissolve, or at least weaken, their commitments to religion and politics. Religious division would be erased by 'true' separatism, which would eventually itself become a religion capable of 'seizing us to the exclusion of all things else'.[44] As a disciple of Charles Kickham, O'Hegarty argued that there should be a clear line of demarcation between ecclesiastical authority over spiritual matters and secular authority over politics,[45] a strain of anti-clericalism that, he was keen to emphasise, was not atheism but 'simply anti-political priestism'.[46] Next to the British government, the political church was the greatest enemy to nationalism in Ireland, and it was essential that any propaganda that conflated nationality and Catholicism be rigorously avoided.[47] In all O'Hegarty's work in this period, he maintained the view that it was up to the nationalist movement to ensure that it had inclusive appeal, and he never entertained wishful thoughts about Ulster unionists spontaneously converting to nationalism for as long as it was closely identified with Catholicism.[48] Nationalism had to be inclusive in terms of individual temperaments and abilities as well as in terms of religion: 'It must give each man a line of action in the sphere of action for which nature or circumstances, or both, fit him: it must inspire, not only the political mind chiefly, as formerly, but equally so the artistic mind, the matter-of-fact mind, the practical mind, even the sentimental mind.'[49] Regardless of religion, social class or personality, O'Hegarty conceived of separatism as a force that would unite and elevate all.

Diligent propagandising was a central feature of O'Hegarty's conception of what it meant to be a good separatist. While some people were prone to being spontaneously 'gripped' by separatism,[50] for the majority the case had to be made in order for them to be won over. For the select few who already had a proper understanding of separatist philosophy, the 'gospel of work and preparation' was 'serious, urgent and responsible' and 'required sacrifices'.[51] Hard work was a virtue he elevated above almost all others. Whereas in 1922 the *Catholic Bulletin* honoured Terence MacSwiney's regular use of rosary beads in Brixton,[52] it was his work ethic that awed O'Hegarty, and he admiringly catalogued his nightly ritual of going to bed at 8 o'clock in order to get up the next morning at 2 o'clock and study during the winter, wearing just an overcoat instead of having a fire in order to avoid falling asleep.[53] MacSwiney's ultimate death through hunger strike was admirable, not because it precipitated a transcendent spiritual redemption of the nation through sacrifice of the flesh, but because it was the ultimate manifestation of earnest hard work in the pursuit of separatist propaganda.[54]

### RISING AND REVOLUTION, 1916–1922

O'Hegarty, although a member of the IRB Supreme Council from 1908 to 1914, did not participate in the Rising or its planning.[55] He did not express any dissent about the event publicly; indeed, in *The Victory of Sinn Féin* he tacitly endorsed the insurrection (which, he emphasised, was the creation of the IRB and not Sinn Féin), stating that after 1916 'there should not have been a shot fired in Ireland'.[56] He had doubts in private, though. The idea of a clandestine 'forlorn hope' insurrection was not abhorrent to O'Hegarty per se. As early as 1907, he had written about the principle of moral insurrection laid down by Fintan Lalor in his address to the 1847 Irish Confederation in the *Peasant*.[57] O'Hegarty also believed that the existence of modern artillery and aircraft made the possibility of a successful national insurrection impossible for subject peoples and had, in fact, started to devise his own scheme for such a rising that involved holding the Shannon. It was important, though, in O'Hegarty's view, that any insurrection in Ireland should be delayed until the Peace Conference,[58] and it is possible to detect glimpses of disapproval of Patrick Pearse and the blood sacrifice ideal in O'Hegarty's published writings of the post-Rising period. In 1919 he described Pearse as 'a mere automaton', lacking in gaiety, 'always strung up to serious pitch', and possessing a mind that was severely literal. Readers were left with no uncertainty about O'Hegarty's view that the architects of 1916 were Tom Clarke and Sean Mac Diarmada, and not Pearse.[59] He similarly minimised the role of Patrick Pearse in the teleology of Irish separatism in his introduction to Tom Clarke's *Glimpses of an Irish Felon's Life* in 1922, when he proclaimed Clarke as the one responsible for the insurrection and the medium for enabling all that had been 'forgotten by the younger generation' to be remembered.[60] In 1924 he went so far as to call Pearse's output as a political propagandist ephemeral and derivative, containing 'nothing which has not been said, and better said, in the last ten years, by various writers in the uncompromising papers, from the "United Irishman" to "Irish Freedom"'.[61] At no point did O'Hegarty praise Pearse for his martyrdom or his depth of religious feeling.

After the 1916 Rising, O'Hegarty stepped up the quantity and intensity of his separatist propagandising. Between 1917 and 1920 he wrote five books: a biography of John Mitchel, a survey of Irish history from the time of the Conquest, an appraisal of Sinn Féin and the separatist movement, a discursive argument for the inclusion of Ulster in an independent Ireland, and a memoir of Terence MacSwiney, all the while editing the IRB-funded newspaper *Irish World*.[62] This frenzied rate of production was certainly aided by his having more free time following his resignation from the Post Office in 1918, when the oath of allegiance became mandatory for all civil servants. His prolific output might also be ascribed to a belief in the importance of maintaining an 'open policy' after any nationalist insurrection. According to O'Hegarty, the absence of an 'open policy' had dictated that Emmet be followed by O'Connell, Young Ireland by the Tenant Right movement, and Fenianism by Parnell.[63] His vast output in the years between the Rising and the Anglo-Irish war indicate the endurance of his optimism about the potential of propaganda to draw the populace away from moderate politics and to be converted to a nationalism that was intellectually based, constructive and non-sectarian.[64]

There was no diminution in his insistence on physical force in these post-Rising books. In the Mitchel biography he repeated his subject's mantra of 'no compromise' for the present day, and transcribed Mitchel's practical advice from 1845 on ambushing trains.[65] His biography of MacSwiney was dense with praise for his subject's warrior-like countenance and doctrinal inflexibility. In describing the 'pith' of MacSwiney's nationalist philosophy, he quoted the monologue of the hero in MacSwiney's play *The Revolutionist*, in which he said, just before dying, that 'nothing matters if they don't give in – nothing – nothing – the last moment – that's the important time – the grip then – What's the good of being alive if we give in?'[66] MacSwiney's martial qualities were relentlessly praised. He was situated as a descendant of the Donegal MacSwineys, a 'fighting clan' who were 'great users of the battle-axe'.[67] His death revealed him to be 'a warrior of the highest caste known to mankind', such that when one looked at his face the word 'Samurai' leapt to mind.[68]

O'Hegarty was emphatic, though, that the 'no compromise' mantra did not equate to immediate, aggressive war. John Mitchel's writings mandated patience: the revolution would come only through a combination of passive resistance, propagandising to 'keep the people in a fighting temper', and finally trusting to 'the national instinct' to begin the revolution at 'the psychological moment'.[69] In 1917, O'Hegarty did not imagine that moment to be close to hand. For all his rhetorical toughness when it came to the 'policy of fight', he thought it would take 'years – many, many years – of discipline and work and suffering' before the people were ready.[70] O'Hegarty's publications after the 1918 general election saw a shift in his attitude to Arthur Griffith, too. With Sinn Féin's overwhelming political success (O'Hegarty was not chosen as a Sinn Féin candidate, much to his disappointment),[71] his disagreement with Griffith about the extent of his political compromise with the constitutionalists fell away, and in *Sinn Féin: An Illumination*, O'Hegarty now wrote about Griffith with fresh enthusiasm as a fellow Fenian and staunch separatist, albeit one with an aloof personality. In spite of Griffith's distaste for physical force, O'Hegarty did not spare the martial imagery in describing him as a warrior: 'Every sentence of his is as clean as a sword-cut, and as terrible in its effect as a battle-axe, and his genius for marshalling facts, like artillery, and concentrating them all at once in the direction he is working at is unequalled.' No man was more responsible than Griffith, O'Hegarty argued, for the nation's present Fenian spirit.[72]

O'Hegarty watched the guerrilla war from behind the desk of his bookshop in Dawson Street, a civilian rather than an active member of the nationalist leadership running the war. He did not fight, nor did he publish any significant writing in the period of heaviest conflict. As Free State and Republican troops lined up for civil war, O'Hegarty was retained by the IRB to edit the *Separatist*, a weekly newspaper established for the purpose of attempting to maintain IRB principles during the crisis. The editorial line was classic O'Hegarty, written with an arch tone in defence of 'principles rather than parties'.[73] O'Hegarty claimed to channel the transcendent 'Separatist ideal', which he wrote about in increasingly anthropomorphic terms. Gone were the 'no compromise' incantations and the clarion calls to physical force that were the spine of his *Irish Freedom* journalism. Now he ascribed to the separatist tradition a wily pragmatism, an instinct to 'make use of every opportunity', whether it be 'the gun, the ballot box, the soldier or the politician'.[74]

O'Hegarty claimed in 1952 that he supported the Treaty from the outset, and perceived the only 'blot' on it to be partition.[75] His contemporary published response to the Treaty was more equivocal. He wrote in the *Separatist* that he did not believe the Treaty fulfilled the precepts of Fenianism or marked the legitimate end point of the Fenian tradition, but he nevertheless supported it on the basis that it brought the ideal 'nearer its consummation'.[76] The pages of the *Separatist* chronicle O'Hegarty's building disillusionment with the possibility of an exalted separatist ideal continuing to bind the movement together. In April 1922 he abandoned calls for unity, despairing that consensus was, by that point, neither possible nor desirable, and all that could be hoped for was an election to settle differences and preserve ordered government.[77] In May, O'Hegarty ran an article by his brother Sean, explaining the plan for army unity devised by the Neutral IRA Association.[78] O'Hegarty's forecast was bleak, though, and he expected that a civil war would come that would break the country 'so utterly that England simply walks in and has her way as she never had before'.[79]

The outbreak of civil hostilities in July saw a radical change in O'Hegarty's formerly adamant adherence to the idea that militarism would unite Ireland and galvanise the national spirit.

Militarism has gone beyond its bounds with us, and, instead of being an adaptable entity, it has become a fetish. A man is not reckoned by his brains or ability, but by his bullets and his power to shoot and destroy. All that is wrong, and must stop. Little boys could be seen some time ago on route marches, carrying revolvers nearly as big as themselves. There has been too much of the heroic and too little of the practical going our way. Boys must be taught the beautiful and not the sordid things of life; they must be taught to appreciate the song of the thrush and the glory of nature, instead of worshipping at the shrine of a Colt, and glorying in the whizz of its speeding bullet. The militarism that has grown upon us must be cast aside as an unclean thing, otherwise we shall perish beneath the weight of its oppression. There must be no more heroics and idle [*sic*] adoration.[80]

When Arthur Griffith died in August 1922, O'Hegarty cast aside all martial imagery of him as a 'battle-axe' seeking the 'swift sword thrust',[81] and instead engaged a more subdued register, recalling him as 'the most constructive and steadfast political intelligence in Ireland' who sought a revolutionary aim through an evolutionary method. Griffith was elevated to the status of the sole initiator of Irish separatism. His newspaper *United Irishman* was now 'the beginning of everything and of everybody, it was the foundation of everything which, in the next twenty years, came to mean anything in Ireland'.[82] O'Hegarty's eulogy for his young protégé at the Post Office, Michael Collins, was far less effusive. He credited Collins with being the 'brain that conceived the war policy', and complimented him on having the courage to maintain it. But O'Hegarty hinted that he believed the policy of guerrilla warfare to have been a mistake per se, remarking that 'I myself contend that so far as the war was won it was won mainly by the civilians.'[83]

### 'AND A MOB WE REMAINED': REMEMBERING THE REVOLUTION AFTER 1922

Nearly all of O'Hegarty's expectations of the revolution were overturned by events between 1916 and 1922. Instead of revolution uniting the nation, Ireland had become physically divided and more deeply sectarian; instead of the leadership working conscientiously and guiding the people to moral and spiritual elevation through education, the movement was seized by men with no conceptual grasp of separatism;[84]

Ulster had been boycotted, instead of educated. Sinn Féin had not only turned into a political party rather than a 'spiritual force', it was a party that did not select him as a candidate. O'Hegarty's message of 'fight' had got through, but not in the way he had envisaged. Instead of violence being exercised in a highly disciplined, spiritually cleansing fashion, young men with poor training and makeshift weapons had participated in a grubby tit-for-tat conflict in which civilians were harmed.

O'Hegarty did not have a historical framework with which to explain these failures, and so reached for a text that was quite different from those written by the Fenians and Young Irelanders who had previously guided his thinking on revolution. H.G. Wells's *The War in the Air*, published in 1909, argued that modernisation had violently eroded 'the old boundaries, the old seclusions and separations' that defined human civilisation, a change he envisaged to have occurred on a grandiose scale, as 'three hundred years of diastole' ended by 'the swift and unexpected systole, like the closing of a fist, resulting in the destruction of the whole of civilisation'.[85] O'Hegarty was powerfully moved by Wells's vision, and explicitly referenced it in his grim assertion that the Irish revolution had 'weakened the ordinary established safeguards for reversion to a primitive unorganised society in which everything would depend upon force'.[86] As Richard Overy has recently observed, this kind of pessimistic determinism was extremely common in Britain in the interwar period, although intellectuals typically looked to the Great War, rather than national revolution, as the source of what they perceived to be a catastrophic fracture with prewar expectations of indefinite human advance.[87] O'Hegarty's anxiety that the Anglo-Irish war had destroyed civilised norms was strikingly resonant with widespread concerns in Britain that wartime violence had brutalised not only ex-servicemen but also the general public, and had led to rioting, industrial unrest and the abuse of state power in the early 1920s. O'Hegarty's argument in *The Victory* represents an interesting inversion of the usual significance that was attributed to the Anglo-Irish war in the discourse of post-war brutalisation. Where many Britons looked to the behaviour of the Black and Tans to confirm their sense that violence had 'slipped its chains' in the post-war years, O'Hegarty drew identical conclusions, but based them on his observations of the violent behaviour of fighters on the nationalist side.[88]

O'Hegarty never recovered his pre-revolutionary optimism about the possibility of mass social transformation in Ireland. Having invested so much energy in the idea of educating the Irish people into separatism

before 1919, by 1925 he regarded even incremental educational improvement as not only impossible, but undesirable. Mass education was
pointless in an agricultural country, he wrote in a survey, and there was
little utility in using the medium of Irish in schools given the poor standards of language competence that existed among the teachers.[89] O'Hegarty became the Secretary of the Department of Posts and Telegraphs
in the Irish Free State and, appropriately for a senior civil servant, dramatically lowered his profile as a commentator on political questions.
He did not publish any books about Irish history or politics for the du-
ration of his civil service career,[90] although his book collection on these
subjects continued to expand.[91] And although he did not write any more
about the revolution for nearly three decades after the publication of
*The Victory of Sinn Féin*, he did offer outspoken commentary on the
way in which other writers represented the revolution. He enjoyed the
imaginative depictions of the revolutionary years generated by Sean
O'Casey, Eimar O'Duffy and Denis Johnston, as well as impressionis-
tic memoirs of the period such as Darrell Figgis's *Recollections of the
Irish War* and W.B. Yeats's *Trembling of the Veil*.[92] Books that had pretensions to being objective histories of the revolution attracted a more
critical reaction, such as Piaras Beaslai's *Michael Collins and the Making of the New Ireland*, Dorothy Macardle's *The Irish Republic* and
Frank Pakenham's *Peace by Ordeal*.[93] He reserved his harshest criticism, though, for socialist interpretations of the revolution. He was
incensed by any attempt to downplay the primacy of nationalism in
the revolutionary period, and cited antipathy to socialist interpreta-
tion as one of the central reasons for his support for the endeavours of
the Bureau of Military History in 1946. The Bureau, he argued, would
neutralise the views of those 'social ideologists' who were attempting
to apply 'this or that post-insurrection ideology' to interpret the revolutionary period.[94] Regrettably, the confidentiality clause that was imposed over the Bureau collection meant that O'Hegarty was never able
to review the material or publish anything based on Bureau materi-
als,[95] but the residue of his hostility to viewing the revolutionary period through a social lens was evident in *A History of Ireland Under the
Union*, published six years later. This final book contained none of the
explicit acrimony toward 'the mob' that O'Hegarty expressed in *The
Victory of Sinn Féin*. It simply excluded the Irish people from the picture altogether. O'Hegarty's account was every bit as deterministic as
the socialist interpretations of the past he despised, but it cast the nationalist movement, rather than class conflict, as the engine of historical change. *A History of Ireland Under the Union* was, O'Hegarty

explained in the preface, almost wholly political history, 'because that is the important part of history'.[96] By excising the people from view, O'Hegarty was able to craft a smooth teleology of nationalist advancement that revealed none of the sense of shock and resentment he had felt at the time at the damage done by guerrilla war.

## CONCLUSION

After O'Hegarty's death in 1955, Mina O'Hegarty wrote of her husband: 'P.S. always believed in the written word.'[97] A commitment to the text is an essential ingredient in understanding O'Hegarty's disappointment with the Irish revolution in the early 1920s. O'Hegarty believed in a utopian separatism before 1916 that was based on the selected writings of Fenians and Young Irelanders. He expected that, by use of propaganda, it would be possible to disseminate separatist thinking in Ireland to a point where it enjoyed the status of a civic religion. In a separatist Ireland, religious divisions would be transcended, the nation would be morally elevated, and the political role of the Catholic Church would be diminished. O'Hegarty's contradictory reaction to the Irish revolution, as he expressed it in *The Victory of Sinn Féin*, was an expression of two competing impulses within Fenianism itself: a rhetoric of uncompromising separatism using whatever force was necessary, and a practical message of indefinite deferral until 'the psychological moment'. Fenianism simultaneously demanded that he celebrate the revolution because it was the achievement of sovereignty by non-parliamentary means, and condemn it because it had so evidently short-cut the stages of education required to develop a separatist mentality that included Ulster. O'Hegarty did not simply blame the civil war for the fact that post-revolutionary Ireland was robustly Catholic, persistently English-speaking, and more divided and materialist than it had been under the Union. His resentment and disappointment flowed to 'the Irish people', who had failed to properly understand the principles of separatist philosophy before reaching for the gun in the War of Independence. O'Hegarty never fully recovered from his pessimism about the catastrophic impact of the revolution on the Irish people, and when he came to write the celebratory chronicle of the course of Irish national liberation, *A History of Ireland Under the Union* in 1952, he was only able to do so by excluding the Irish people from the scope of his analysis.

O'Hegarty's path to disillusionment demonstrates the importance of looking beyond the categories of 'revolutionary' and 'constitutionalist' in this period of Irish history. *The Victory of Sinn Féin* shows that it was not necessary to be a constitutionalist to be a nationalist critic of the Irish revolution. O'Hegarty, with his pre-1916 incantations to 'dig up the hatchet', 'sharpen it' and 'die for Ireland', stood firmly in the revolutionary camp, but he was nevertheless shocked by the extent to which revolutionary violence in practice yielded none of the redemptive benefits of violence in theory. This sense of disappointment and shock was not readily acknowledged by many nationalists at the time and has left few traces on the historical record. It was, nevertheless, an important dimension of the experience of revolution felt by many people who were involved in the advanced nationalist movement before 1916, and is something that merits further academic exploration.

## NOTES

1. Senia Pašeta, *Before the Revolution: Nationalism, Social Change and Ireland's Catholic Elite, 1879–1922* (Cork: Cork University Press, 1999); 'Ireland's Last Home Rule Generation: The Decline of Constitutional Nationalism in Ireland, 1916–30' in Mike Cronin and John Regan (eds), *Ireland: The Politics of Independence, 1922–49* (London: Macmillan, 2000), pp.13–31; and *Thomas Kettle* (Dublin: University College Dublin Press, 2008).
2. Paul Bew, 'Moderate Nationalism and the Irish Revolution, 1916–1923', *Historical Journal*, vol. 42 (1999), pp.729–49.
3. Cf. George Russell, *The Interpreters* (London: Macmillan, 1922); Eimar O'Duffy, *The Wasted Island* (Dublin: Martin Lester, 1919); Desmond Ryan, *The Invisible Army: A Story of Michael Collins* (London: Arthur Barker, 1932).
4. P.S. O'Hegarty, *The Victory of Sinn Féin: How it Won it and How it Used it* (Dublin: Talbot Press, 1924), pp.40–3.
5. Ibid., p.173.
6. Ibid., pp.167, 169, 60.
7. Ibid., pp.52–3.
8. Ibid., p.62.
9. Ibid., pp.55–6.
10. Ibid., p.179.
11. P.S. O'Hegarty to George Lyons, February 1937, National Library of Ireland (NLI) MS 33,675/A/2/(60).
12. *Honesty*, 28 February 1925.
13. Ibid.
14. *The Leader*, 31 January 1925.
15. E. Bloxham, 'Letter to the Editor – The Victory of Sinn Féin', *Irish Statesman*, 24 January 1925; Marion E. Duggan, 'Letter to the Editor – The Victory of Sinn Féin', *Irish Statesman*, 31 January 1925; *The Leader*, 31 January 1925.
16. Y.O., 'Review of *The Victory of Sinn Féin* by P.S. O'Hegarty', *Irish Statesman*, 20 December 1924.
17. James O'Connor, *A History of Ireland 1798–1924* (London: Edward Arnold, 1925), p.294.
18. Dan Breen, *My Fight for Irish Freedom* (Dublin: Talbot Press, 1924).
19. Tom Garvin, introduction to P.S. O'Hegarty, *The Victory of Sinn Féin* (Dublin: University College Dublin Press, 1998).

20. P.S. O'Hegarty, *A History of Ireland Under the Union, 1801 to 1922. With an epilogue carrying the story down to the acceptance in 1927 by de Valera of the Anglo-Irish Treaty of 1921* (Dublin: Methuen & Co., 1952), p.738. Underlining in the original.
21. Ibid., p.739.
22. Ibid., p.735.
23. Cian O hEigeartaigh, 'P.S. O'Hegarty: 1879–1955', *Irish Times*, 4 January 1980.
24. Keiron Curtis, 'P.S. O'Hegarty and the Ulster Question', *Irish Political Studies*, vol. 22 (2007), p.118.
25. Peter Hart, *Mick: The Real Michael Collins* (London: Macmillan, 2005), pp.39, 71; O'Hegarty, *Victory of Sinn Féin*, p.24.
26. Kevin Girvin, *Sean O'Hegarty* (Cork: Aubane Historical Society, 2007), p.184.
27. Mina O'Hegarty to James Starkey, 2 January 1956, Trinity College Dublin (TCD), MS 4630–49/2694.
28. Desmond Ryan, *Remembering Sion: A Chronicle of Storm and Quiet* (London: Arthur Barker, 1934), p.52.
29. Sarsfield [P.S. O'Hegarty], 'Sinn Féin and Moral Insurrection', *The Peasant*, 13 July 1907.
30. P.S. O h-Eigeartaig [P.S. O'Hegarty], 'The Success of the Policy of Fight', *The Peasant*, 20 July 1907.
31. Landen, [P.S. O'Hegarty] 'The Criminality of Constitutionalism', *Irish Freedom*, 15 January 1912.
32. Landen [P.S. O'Hegarty], 'The Arming of Ulster', *Irish Freedom*, 15 December, 1910.
33. P.S. O h-Eigeartaig [P.S. O'Hegarty], 'The Emancipation of Women', *Irish Freedom*, 15 September 1912.
34. P.S. O h-Eigeartaig [P.S. O'Hegarty], 'The Success of the Policy of Fight', *The Peasant*, 20 July 1907.
35. O'Hegarty's witness statement to the Bureau of Military History, 22 April 1953, quoted in Girvin, *Sean O'Hegarty*, pp.188–9.
36. M.J. Kelly, *The Fenian Ideal and Irish Nationalism, 1882–1916* (Woodbridge: Boydell Press, 2006), pp.185–6, 189–92.
37. Griffith wrote prefaces to the following volumes: Mitchel's *Jail Journal* (Dublin: M.H. Gill & Son, 1913), Michael Doheny's *The Felon's Track* (Dublin: M.H. Gill & Son, 1914) and *James Fintan Lalor: Patriot and Essayist, 1807–1849* (Dublin: Talbot Press, 1918), as well as editing the volume *Thomas Davis: The Thinker and Teacher* (Dublin: M.H. Gill & Son, 1914).
38. Marnie Hay, *Bulmer Hobson and the Nationalist Movement in Twentieth-Century Ireland* (Manchester: Manchester University Press, 2009), p.46.
39. Sarsfield [P.S. O'Hegarty], 'Sanity and Reaction', *Irish Nation*, 6 November 1909.
40. Quoted in Kelly, *Fenian Ideal*, p.185.
41. Richard Davis, *Arthur Griffith and Non-Violent Sinn Féin* (Dublin: Anvil Books, 1974), p.147.
42. Kelly, *Fenian Ideal*, p.192.
43. P.S. O h-Eigeartaig [P.S. O'Hegarty], 'Sinn Féin and Free Speech', *The Peasant*, 9 November 1907.
44. Sarsfield [P.S. O'Hegarty], 'The Crisis', no. 23, 16 May 1907.
45. Kickham in *Irish People*, 27 February 1864, quoted in T.W. Moody, *The Fenian Movement* (Dublin: Mercier Press, 1978), p.109.
46. P.S. O'Hegarty to Terence MacSwiney, 23 March 1904, MacSwiney Papers, University College Dublin Archives (UCDA), P48b/376.
47. Sarsfield [P.S. O'Hegarty], 'Fenianism in Practice: An Irish Ireland Philosophy,' *The Republic*, 11 April 1907.
48. Sarsfield [P.S. O'Hegarty], 'The Sectarian Danger', *Irish Volunteer*, 15 March 1914.
49. Sarsfield [P.S. O'Hegarty], 'Fenianism in Practice: An Irish Ireland Philosophy', *The Republic*, 28 February 1907.
50. Ibid.
51. P.S. O'Hegarty, *John Mitchel: An Appreciation* (Dublin: Maunsel & Co, 1917), p.135.
52. *Catholic Bulletin*, June, 1922.
53. P.S. O'Hegarty, *A Short Memoir of Terence MacSwiney* (Dublin: Talbot Press, 1922), p.12.

54. P.S. O'Hegarty, 'Review of *Michael Collins and the Making of a New Ireland* by Piaras Béaslaí', *Irish Statesman*, 27 November 1926.
55. P.S. O'Hegarty, 'Recollections of the IRB', 7–11 November 1917, NLI, MS 36,210.
56. O'Hegarty, *Victory of Sinn Féin*, pp.166–7. In *Sinn Féin: An Illumination* (Dublin: Maunsel, 1919), O'Hegarty also corrected public misapprehensions that the Rising had been organised by Sinn Féin (see p. 52).
57. P.S. O h-Eigeartaig [P.S. O'Hegarty], 'The Success of the Policy of Fight', *The Peasant*, 20 July 1907. See also Sarsfield [P.S. O'Hegarty], 'Sinn Féin and Moral Insurrection', *The Peasant*, 13 July 1907.
58. P.S. O'Hegarty, 'Recollections of the IRB', 7–11 November 1917, NLI, MS 36,210.
59. P.S. O'Hegarty, 'P.H. Pearse', *Irish Commonwealth* (1919), Pearse Papers, NLI, 8265/ 103.
60. P.S. O'Hegarty, *Introduction to Glimpses of an Irish Felon's Prison Life by Thomas J. Clarke* (Dublin: Maunsel, 1922), p.xiii.
61. P.S. O'Hegarty, 'Padraig Mac Piarais', *Irish Book Lover* (September–October 1924).
62. *John Mitchel: An Appreciation* (Dublin: Maunsel, 1917); *The Indestructible Nation: A Survey of Irish History from the English Invasion* (Dublin: Maunsel, 1918); *Sinn Féin: An Illumination* (Dublin: Maunsel, 1919); *Ulster: A Brief Statement of Fact* (Dublin and London: Maunsel, 1919); *A Short Memoir of Terence MacSwiney* (Dublin: Talbot Press, 1922). The latter, although published in 1922, was written after MacSwiney's death in 1920 (p.i).
63. O'Hegarty, *Sinn Féin*, p.14.
64. Ibid., pp.v–vi.
65. P.S. O'Hegarty, *Mitchel: An Appreciation*, p.19.
66. O'Hegarty, *Short Memoir of MacSwiney*, p.98.
67. Ibid., p.1.
68. Ibid., p.97.
69. O'Hegarty, *Mitchel: An Appreciation*, pp.132–3.
70. Ibid., p.33.
71. Hart, *Mick*, p.183.
72. O'Hegarty, *Sinn Féin*, pp.28, 30.
73. 'The Separatist Position', *The Separatist*, 18 February 1922.
74. 'The Fenian Tradition and the Present Situation', *The Separatist*, 18 February 1922.
75. O'Hegarty, *Ireland Under the Union*, p.754.
76. 'The Fenian Tradition and the Present Situation', *The Separatist*, 18 February 1922.
77. 'Nearer and Nearer', *The Separatist*, 29 April 1922.
78. Sean O'Hegarty, 'What it Means', *The Separatist*, 13 May 1922. For more on Sean O'Hegarty's plans for army unity, see Bill Kissane, 'Civil Society Under Strain: Intermediary Organisations and the Irish Civil War', *Irish Political Studies*, vol.15 (2000), p.13, and Peter Hart, *The IRA and its Enemies: Violence and Community in Cork, 1916–1923* (Oxford: Clarendon Press, 1998), p.264.
79. O'Hegarty 'What it Means'.
80. *The Separatist*, 8–15 July 1922.
81. O'Hegarty, *Sinn Féin*, p.30.
82. *The Separatist*, 19 August 1922.
83. *The Separatist*, 26 August 1922.
84. O'Hegarty, *Victory of Sinn Féin*, p.134.
85. H.G. Wells, *The War in the Air* (London: T. Nelson & Sons, 1909), pp.327, 336–7.
86. O'Hegarty, *Victory of Sinn Féin*, p.169.
87. Richard Overy, *The Morbid Age: Britain Between the Wars* (London: Allen Lane, 2009), p.10.
88. Jon Lawrence, 'Forging a Peaceable Kingdom: War, Violence and Fear of Brutalization in Post-First World War Britain', *Journal of Modern History*, vol. 75 (2003), pp.557–89.
89. Draft letter from P.S. O'Hegarty to McKenna, [July 1925], O Broin Papers, NLI, MS 31,669.
90. A Civil Service regulation forbade civil servants from 'contributing to newspapers or other publications any letters or articles conveying information, comment or criticism on any matter of current political interest'. National Archives of Ireland (NAI), S 13186.
91. P.S. O'Hegarty, 'Notes on my Books', 14 April 1953, TCD, MS 4630–49/2693,
92. P.S. O'Hegarty, 'A Drama of Disillusionment', *Irish Statesman*, 7 June 1924; P.S. O'Hegarty, review of *The Trembling of the Veil* by W.B. Yeats, *Irish Review*, 6 January 1923.

93. P.S. O'Hegarty, review of *Michael Collins and the Making of a New Ireland* by Piaras Béaslaí, *Irish Statesman*, 27 November 1926; Moya Llewelyn Davies to P.S. O'Hegarty, 28 August 1941, NLI, MS 41,780/5.
94. P.S. O'Hegarty, 'Getting our History put Straight', *Sunday Independent*, 28 April 1956.
95. Evi Gkotzaridis, *Trials of Irish History: Genesis and Evolution of a Reappraisal 1938–2000* (Oxford: Routledge, 2006), pp.85–6.
96. O'Hegarty, *History of Ireland Under the Union*, prefatory note.
97. Mina O'Hegarty to James Starkey, 17 February 1956, TCD, MS 4630-49/2671.

# CHAPTER SIX

# Throttling the IRA: Fianna Fáil and the Subversive Threat, 1939–1945

## CAOIMHE NIC DHÁIBHÉID

Aspects of the relationship between Fianna Fáil – the Republican Party – and the extreme republican movement have attracted attention from a number of commentators, who have tended to centre on the interactions between the IRA and Fianna Fáil in the late 1920s and mid-1930s, when the fluidity of ideological boundaries between the two parties appeared to allow for a unity of purpose and to create a community of republican brethren. In this vein, both Brian Hanley and Richard Dunphy have noted the ambivalence that characterised relations between the Fianna Fáil party and the IRA during this period, with overlapping memberships, common aims and common enemies.[1] The disintegration of this relationship has, conversely, attracted less attention. Ronan Fanning's reflections on the mental processes by which Éamon de Valera divested himself of the IRA occupies a lonely position in the historiography of Irish republicanism, despite its appearance over twenty-five years ago.[2] Much as other accounts have posited the proscribing of the IRA by the Fianna Fáil government on 18 June 1936 as an appropriate book-end for the question of Fianna Fáil–IRA relations, Fanning's termination of his study in 1940 – a periodisation determined by the date of de Valera's invocation of the 'ultimate law' against the destabilising IRA threat during the war years – thereby neglects to delineate the nature of that menace and the vigour of the government's response. De Valera's officially-sanctioned biography is similarly tight-lipped on the issue of the republican movement during the 'Emergency', limiting a discussion of the entirety of the government crackdown on the IRA to an emotive portrayal of de Valera stricken by 'sorrow and self-reproach' but determined, 'no matter how much his decisions pained him, that he would show no signs of weakness'.[3]

This chapter, in contrast, will examine the precise nature of the government's response to the dangers presented by the extreme republican movement during the war years. It will demonstrate that this periodisation, far from representing a postscript to a political decision already made, rather constitutes an important episode in determining the attitude of a republican, 'slightly constitutional' government to a revolutionary movement. Although a non-belligerent, and one of the few neutral countries at the outset of war who retained that status at its end, the crucible of the war years provided a severe test of many aspects of Irish society and political life. The stability of the core institutions – many of which had been reworked only two years prior to the outbreak of war – was reinforced considerably; the capacity of the Irish people to accept all kinds of privations and curtailments of civil liberties in pursuit of a loftier goal was established; and an explicit choice had finally to be made between the dream of Irish unity and the reality of Irish sovereignty. Central to this process is the radical repositioning of the Irish government's attitude towards the IRA; the title of this chapter is drawn partially from an intervention by Gerald Boland, minister for justice, in Dáil Éireann in January 1942. He told the house bluntly, 'We have to stop [the IRA], we have to throttle this thing and put it down.'[4] Boland's 'no holds barred' declaration represents an effective summation of the Fianna Fáil government's rapidly hardening position vis-à-vis the IRA over the course of the war years. This chapter will examine the evolution of this position, playing particular attention to the interaction between political will and judicial action during the period in question.[5]

## EARLY EXCHANGES: LEGAL FRAMEWORKS AND ARMS RAIDS

Once war had been declared on 3 September 1939, the tensions that had been building between the Irish government and the IRA since the latter's bombing campaign in England had begun immediately took on a much graver aspect. Central to this worsening relationship was the government's enactment of stern emergency legislation to deal with the exigencies of war. The Emergency Powers Bill was rushed through the Dáil, expanding the powers already available to the government under the Offences Against the State Act to include extended powers of search and arrest for Gardaí and important changes in the functioning of the courts, inquests and juries.[6] In a significant move, de Valera replaced Paddy Ruttledge as Minister for Justice with Gerald Boland: the latter was a steely IRA veteran whose loyalty to de Valera

combined with personal experience of the steps needed to tackle subversion to create an immovable object in the face of increasing IRA
violence inside neutral Ireland. Boland's first act as minister was to
draw up a list of names scheduled for arrest under the Offences Against
the State Act; by the end of September 1939 ninety-three suspects had
been arrested, with sixty-seven held at Arbour Hill prison and a further
fifteen awaiting trial before the Special Criminal Court.[7] But soon a
coterie of republican prisoners inside Arbour Hill embarked upon the
traditional republican weapon: the hunger strike. Most prominent
amongst them was Patrick McGrath, a veteran of the Easter Rising and
War of Independence who still carried a British bullet lodged in his
chest. The prospect of de Valera 'allowing' such an eminent former
comrade to die prompted a large outpouring of emotion within
republican circles and a *crise de conscience* within the government.
Public expression of this disquiet was, however, severely hampered by
the strict censorship regime: newspaper editors had already been
instructed that 'the publication of anything which could give anyone
an excuse for supporting the so-called IRA of today can only do harm
at the present time'.[8] Privately, though, the government was receiving
a flood of letters and resolutions appealing for the release of McGrath,
from across the wide spectrum of nationalist opinion and largely focused on McGrath's history within the independence struggle.[9] Despite de Valera's emotive speech to the Dáil indicating the resolve of his
government to stand firm, having chosen 'the latter of two evils', there
was evident unease within the cabinet at the prospect of allowing un-
tried prisoners to die in custody.[10] The Taoiseach's strongly worded
speech was fatally undermined when, on 15 November, McGrath and
the two other hunger-strikers were released from Mountjoy to Jervis
Street Hospital; this was compounded on 7 December when the state
entered a *nolle prosequi* on all charges pending against McGrath under
the Offences Against the State Act.[11] Boland later maintained that Mc-
Grath was released for health reasons – the government had been informed that there was no chance of his recovery – but the overriding
impression was that de Valera's mettle had been tested, and had been
found wanting.

The release of McGrath was an undoubted fillip to republican
morale; even better was the next battle, in the courts, with the republican movement's challenge to the constitutionality of the Offences
Against the State Act. Barrister and republican Seán MacBride, acting on
behalf of Seamus Burke, made a habeas corpus application before Justice George Gavan Duffy; his argument centred around the provision

in the Act which stated that 'whenever a Minister of State is satisfied that any particular person is engaged in activities calculated to prejudice the preservation of the peace, order, or security of the State, such Minister may by warrant under his hand order the arrest and detention of such person under this section'.[12] Gavan Duffy crucially upheld MacBride's argument that when a minister satisfied himself that a person was engaging in activities prejudicial to the security of the state, he was exercising judicial functions; this indicated an important distinction from the relevant clause of the previous Public Safety Act, which merely stipulated that a minister should be of the opinion that such activities were being engaged in. Burke was duly released shortly after judgement had been delivered; as was expected, a further fifty-four prisoners were also released, largely emptying the jails of republican prisoners by December of 1939.[13]

The key legal framework for the prosecution of the IRA having been struck down, the government was unsure how to proceed, although the Secretary of Justice argued forcefully for a radical overhaul of the Offences Against the State Act, insisting that 'trial by jury has no real roots in this country'.[14] The cabinet evidently decided to wait until the new year to begin the process of amending the emergency legislation. But on the evening of 23 December the Magazine Fort in Phoenix Park, the principal ammunition store for the Irish Army, was raided by the IRA, whose well-prepared party arrived with lorries ready to transport the yield. Over one million rounds of ammunition were taken along with a negligible amount of weaponry.[15] Even more disquietingly, the raid revealed systemic failures in the conduct of the Irish Army and alarming reluctance on the part of the Magazine Fort soldiers to put up anything even remotely resembling resistance; as T.F. O'Higgins scornfully remarked, the soldiers meekly submitted 'without as much as a blackthorn being used'.[16] If this was how the Irish Army reacted to a few IRA men with pistols, the prospect of successfully repelling any serious military invasion was worrying. But in pulling off this audacious coup, the IRA had shown their hand too early. The shock administered to the public sense of security by the raid resulted in the notification of old arms dumps to the authorities, producing the farcical situation whereby more ammunition was recovered than was originally stolen.[17] More than anything, the raid pushed the government to react strongly to what had been a growing sense of crisis since the release of the hunger-strikers and the habeas corpus judgement. Despite the reservations of the opposition, the required amendments to both the Emergency Powers Act and the

Offences Against the State Act were swiftly passed. The prohibition on interning Irish-born citizens in the original of the former was removed, and in both Acts the opinion of a minister was enough to secure the arrest without warrant and internment of any individual. In one stroke, the habeas corpus victory was null and void: no impediment to internment remained. But by the time the Supreme Court confirmed the constitutionality of both new Acts, on 9 February 1940, the republican movement had switched its attention from points of constitutional law to the old certainties of murder, execution and protest.

### 'THE MARTYR COMPLEX'

An important interlude came with the trial and execution in London of Peter Barnes and James McCormack, convicted of planting explosives in the centre of Coventry, which killed five people. As the date of the execution approached, a customary agitation for reprieve was mounted by the republican movement; more surprising, however, was the response of the Irish authorities. Widespread coverage of the agitation for reprieve was allowed, even encouraged, in the press. The government was evidently sensitive to an attack on its republican flank, and used the death sentences as a way of reclaiming some of the ground they might have been considered to have lost after the previous year's moves against the IRA. The last thing de Valera could allow was a mass mobilisation on a nationalist issue outside the control of Fianna Fáil; as Joseph Walshe dryly underlined to John Cudahy, then American representative in Dublin, 'the martyr complex in Irish politics was something to be avoided like the plague'. With this in mind, the government moved to explicitly take control of the reprieve movement, making representations for clemency to the British government via John Dulanty in London, and to Sir John Maffey in Dublin. Cudahy was dismayed by the Irish government's apparent hypocrisy on the issue, confessing to Washington that he found it 'difficult to reconcile this point of view that foreign governments may not place IRA members in "deterrent confinement" whereas the Irish Government maintains that it can arrest its own citizens on suspicion and hold them indefinitely without trial'.[18]

What Cudahy failed to understand, however, was that it was precisely because a foreign government was moving against Irish republicans that the Irish government was compelled to act. Anything short of that would have been perceived as weakness on the national question and presented the possibility of being outflanked.[19] This feature would recur two years later, with the execution of Tom Williams north of the border rendering even more starkly the helpless hypocrisy of the Dublin government on such issues. After the failure of the reprieve movement for Barnes and McCormack, the IRA sought to build on any republican sympathies that resurfaced among the Irish public after the executions. But if the IRA hoped to secure popular support, murdering Gardaí, as Tomás MacCurtain did during a scuffle in Cork city on 3 January, was not the way to go about it. When MacCurtain was arrested following the shooting of Detective Roche, he commented to the Gardaí: 'I am surprised that you did not know before now that we are armed and that we are going to use them'; an ominous indication of the IRA's attitude towards the Gardaí.[20] While MacCurtain awaited trial, he was sent to Mountjoy, where he joined the recently arrested Jack McNeela and Jack Plunkett.[21] This group of prisoners soon began flexing their perceived muscles, and on 25 February a new hunger strike began: MacCurtain, McNeela, Anthony D'Arcy, Michael Traynor, Thomas Grogan, James Lyons and Jack Plunkett all began refusing food until their demand that two fellow prisoners be transferred to military custody was met. This was potentially extremely serious for the government: two of the hunger-strikers this time round were relatives of republican martyrs – Thomas McCurtain, murdered Lord Mayor of Cork, and Joseph Mary Plunkett, executed in 1916 – with privileged access to the vagaries of nationalist psychology. De Valera was deeply worried, telling the newly arrived American representative David Gray that '[h]e was in the throes of a domestic political crisis with international implications ... the IRA were anxious to get German help to depose him and presumably execute him for war crimes'.[22] In spite of de Valera's fears, the cabinet stood firm, and in facing down the hunger-strikers, the government nullified what had always been considered the most potent of weapons in Irish republican armoury. The final stages of the *danse macabre* were reached on 16 and 19 April, when Tony D'Arcy and Jack McNeela – the latter a nephew of Fianna Fáil veteran TD Michael Kilroy – expired on the fifty-first and fifty-fourth day respectively of refusing food.

A heated inquest into the death of McNeela followed, during which Boland was subjected to a bruising cross-examination by MacBride, who loftily placed the minister 'in the dock as far as the Irish nation is concerned'.[23] The jury's riders, that political prisoners should not be subjected to criminal status and that an intermediary priest should have been granted access to Mountjoy earlier in order to convince the hunger-strikers to desist, were perceived as a republican victory, and as a signal that the IRA was not unduly disheartened by the deaths of Mc-Neela and D'Arcy, on 25 April an attempt was made to blow up the Special Branch section of Dublin Castle, injuring two Gardaí. This attack was followed by a 'raging gun battle' in Merrion Square on 7 May: an attempt to seize British diplomatic mail was prevented by two Gardaí, who bravely repelled the IRA gunmen although they were grievously wounded. In an important public intervention, de Valera addressed the nation on radio and issued a sombre warning: 'The policy of patience has failed and is over … if the present law is not sufficient, it will be strengthened; and in the last resort, if no other law will suffice, then the Government will invoke the ultimate law – the safety of the people.'[24]

This address was made in the context of a rapidly deteriorating international situation, with Nazi Germany sweeping all before it in continental Europe and Britain poised to stand alone. With external events threatening to precipitate catastrophe in Ireland – by the summer of 1940, an unidentified German spy remained at large while fears of an invasion by either of the opposing powers ran high – on the domestic front more legislation was being drawn up to deal with the renewed gravity of the IRA threat. The Emergency Powers Amendment (No. 2) Act provided for the establishment of military courts to try civilians – that is, members of the IRA – that could only pass a sentence of death on those convicted, from which there would be no appeal.[25] As the legislation was passing through parliament, MacCurtain was finally brought before the Special Criminal Court on 11 June 1940, refusing either representation or to recognise the court. MacCurtain was sentenced to death by hanging, to be carried out on 5 July, and immediately a campaign swung into action. A mass of letters, telegrams and resolutions urging for reprieve descended on the government, mostly from veterans' associations of the Old IRA, who appealed to the memory of MacCurtain's martyred father.[26]

MacCurtain's legal team – MacBride and Albert Wood KC – sent a detailed memorandum to the Cabinet urging a reprieve on legal grounds, which included the failure of the Gardaí to produce a warrant for MacCurtain's arrest, emphasised the confusion of the struggle that had resulted in the fatal shot, and the effect of the murder of Mac-Curtain senior by policemen in 1920, 'a fact which, in our opinion, has subconsciously operated in the mind of the accused in the course of the fatal struggle'.[27] Although Maurice Moynihan later maintained that there was unanimity within the government that the murderers of Gardaí would face the ultimate penalty, inside the cabinet there was evident unease in some quarters at the prospect of executing the son of an old and venerated comrade. Seán T. O'Kelly was the most susceptible to feelings of guilt, and, with MacBride, hatched a plan to overturn the sentence. MacBride made an eleventh-hour habeas corpus application to Gavan Duffy in the High Court, which, as he calculated, was refused, and he immediately lodged an appeal in the Supreme Court.[28] The Supreme Court was unable to convene, owing to Justice Murnaghan's absence walking his dog, and the execution was duly postponed. O'Kelly having gone to work on his cabinet colleagues, MacCurtain's sentence was commuted to life imprisonment on 10 July. Although some within the IRA may have shared MacCurtain's evident dismay at the reprieve – an anointed martyr such as him would have been a welcome public relations boon – the republican movement had reason to feel optimistic by the summer of 1940. Long-standing secret contact with the intelligence agencies of Nazi Germany appeared to be bearing fruit and Britain stood alone against Nazi hegemony in Europe. The sense of ongoing crisis within the Irish political establishment was heightened by another potentially destabilising episode: a shoot-out on the Rathgar Road in August 1941 resulted in the death of Detective-Officer John Hyland and the arrest of Patrick McGrath – having made a miraculous recovery from his impending death – and Thomas Harte. The venom between the IRA and the forces of the state was further compounded by the death of John Joe Kavanagh, shot dead by Special Branch while tunnelling into Cork Jail in what was evidently an attempt to 'escape' prisoners inside. Such instances, and rumours that detectives had 'orders to shoot at sight', certainly contributed to pre-existing tensions; that the IRA were increasingly resembling desperados in their viciousness, as in the shoot-out at Rathgar Road, indicates the raised stakes in the unofficial blood feud with Special Branch, which had been simmering since 1938.[29]

The government response to the murder of Hyland was deceptively swift: although it appeared that the establishment of the Special Military Court was an instantaneous reaction, the work of Seosamh Ó Longaigh has demonstrated that this development was part of an ongoing government initiative to toughen up its policy vis-à-vis the subversive threat.[30] The Military Court was free to impose only one penalty on conviction, the death sentence, and no appeal was permitted. Moreover, the Military Court was responsible for the prosecution of a much wider range of offences than was previously the case, from possession of firearms and acts of sabotage to membership of an unlawful organisation. Sentences were to be carried out within twenty-four hours, thereby avoiding the prospect of destabilising public protests. Speaking in Dáil Éireann in 1946, Gerry Boland spoke plainly of the Military Court's design: 'This court has been described outside as a terror court. I have no objection to its so being described. That is exactly what it was. It was a terror court – a court set up to meet terror in a drastic and summary manner.'[31]

The Military Court was convened for the first time in the evening of 16 August under the Emergency Powers (No. 41) Order; the next day McGrath and Harte were charged before it and, the following week, convicted and sentenced to death by firing squad. The government declined to commute the sentence.[32] It was at this point that the two, who had refused legal representation in keeping with what appears to have been a fluctuating IRA policy, engaged MacBride to appeal on their behalf – notwithstanding the prohibition against appeal in the terms of the Emergency Powers (Amendment) No. 2 Act. MacBride attempted to repeat the pattern that had proved so successful in previous cases by appealing directly to Justice Gavan Duffy in his home for a habeas corpus order. This, however, failed: Gavan Duffy, working off the basis of the Emergency Powers Act and not the Offences Against the State Act, declined to grant an absolute habeas corpus order, commenting that 'in view of the public importance of the emergency legislation it was, perhaps, regrettable that the objections taken by counsel should happen to be of a rather technical character'.[33]

This was a thinly-veiled criticism of MacBride's professional approach to the case and to his argumentation, much of which was subsequently reproduced before the Supreme Court. MacBride's arguments were highly technical, focusing on the validity of the entire Emergency Powers Act, the procedural steps taken by the President to sign the bill into law, and the existence of a state of war inside Ireland. MacBride also raised the question of the suitability of a military court to try civilians, a somewhat hypocritical claim for the legal representative of a self-styled army, some of whose members had recently hunger-striked to death for the right to be held in military custody. But the hypocrisy ran both ways: that the state should deny military status to IRA prisoners and internees, but insist on the right to try them summarily before military courts comprised of army officers and held in military barracks, indicates the convoluted logic inherent in the state's response to the subversive threat during the war years. An argument that appeared to have more currency, however, was MacBride's contention that 'whatever law or orders the appellants had been tried under had been non-existent at the time of their arrest'. This was compounded by the failure of the government to lay the same law or orders either before the Oireachtas or before the public, even at the time of trial of McGrath and Harte.[34] At any other time, such an omission would almost certainly have ensured the quashing of the sentence handed down, but the Supreme Court judgement, like Gavan Duffy's in the High Court, was robust, unanimously dismissing all of MacBride's arguments without hearing counsel for the state.[35]

In the run-up to the executions, the customary clamour was raised in favour of clemency, although not as vociferously as with MacCurtain.[36] Nonetheless, strong private pressure was exerted upon persons of influence within and outside of government: David Gray reported that 'the full force of patriots descended on this legation', delivering dire warnings of bloody civil war and full reprisals against cabinet ministers.[37] There was a qualitative difference to the appeals for clemency this time, however. Instead of merely petitioning for mercy for the condemned men, fuller proposals were delivered to the government detailing the basis along which a truce with the IRA might be agreed. This appeared to have been in the ether since the MacCurtain case: rhetoric along these lines was being promulgated by Córas na Poblachta, a newly-formed republican political organisation. Although MacBride declined to formally align himself with the new organisation, he acted as a conduit between the wider republican movement and the government, visiting government buildings on the eve of the McGrath executions to deliver terms for a truce.[38] De Valera declined to reply, and the truce initiative failed. The government had no real incentive to agree to the proposal; it finally had the legal machinery in place to effectively deal with the IRA threat, and any agreement would place it in an almost impossible political position vis-à-vis the opposition. The question of trust was, moreover, paramount, and any residual trust that had existed between the Fianna Fáil government and the estranged members of the republican family had been blown away by the discovery of the IRA's collusion with German agents.

Attempts to broker a truce having foundered, McGrath and Harte's sentences stood. The government's yielding to McGrath the previous November had counted against the veteran this time round; by reimmersing himself within the violent republican milieu, McGrath had effectively squandered any lingering goodwill within the government. De Valera was particularly pained by the case, blaming himself for five needless deaths. Other cabinet ministers took a similar view, Seán MacEntee concluding that the case 'again emphasised the inadvisability of yielding to hunger strike tactics'.[39] The executions were carried out early on the morning

of 6 September. For the government, and the wider society, it indicated a reassuring willingness to stand firm in the face of the subversive threat. The choice had been to govern or to abdicate, and de
Valera had finally fulfilled the promise he had made to invoke 'the ultimate law' to preserve the security of the state. A postscript to the
McGrath and Harte case came when Thomas Hunt was later captured,
tried and convicted of aiding and abetting in the murder of Hyland; his
sentence of death was commuted to life imprisonment by Gerry
Boland, who viewed him as 'more a tool than anything else'.[40] Similar
clemency was not directed towards Richard Goss, who in August 1941
was executed for his part in a miniature skirmish in County Longford,
where shots were fired at the Irish Army. The resolve of the government to press ahead with an execution even on a relatively minor
charge of 'shooting at military', indicates that a new level of determination had been scaled in the campaign to break the IRA as a force in
Irish political life. The latter part of the year and the early months of
1942 would see these efforts redoubled, as the very fundamentals of
law were set aside to crush the illegal organisation.

### INCREASED VIOLENCE

With the perniciousness of the Stephen Hayes affair serving as a timely
reminder of the continued ability of the IRA to function – albeit at
drastically reduced capabilities – as a subversive organisation, the discovery of the body of Michael Devereux in October 1941 prompted
renewed vigour on the part of the government.[41] Devereux, a 24-year-
old lorry driver from Wexford, had been executed as a spy by fellow
IRA members on a Tipperary mountainside. Once Devereux's body
had been discovered, four men were taken into custody: George Plant,
Joseph O'Connor, Michael Walsh and Patrick Davern. Davern and
Walsh both made statements to Gardaí detailing the whole affair; these
statements were expected to form the basis of the prosecution case
against Plant and O'Connor, who were charged with murder and
procuring murder respectively, and Walsh and Davern were listed as
witnesses for the state. Inside Mountjoy, however, untold pressures
were brought to bear on both men by fellow prisoners, and at the ensuing trial of Plant and O'Connor, Walsh, Davern and a third witness,
Simon Murphy, refused to testify, claiming their statements had been
extracted by force. The case sensationally collapsed and for a brief moment it seemed as though this bold move had out-manoeuvred the
state. But the government reacted swiftly and more decisively than the

republican movement could have imagined: a *nolle prosequi* was entered for Plant and O'Connor, and the two defendants were immediately charged again with the murder of Devereux, along with Walsh and Davern. Under Emergency Powers (No. 41F) Order, the case was transferred to the sterner location of the Military Court; more crucially, the government issued Emergency Powers (No. 139) Order which allowed unsworn, unsigned statements to be admitted as evidence in a court of law, regardless of whether the author of the statement should give evidence or not. It further provided that 'if, on any occasion during the trial before a court to which this order applies, the court considers it proper that it should not be bound by any rule of evidence, whether statutory or at common law, the court shall not be bound by such rule'.[42] This was an unprecedented step, altering at a stroke the basis of law as it had been practised in Ireland. MacBride quickly launched a legal challenge, seeking habeas corpus and prohibition from trial, first in the High Court and then the Supreme Court. Appearing with Cecil Lavery, MacBride submitted that

> a Military Court – whose appointment was at the hands of a political executive, and subject to the whims of a political executive – vested with powers of life and death over others, without trial under any rule of law or rule of evidence, was not in accordance with the object set out in the preamble to the Constitution: the common good.[43]

Without the normal rules of evidence, MacBride argued, the Military Court failed to constitute a judicial tribunal as envisaged in the constitution, and as such was repugnant. But in rejecting their arguments, the High Court and Supreme Court intimated that notwithstanding the monstrous encroachment into individual liberties and the rule of law represented by the order, the ultimate law invoked by de Valera in 1940 took precedence. At the ensuing eleven-day trial, in which the judicial powers under the new order were invoked, the statements of Walsh and Davern were accepted as evidence. After forty-five minutes' deliberation, the Military Court returned a verdict: O'Connor was acquitted (but immediately rearrested and interned) while Plant, Walsh and Davern were all found guilty and sentenced to death by shooting – the only sentence possible. The sentences of Walsh and Davern were later commuted, but Plant's stood. He was transferred to Portlaoise Prison on 4 March, allegedly with his coffin alongside him in the back of the lorry, where MacBride observed the calmness with which he prepared himself for death.[44] Plant's family, not having been notified in time, learned of his death on the radio.[45]

Republican and nationalist attention was diverted for much of 1942 by the impending executions of six IRA members north of the border for the murder of Constable Patrick Murphy; the case, with massive attendant publicity, provided the southern government with an opportunity to unblushingly demonstrate its ability to completely separate southern illusions from northern realities: that justice in the northern state was at least administered in a courtroom, with a judge and jury, not by military court martial, did not prevent the government from making an official plea for a reprieve. Clemency was exercised in five of the cases; the sixth man, the IRA O/C Thomas Williams, was executed on 2 September. The rush of feeling stirred up by the execution also provided something of a fillip to the IRA both north and south, although neither proved capable of capitalising on it. Unable to adhere to the GHQ decision to restrict IRA activities to operations in Northern Ireland, the Dublin leaders made a drastically ill-advised decision to target Detective-Sergeant Denis O'Brien, their chief adversary within Special Branch. Perhaps the best-known of the 'Broy Harriers', O'Brien was closely associated with the old republican establishment: his brother, Paddy O'Brien, had been O/C in the Four Courts, both brothers were 1916 and War of Independence veterans, and another brother was private secretary to Seán Lemass.[46]

On the morning of 9 September 1942, three IRA gunmen lay in wait outside O'Brien's home in Rathfarnham; as he drove down the avenue on his way to work, they opened fire with rifles and a machine gun, killing the detective instantly. O'Brien's close ties to senior figures within Fianna Fáil's republican past and present meant that his murder was not only an attack upon the preservation of law and order in the state, but a personal blow to members of the government. This murder marked a new low in the confrontations between the IRA and Special Branch since the war had begun: where previous killings had occurred during raids and shoot-outs, this 'deliberate and planned assassination' was testimony to a brutality which was increasingly coming to resemble a vendetta.[47] As well as instigating a new stage in the blood-feud between the IRA and the Gardaí, the murder of O'Brien provided a further opportunity for the de Valera government to demonstrate its unblushing double standards to IRA crimes inside and outside its jurisdiction. The press censor instructed Irish newspapers to describe the crime as murder wherever possible and the perpetrators as murderers, not gunmen. This, as Dónal Ó Drisceoil has shown, was in direct contradiction to the instructions issued less than a week previously, when the opposite terminology was ordered for coverage of the Williams execution. Hence the ostentatious pieta presented in the *Irish Times*, with an elaborate description of the dead man's wife cradling her husband's body in her arms, after an operatic account of the murder, prompting David Gray's scornful comment that 'murder by the IRA is murder only in Eire and not when committed north of the border'.[48]

A catalogue of ugly incidents followed the O'Brien murder, as police intensified their efforts to arrest the chief suspects. In Cavan, a raid on a wedding-house resulted in the deaths of IRA volunteer Patrick Dermody and Detective Michael Walsh; a second IRA man, Harry White, escaped injured.[49] The death list further increased on 24 October after another shoot-out in Donnycarney; this time, Detective George Mordaunt was killed. Harry White again escaped, but Maurice O'Neill was captured. This was an unprecedented series of events: despite the long-standing bitterness between the IRA and the Gardaí, the murder of three policemen in the space of two months evoked memories of an earlier struggle against another force, something the government was determined to avoid. Such heightened domestic tensions – with, it should be remembered, a general election expected the following year – explain the virulence with which O'Neill was prosecuted in the Military Court. He was charged not with the murder of Detective Mordaunt, but with 'firing at detectives with intent to resist arrest'. It was a most unpropitious time to be facing such a charge; not only was the murder of Mordaunt uppermost in the mind of the government and the court, but the killers of O'Brien had yet to be apprehended. With less than three days to prepare a defence for a death charge, MacBride gamely represented O'Neill, basing the defence around the suggestion that the police fired the first shot and that O'Neill was merely acting in self-defence. In an unusual move for an IRA defence, O'Neill was put on the stand, giving blunt evidence that his IRA unit was preparing to travel to the North and that the gun he carried was for training purposes only.[50] In MacBride's closing address, he made a final plea for clear heads on the precise nature of O'Neill's charge. 'Everybody deeply regrets the tragedy which resulted in Detective Mordaunt's death and everyone prays that we will be spared similar tragedies,' he said, '[a]t times, during the cross-examination of the prisoner I felt that conviction was being sought for this and for other tragedies. But the more the court is deeply shocked by the death of Detective Mordaunt the more scrupulously careful it must be not to allow this consideration to weigh against the prisoner.'[51]

Such considerations, however, could have no effect on the outcome of the trial. O'Neill had been charged with firing at detectives, that charge had not been disproven, and any charge before the Military Court carried the death penalty. O'Neill was sentenced to death. A campaign emanating principally from O'Neill's native county Kerry did make its presence felt in the aftermath of his sentencing. As well as the North Kerry Old IRA, the Kerry County Board of the GAA and Kerry County Council, the South Kerry branch of Fianna Fáil also wrote in the strongest terms to plead for a reprieve.[52] Despite residual Fianna Fáil ties to Kerry, wrought in the bloody executions of the civil war, the government declined to commute the sentence. Feelings in Kerry ran high on the night of the execution: Michael McInerney reported later that 'about 100 members of the LDF resigned, shots were fired at the Garda barracks in Tralee and shopkeepers closed their shops for the day'.[53]

## POLITICAL IMPLICATIONS

What were the political results of all these upheavals? Stung by the local elections results of 1942 – in Dublin alone Fianna Fáil dropped from twelve seats to two – the government was reluctant to call the long-awaited general election.[54] There were a number of parties eager to see if the gains in the previous year's local elections and a general popular discontent with the government – produced especially by wartime short-ages, rationing and a highly unpopular wage freeze – would tell at the polls. The state of Irish politics was, therefore, as delicately poised as it had been for a decade, and a sense of new possibilities was in the air.[55] The republican movement was also sensitive to the new alignments currently taking shape within the Irish political establishment; although the tentative steps taken by Córas na Poblachta had not resulted in any gains at the local elections, from the spring of 1943 there was a definite trend towards political engagement that had been absent from the movement since the Russell takeover four years previously. The first public announcement of a détente regarding political participation came with a one-day conference called by the National Association of the Irish Republican Army Old Comrades on 17 March 1943.[56] A standing committee was elected at the conference, comprising Seán MacBride as Chairman, Dónal O'Donoghue and May Laverty as Secretaries, and Roger McHugh and Luke Duffy as Honorary Treasurers. The last name is most significant: Duffy was the current secretary of the Labour Party. His attendance at the conference and his nomination as an officer of the standing committee arguably indicated some measure of official Labour approval for the initiative, although he was censured by the party's more conservative Administrative Council for his presence.[57]

The conference, as well as MacBride's chairmanship, should not however be interpreted as a break from the violent strand of republicanism represented by the IRA; rather, the illegal organisation was intimately associated with the strategies drawn up for this new approach. On 30 March 1943 Hugh McAteer wrote to Charles Kerins that he was 'very pleased to see by the Press reports that a start has been made in launching the new Republican party'. He further queried whether 'Seán McBride intends to implement the suggestions I made in my last dispatch, re. contesting of certain seats and attitude of non-hostility towards Labour in other areas.'[58] The accommodationist attitude towards other parties revealed in this letter is an interesting development in the hitherto self-absorbed mentality of extreme republicanism. Subsequent letters between GHQ members McAteer and Charlie Kerins reveal a more sustained process of reflection and dialogue on electoral affairs, in a manner unthinkable for the staunchly 'non-political' IRA in previous years:

> I have come to the conclusion that it would be inadvisable to put forward a Republican candidate [in Kerry], as this would split the anti-Fianna Fáil votes, with the result that the Fianna Fáil candidates would be re-elected. The present Labour and Farmer candidates, though not members of the Army, have very sound Republican principles.[59]

From the republican point of view, the rationale for electoral cooperation was simple:

> All the parties have the blood of Republican martyrs on their hands but Fianna Fáil are the worst. They murdered Republicans in the name of Republicanism and stooped to meaner methods than were ever used by the first Free Staters or the English. On that account we want to see them kicked out no matter what party takes their place.[60]

During the election campaign MacBride maintained his distance from Córas na Poblachta, who mismanaged the campaigns of their two best-known candidates, Seán Dowling and Simon Donnelly (both well-known Old IRA members), by running them in the same constituency, Dublin South.[61] In the event, all the republican candidates (including republican internee Seán McCool) polled dismally, uniformly losing their deposits. But the two main parties also performed badly in the election: despite another catchy slogan ('don't change horses in mid-stream'), Fianna Fáil lost ten seats and its overall majority, while Fine Gael lost thirteen.[62] The beneficiaries were, overwhelmingly, Clann na Talmhan and Labour, both parties which appeared to endorse wider republican aims. New Labour TD Roddy Connolly, son of James, made explicitly clear Labour's electoral debt to the republican constituency in his maiden speech:

> it should be obvious to the Minister that the 80,000 extra votes which the Labour Party obtained at the election were, perhaps, due very largely to the fact that quite a number of Republicans, those with Republican traditions, had come over towards the Labour Party, and that their activities had resulted in that accretion of strength. Naturally, if that is so, the Labour Party must become responsive to this new impact on its political make-up.[63]

Labour was responsive to this new impact, arguing vigorously in the Dáil for the release of the hunger-striking prisoners and setting a precedent for future advocacy of republican issues over the subsequent years.

While elements within the republican movement were demonstrating a new openness to political ideas, the elevated passions of the height of the IRA campaign against the state briefly recurred. Early on the morning of 15 June 1944, Kerryman Charles Kerins – the 'chief of staff of a one man army' – was arrested at the home of Doctor Kathleen Farrell in Rathmines. Gardaí and government had long been certain that Kerins had given the order for the O'Brien murder, even if he had not actually carried it out, a belief borne out by Harry White's later recollection that Kerins had warned him to 'stay out of the way' on the morning of the shooting.[64] On 2 October Kerins's trial for murder opened before the Special Criminal Court: the state's evidence was largely circumstantial, resting on a fingerprint of Kerins found on a bicycle close to the murder scene, weapons and IRA documents discovered at a boarding house in Dublin, and some very shaky identifications. Many of the witnesses who appeared in court refused to identify Kerins and were treated as hostile witnesses by the state, a testament to the fear that still governed public attitudes towards the IRA.[65] After being found guilty, Kerins lambasted the judicial system, declaring: 'if this is an example of de Valera's justice, freedom and democracy, then I should like to know what dictatorship and militarism are'.[66] The Court of Criminal Appeal having refused leave to appeal on 15 November, Kerins's legal team applied for permission to appeal to the Supreme Court. Arguing that Kerins's 'trial was not satisfactory and the evidence ... insufficient', MacBride and Lavery submitted that key witnesses – who had given evidence at the trial of Michael Quill for the same offence – were not called. The circumstantial nature of the fingerprint evidence and documents linking Kerins with the IRA was also queried, and, finally, that the prosecution had been permitted to make a closing speech was severely criticised.

The attorney-general refused a certificate to appeal to the Supreme Court, and the execution date of 1 December was allowed to stand. Immediately, however, a massive campaign for clemency was launched: petitions containing the signatures of such diverse figures as Seán O'Faolain, Harry Kernoff, Seán Keating, Colm Gavan Duffy, Austin Clarke, Eileen Davitt, Rosamond Jacob and Mrs Mellows were received, and in total almost 100,000 signatures were collected. A reprieve committee was established, including Con Lehane, Kathleen Lynn, Peadar O'Donnell, Hanna Sheehy-Skeffington, Moss Twomey, Roger McHugh, and Denis Guiney (a prominent businessman and Fianna Fáil supporter), while a number of local Kerry organisations – including Kerry County Council – also agitated for clemency.[67] But the government took a robust line with the reprieve campaign, refusing to allow any publicity around, for instance, the meeting at the Mansion House on 27 November, where a number of Labour TDs spoke; similarly, attempts to advertise that and future public meetings were suppressed, including a seemingly innocuous appeal to 'all Kerrymen and women living in Dublin' to attend a meeting outside Clery's department store on 30 November.[68] While the Kerins reprieve campaign did succeed in questioning the extent and purpose of censorship in Ireland during the war years, chances of securing a reprieve for Kerins were always slim. As detailed above, O'Brien's murder was perceived as a personal slight to some members of the Fianna Fáil cabinet; equally, the Gardaí were determined that someone should be brought to justice for the murder of their colleague. The flimsiness of the evidence linking Kerins to the actual murder was set aside for the wider aim of vengeance.

Kerins was hanged in the early hours of 1 December; particularly galling to republicans was that the British hangman, Albert Pierrepoint, had performed the execution.[69] Kerins remains the last republican executed in Ireland, north and south, for a political crime. In 1948 his remains, along with those of all other republicans executed during the war years, were released to his next of kin by the inter-party government, a move undoubtedly pressed by his legal representative, the then

Minister for External Affairs.[70] The authorities believed that the Kerins reprieve campaign was being used as a front to reorganise the IRA; certainly, as we have seen, attempts were being made to reorganise the republican movement.[71] MacBride had participated in a meeting convened by Patrick McLogan, former MP for Armagh, in October 1944, and a month previously a similar gathering brought together Moss Twomey, Simon Donnelly and Mrs Austin Stack.[72] But these meetings are best interpreted as forging a new political way forward for the republican movement as a whole, not as a reorganisation of the IRA. That organisation had been thoroughly shattered by the security crackdown throughout the war years; even before the arrest of Kerins, the whole infrastructure of the IRA had broken down. Cognisant of this, the authorities initiated a gradual release of the interned prisoners, which commenced in the autumn of 1943; this process accelerated through 1944, and by March 1945 only 115 remained in the Curragh.[73]

CONCLUSION

Three years after the end of the war, a new republican political party, Clann na Poblachta, secured ten seats in the general election; their electoral success, led by Seán MacBride, enabled them to hold two cabinet seats in the first interparty government of 1948. Although this republican 'new departure' was not officially sanctioned by the IRA, and the weariness of sixteen years of unbroken Fianna Fáil government undoubtedly told on the electorate, the short-lived success of Clann na Poblachta can be read as a product, in some manner, of the hostilities between the government and the republican movement during the war. The catalogue of murder and executions in Ireland during the Emergency was sobering, and represented the most sustained outbreak of political violence in the state since the end of the civil war. Although as Fanning has demonstrated, de Valera had long rejected the IRA's political vision, the Second World War provided the immediate catalyst for the government's resolve to crush subversion within the state. The seriousness of external events was undoubtedly a determining factor in shaping the government response, as well as the reaction of the wider population. Without the vast apparatus of emergency legislation rushed through the Oireachtais, the necessary legal measures to defeat the IRA might not have existed. Similarly, without the undoubtedly repressive censorship regime, the possibility of destabilising public protests around the executions and hunger strikes might well have gathered a head of steam, precipitating a political crisis, both internally and externally.

Both of these issues, however, raise difficult questions as to the proper response of a liberal democratic state to internal terrorism. The use of state violence – in the case of Jackie Griffith, indiscriminate and no-warning violence – in pursuit of the preservation of democratic sovereignty might be considered a self-negating measure; equally, the widespread repression which existed through the emergency powers legislation – targeting the ordinary citizen as well as the subversive – merits further academic exploration. The fate of civil liberties in Ireland during the Second World War was not altogether a happy one.

In dealing with republican subversion during the Emergency, Fianna Fáil had to explicitly confront their erstwhile revolutionary comrades. Although the bulk of the Fianna Fáil cabinet were men with 'good fighting records', their shift to constitutionalism in 1926 had, to their credit, been complete. That it took the party a subsequent ten years to muster up the stomach to face down their former brothers-in-arms should not altogether detract from the serious political and personal rationalisation that the process must have evoked. That it was a Fianna Fáil government, stemming as the party did from the anti-Treaty, more ostentatiously republican section of the community, was an important development: in upholding execution warrants and in allowing the hunger strikes to play themselves out, the government sent an effective signal that it would not permit Irish democracy to be jeopardised, whatever the emotional or sentimental attachments which might have existed within the broader republican movement. More fundamentally, however, in demonstrating the determination of the government to uphold Irish sovereignty and the rule of law at all costs, de Valera and his cabinet definitively demonstrated the excision of political violence from the Irish constitutional mainstream.

### NOTES

1. Brian Hanley, *The IRA, 1926–1936* (Dublin: Four Courts Press, 2002), *passim*; Richard Dunphy, *The Making of Fianna Fáil Power in Ireland, 1923–1948* (Oxford: Clarendon Press, 1995), pp.137–41.
2. Ronan Fanning, '"The Rule of Order": Éamon de Valera and the IRA, 1923–40' in John P. O'Carroll and John A. Murphy, *De Valera and his Times* (Cork: Cork University Press, 1983), pp.160–72.
3. The Earl of Longford and Thomas P. O'Neill, *Eamon de Valera* (Dublin: Gill & Macmillan, 1970), p.357.
4. *Dáil Éireann Debates*, vol. 85, col. 1460ff., 28 January 1942.
5. This chapter will not dwell significantly on the interactions between the IRA and German agencies; rather, my focus here is domestic political affairs, and how the republican wartime campaign impacted these. Obviously, however, the German link – and Allied perceptions of the German link – remains an important subtext for much of what will follow.
6. Dónal Ó Drisceoil, *Censorship in Ireland, 1939–1945: Neutrality, Politics and Society* (Cork:

Cork University Press, 1996), pp.17–26; Seosamh Ó Longaigh, *Emergency Law in Independent Ireland, 1922–48* (Dublin: Four Courts Press, 2006), pp.230ff.

7. *Dáil Éireann Debates*, vol. 77, col. 247, 27 September 1939.
8. Quoted in Ó Drisceoil, *Censorship in Ireland*, p.235.
9. See, for example, Liam Tobin to Éamon de Valera, 8 November 1939, quoted in Eunan O'Halpin, *Defending Ireland: The Irish State and its Enemies since 1922* (Oxford: Oxford University Press, 1999), p.247; and Nancy O'Rahilly to Éamon de Valera, 15 November [1939], Margaret Pearse to Éamon de Valera, 15 November 1939, National Archives of Ireland (NAI), D/T, S11515.
10. Memorandum on the Policy of the Government with Regard to Offences against the State, p.10, IRA Activities in Ireland, 1939–1950, NAI, D/T, S11534A.
11. *Irish Times*, 16 November and 8 December 1939.
12. Offences Against the State Act (1939), Section 55, www.irishstatutebook.ie/1939/en/act/pub/0013/index.html, accessed 10 November 2009; *Bunreacht na hÉireann*, Article 40.4.1.
13. *Irish Times*, 4 December 1939.
14. Roche to Boland, quoted in Ó Longaigh, *Emergency Law in Independent Ireland*, pp.241–2.
15. There was a foiled attempt to raid Islandbridge armoury the same night, apparently a 'prelude to a mass attack on the North'. Christy Quearney quoted in Uinseann MacEoin, *The IRA in the Twilight Years, 1923–1948* (Dublin: Argenta Press, 1997), p.775. This appears to have been a commonly held view within the IRA: Mick Fitzgibbon and Joe Dolan, both IRA members, expressed similar sentiments, pp.486 and 588.
16. *Dáil Éireann Debates*, vol. 78, col. 1415, 3 January 1940.
17. 'Ammunition and Arms found in Various parts of the Country during 1940', NAI J8/764; Lieutenant Colonel John P. Duggan, quoted in Benjamin Grob-Fitzgibbon, *The Irish Experience During the Second World War: An Oral History* (Dublin: Irish Academic Press, 2004), p.205. See also Seamus Prendergast, 'Personal Memories of Magazine Raid – December 1939', *Carloviana* (January 2002), p.51; Conor Brady, *Guardians of the Peace* (Dublin: Gill & Macmillan, 1974), p.235.
18. Maffey to Machtig, 31 January 1940, The National Archives, London (TNA), DO 130/9; J. Cudahy to Secretary of State, despatch no. 308, 13 February 1940, The National Archives and Records Administration, College Park, Maryland (NARA), MF 1231, roll 9, Political Affairs.
19. Eunan O'Halpin's argument that the British felt de Valera's representations for reprieve were signs of his vulnerability to an IRA coup pushes this line too far, however. See Eunan O'Halpin, *Spying on Ireland: British Intelligence and Irish Neutrality During the Second World War* (Oxford: Oxford University Press, 2008), p.77.
20. *Irish Times*, 2 February 1940.
21. This had been sent by the Germans to the IRA and was intended for communication purposes only. The IRA were unable to resist the temptation to broadcast internal propaganda, however, and soon G2 traced the signal. The saga of increasingly inept German attempts to replace this transmitter is best captured in M. Hull, 'The Irish Interlude: German Intelligence in Ireland, 1939–1943', *Journal of Military History*, no. 66 (July 2002), pp.695–718.
22. David Gray, 'Behind the Green Curtain', chapter 2, unpublished memoir. I am grateful to Professor Paul Bew for providing me with a copy of this manuscript
23. *Irish Independent*, 23 April 1940. Boland later described the encounter as 'one of the worst experiences I've ever had'. Robert Fisk, *In Time of War: Ireland, Ulster and the Price of Neutrality* (London: Andre Deutsch, 1983), p.345.
24. Mine explosion at Detective Branch Headquarters, Dublin Castle, NAI, J8/792; Brady, *Guardians of the Peace*, p.236; Maurice Moynihan (ed.), *Speeches and Statements by Éamon de Valera, 1917–1973* (Dublin: Gill & Macmillan, 1980), p.433.
25. *Dáil Éireann Debates*, vol. 80, col. 1739, 19 June 1940.
26. NAI, D/T, S11974. Among the individuals who appealed for clemency were Owen Sheehy-Skeffington, Rosamond Jacob and Eoin O'Duffy.
27. Considerations submitted by Albert Wood, KC and Seán MacBride, BL, 18 June 1940. NAI, D/T, S11974.
28. Uinseann MacEoin, *Survivors* (Dublin: Argenta Publications, 1980), p.124; George M. Goulding, *George Gavan Duffy: A Legal Biography* (Dublin: Irish Academic Press, 1982),

p.131; Seán MacBride, *That Day's Struggle: A Memoir, 1905–1951*, ed. C. Lawlor (Dublin: Currach Press, 2005), pp.126–7.

29. Kathleen Lynn Diaries, 22 August 1940, Library of Royal College of Physicians, Dublin. MacBride initially represented the next of kin at the inquest into the shooting of Kavanagh, but after a lengthy adjournment was replaced by barrister Seán Collins. On receipt of an order from the Minister for Justice, the coroner discharged the jury and returned a verdict limited to establishing the cause of death. *Weekly Irish Times*, 21 September 1940.
30. Ó Longaigh, *Emergency Law in Independent Ireland*, pp.246–59.
31. *Dáil Éireann Debates*, vol. 101, col. 1116, 29 May 1946.
32. *Irish Times*, 22 August 1940.
33. *Irish Independent*, 27 August 1940.
34. *Irish Times*, 3 September 1940.
35. [1941] Irish Reports, 77. See also Fergal F. Davis, *The History and Development of the Special Criminal Court, 1922–2005* (Dublin: Four Courts Press, 2007), pp.86–7.
36. Petitions for the reprieve of Patrick McGrath and Thomas Harte, NAI, D/T S12048B.
37. Gray, 'Behind the Green Curtain', chapter 14.
38. 'The IRA to cease drilling, carrying arms, manufacturing arms or explosives, transporting arms or explosives into the six counties, to cease the publication of War News in the twenty-six counties and to cease broadcasting from the twenty-six counties. The campaign in England to be called off.' In return, the government would 'instruct police to suspend all activities against IRA, to suspend sentences against IRA in prison and to gradually release prisoners'. Seán MacBride to Éamon de Valera, 5 September 1940, NAI, D/T S12069.
39. 'Notes on IRA Activities, 1941–47', University College Dublin Archives (UCDA), Seán Mac-Entee Papers, P67/550. Seán Lemass, Minister for Supplies, was evidently more troubled by the prospect of a Fianna Fáil government executing former republican comrades. See John Horgan, *Seán Lemass: The Enigmatic Patriot* (Dublin: Gill & Macmillan, 1997), p.189.
40. *Dáil Éireann Debates*, vol. 101, col. 1132, 29 May 1946.
41. Hayes, IRA Chief-of-Staff, was suspected of acting as a state informer by his comrades in the IRA Army Council. His court martial, torture and writing of his infamous 'confession', which alleged government complicity in a number of ill-fated IRA operations, administered a significant shock to the public sense of security in the summer of 1941.
42. 'Emergency Powers (No. 139) Order', quoted in Ó Longaigh, *Emergency Law in Independent Ireland*, pp.262–3.
43. *Irish Times*, 15 January 1942.
44. MacBride, quoted in Tim Pat Coogan, *The IRA*, 3rd edition (London: Harper Collins, 1995; first published 1971), p.158; Pierce Fennell, quoted in MacEoin, *IRA in the Twilight Years*, p.572; NAI, D/T S 12741.
45. Michael Moroney, 'George Plant and the Rule of Law: The Devereux Affair', *Tipperary Historical Journal* (1988), p.11.
46. *Irish Times*, 11 September 1942. O'Brien featured in all of the IRA reverses and humiliations, from the Hayes debacle to the Devereux affair. As well as forming part of the Special Branch unit that raided Rathgar Road, resulting in the capture and subsequent execution of McGrath and Harte, he was also noted for his prowess in the interrogation room and his willingness to open fire on IRA suspects in the field: he was personally responsible for wounding Liam Rice and Charlie McGlade in recent engagements. Harry White and Uinseann MacEoin, *Harry: The Story of Harry White as Related to Uinseann MacEoin* (Dublin: Argenta Press, 1985), p.105; Brady, *Guardians of the Peace*, p.237; Moroney, 'George Plant and the Rule of Law', pp.5–6.
47. Brady, *Guardians of the Peace*, p.237; O'Halpin, *Defending Ireland*, pp.249–50.
48. Gray memorandum on censorship in Ireland, quoted in Ó Drisceoil, *Censorship in Ireland*, p.240; *Irish Times*, 10 September 1942.
49. *Irish Press*, 2 October 1942.
50. *Irish Press*, 5 November 1942.
51. *Irish Times*, 6 November 1942.
52. Maurice O'Neill Reprieve Petitions, NAI, D/T S13004.
53. Ibid.
54. *Dáil Éireann Debates*, vol. 89, col. 2357, 5 May 1943; see also Brian Girvin, *The Emergency: Neutral Ireland, 1939–1945* (London: Macmillan, 2005), p.241.
55. Michael Price, of the CPI faction within the Labour Party, predicted that the 1943 poll would

be 'the most momentous general election since 1922'. Quoted in Niamh Puirséil, *The Irish Labour Party, 1922–1972* (Dublin: University College Dublin Press, 2007), p.99. See also Dunphy, *The Making of Fianna Fáil Power in Ireland*, pp.286–9.

56. *Irish Times*, 19 March 1943. This association appears to be distinct from the National Association of Old IRA. The personnel, alignments and activities of a number of old republican comrades organisations is an area that would merit further research.

57. Puirséil, *Irish Labour Party*, p.88. Attendees included representatives from the republican movement old and new – Peadar Cowan, Seán Dowling, Maureen Buckley, Roger Sweetman, Roger McCorley, Con Lehane and Mick Fitzpatrick.

58. *Irish Times*, 5 October 1944. This was another of the documents revealed during the Kerins trial.

59. Ibid.

60. Copy of *Republican News*, June 1943, IRA Activities in Ireland, 1939–1950, NAI, D/T S 11534A. The same issue referred to Seán MacEntee as 'a ministerial corner-boy... a skunk who disowned Pearse and Connolly and [in his court martial in 1916] declared that but for being late for a train he would be in the British Army in France instead of being mixed up in what he called "that unfortunate insurrection"'.

61. Brian M. Walker (ed.), *Parliamentary Election Results in Ireland, 1918–92: Irish Elections to Parliaments and Parliamentary Assemblies at Westminster, Belfast, Dublin, Strasbourg* (Dublin: Royal Irish Academy, 1992), p.156.

62. Cornelius O'Leary, *Irish Elections, 1918–77: Parties, Voters and Proportional Representation* (Dublin: Gill & Macmillan, 1979), p.35; Puirséil, *Irish Labour Party*, p.101.

63. *Dáil Éireann Debates*, vol. 91, col. 543, 9 July 1943.

64. White and MacEoin, *Harry*, p.104. The murder was actually carried out by Archie Doyle, probably with Michael Quille, who had already been acquitted. Doyle had previously been part of the unit that murdered Kevin O'Higgins in 1927.

65. For a record of the trial, see *Irish Times*, 3–11 October 1944. After the state case had been heard, Kerins was again given an opportunity to present a defence; again, declining, he declared scornfully that '[the President of the Court] could have adjourned it for six months as far as I am concerned, as my attitude towards the Court will always be the same'.

66. *Irish Independent*, 11 October 1944.

67. Charlie Kerins Reprieve Petitions, NAI, D/T S 13567/1; Charles Kerins Reprieve Petitions, National Library of Ireland (NLI), MS 31756(3).

68. Charlie Kerins Reprieve Petitions, NAI, D/T S 13567/1; Ó Drisceoil, *Censorship in Ireland*, pp.242–3.

69. Pierrepoint's autobiography details the extreme secrecy with which he had to conduct his activities in Ireland, travelling under an assumed name. Albert Pierrepoint, *Executioner* (London: Harrap, 1974).

70. Memorandum on remains of Richard Goss, 26 July 1948, NAI, D/T S 12540.

71. De Valera was explicit on this: '[t]he advertisements were stopped by virtue of our right to maintain order and preserve the State, to prevent organisations getting ahead and using this as a cloak for reorganisation' (*Dáil Éireann Debates*, vol. 95, col. 1459, 1 December 1944). A half-hearted attempt to reconvene the IRA was made in late 1945, but this was swiftly stamped out by the Gardaí. By 1947 the Department of Justice reported that '[t]he IRA has disintegrated ... it can no longer be regarded as a serious menace to peace and good order' (quoted in Ó Longaigh, *Emergency Law in Independent Ireland*, p.273).

72. Notes on IRA Activities, 1941–47, p.80, and Profile of Seán MacBride, MacEntee Papers, UCDA, P67/550.

73. Ó Longaigh, *Emergency Law in Independent Ireland*, p.302; John Maguire, *IRA Internments and the Irish Government: Subversives and the State, 1939–1962* (Dublin: Irish Academic Press, 2008), pp.49–50.

# CHAPTER SEVEN

# The Politics of Terminology: Seán Lemass and Northern Ireland, 1959–1966

## STEPHEN KELLY

This chapter offers a reassessment of a defining theme of Seán Lemass's Northern policy as president of Fianna Fáil and Taoiseach from 1959 to 1966. Using the most recently available archival material, the chapter examines Lemass's usage of political terminology to forge a new approach to the old problem of partition. Placed within the framework of his eagerness to develop cross-border economic co-operation between Dublin and Belfast, two central issues are analysed: first, Lemass's desire that Irish nationalists would cease to constantly use the term 'Six Counties' to refer to Northern Ireland; and second, his policy of granting de facto recognition to the Northern Ireland state in the context of a federal agreement, whereby the Northern Ireland government would retain its own parliament in Belfast, with the powers currently held by Westminster transferred to the Dublin parliament.

The chapter presents Lemass as, first and foremost, a pragmatist: republican sentimentality and tradition had no place in his Northern policy. From the inception of the Northern Irish state, the Irish government had refused to accept its legitimacy as a political unit.[1] For many nationalists, in both parts of Ireland, the Stormont government was illegitimate; republicans repeatedly pronounced that no one in Ireland, including the unionist population, had voted for what they termed the 'Partition Act'. Lemass realised – unlike many within Fianna Fáil and the wider nationalist community – that the Irish government was hampered by the logic of its own official discourse. Through a revision of political terminology, Lemass attempted to escape Ireland's revolutionary past and forge a firmly constitutional future. Through the subtle use of terminology and the encouragement of north–south economic co-op-eration, Lemass slowly cultivated the seeds of change as he attempted to shift party and public attitudes towards an acceptance of partition and of Northern Ireland.

Lemass was eager, and indeed now able, to offer a new interpreta-tion of partition. He wished to portray partition not so much as the ar-tificial division of the country, but as a tangible political, social and cultural division – a division that could only be healed through a process of understanding and co-operation between north and south. For Lemass, the economy was central to his aspiration for Irish unity. As Taoiseach, he sought to adapt Fianna Fáil's traditional Northern policy to the new economic realities of the 1960s. Significantly, under the Lemass government, economic and partition policies became intrinsically linked.

It would be incorrect, however, to argue that Lemass's Northern policy was a marked departure from that of his predecessor Éamon de Valera. Under Lemass's leadership no radical policy development regarding partition occurred; as with de Valera, he did not advocate a substantial change of principle or priorities regarding Northern policy. Lemass freely admitted that his policy for unity was 'not a new policy', but was instead 'a reaffirmation of the traditional republican policy', from Wolfe Tone, Thomas Davis, Pádraig Pearse and de Valera.[2] His government maintained that the British government was required to make a declaration that Irish unity was in London's interests;[3] that Ul-ster unionists could not be coerced into a united Ireland;[4] and finally, that a federal solution between Dublin and Belfast constituted a legit-imate settlement of partition.[5]

The historiography of Lemass's contribution to the Northern Ireland question has varied greatly. Clare O'Halloran has remarked that 'the Lemass era had only limited implications' for the partition question.[6] Paul Bew and Henry Patterson have further argued that Lemass 'contributed absolutely no new ideas in the Republic to the "debate" about the North'.[7] Bew and Patterson, admittedly writing sev-eral years before the release of crucial governmental state papers on both sides of the border, underestimate Lemass's ability to shift public and party attitude, however circumspectly, on Dublin's approach to Northern Ireland. Indeed, Patterson has recently argued that Lemass was 'far from silent on Northern Ireland',[8] while in 2007 Bew acknowledged that Lemass's Northern policy was 'complex and tortuous'.[9] It is Tom Garvin, however, who strikes the most balanced analysis. Although Northern Ireland 'baffled' Lemass, and he was never quite able to radically shift from the orthodox Fianna Fáil approach, he did make 'real and conscientious efforts to shake off inherited passionate convictions'.[10] Simply put, Lemass preferred realities to aspirations: 'he dealt with the North as it was, not as what he hoped it might be'.[11]

To date, only John Horgan has attempted to examine in sufficient detail Lemass's attempts to refrain from the use of the 'public reiteration' of the Irish government's territorial claim in the constant use of the term 'Six Counties' to refer to Northern Ireland.[12] He has, however, underestimated the internal debate within Fianna Fáil that developed on the issue of terminology from the late 1950s.[13] Michael Kennedy,[14] and again to a lesser extent Horgan,[15] have analysed in detail Lemass's policy of seeking to offer the Northern Ireland government and parliament de facto recognition, based on a federal agreement between Dublin and Belfast. Nevertheless, both have failed to expound on Lemass's orchestrated scheme to place the 'de facto debate' on the political agenda so as to induce economic cross-border co-operation between Stormont and the Irish government.

## THE EVOLUTION OF TERMINOLOGY: FROM A 'SIX COUNTIES' TO A 'NORTHERN IRELAND' POLICY

Although it is apparent that Lemass was unwilling to make any drastic alteration to Fianna Fáil's Northern policy, he did seek to move away from the anti-partitionist rhetoric that had dominated the party's stance on partition since its foundation; that said, on suitable occasions, Lemass could also regress to the comforts of nationalist rhetoric.[16] The single greatest change was Lemass's subtle development of political terminology regarding Northern Ireland. Through the imaginative use of language, he attempted to create a climate that favoured a softer policy of near recognition of Northern Ireland, so fostering closer north–south relations. Lemass epitomised the 'politics of nuance',[17] in which shades of difference in the articulation of certain ideas had profound implications for political ideology and action.[18] Importantly, he introduced a process of reinterpretation – rather than replacement – of key principles of Fianna Fáil's attitude to partition. This change was, however, always limited, as Lemass was unable to proceed any faster than his supporters would allow, owing to the constant battle within the party between the traditionalists and modernisers over partition policy.

On the day he became Taoiseach, Lemass illustrated his wish to end

Irish nationalists' constant use of irredentist language. In a break from the past, he said that he preferred to cease to use the negative term 'anti-partition' and replace it with the more positive phrase 'restoration of national unity'.[19] Symbolically, this was a huge step forward. The old phrase had become synonymous with de Valera and Fianna Fáil, and was particularly associated with the ill-fated All-Party Anti-Partition Committee that had so recklessly spearheaded the irredentist campaign in the south during the late 1940s and early 1950s.[20] Within Fianna Fáil, some supporters had been calling for the party hierarchy to refrain from using the term since the mid-1950s. Matthew Feehan, a member of the Fianna Fáil national executive during the mid-1950s, explained that 'to be anti-anything is negative ... therefore we should discontinue the use of the term Anti-Partition'.[21]

Lemass's most important public pronouncement on his desire to leave behind the outdated nationalist rhetoric came at his first Fianna Fáil Ard Fheis as Taoiseach, in November 1959. Lemass remained loyal to a central tenet of Fianna Fáil's Northern policy, maintaining that it was 'impossible' to recognise the existence of the Northern Ireland state.[22] He was, however, willing to move the goalposts by acknowledging the existence of partition.[23] This was unprecedented, a brave gamble on Lemass's part; it is easy, as John Horgan has observed, to underestimate the political tremor that was caused by a Fianna Fáil Taoiseach's decision to include the two words 'partition' and 'recognise' in the same sentence.[24] Of even greater significance was Lemass's reference, throughout his speech to the party faithful, to the 'parliament and government of Northern Ireland' and 'the Constitution of Northern Ireland'.[25] It was an initiative that de Valera was unlikely to have contemplated. Lemass's usage of terminology highlighted a distinctive feature of his Northern policy and his willingness to progress beyond the traditional Fianna Fáil anti-partitionist mentality. Since the early years of the Irish Free State, the standard practice in political and administrative circles in southern Ireland was the constant usage of the term 'Six Counties' to refer to Northern Ireland. This formula was an easy way for Irish nationalists to propagate their non-recognition of the Northern Ireland state, and was endorsed, not only by de Valera, but also by the leaders of Fine Gael and the Labour Party.

Lemass, however, was no longer willing to adhere to such nationalist rhetoric. Although he had no intention of succumbing to unionist demands that Northern Ireland should be recognised de jure as part of the United Kingdom, Lemass did want to deal with the political realities of north–south relations.[26] He believed that 'the use of terms like

"Belfast government", "Stormont government", "Belfast authorities" has been the outcome of "woolly thinking" on the partition issue'.[27] In private, he explained that if Ulster unionists were to ever agree to enter a united Ireland under a federal solution, it was nonsensical that the Irish government continue to refrain from using the title 'government of Northern Ireland'. Thus, Lemass explained that it would be merely 'commonsense that the current name would be kept'.[28] Lemass also believed that if he was to achieve his policy of establishing effective co-operation in the economic sphere with Ulster unionists, the Irish government, as expressed by Lemass's son-in-law and future Taoiseach, Charles Haughey, 'needed to take a less rigid line in the matter of nomenclature'.[29]

Both the *Irish Times* and *Irish Independent* drew attention to this new policy, suggesting that the use of a 'changed terminology' had now been informally communicated to the media and was a welcome departure from the use of the derogatory term 'Six Counties'.[30] The director of the Government Information Bureau, Pádraig Ó hAnracháin, a confidant of Lemass, informed the political correspondent of the *Irish Independent*, P. Quinn, that although 'no government decision' had been communicated to the officials concerned, Lemass had 'officially encouraged' such an approach.[31] The British warmly welcomed Lemass's willingness to abandon the use of the 'Six Counties'. The British ambassador, Sir Alexander Clutterbuck reported back to Whitehall that Lemass's references in the Dáil to partition were 'couched in notably moderate terms'.[32]

Support for Lemass's new initiative from within Fianna Fáil was mixed. Although not attacking Lemass personally, the available evidence suggests that there was a certain level of discontent among party deputies. Leading frontbenchers Jack Lynch, Seán MacEntee and Charles Haughey welcomed the change in policy.[33] Frank Aiken, minister for external affairs and a northern-born founding member of Fianna Fáil, was the main opponent of the change in nomenclature, but there were others within the party who disagreed with Lemass's departure.[34] The division between senior Fianna Fáil members surfaced following a statement in the Dáil in July 1959 by party TD for Dún Laoghaire-Rathdown, Lionel Booth. Booth, himself a Protestant and well-respected businessman, passionately pleaded to all members of Dáil Éireann to ban the word *partition* 'forever from the language'. He remarked that it was a 'misleading word' that only increased the 'whole misconception'. Echoing the words of his party leader, he too explained the futility of the usage of terms such as 'puppet government', 'occupied territory' and 'police State'.[35]

At a meeting of the party's parliamentary party, on 15 July 1959, held a week after Booth's comments in the Dáil, Michael Joseph Kennedy, Longford–Westmeath TD and parliamentary secretary to the minister for social welfare, Seán MacEntee, made a *cri de cœur* in opposition to Booth's remarks. Lemass was forced to intervene, explaining that partition was 'a very difficult question' and notified deputies to be 'extremely careful' when it came to making public utterances on partition.[36] At a subsequent meeting of the party's national executive, a letter was read from Booth's own local Fianna Fáil branch, denouncing his Dáil statement on partition. Again Lemass spoke on Booth's behalf, and reassured those present that he discussed with Booth 'the advisability of his taking an early opportunity of removing any misconceptions created by his remarks'.[37]

This episode exposed the fault line within Fianna Fáil on the subject of terminology. Lemass's own comments at the Ard Fheis in November 1959 and the subsequent media attention surrounding his usage of the term 'Northern Ireland' caused such controversy among Fianna Fáil supporters that in June 1960 he was forced to speak in the Dáil on the issue. The *Belfast Telegraph* opportunistically reported that Lemass's willingness to use the term was to be 'interpreted as an acknowledgement of the constitutional position' of Northern Ireland and that TDs had been encouraged to use the term in Parliamentary Questions or in 'any context'.[38]

Prior to his much anticipated speech in the Dáil, Lemass's department circulated a draft version of the address to both Aiken and MacEntee to seek their views. Interestingly, no reply was received from Aiken. From the available evidence, however, it is apparent that he disliked Lemass's new initiative; indeed, in September 1963, Aiken's department, while agreeing that it would not be improper to 'use the term "Northern Ireland" … from time to time officially', maintained that there was 'no question of a wholesale departure from the use of the term "Six Counties".[39] MacEntee on reading the draft copy informed Lemass that he had 'no observations to make'.[40]

During the course of Lemass's Dáil speech in June 1960, he was visibly reluctant to officially record that the government had decided to use the term 'Northern Ireland'. Instead, he informed deputies that 'no final decision had been taken by the government on the name of Northern Ireland or to give formal or official recognition to the government of Northern Ireland'.[41] Lemass, ever the pragmatist, was forced to deny the reality of what he was doing and instead he left the matter as undecided so as to satisfy both sides within the party. This approach had, however, its own problems, as it merely encouraged the development of a wide variation in practice between government departments and various ministers. Lemass could himself be criticised for the ambiguity inherent within government policy on the issue. Lemass's usage of terminology as Taoiseach in the Dáil varied greatly: in February 1961, he used both 'Northern Ireland' and 'Six Counties' in the same debate in the Dáil.[42] It did become policy invariably to use the term 'Northern Ireland' instead of the 'Six Counties' within the department of the Taoiseach, although Lemass never officially sanctioned this change. In March 1966, shortly before his retirement as Taoiseach, Lemass privately admitted that he had 'no strong views either way'.[43] Throughout his time as Taoiseach, whenever the issue of terminology arose, the standard practice within his department was to cite his Dáil speech of 21 June 1960 as official government policy.[44] This was to remain the official government response throughout the 1960s, with Lemass's successor, Jack Lynch, happy to leave the matter as undecided.[45]

It is difficult, a generation removed, to convey how significant Lemass's decision was to replace the phrase 'Six Counties' with that of 'Northern Ireland'. This apparently symbolic gesture was, in the early 1960s, a great leap forward. One must understand how powerful and intoxicating the usage of anti-partitionist rhetoric was to the nationalist psyche; abandoning such language was a brave departure on Lemass's behalf. His wish to foster a new discourse of this nature was complicated from the start: it was, after all, advanced by a state whose very constitution claimed jurisdiction over the 'Six Counties'. Thus, Lemass's usage of terminology was an important departure, and signalled his desire to reconstruct one of the most contentious ideological symbols of the traditional Fianna Fáil mentality.

LEMASS AND THE 'DE FACTO DEBATE' ON NORTHERN IRELAND

As we have seen, on becoming Taoiseach, Lemass had sought to persuade Irish nationalists to cease using archaic anti-partitionist language of a bygone generation. During his second term as Taoiseach (1961–5), he now attempted to transform his policy of nuance into a policy of practical recognition of Northern Ireland. Central to this approach was Lemass's desire to convince Ulster unionists that the Irish government was willing to offer de facto recognition to Northern Ireland, based on the commitment that a federal agreement could be reached between both jurisdictions to secure Irish unity.

Since the early 1920s de Valera, irrespective of Belfast's continued rejections,[46] had routinely offered a federal proposal to Ulster unionists as a solution to partition.[47] De Valera had even ensured that Article 15.2 of the Irish constitution of 1937 entailed a provision for a subordinate legislature, by which the Northern Ireland parliament would agree to transfer the powers reserved for the British imperial parliament to Dublin. With de Valera now assigned to the comforts of Phoenix Park as president of Ireland, Lemass now hoped that he could entice Ulster unionists to reconsider Dublin's federal offer.

The 'de facto debate' was a major obstacle for Lemass as he attempted to encourage closer economic co-operation between Dublin and Belfast. His first major policy development on partition as Taoiseach was his offer to the Northern Ireland government of a 32-county free trade area between north and south for goods of Irish or Northern Irish origin.[48] This offer, however, was rejected by the Northern Ireland prime minister, Lord Brookeborough, because of Belfast's belief that the Irish government was doing little to stop renewed IRA activity,[49] and, more importantly, due to Dublin's refusal to recognise the parliament and government of Northern Ireland. Indeed, throughout Brookeborough's premiership, Ulster unionists had maintained that cross-border co-operation was 'impossible', given Dublin's refusal to grant official recognition to the Northern Ireland state.[50] An editorial in the *Irish Times* recorded the dilemma that faced the Taoiseach: 'Lemass cannot hope to negotiate with a body whose existence he does not recognise.'[51]

It was not until the IRA announcement of an end to its Border Campaign (1956–62) in February 1962 that Lemass was finally in a position to seize the opportunity he had so earnestly awaited to kick-start his campaign to persuade the Northern Ireland government to agree to cross-border co-operation with Dublin. Lemass was aware that if he were to convince Belfast to agree to economic co-operation with Dublin, he would be required to make concessions to Ulster unionists on the issue of recognition of the Northern Ireland state.  Under Lemass's guidance a small group of Fianna Fáil deputies commenced a kite-flying campaign that sought to move the debate between Dublin and Belfast away from a territorial dispute, instead focusing on the mutual benefits of cross-border co-operation. On 16 April 1963, George Colley, backbench party TD for Dublin north-east, spoke at a major symposium discussing north–south co-operation at the Shelbourne Hotel, Dublin. Colley's speech was important for the emphasis that he placed on the recognition of Northern Ireland. The timing of the symposium was not coincidental: it had been hurriedly arranged in the weeks after Terence O'Neill succeeded Lord Brookeborough as Northern Ireland prime minister in late March 1963. O'Neill's appointment was warmly welcomed by Dublin. He had no record of drum-beating militancy or fundamentalist Protestantism; he was reported to be a 'dynamic man' who, like Lemass, wished to transform the economic conditions in his jurisdiction.[52] One Northern Irish paper wondered whether O'Neill would permit north–south economic co-operation even if Dublin had not granted formal recognition to the Belfast government.[53] Lemass held a similar opinion. Thus the symposium was an orchestrated effort by Lemass to make conciliatory noises to the new Northern Ireland prime minister in the hope that north–south economic co-operation could be resurrected without a demand from Belfast for de jure recognition of its government and parliament.

Speaking several years later to Michael Mills of the *Irish Press*, Lemass recalled how he exploited the press as a means of accelerating executive action 'as part of the art of political leadership'.[54] He was ready to 'plant a good story, fly a kite' in order to test public opinion.[55] By using Colley as a front man, Lemass was attempting to manoeuvre his party, Ulster unionists, and the general public ever closer to his line of thinking. Mary Colley, wife of George Colley, remembered that it was under Lemass's instructions that her husband delivered the speech. She recalled that during this period a faction within Fianna Fáil, which included her husband, Lemass and Jack Lynch, had commenced a 'gradation of initiatives' that sought to 'open up a new way' towards the party's official stance on Northern Ireland.[56]

Speaking to a packed ballroom in the Shelbourne Hotel, Colley dealt with the sensitive question of recognition of the Northern Ireland government. He said it was 'the greatest – perhaps only barrier to effective co-operation between north and south on economic matters'. His choice of terminology was noteworthy:

> The government of Northern Ireland is in effective control of the territory of Northern Ireland and as such we in the South have always accorded de facto recognition to the government. Consequently the demand from the North is not for de facto recognition but for de jure recognition of the constitutional position of Northern Ireland … What we have not been prepared to do is grant de jure recognition to the claim of the British parliament to legislate for any part of Ireland.[57]

Colley's usage of the terms 'Northern Ireland' and 'recognition' in the same sentence was a deliberate attempt by the Fianna Fáil deputy to place on record Dublin's changing official position on the issue of the recognition of the Northern Ireland government. Four years previously, speaking at the 1959 Fianna Fáil Ard Fheis, Lemass had similarly acknowledged 'that partition existed'.[58] Colley now went further, and although recording that the government would never grant de jure recognition to Northern Ireland, as this would give legitimacy to the British government's territorial claim on Northern Ireland, he did publicly concede that Dublin recognised the de facto existence of the Northern Ireland state.

Since the late 1950s, Lemass had been at the forefront of an ongoing internal debate within Fianna Fáil on the issue of de facto recognition of Northern Ireland. Working closely with a small select group within the party, which included Lionel Booth,[59] national executive committee member, solicitor and future attorney-general (1977 to 1981) Anthony Hederman,[60] and party senator Eoin Ryan,[61] Lemass had privately argued that if Irish unity was to be obtained based on a federal solution, the Belfast government would need to be recognised de facto.[62]

During the late 1950s, respected Irish nationalists outside of Fianna Fáil circles also attempted to nurture innovative thinking on Dublin's relationship with Belfast and particularly the de facto recognition of the Northern Ireland government. The catalyst for this was the publication of a pamphlet by a young lawyer, Donal Barrington, entitled *Uniting Ireland*. Barrington argued that although all southern parties agreed that 'unity of wills' was the sole prerequisite for the ending of partition, this agreement needed to be translated into practical terms if it was to ever convince Ulster unionists to enter a united Ireland. Thus, recognition of the Northern Ireland government was imperative if any inroads were to be achieved.[63] There is some evidence to suggest that Lemass had become receptive to such innovatory thinking; Liam de Paor claimed that the policy suggested by Barrington 'was, in effect, put into operation by Mr Lemass's government'.[64] Veteran nationalist John Horgan,[65] senator Owen Sheehy-Skeffington,[66] the northern Protestant nationalist Ernest Blythe,[67] and future Fine Gael leader and Taoiseach Garret FitzGerald had all argued that de facto recognition merely implied that the Irish recognised the existence of the 'Six Counties' as a provincial administration and not as the government of a sovereign state.[68]

Although Lemass did not attend the symposium on north–south relations at the Shelbourne Hotel, he was the instigator of Colley's speech. The decision of a Fianna Fáil deputy to publicly recognise the Northern Ireland government and parliament, de facto, was clearly a preconceived and co-ordinated attempt by Lemass to meet O'Neill halfway on the issue of recognition. Lemass did not have to wait long to receive a reply from Ulster Unionists: O'Neill soon poured cold water on the prospect of a north–south meeting prior to recognition. Speaking at Stormont, he categorically ruled out 'general discussions so long as the Dublin government refused to recognise the constitutional position of the six counties'.[69] O'Neill's remarks led to a stalemate. He underestimated the importance of Colley's speech, which was the first occasion on which a member of Fianna Fáil had effectively recognised the legitimacy of the Northern Ireland government.

O'Neill's rebuttal of Colley's speech was also a reflection of the pressure that he faced from traditionalists within the Ulster Unionist Party. Michael Kennedy has argued that O'Neill was in 'no position to officially open relations with Dublin', given the strength of the hardcore traditionalist wing within the Ulster Unionist Party.[70] In other words, O'Neill could not move as quickly as Lemass would have liked. This observation was made clear by Sir Robert Gransden, agent for the Northern Ireland government in London from 1957 to 1962. Speaking in July 1963 to a Dublin civil servant, Gransden noted that although O'Neill's continued demand that the Irish government grant official recognition to Northern Ireland government was 'unrealistic', he explained that Dublin must realise that the Stormont government 'cannot get out of step with the thinking of its own supporters and we should recognise that, if the prime minister there attempted to do certain things, he might be "shot out on his ear"'.[71]

Faced with yet another rejection from Belfast for crossborder co-operation prior to the ceding of official recognition, Lemass decided that the time had arrived for him to personally deliver a public statement on the Irish government's policy of recognition. His decision to speak in Tralee, county Kerry, in July 1963, at a dinner given in honour of veteran Fianna Fáil TD, 'the Ballymac man' Tommy McEllistrim, was a courageous undertaking; Kerry had traditionally been a hotbed of militant republicanism, and had a strong Fianna Fáil grassroots tradition. Although the Government Information Bureau maintained that the speech did not mark 'any change from past policy',[72] the reality was that it was one of Lemass's most important pronouncements on Northern Ireland policy during his time as Taoiseach. It presented a calculated policy statement that had been fermenting for the previous several years. Aimed directly towards Ulster unionists, the speech deliberately and significantly omitted any mention of the role of the British government in ending partition. Lemass delivered his speech to a packed room of Fianna Fáil grassroots supporters. He lamented that the Ulster unionist demand for recognition was a gimmick and 'an excuse for inaction'. Nevertheless, using the de facto/de jure argument that Colley had given a trial run at the symposium on north–south relations the previous April, Lemass explained that he understood O'Neill's demands for recognition of the Northern Ireland government. He had no problem recognising the Northern Ireland state de facto: if the Northern majority were to agree to a united Ireland based on a federal agreement between Dublin and Belfast, Ulster unionists would still require their own government and parliament. His choice of words was significant: 'We recognise that the government and parliament there exist with the support of the majority in the six county area – artificial though that area is.'[73]

While Lemass had not recognised Northern Ireland as part of the United Kingdom, placed within his calls for a federal agreement was a de facto recognition of the Northern Ireland state. The *Irish Times* noted that 'grudging and half-hearted though this admission, it none the less represents an important step forward'.[74] Lemass had referred to Northern Ireland as 'an artificial area'; this was, however, to be expected, given it was a Fianna Fáil gathering of the party's grassroots. Significantly, no southern political leader since the foundation of the Irish state had ever been so explicit in public on the issue of recognition. Indeed during the mid-1920s, Desmond FitzGerald, as minister for external affairs under the Cumann na nGaedheal government, and a supporter of granting de facto recognition to Northern Ireland, had merely inferred rather than stated openly his preferred policy.[75] Although de Valera had publicly spoken of a 'concurrence of wills' approach, based on agreement between Dublin, Belfast and London, as a solution to partition, he had always maintained Dublin would not recognise the constitutional position of Northern Ireland.[76]

Nationalist reaction both north and south of the border to Lemass's recognition of the de facto existence of the Northern Ireland government was tinged with a sense of betrayal of the republican orthodoxy. An editorial in one southern paper noted that to give recognition to the Northern Ireland government would 'make a mockery of all that Ireland has fought for over the centuries'.[77] The *Derry Journal* was likewise dismissive of the recognition debate. Quoting Ernest Blythe's repeated calls for the Irish government to grant de facto recognition to the Northern Ireland government and parliament, the paper rhetorically pondered: 'how a particular six county portion of the historic Ireland could suddenly have acquired the quality of a separate and indefeasible entity as if of a God-given right, but which was never heard of as any such entity until Lloyd George came about'.[78]

Ulster unionists gave Lemass's Tralee speech a guarded welcome. The Ulster Unionist MP for south Down, Captain L.P.S. (Willy) Orr, said that it presented a 'change of spirit' from Dublin, although he regretted that really 'the speech contained nothing new',[79] a view which the Northern Ireland minister for commerce, Brian Faulkner similarly expressed.[80] O'Neill waited for some time before he officially replied to Lemass's speech, taking the temperature of his supporters before making his own position clear. He described Lemass's speech as 'not without courage'. However, he did maintain that it was Northern Ireland's 'indisputable right' to remain within the United Kingdom.[81]

Lemass's trip to America in October 1963 undermined any likelihood of a positive response from O'Neill. Indeed Lemass's time abroad exposed his sometimes muddled approach to his Northern Ireland policy. His speeches in America sought to expose the discriminatory practices of the Protestant majority against the Catholic minority within Northern Ireland. Such pronouncements, however, were at variance with his conciliatory speeches in Ireland over the previous number of months, which had sought to nurture cross border co-operation. In his American speeches he challenged the very legitimacy and permanence of the Northern Ireland state.[82] Speaking at the National Press Club in Washington, he was critical of the Northern Ireland electoral system, and spoke for the need of a system 'which would give proper representation to all sections' of the community irrespective of their religion.[83]

O'Neill reacted bitterly to Lemass's speeches: 'where is the Tralee speech now?' he asked mockingly.[84] Privately it was reported to Lemass that his speeches in America had been a source of 'embarrassment' to O'Neill, who, as a result of the remarks, found himself in a 'very awkward' position with his supporters.[85] When O'Neill eventually decided to publicly reply to Lemass, at a unionist rally in county Antrim in November 1963, he was impenitent, maintaining that Lemass's comments in America 'have wiped out all those remarks which he made in Tralee last July'.[86] Lemass had overplayed his hand in America and his trip abroad merely resulted in a return of megaphone diplomacy between Dublin and Belfast. He realised that a bold initiative was necessary if he were to have any chance of saving his ambition to formally establish north–south cross-border relations. Thus, in early December 1963 Lemass sent his party colleague, Lionel Booth, to Belfast to speak on his leader's behalf. Just as Booth had sought to encourage Fianna Fáil supporters to cease using anti-partitionist terminology during the late 1950s,[87] he now attempted to reassure Ulster unionists that Irish unity could only be achieved with their consent.

Speaking to a packed audience at a Methodist church on University Road, Belfast, Booth, who was himself a Protestant and was educated in the Leys School, a Methodist-funded institution in Cambridge, guaranteed his audience that there could be 'no change' to the political set-up of Northern Ireland unless by the 'free consent of the people of the North'.[88] Booth's assurance that the constitutional position of Northern Ireland could not be altered without agreement from Ulster unionists was hugely significant. In effect, his words recognised that partition could not be ended without the consent of the majority of Northern Ireland, as enshrined in the Ireland Act, passed in Westminster in 1949.

The 'principle of consent' from an Irish nationalist perspective was not formally adopted by a political party until September 1969 by Fine Gael, when it was then taken to mean that the reunification of the national territory as defined in Article Two of the Irish Constitution required the majority consent in Northern Ireland.[89] While it is true that Lemass never publicly spoke about the 'principle of consent', his Tralee speech of July 1963 had recognised, irrespective of his comments on the 'artificial' position of the area, that the Northern Ireland state existed with the support of the majority of its citizens.[90] Thus having ruled out physical force to end partition,[91] and acknowledging that the Northern Ireland government and parliament was maintained with the support of the majority, it seems fair to assume that in private he was of the opinion that Irish unity could only be achieved when Ulster unionists agreed to a united Ireland.[92]

Indeed, the available evidence would suggest that within Fianna Fáil there was a determination to re-examine the issue. As early as 1938, Seán MacEntee had privately expressed to de Valera that Irish reunification could not be achieved without the support of the Protestant majority in Northern Ireland.[93] Most tellingly, in March 1967, shortly after Lemass's retirement as Taoiseach and leader of Fianna Fáil, Charles Haughey wrote to Frank Aiken, advising his party colleague that because Northern Ireland had over time become a 'firmly established political reality', Dublin must acknowledge that Irish unity could only be secured 'through a majority decision of the people of the North, moulded by the positive publicity of the government in the Republic'.[94]

Lemass, as ever unwilling to create a divide within Fianna Fáil, never formally adopted the 'principle of consent' as official policy. He was painfully aware that to officially concede on the issue would have been met with fierce resistance from the fundamentalists within the party, who would have viewed such a move as a 'sell-out' and the abandonment of the republican tradition. In fact, the 'principle of consent' did not become official Fianna Fáil policy until the late 1980s. Although under Jack Lynch's leadership (1966–79) there was support for the policy, a faction remained within the party that interpreted the 'principle of consent' on the basis that the unionist population of Northern Ireland represented the 'national minority' of the entire island of Ireland, and were thus required to accept the wishes of the 'national majority' for an independent and united Ireland.[95] Under Charles Haughey's reign (1979–92) – irrespective of his previous views on the subject as expressed to Aiken in 1967 – the 'principle of consent' was rigorously attacked by Fianna Fáil. Indeed, it was not until the Anglo-Irish Agreement of 1985, which formally recognised the 'principle of consent', that a reinterpretation of the issue was undertaken by the party; this occurred after the Fianna Fáil leadership accepted the Agreement as an internationally binding treaty.[96] Booth's speech in Belfast was not reported widely within the press on either side of the border, with the result that his reference to 'the free consent of the people of the North' was not accorded the importance that it deserved.[97]

The 'de facto debate' remained silent for the remainder of 1963 and throughout 1964, Lemass wishing to sidestep the issue of recognition and instead trying to persuade Ulster unionists that the dispute over the constitutional position of Northern Ireland should not inhibit cross-border north–south co-operation.[98] The issue, however, was back on the political agenda following Lemass's much heralded visit to Northern Ireland in January 1965 to meet Northern Ireland prime minister, Terence O'Neill. The meeting between Lemass and O'Neill in Belfast, on 14 January 1965, was highly symbolic. Not since the James Craig–William Cosgrave meeting forty years previously in 1925 had an official meeting occurred between the prime ministers of the two states in Ireland. Indeed, the sensational reaction to the Lemass–O'Neill meeting was not rivalled until the celebrated handshake between Taoiseach, Bertie Ahern, and the first minister of Northern Ireland, Ian Paisley, in 2007. Although no constitutional or political issues were raised at the meeting, Lemass's visit to Northern Ireland did reignite the 'de facto debate'. On his return to Dublin following his meeting with O'Neill, Lemass attempted to play down the importance of the meeting in a pre-emptive manoeuvre against those hardliners both within and outside Fianna Fáil who viewed the meeting as a signal that the party had abandoned its republican ethos. The *Kerryman* warned that although Lemass had set out bravely on a new approach to Northern Ireland, it would earn him criticism from 'diehards in our midst' and could even 'harm him politically'.[99] Lemass had taken a calculated gamble in travelling to Belfast and, as Tom Garvin has observed, was trying to transcend a considerable amount of remembered history, bitterness and political passion.[100] This would explain Lemass's reluctance, on his return to Dublin, to make any public comment on the issue of recognition of Northern Ireland. He did not want to return to a subject that he knew could have a destabilising effect within Fianna Fáil: the reality was that his visit confirmed de facto recognition of Northern Ireland, which Lemass had already conceded in his Tralee speech in July 1963.

When he did decide to speak on the issue of recognition, on 10 February 1965, he was intentionally vague on the issue, skilfully dodging explicit granting of recognition to the Northern Ireland state. He spoke of the pre-Treaty acceptance by the original Dáil of the continued existence of the Northern Ireland parliament on the understanding that Ulster unionists would agree to enter an all-Ireland constitution.[101] In the same way that Lemass never formally ordered that the term 'Northern Ireland' should be used in place of the term 'Six Counties', during his time as Fianna Fáil president and Taoiseach, the Irish government never formally acknowledged the de facto position of Northern Ireland.[102] Indeed under Jack Lynch's leadership, Fianna Fáil routinely implied that de facto recognition of the Northern Ireland parliament and government was only envisaged within the context of a federal agreement between Belfast and Dublin.[103] Thus when Lemass retired as Taoiseach in the winter of 1966, he left behind a Northern policy that was both innovative, but ultimately unofficial. In any respect, the progress that might have resulted from a continuation of Lemass's Northern policy was ultimately undone by the onset of the Troubles in Northern Ireland.


CONCLUSION

Seán Lemass's time as president of Fianna Fáil and Taoiseach signified a willingness of Irish nationalists to move away from their archaic anti-partitionist past. Through the delicate usage of political terminology, Lemass sought to convince Ulster unionists that they had nothing to fear in a federalised united Ireland. Retrospectively, Lemass's decision to alternate the phrase 'Northern Ireland' with 'the Six Counties' may not seem altogether significant. However, one must remember the extent to which the usage of anti-partitionist terminology resonated in the collective consciousness of nationalist Ireland. Lemass was a risk-taker, a man of action. His Northern policy was motivated by his desire for the economic reinvigoration of Ireland. He realised that many within Fianna Fáil, which included frontbench stalwarts such as Frank Aiken, would not support his new initiatives, yet sentimentality had no place in Lemass's Northern policy.

It is important to acknowledge that Lemass's approach to partition did not represent a fundamental transformation of Fianna Fáil's Northern policy. As leader of Fianna Fáil, 'the Republican Party', Lemass understood that he had a responsibility to remain loyal to party supporters. There were elements of his approach to partition that showed his ritual obedience to the Fianna Fáil tradition. He still maintained during his years as Taoiseach that partition was 'an absurdity';[104] that a British declaration in support of Irish unity was necessary; and that the Irish government would never recognise de jure the official status of Northern Ireland as a sovereign state.

Nevertheless, Lemass's willingness to move the debate away from a purely territorial dispute between Belfast and Dublin was a significant milestone – if simply for the fact that it represented such a huge step forward from de Valera's perceived immobilism towards Ulster unionists. Lemass's determination to offer Ulster unionists de facto recognition of the Northern Ireland parliament and government, placed within the context of a federal solution to secure Irish unity, was in his eyes a purely pragmatic policy. His orchestrated attempts, through the use of senior Fianna Fáil representatives, to propagate the legitimacy and viability of his federal proposal to Ulster unionists exposed a cunning characteristic of Lemass's personality: a quality that was essential if he were to encourage party supporters to adhere to *his* Northern policy.

A justified criticism of Lemass, as made by Tom Garvin, was that he could be accused of retaining a 'certain innocence about Northern realities, in particular the implacable collective resistance of the unionist population to anything that looked even vaguely like a Dublin takeover bid or anything that seemed to threaten the union with Britain'.[105] There was, indeed sometimes, a certain naivety on Lemass's behalf. He genuinely seemed to believe that because he had simply offered Ulster unionists a federal solution, they would eventually agree to this proposition. Nevertheless, what he did offer, as leader, was a willingness to disregard traditional illusions and prejudices, and to deal with the Northern Ireland as it was and not how he wished it to be. He was determined to escape Dublin's revolutionary past and create a firmly constitutional future. As Garret FitzGerald has observed, what made him distinct from the traditional Fianna Fáil stance on Northern policy, as espoused by his predecessor Éamon de Valera, was that Lemass was simply 'sensible' when it came to Northern Ireland.[106]

## NOTES

1. Michael Laffan, *The Partition of Ireland, 1911–1925* (Dublin: Dublin Historical Association, 1983), p.123.
2. Speech by Lemass at a Fianna Fáil dinner, Imperial Hotel, Castlebar, 14 December 1959, National Archives of Ireland (NAI), Department of the Taoiseach (DT) 97/9/1504. See also speech by Lemass at a dinner of the south Louth Fianna Fáil Comhairle Ceantair, White Horse Hotel, Drogheda, 5 February 1961, NAI, DT 97/9/1550.
3. Meeting between British Prime Minister, Harold Macmillan and Lemass, 13 July 1959, NAI, Department of External Affairs (DFA) P203/2. See also meeting between Macmillan and Lemass, 18 March 1964, The National Archives, London (TNA), Prime Minister Files (PREM) 11/5151.
4. See speech by Lemass, 5 February 1961, NAI, DT S 9361 K/61. See also speech by Lemass at a Fianna Fáil dinner, Imperial Hotel, Castlebar, 14 December 1959; NAI, DT 97/9/1504.
5. See Lemass's Oxford address, 15 October 1959; reprinted *Irish Times*, 16 October 1959.
6. Clare O'Halloran, *Partition and the Limits of Irish Nationalism: An Ideology under Stress* (Dublin: Gill & Macmillan, 1987), p.xviii.
7. Paul Bew and Henry Patterson, *Seán Lemass and the Making of Modern Ireland, 1945–66* (Dublin: Gill & Macmillan, 1982), p.11. See also Jonathan Bardon, *A History of Ulster* (Belfast: Blackstaff Press,), p.629.
8. Henry Patterson, 'Seán Lemass and the Ulster Question, 1959–65', *Journal of Contemporary History*, vol. 34 (1999), p.146.
9. Paul Bew, *Ireland: The Politics of Enmity, 1789–2006* (Oxford: Oxford University Press, 2007), p.487.
10. Tom Garvin, *Judging Lemass: The Measure of the Man* (Dublin: Royal Irish Academy, 2009), p.220.
11. Ronan Fanning, *Independent Ireland* (Dublin: Helicon, 1983), p.169.
12. John Horgan, *Seán Lemass: The Enigmatic Patriot* (Dublin: Gill & Macmillan, 1999), p.260.
13. Ibid., pp.260–5.
14. See Michael Kennedy, *Division and Consensus: The Politics of Cross-Border Relations in Ireland, 1925–1969* (Dublin: Institute of Public Administration, 2000), pp.191–216.
15. Horgan, *Lemass*, pp.262–3.
16. During his Oxford address, Lemass relentlessly referred to Ulster unionists as 'partitionists'. *Irish Times*, 16 October 1959.
17. This author has borrowed this term from Katy Hayward's article, 'The Politics of Nuance: Irish Official Discourse on Northern Ireland', (*Irish Political Studies*, vol. 19 no. 1 [2004], pp.18–38).
18. Ibid., p.19.
19. *Irish Press*, 30 June 1959.
20. See meetings of the All-Party Anti-Partition Committee, January 1949–October 1971, Frank Aiken Papers, University College Dublin Archives (UCDA), P104/8630–70.
21. See Mullins to Feehan, December 1954, Fianna Fáil Papers, UCDA P176/46. In 1955 the Tomas Ó'Cléirigh cumann, Dublin north-east, also informed party headquarters that the term should be replaced with a more 'positive' term such as 'Liberation' or 'National Union'. See memorandum on partition submitted by Tomas Ó'Cléirigh cumann, Dublin north-east, 15 January 1955, pp.2–3, UCDA, P176/46.
22. *Irish Times*, 11 November 1959.
23. *Irish Press*, 11 November 1959.
24. Horgan, *Lemass*, p.258.
25. *Irish Press*, 11 November 1959.
26. Lemass to Ernest Blythe, 7 December 1962, NAI, DT S 16272 D/62.
27. Lemass to Vivion de Valera, 14 May 1960, NAI, DT S 16699B.
28. Ibid.

29. This was the opinion of Charles Haughey, a view Lemass certainly held. Haughey to Aiken, 14 March 1967, UCDA, P104/8822.
30. See *Irish Times*, 23 May 1960, and *Irish Independent*, 24 May 1960.
31. Conversation between Ó hAnnracháin and Quinn, 23 May 1957, NAI, DT S 1957/63.
32. Clutterbuck to Home, 1 September 1959, TNA, Dominions Office 35/5379. See Garvin, *Judging Lemass*, p.217.
33. Lemass to Jack Lynch, 18 March 1966, NAI, DT S 96/6/23; reply received by the Department of the Taoiseach from MacEntee, NAI, DT 1957/63; and Haughey to Aiken, 14 March 1967, UCDA P104/8822.
34. John Molloy, Secretary of the Department of External Affairs to Secretary of the Department of Education, 27 September 1963, NAI, DT S 10467/ F/64.
35. *Dáil Éireann Debates*, 7 July 1959, vol.176, cols. 644 and 647.
36. Meeting of Fianna Fáil parliamentary party, 15 July 1959, UCDA, P176/447.
37. Meeting of Fianna Fáil national executive, 27 July 1959, UCDA, P176/348.
38. *Belfast Telegraph*, 25 May 1960.
39. Secretary of the Department of External Affairs to Secretary of the Department of Education, 27 September 1963, NAI, DT S 10467/F/64. Also in April 1963, Aiken 'advised' his department that he 'considered it preferable to continue to use the term "Six Counties" throughout the monthly publication, *Trade Statistics of Ireland*, rather than "Northern Ireland"' – a policy that 'the Taoiseach accepted'. T. O'Cearbhaill to C.H. Murray, Assistant Secretary of the Department of Finance, NAI, DT S 1957/63.
40. Reply received by Department of the Taoiseach from MacEntee, 20 June 1960, NAI, DT S 1957/63.
41. *Dáil Éireann Debates*, 21 June 1960, vol. 183, col. 2.
42. *Dáil Éireann Debates*, 8 February 1961, vol. 186, col. 10. See also *Dáil Éireann Debates* on 7 March 1963, vol. 200, col. 892, when he used the term 'Six Counties'; also *Dáil Éireann Debate*, 13 December 1962, vol. 198, col. 1408, when he used the term 'Northern Ireland'.
43. Lemass to Jack Lynch, 18 March 1966, NAI, DT S 96/6/23.
44. See NAI, DT S 1957/63.
45. See speech by Lynch, *Dáil Éireann Debates*, 11 November 1969, vol. 242, cols. 1086–7.
46. See speeches by Lord Craigavon, Northern Ireland prime minister (1921–40), *Belfast News Letter*, 2 May 1939, and Sir Basil Brooke (later Lord Brookeborough), Northern Ireland prime minister (1943–63), *Irish Independent*, 3 April 1948.
47. *Irish Independent*, 20 July 1923, and *Evening Standard*, 17 October 1938.
48. See Lemass's Oxford address, 15 October 1959; reprinted in *Irish Times*, 16 October 1959.
49. *Irish Times*, 15 January 1960.
50. See speeches by Brookeborough, *Irish Times*, 23 October 1954; *Irish Independent*, 7 April 1955; and *Northern Whig*, 5 February 1958.
51. *Irish Times*, 30 July 1963.
52. *Irish Times*, 26 March 1963.
53. *Belfast Telegraph*, 27 March 1963.
54. *Irish Press*, 4 February 1969.
55. Brian Farrell, *Seán Lemass* (Dublin: Gill & Macmillan 1983), p.106.
56. Author's interview with Mary Colley, 18 May 2009.
57. *Irish Press*, 17 April 1963.
58. *Irish Press*, 11 November 1959.
59. Speaking in the Dáil in July 1959, Booth spoke in support of recognising the Northern Ireland government de facto. He argued that not to do so was a policy of futility, and accused mainstream nationalism as being 'far too greedy'. *Dáil Éireann Debates*, 7 July 1959, vol. 176, col. 646.
60. At a meeting of the Fianna Fáil national executive in February 1958, Hederman had 'requested that the Irish government should recognise the government of Northern Ireland de facto'. Meeting of Fianna Fáil national executive, 10 February 1958, UCDA, P176/348.
61. Ibid. At the meeting Ryan had seconded Hederman's motion for the de facto recognition of Northern Ireland.
62. Lemass to Vivion de Valera, 14 May 1960, NAI, DT S 16699B.
63. Donal Barrington, *Uniting Ireland* (Dublin: n.p., 1957). A copy is available from NAI, DT S 9361 G.
64. Liam de Paor, *Divided Ulster* (Harmondsworth: Penguin, 1970), pp.137–8.

65. See comments by Horgan, *Irish Times*, 16 December 1957.
66. See *Seanad Éireann Debates*, 29 January 1958, vol. 48, cols. 1404–6.
67. See comments by Blythe, *Irish Times*, 5 August 1957.
68. See Garret FitzGerald's comments, *National Observer*, June 1959.
69. *Irish Press*, 1 May 1963.
70. Kennedy, *Division and Consensus*, p.198.
71. Note by Hugh McCann, 15 July 1963, NAI, DT S 9361K/63.
72. *Irish Times*, 2 August 1963.
73. *Irish Press*, 30 July, 1963.
74. *Irish Times*, 30 July 1963.
75. O'Halloran, *Partition and the Limits of Irish Nationalism*, p.121.
76. *Dáil Éireann Debates*, 24 June 1947, vol. 107, col. 79.
77. *Sunday Independent*, 14 July 1963.
78. *Derry Journal*, 12 July 1963.
79. *Irish Times*, 2 August 1963.
80. *Irish Times*, 31 July 1963.
81. *Irish Press*, 12 September 1963.
82. See *Irish Times*, 17 October 1963, and *Irish Press*, 18 October 1963.
83. *Irish Press*, 16 October 1963.
84. Michael Kennedy, 'Northern Ireland and Cross-Border Co-operation' in Brian Girvin and Gary Murphy (eds), *The Lemass Era: Politics and Society in the Ireland of Seán Lemass* (Dublin: University College Dublin Press, 2005), p.114.
85. Cremin to McCann, 5 December 1963, NAI, DT S 9361K/63.
86. *Irish Press*, 8 November 1963.
87. *Dáil Éireann Debates*, 7 July 1959, vol. 176, col. 646.
88. Booth also remarked that 'his ancestors had come to Ireland with Oliver Cromwell and that his Portadown born wife's ancestors had come over with King William', so he could relate to Ulster unionists more than most southern Irish politicians. *Irish Times*, 9 December 1963.
89. Gareth Ivory, 'Revisions in Nationalist Discourse Among Irish Political Parties', *Irish Political Studies*, vol. 14, no. 1 (1999), pp.89–90.
90. *Irish Press*, 30 July 1963.
91. See Lemass's Oxford address, 15 October 1959; reprinted in *Irish Times*, 16 October 1959.
92. See Horgan's comments on the issue of 'consent' in *Lemass*, pp.286–8.
93. MacEntee to de Valera, 17 February 1938, UCDA, Seán MacEntee Papers, P67/155 (MacEntee never sent the letter to de Valera).
94. Haughey to Aiken, 14 March 1967, UCDA, P104/8822.
95. Ivory, 'Revisions in Nationalist Discourse', p.90.
96. Ibid., p.94. See also Gareth Ivory, 'Fianna Fáil, Constitutional Republicanism and the Issue of Consent: 1980–1996', *Éire-Ireland*, vol. 32 (summer 1997), pp.93–116.
97. See *Belfast Newsletter* and *Irish Press* for December 1963.
98. See Lemass's Arklow speech, *Wicklow People*, 18 April 1964.
99. *The Kerryman*, 23 January 1965.
100. Garvin, *Judging Lemass*, p.6.
101. *Dáil Éireann Debates*, 10 February 1965, vol. 214, cols. 3–4.
102. See Lemass's speech, 'One Nation', to the Oxford Union, 15 October 1959; *Irish Times*, 16 October 1959.
103. See Lynch's Tralee speech, 20 September 1969; *Irish Times*, 21 September 1969.
104. *Irish Press*, 4 April 1960.
105. Garvin, *Judging Lemass*, p.219.
106. Author's interview with Dr Garret FitzGerald, 19 January 2009.

# CHAPTER EIGHT

# 'A Third Road': Constitutional Nationalism, Militant Republicanism and Non-Violence in the Civil Rights Era

## SIMON PRINCE

On 4 October 2008, John Hume and Martin McGuinness spoke at the commemoration marking the fortieth anniversary of the first Derry civil rights march. The different Irish nationalist traditions, constitutionalism and physical force, were each laying claim to the legacy of the civil rights movement.[1] The main organiser of the march, Eamonn McCann, belonged to neither of these traditions and chose not to take part in the official commemoration. He instead launched a pre-emptive attack in a local newspaper upon the assumption that the past 'could be understood entirely and could not be understood other than in terms of Orange and Green, Protestant and Catholic, unionist and nationalist'. An act of non-violent confrontation by revolutionary socialists had started the civil rights movement, but this had 'virtually been written out of history'.[2] In part, this was because the crisis sparked by the radicals inadvertently revived the old traditions of constitutional nationalism and militant republicanism. After a brief moment at the centre of events, the organisers of the 5 October 1968 march had been pushed back to the political margins. As a former leftist explains in Anne Devlin's play *The Long March*, 'we thought we were beginning a new journey: the long march. What we didn't see was that it had begun a long time before with someone else's journey; we were simply going through the steps in our time.'[3]

The story of the civil rights era is normally told as a short story, no more than a chapter or two in an autobiography or a general history.[4] This smoothes the story into the familiar template of Irish history that McCann describes, and also gives it a conventional narrative structure in which events build steadily to a climax. However, there is a different tradition of Irish short-story-telling that is exemplified by James Joyce's *Dubliners*; one where characters are unable to change their unhappy lives and escape from the restricted routines of the mundane worlds they inhabit.[5] The story of the civil rights era is more a story of paralysis and possibilities denied than a story of tragic heroism, more a story of aimless circles than straight lines towards clear goals.

This chapter offers a series of brief case studies that look at how a range of activists tried to break away from the recurring failures of constitutional nationalism and militant republicanism by practising non-violent direct action. In each case, their efforts were largely unsuccessful. What this illustrates is that there were great difficulties involved in adopting and adapting a foreign idea; that Northern Ireland's communal divide presented problems to putting such a strategy into effect; that violence was a constant threat; that the constitutional and physical-force traditions were still potent even when they appeared moribund; and that neither the civil rights movement nor the Troubles were inevitable. The chapter's opening section sets out the recurring cycle that opposition politics seemed to be trapped inside, the alternative road offered by non-violence, and the first failed attempt to use it in Northern Ireland after the Second World War. The chapter then moves on to 1963 and the direct action campaign directed against Dungannon council's housing policy. The third section returns to Dungannon five years later and examines how another squatting incident led to the first civil rights march. The final two sections explore how the Derry radicals succeeded in smashing out of the old cycle and how afterwards a new one took shape, giving new form to the two traditions.

## THREE ROADS

In January 1957, Eddie McAteer, the Nationalist MP for Foyle, analysed the Irish Republican Army's (IRA) 'Border Campaign' for the Department of External Affairs in Dublin. 'The present outbreak of violence would be quelled,' he wearily predicted, 'only [to] break out again with "another IRA" in five or ten years.'[6] Dublin valued McAteer's judgement because he had close ties to the republican movement: his brother, Hugh, had served as the IRA's chief of staff during the early

1940s. McAteer respected his brother and shared his commitment to Irish unity, but he never believed in armed struggle.[7] He chose constitutional nationalism over militant republicanism; this was a decision that he never came to regret, although repeated disappointments did lead him to become ever more cynical.

When McAteer had been first elected to Stormont, in 1945, he had been altogether more idealistic. The Allies were promising to build a new world order, national revolutions in Asia were starting to sweep away the old colonial system, and the traditionally sympathetic Labour Party had come to power at Westminster. McAteer therefore had reason to hope that Irish self-determination, as he understood it, would finally be conceded and partition ended. He pushed out time-serving hacks within the party and led into political office a new generation of Nationalists that wanted to pursue the interests of Northern Catholics with more energy. The Anti-Partition League (APL) was set up to bring all strands of constitutional nationalism in the North together around a common platform, and to participate in parliamentary elections. Nationalists did not just stand; they also intended to sit in Stormont, exposing the injustices perpetrated by the unionist regime from within the system and to argue for Irish unity. The APL took the chance to use Westminster as a forum to raise grievances, too, and co-operated closely with Labour's Friends of Ireland. Support came as well from the southern political parties: they formed the Mansion House Committee to fund Nationalist candidates in the 1949 Stormont elections. That same year, a representative of the new Republic of Ireland accompanied an APL delegation on a tour of the United States, with the aim of persuading Irish Americans to lobby their government over the issue of partition.[8]

McAteer and the APL also tried to take politics on to the streets, staging a series of publicity-seeking marches through Derry. The second of these marches, on St Patrick's Day 1952, was beaten off the streets by the Royal Ulster Constabulary (RUC) amidst violent scenes that would later be compared to those that had erupted on 5 October 1968. The political consequences, however, were not comparable.[9] McAteer stressed before the first march that the 'important thing' about such actions was to ensure that they were 'seen by foreign observers', and his were not seen.[10] Indeed, the APL as a whole was marching into obscurity: Stormont was deaf to Nationalist complaints, the Labour cabinet remembered Northern Ireland's wartime service and Southern Ireland's neutrality, Dublin's help was half-hearted at best, and Washington was not going to alienate its Cold War ally over what was seen as a minor matter. The resulting frustration was exploited by the IRA in order to launch a border campaign and to renew the armed struggle. McAteer joylessly reminded everyone that he had long been warning that this would happen if the constitutional road was blocked, that 'continual repression of and contempt for the basic rights of the Nationalist minority would shatter everyone's faith in normal political action'.[11]

The IRA's own statements on the Border Campaign echoed in some ways McAteer's assessment that the Irish body politic was suffering from a recurring outbreak. 'This is the age-old struggle of the Irish people versus British aggression,' read the Proclamation of December 1956. 'This is the same cause for which generations of our people have suffered and died.'[12] The IRA underscored this particular point by naming its four 'flying columns' after Republican heroes drawn from over a hundred years of risings and wars: Patrick Pearse, Tom Clarke, Bartholomew Teeling and Liam Lynch.[13] The plan was for the columns to cross over into Northern Ireland's border counties and combine with local units to create 'liberated zones'.[14] However, apart from a spasm of support at the start, the violence failed to inspire the Irish people, on either side of the border. Sympathy for the bravery and patriotism of volunteers did not stretch to welcoming the killing of policemen and the resulting risk of a sectarian backlash. Without popular backing, the North's security apparatus found it relatively simple to contain the IRA threat that it had been created to counter. Éamon de Valera's return to government in Dublin helped Stormont, too, as he introduced internment in the South and sped the decline in IRA activity.[15] In February 1962 the IRA finally faced up to the failure of the campaign.[16]

Just over five years after this outbreak of violence had been quelled, McAteer feared that history was again going to repeat itself. McAteer, who was now the Nationalist leader, gave a speech at the 1968 party conference pleading with Catholics to 'be realistic', as 'we are an entrapped minority' and 'are very much on our own here in the North of Ireland'. The Labour government, Dublin and Irish America were preoccupied with their own suffering and successes. Change, then, was not going to come from over the border or from overseas, but instead from their Protestant neighbours. This was, of course, if change was ever going to come: McAteer suspected that 'the way to power and advancement in the Unionist Party is by kicking the Nationalist people'. Despite these doubts, the Nationalist leader continued to preach patience. McAteer begged those 'amongst us who are thinking about

going home and taking up their pikes' not to be 'goaded into precipitate action which could only set the clock back a very considerable
time'. The use of 'pikes' was a clear reference to the republican rising
of 1798, but there were other Nationalists who believed that the dead
end of armed struggle was not the only alternative road. Austin Currie, the young Nationalist MP for East Tyrone, told the conference: 'if
we cannot obtain justice through normal channels then we should do
so through the only effective means at our disposal'. For Currie, this
meant non-violent direct action – and he persuaded the party to make
'a detailed examination of the implications that would arise from the
adoption of a policy of civil disobedience'.[17]

Currie had studied American history at Queen's University Belfast,
and followed the progress of the civil rights movement in the media.
Like many other opposition activists in Northern Ireland, he believed
that there were lessons to be taken from across the Atlantic.[18]
Although the injustices inflicted upon blacks dwarfed those experienced
by Catholics, there were sufficient structural similarities to make the
American example relevant to Northern Ireland. In both cases, an
effectively autonomous region was ruled by a single party in the interests of the majority community and against those of the minority.[19] The
radical theologian Reinhold Niebuhr, who sympathised with black suffering and would later influence Martin Luther King's thinking, saw in
the 1930s that this situation in the American South made it 'hopeless' to
expect freedom to come by 'trusting in the moral sense of the white race'
or through 'violent revolution'. But how was it to come if words and
weapons were equally useless? Niebuhr knew – 'with a dogmatism which
all history justifies' – that 'the white race in America will not admit the
Negro to equal rights if it is not forced to do so', and he thought that he
had found a force that combined coercion with morality. This was
Mahatma Gandhi's Satyagraha or 'soul force'.[20] Gandhi had forged a
weapon that he regarded as different from, and infinitely superior to,
the force which the government commanded.[21] While Gandhi believed
that the object of non-violent struggle should be to convert rather than
coerce, Niebuhr claimed that the strategy of non-violence practised in
India did 'coerce and destroy'. However, soul force was a 'type of coercion' that 'preserves moral, rational, and co-operative attitudes
within an area of conflict and thus augments the moral forces without
destroying them'. Where violence pushes the sides to a conflict further
and further apart, non-violence keeps open the lines of communication
and the chance of a settlement. Niebuhr also recognised that using
non-violence further weakened an opponent by 'rob[bing] [him] of the

moral conceit by which he identifies his interests with the peace and order of society'. The authorities and their apologists might still try to brand the protesters as terrorists, traitors, criminals and so on, yet neutral elements both inside and outside the dominant group would most likely see through these underhand tactics.[22]

Niebuhr predicted that the 'emancipation of the Negro race in America probably waits upon the adequate development of this kind of social and political strategy'; he was right.[23] However, successfully putting the theory into practice was to require years and years of struggle. Unearthing an idea that was rooted in the history and culture of India and transplanting it to American soil was far from easy, and many times the seed of the idea failed to bloom.[24] Non-violence did not come naturally to blacks anymore than it did to Indians; non-violence had to be taught and enforced, and that required institutions and organisation. So, over three decades were to pass between Niebuhr making his prediction and King using 'a Niebuhrian stratagem of power' to win the great non-violent victories for civil rights at Birmingham and Selma, Alabama.[25]

McAteer did not need to look to the United States or hold a policy debate to learn about the problems and potential of using Satyagraha outside of India: he had himself tried and failed to stage a civil disobedience campaign in Northern Ireland. In 1948, as frustration with constitutional politics was starting to grow, he had invoked 'the mighty spirit of the late Mahatma', who had 'pointed a third road', that of 'non-co-operation, no violence [*sic*]'. 'If the British Government's only answer to our pleadings is that the problem is not urgent,' he argued in *Irish Action*, 'then let us make it urgent!' McAteer set out in this pamphlet methods to make it urgent, to make the 'local misgovernment' practised by Unionists 'impossible'. These ranged from 'acting stupid' when dealing with government officials to holding back taxes and occupying public buildings.[26] McAteer himself refused to pay his rates, which led to a court case in 1951. The following year he tried to force his way on to the mayor of Derry's chair, a gesture which symbolised that power in the city rightly laid with Catholics.[27] But McAteer seemed to be the only one taking part in his campaign. Among the millions of other Irish nationalists, it was treated with indifference and, in some cases, outright hostility; as early as January 1949 the *Irish Times* commented: 'McAteer's formula can only lead to disaster.'[28] There were flaws in the formula, not least of which was McAteer's belief that 'organisation has distinct disadvantages' and that 'Each individual must constitute a complete action cell.'[29] The 'science of non-violence', as

Gandhi put it, would be experimented with again and again by Northern Irish activists in the years ahead, yet the formula was never perfected.[30]

## DUNGANNON

When the Campaign for Social Justice (CSJ) looked back in 1969 at 'How the Civil Rights Movement Began', it selected as the starting point the direct action protests that young Catholic mothers had staged six years previously against Dungannon Urban District Council's housing policy.[31] Historians such as Henry Patterson have tended to agree with this conclusion, but if the campaign was any kind of start, then it was a false start.[32] Although the Dungannon housewives were to get more impressive results than McAteer from their experiments with the science of non-violence, the formula was still not right for Northern Ireland. Another difference from McAteer's efforts was that this campaign took inspiration from the United States and King, not from India and Gandhi. On the day that the BBC screened a *Panorama* report from Birmingham, Alabama, and federal troops were deployed to the most thoroughly segregated city in the American South, sixty-seven women without homes of their own marched into the Protestant centre of Dungannon.[33] They carried placards with slogans such as 'Racial Discrimination in Alabama Hits Dungannon', and picketed the council offices until they were allowed in to present their 'Declaration of Independence'. The delegation asked the councillors to end the unofficial policy of segregation, whereby public housing in unionist wards went to Protestants and in nationalist wards to Catholics. Instead, they wanted homes to be awarded on a points system based on need that would ensure a fair distribution of tenancies. The councillors declined to make any firm commitments, so the women warned them that if there was 'no alternative' then they would take illegal, direct action and 'squat in the condemned houses'.[34]

As the Dungannon campaign developed, the ways in which it broke with previous forms of protest soon became obvious. 'There were no bands, no sashes and no fuss,' the nationalist *Dungannon Observer* noted of an early march, 'just a group of well-dressed and attractive young women ... their prams, [and] their older children.'[35] Respectability was a tactic that had long been used by the American civil rights movement. Southern racists defended segregation by portraying blacks as naturally lazy, ignorant, violent and irresponsible. So, civil rights activists behaved in accordance with prevailing middle-class standards of respectability and thus turned this stereotype back on the segregationists; they made themselves seem deserving of full citizenship and their opponents appear to be little more than animals. Respectability also helped to make femininity a weapon rather than a weakness: it was white men rather than black women who had forgotten how to behave.[36] In Dungannon, too, respectability helped hide just how radical this female, Catholic challenge to the male, Protestant status quo was. Here were mothers pressing the system to give them homes for their families, not men marching or fighting to overthrow the system, but their demands still threatened Unionism's control of councils across the country.[37]

The marches, though, failed to move the Dungannon councillors, and in August 1963 the final decision was made to allocate every one of the 142 tenancies on a new estate to families who already had homes. Many of the properties that these families were vacating were now earmarked for destruction as part of the slum clearance programme. The Dungannon movement now felt there really was 'no alternative'. 'One family moved into [the empty prefabs at] Fairmount Park,' the *Dungannon Observer* reported, 'then another. Soon the "squatters" came in a stream. The dam had burst.'[38] Within a couple of days, the number of squatters had swelled to 120 people, occupying thirty-five of the prefabs.[39] The council overreacted: the electricity and running water were turned off and legal action to eject the squatters was also considered. Liberal unionist opinion saw through these underhand tactics, however. 'The Dungannon Council's postwar housing record,' commented the unionist *Belfast Telegraph*, 'is not one of signal achievement. In these circumstances it is negative to assert that the squatters "will not be considered" when houses become available.' The editorial concluded that 'Stormont should adopt a tougher line with those local authorities whose building programmes fall short of requirements.'[40]

This was the high point of the Dungannon direct action campaign. Gender and class had been working for the movement; now they began working against it. After the early protests, a local doctor's wife, Patricia McCluskey, had become the leader of the campaign – almost from the instant she got involved. In an interview with the unionist *Tyrone Courier and Dungannon News*, McCluskey laid out her qualifications for this new role: she had worked to rehouse people who had been bombed out during the Second World War, she had been a teacher and she had visited German refugee camps.[41] She did indeed prove an effective spokesperson and a capable organiser, yet she was also a restraint upon more radical action. McCluskey had actually tried to stop the Fairmount Park squatting, as she was concerned about the social stigma that came with stepping outside the law and the problems that this could cause for the young women in her care. Despite these doubts and concerns, however, she was quick to appropriate the protest as her own – keeping the leadership and fielding questions from journalists. Her husband, Conn McCluskey, would later justify this to Tara Keenan Thomson by saying: 'these girls really weren't good enough for politics'.[42] Conn may well have felt that women in general were not good enough for politics; the delegation he took to Stormont to negotiate a settlement was made up entirely of men. A campaign that had been started by young, working-class women was brought to a conclusion by middle-aged, middle-class men. And the women involved were largely happy about how things ended. Thomson was told by one woman: 'We wanted [the delegation] to speak for us to see if they could get houses and they did!'[43] Stormont made the council agree to expand an estate that was being built in the Catholic ward and to consider the squatters for rehousing there after the protest ended. The minister responsible for local government wrote to the local Nationalist MP that the 'result is, I think, a happy one and should ensure that the families in Dungannon who are most in need of housing will receive houses fairly quickly'.[44]

Letters to the *Dungannon Observer* had suggested a Northern Irish version of the March on Washington, described Catholics as 'white Negroes', and pointed out parallels with Birmingham.[45] The McCluskeys, though, had no desire to develop the Dungannon campaign into a mass movement using tactics of non-violent confrontation to gain full civil rights. Instead, they wanted to build on the last stage, when professional men had debated the facts of the case and reached an amicable settlement. The couple therefore recruited 'people whom we judged to be entirely reputable': these included an architect, an ear, nose and throat surgeon, a dentist, a wealthy businessman and a science professor. And they kept the numbers small – ten men and three women – 'because large groups of Irish people are prone to discuss matters too fully without making final decisions, and eventually split up'.[46] The CSJ, which Margaret McCluskey formally launched in January 1964, aimed to follow the elite pressure group approach of Britain's National Council for Civil Liberties rather than the mass civil disobedience practised by King's Southern Christian Leadership Conference. The group's 'first objective' would be to 'collect comprehensive and accurate data on all injustices done [and] to bring them to the attention of as many socially minded people as possible'.[47] Just as popular sentiment had been used to push Stormont into imposing a deal on the council, the reasoning went, so could Westminster be moved to right the devolved government's wrongs. As one of the CSJ's first pamphlets put it, 'Pressure of British opinion, properly directed ... could ensure the removal of any bias against Nationalists and Catholics because of their political or religious convictions.'[48]

The CSJ was appealing to the moral sense of the British people, and they were to find that this was hopeless. Patricia McCluskey, however, did enjoy some superficial successes: two years after she had addressed a meeting of housewives in Dungannon, she was speaking at the Palace of Westminster to MPs and peers. The resulting Campaign for Democracy in Ulster (CDU), a ginger group within the Labour Party, worked closely with the McCluskeys, their 'true friends', to press the government into intervening in Northern Irish affairs.[49] They failed. Roy Jenkins, the cabinet minister responsible for the province, later admitted that the issue 'was about 12th on my agenda'.[50] His successor at the Home Office, Jim Callaghan, dismissed the CDU by noting that there was always a group 'interested in Northern Ireland ... just as there is always a group interested in relations ... with South Africa, or with any other part of the Commonwealth ... there was as much interest and detachment as that'.[51] The grassroots of the party shared the leadership's indifference. A confidential memorandum prepared for the CDU's central committee concluded that the group's 'efforts appear to be in vain': 'the British Left ... are far too concerned to save socialism from extinction than to bother about Northern Ireland, about which the mass of the British people know little and care less'.[52] The constitutional road appeared blocked. As Callaghan explained in 1992, it 'needed a crisis to enable us to take action', not pamphlets, letters, questions in Parliament and meetings.[53] Two decades after *Irish Action*, no one yet had adequately answered the young McAteer's call to make the matter an urgent one for the British government.

## DUNGANNON, AGAIN

Far from increasing in numbers and militancy as the years passed, direct action disappeared from the Dungannon area until late 1967, and when it did return to the local political scene it was on a much smaller scale. Currie and the local Republican Club worked together to squat Catholics in empty council houses – usually just one or two families every few months.[54] This new campaign was not making much of an impact until the rural district council awarded a tenancy to a Protestant teenage girl who was working for a prospective Unionist MP. As the commission of inquiry chaired by Lord Cameron judiciously put it, she was by 'no stretch of the imagination ... a priority tenant'.[55] Currie later remembered saying at the time: 'if I live to be a hundred I'll never get a better case to symbolise the situation in Northern Ireland'.[56] On 20 June 1968, Currie and two other men went to the house in the village of Caledon, forced their way inside, and barricaded the doors. The tenant's brother smashed the door down with a sledgehammer and saw the squatters off the property and into the headlines.[57]

Nationalism and republicanism were exploring non-violence not as an alternative to constitutional politics and the politics of the gun, but rather as a parallel and related strategy to them. Currie's actions can in some ways be seen as being directed against the uneasy coalition of opposition parties and groups that had formed around the civil rights issue, as much as against the Unionists. Indeed, the leverage Currie won over his own party leadership and over key figures within the coalition was far greater and far more significant than that which he gained over the local council or Stormont. Just two days after the protest, Currie told a rally in Dungannon that they were in the same position as blacks in the American South, and that '[t]here will be other Caledons'. Joining him on the platform were McAteer, Patricia McCluskey, the republican Kevin Agnew and the Westminster MP for West Belfast, Gerry Fitt.[58] Currie chose to spend his newly acquired political capital on organising Northern Ireland's first civil rights march. 'I put the proposal [to Conn McCluskey],' Currie recalled, 'that it was time to get away from just disseminating facts and figures, time to get away from the civil liberties groups in Britain ... and to take it to the streets.'[59] Conn McCluskey, in turn, requested a meeting of the executive committee of the Northern Ireland Civil Rights Association (NICRA), and Agnew agreed to host it.[60] Some NICRA members were already open to Currie's idea. As the future NICRA chairman Frank Gogarty explained, Northern Irish activists had been following with interest the Poor People's March on Washington.[61] They had not been following it closely enough, however. Fred Heatley, a NICRA committee member, remembered that 'the tactics of Martin Luther King in America had been absorbed inasmuch that it was felt by some that only public marches could draw wide attention to what we were trying to achieve'.[62] NICRA therefore consented to sponsor Currie's march from Coalisland to Dungannon on 24 August 1968. The press release announced that the time had come to challenge discrimination 'by more vigorous action than Parliamentary questions and newspaper controversy'.[63]

The civil rights campaign now seemed to be belatedly moving in the direction that its godfathers had originally planned for it. NICRA's long, difficult birth and the first year or so in which it fought to survive may not fit comfortably into the wider story of non-violence in the long 1960s, yet they need to be sketched out to illuminate this story. So, the narrative now will track back a decade. Discrimination was meant to help prop up Unionist control, but C. Desmond Greaves of the British-based Connolly Association had recognised as early as 1955 that it was a point of weakness as well. Being a veteran Communist, Greaves argued that civil rights were denied to hold back the Protestant and Catholic working classes from coming together.[64] Working-class solidarity, the fall of the 'Orange Tories', independence from Britain, the unification of Ireland – all of this would spring from the civil rights struggle. Greaves thought that this struggle had to be led by Ireland's Labour movement, in which he also included the island's Communist parties. And this appeared to be exactly what was about to happen when the Communist-controlled Belfast Trades Council put on a conference about discrimination in May 1965.[65] The Northern Ireland Labour Party (NILP), though, made sure that the vast majority of trades unions did not get involved in a campaign fronted by its great rivals.[66] The following year, the NILP launched its own civil rights initiative, calling on the Unionist government to accept 'the basic principle that equal citizenship should confer equal civic rights in every part of the United Kingdom'.[67] The attorney-general responded to the petition by warning ministers that Stormont should not 'water down its rights or weaken its position so as to result in its own ultimate destruction'.[68] The road followed by the Old Left had reached a familiar dead end.

Two former members of the Connolly Association, Roy Johnston and Tony Coughlan, chose to try to take another vehicle, the IRA, along the third road. Johnston volunteered and soon became the IRA's political education officer, while Coughlan stayed independent; yet it was the latter who devised the civil rights strategy. In August 1966, Coughlan proposed that Stormont 'should be squeezed by popular demands from ... the discriminated against, the oppressed ... demands for reforms, for civil rights'. He recommended that 'full attention should be paid to securing the maximum and broadest unity of action' and that the 'whole gamut of civil resistance' should be used.[69] This position was the closest any Irish activist had come to the approach that had brought success in America, as, unlike McAteer and the McCluskeys, Coughlan wanted a wide coalition and systematic planning. So, meetings were held within the movement to win round the grassroots before other opposition parties and groups were invited to attend a civil rights seminar. Those who came to this event listened to a lecture from one of the founders of the Irish and British anti-apartheid movements and discussed the black struggle for equality in America. Out of these contacts came an organising committee; NICRA was finally introduced to the world in January 1967.[70]

Coughlan had warned that republicans would have to 'give way to others for the sake of unity where that is necessary', but doing so led to the abandonment of most of the planned acts of civil resistance.[71] By the summer of 1967 Northern republicans were complaining to Johnston that NICRA had done nothing to address civil rights issues in their local areas. When he raised these concerns with Betty Sinclair, the association's Communist chairwoman, she explained that NICRA had 'too much in the way of groups' and as a result could not 'do its job properly'.[72] The Communists, whose support base was overwhelmingly Protestant, were fighting to stop the campaign for civil rights becoming one for Catholic rights. Sinclair, for example, had stressed from the start that the property-based franchise denied the vote to Protestant workers too, and that their children were stuck in substandard schools.[73] Nevertheless, the civil rights strategy invariably remained focused on actual and alleged Catholic wrongs: the effect was to further deepen the community divide, rather than bridging it. This central weakness paralysed NICRA, turning it into yet another civil liberties group rather than a civil rights movement. NICRA's own authorised history admitted that during the first eighteen months its 'main activity was writing letters to the Government'. As other groups had already discovered, this tactic only yielded replies from Stormont 'denying that a particular abuse had occurred and suggesting that even if the NICRA allegation was true, there was probably a very good reason for the abuse'.[74]

Sinclair was one of the main opponents of Currie's suggested shift to the streets.[75] As a young Communist during the interwar years, she had seen what happened when the same shift was made by the Marxist Revolutionary Workers' Group. Communal violence around the Orange marching season in 1935 left ten dead, hundreds displaced, and Sinclair's party in decline.[76] But, as Kevin Boyle, one of McCann's comrades, later recalled: 'the people warning of the risks would always have grey hair. We couldn't be told, each generation cannot be told.'[77] Currie was born after the Belfast riots of the 1930s, and was not even a teenager when McAteer had been batoned off the streets of Derry in the 1950s: he did not have first-hand knowledge of the risks that he was taking. This mattered. King had argued in an article about the Selma marches in 1965 that 'the responsibility of weighing all the factors and estimating the consequences rests heavily on the civil rights leaders'. The temptation to 'go forward recklessly' had to be resisted, as it could have 'terrible consequences'.[78] Even the most successful formulas for non-violence were still volatile and unstable.

That the Coalisland–Dungannon march did not have terrible consequences is partly due to this very failure to grasp what had been happening in America. In the same article on Selma, King had explained that the 'goal of the demonstrations' was to 'dramatise the existence of injustice', to bring about a 'confrontation with injustice'.[79] However, non-violent confrontation was not what most people marching from Coalisland to Dungannon had set out to achieve, and those that did want it either did not know what they had to do or were stopped from doing it by the shape the protest took. As Sinclair had feared, this new departure resembled a traditional nationalist parade: five bands accompanied the march, Nationalist MPs were in the front ranks, IRA volunteers acted as stewards, and the Irish national anthem was sung. Currie and Fitt gave confrontational speeches, in which they used sectarian insults such as 'Orange bigots' and 'black bastards', yet their actions did not match this rhetoric. Fitt had claimed he would have led the march into the RUC lines, 'if it weren't for the presence of women and children'.[80] King, by contrast, had actually sent children into the arms of policemen, the teeth of German Shepherds, the water hoses of fireman, and the cells of the local jail, to save his Birmingham campaign.[81] Although the republican leadership was more comfortable with confrontation than the constitutional politicians, the marshals were still ordered to keep the crowd back from the RUC. A confidential document acquired by Special Branch stressed that there had to be 'no resistance'.[82] Youthful leftists from Belfast and Derry tried to resist by throwing 'stones, broken placards, and poles' at officers, but, as Currie remembered, they were 'prevented by the stewards from engaging in confrontation with the police'.[83] When the marchers finally began to disperse, some of the leftists clashed with loyalist counter-demonstrators before being cleared off the streets by the RUC – who were made to appear the neutral guardians of law and order.[84]

The following morning, Prime Minister Terence O'Neill read the

*Sunday Times* 'from cover to cover' and came across 'not a word about it': the world's press had no interest in covering a peaceful protest in rural Northern Ireland.[85] Northern Catholics had also largely ignored the march, with less than a tenth of the predicted 20,000 people turning up on the day.[86] Billy McMillen, a member of the IRA's Belfast brigade, concluded that the march as a 'disappointing anti-climax'.[87] Those outside the civil rights coalition were to deliver an even harsher verdict. Two days after the march, Coalisland's church hall was filled with people from the Dungannon area waiting to hear what the parish's senior curate had to say about what had happened. The police reported that the priest 'expressed the view that the march was a failure' and that the 'meeting endorsed these views'.[88] As King's 'long years of experience' had taught him, it was 'ineffective' to stage 'token marches avoiding direct confrontation', to stop short of 'revealing the continued presence of violence'.[89]

## DERRY

The radicals who had tried to confront the RUC in Dungannon were the organisers of the second civil rights march in Derry; with this protest, they succeeded in revealing the continued presence of violence in Northern Ireland. As McCann wrote in his memoirs, 'our conscious, if unspoken, strategy was to provoke the police into overreaction and thus spark off mass reaction against the authorities'. Everyone in Derry, McCann acknowledged, knew that the 'one certain way to ensure a head-on clash with the authorities was to organise a non-Unionist march through the city centre'.[90]

The Derry radicals were 'a complementary mix' of Labour militants, the republican left, and independent socialists.[91] This group did not defer to leaders in Belfast or Dublin, but instead 'used to just decide to do things standing at the corner. Someone would say "let's do such and such" and we'd say "yeah, let's go!" And then we'd do it. Immediately.'[92] During the first half of 1968, they had interrupted meetings of the corporation, picketed the Guildhall, staged a sit-down protest at the opening of the new bridge across the River Foyle, set up tenants' associations, resisted evictions, helped homeless families squat in empty houses, and blocked off roads with a caravan. When a policeman asked one of the demonstrators why he was stopping traffic, the officer was told: 'I hope that you will bring this matter to Court; then I will get the publicity I am looking for.'[93] However, the radicals were getting neither the publicity nor the support that they needed to

bring about what King called 'the presence of justice'.[94] They therefore chose to follow more closely the examples set by King and indeed
other western European leftists, by seeking a direct confrontation with
the police.[95]

Once again, when other people and groups were brought on board,
the militancy was muted. A NICRA delegation headed by Conn Mc-
Cluskey came to Derry on the eve of the civil rights march to inform
the organisers that the ban would not be challenged. The radicals,
though, had prepared for this eventuality: the NICRA members were
not taken to a private meeting with the planning committee, but to a
public meeting packed with leftists from across the country who had
no intention of conceding or even compromising. Gogarty eventually
broke off from his fellow delegates to side with the radicals, which
forced NICRA to back down to avoid splitting the coalition.[96]

The following day, 5 October 1968, people from every opposition
group in Northern Ireland gathered at the Waterside railway station.
IRA volunteers pushed politicians into the police line and Fitt cut his
head forcing his way through the cordon, but the officers largely maintained their discipline and even allowed an illegal meeting to be held
in front of them.[97] Sinclair used this opportunity to try to turn Derry
into a repeat of Dungannon, and called on the marchers to disperse
peacefully.[98] Civil rights activists were once more showing that they
either did not know how, or did not care, to bring about non-violent
confrontation; the radicals, however, had plans of their own. McCann
told the crowd that he was 'not advising anyone to rush the police cordon', but nor was he going to 'stop anyone' – and neither were the
marshals. When the meeting ended, over an hour after the march had
first moved off, the leftists threw broken placards at the police and
taunted them with chants of *Sieg Heil*.[99] About five minutes later, as the
Cameron commission concluded, 'the police broke ranks and used their
batons indiscriminately on people', in front of the television cameras.[100]
'The civil rights *movement* began then,' McCann told the *New Left
Review* in April 1969.[101]

'We have become a focus of world opinion,' O'Neill complained to
his cabinet after the march, which shattered the image that he had been
promoting of a 'calm' Northern Ireland, where 'slow but steady
progress' was being made. Westminster would now 'no longer be able
to stand aloof', bringing 'nearer a dreadfully dangerous review of our
whole constitutional position'.[102] The Derry radicals had hit upon the
right formula for Northern Ireland; the crisis had come. However, as
King had cautioned, the 'working out of this process has never been

simple or tranquil'.[103] Derry was certainly not tranquil on the weekend of the march, which exposed one of the weaknesses in the simple short cut the radicals had taken along the third road. On 6 October 1968, Catholic teenagers from the Bogside invaded the city centre and started to smash the windows of a Protestant-owned department store.[104] This contrasted sharply with how the children of Birmingham had behaved five years before, when they had taken over the downtown area of their city: weeks of workshops on non-violence had taught them to stage sit-ins, pickets and marches through the segregated shops.[105] Pacifist groups had offered to share their expertise with Northern Irish activists, but these invitations had not been pursued; it was only in the summer of 1969 that the Fellowship of Reconciliation organised a camp in Derry.[106] 'We had no understanding of the personal discipline involved in non-violent politics,' McCann later admitted.[107] The movement lacked discipline, but it did not lack energy; it was the constant conflict between the city's police and its youth that, as McCann argued in his memoirs, 'powered the civil rights campaign through its first frenetic months'.[108] While violence may not have been the essence of the civil rights movement, it was nonetheless there from the very start. Non-violent confrontation as practised by the leftists had succeeded in dramatising the existence of injustice. Yet, it fed off violence and neither the radicals nor indeed anyone else had the means of restraining this violence – which made it even more difficult to bring about the presence of justice.

NEW FORMS, OLD ROADS

On 5 October 1968 the Derry radicals had brought into being 'a ready-made mass movement'.[109] The New Left worldview had inspired a small band of young people to believe that a socialist future was possible for Ireland, and that they should take unusual, risky actions to achieve it. This way of thinking had taken Northern Ireland along the third road, the road of non-violent direct action, but it could not direct the thousands of people who were now on the streets. Other, older, ways of thinking could. The nationalist and republican traditions were embedded in poetry, books, newspapers, plays, songs, ceremonies, commemorations and monuments – put simply, Irish culture.[110] Constitutional nationalism and militant republicanism were still relevant to Irish culture and to the current political situation, so they were reworked for the Troubles. A crisis that constitutional nationalism and militant republicanism could not have caused was to help resurrect both these political traditions; the civil rights movement's long and difficult birth was to be followed by a short and difficult existence. As early as July 1969, the Derry Labour Party was claiming that it had become 'a sick joke' to describe the movement as '"non-violent", "non-sectarian", and "non-political"'.[111]

The following month, August 1969, McCann tried to understand how this had happened by looking back to the days after 5 October 1968. 'People who had scorned and slandered the organisers of the march,' he wrote, 'now came with offers of advice, offers of assistance and protestations of support. They did it very well. By October 9th they had created and had begun to dominate a new organisation – the [Derry] Citizens Action Committee [DCAC].'[112] McCann had walked out of the meeting that set up the DCAC, telling reporters that it was 'middle-aged, middle class and middle of the road'.[113] However, this was not so much an insult as an accurate assessment of the qualities that the conservative Catholic population of Derry were looking for in the men at the head of the movement. Indeed, the DCAC's Paddy Doherty recalled that there was 'general relief that control of the campaign for civil rights had passed from Eamonn McCann and his followers to … more solid, representative leaders'.[114]

The moderates immediately put a stop to plans that the radicals had to hold a one-hour strike and to restage the march because of the danger of further violence.[115] Although DCAC members continued to talk about 'non-violence', what they meant was that they wanted their marches and meetings to be peaceful. The new leaders and the new movement were more comfortable with the traditional nationalist protest repertoire than with the tactics of civil disobedience.[116] This was the case even with the strategies that had their roots in Ireland: a boycott of segregated stores had been at the heart of King's Birmingham campaign, but John Hume, the DCAC's vice-chairman, was 'totally and completely against this sort of action because it was unjust'.[117] The popularity of Hume and his approach was demonstrated in the February 1969 Stormont elections, when he easily defeated both McAteer and McCann to become MP for Foyle.[118] McAteer lamented that Hume had simply achieved the 'efficient takeover of the work which has been carried on for many years by us'.[119] Hume would get much further with this work than McAteer did because the Troubles meant that the Unionists, the British, the Southern Irish and the Americans now wanted to deal with the leader of constitutional nationalism.

While thousands marched behind Hume and voted for him in the election, hundreds disregarded his calls to remain peaceful. On 3

January 1969, for example, Hume addressed a crowd of about 800 people who had gathered outside a Paisleyite prayer meeting in the Guildhall, asking them to leave the scene. They did not; instead they set fire to a car, looted shops and clashed with the Paisleyites, the RUC and the stewards. The district inspector policing the event reported that the 'Citizens' Action Committee had lost control'.[120] The gangs of Catholic youths that were ambushing Protestants and fighting with the police were soon singing republican songs and shouting slogans such as 'Up the IRA'.[121] For those who wanted to hit back, militant republicanism offered them a way of making sense of their situation. It explained that Northern Ireland was by its very nature sectarian and could not be reformed, that the IRA was the sole defender of their community against loyalists in and out of uniform, and that armed struggle was the only road to a united Ireland. As McCann explained to the *New Left Review*, the 'idea of revolution is not at all alien to the Irish working class ... and when one calls for revolution, no matter what one actually demands there is always a link ... to 1916'.[122] A short, straight road did not stretch from the Waterside railway station to the paramilitary violence of the Troubles, but some people, however, did take a long, twisted road to taking up arms. The crisis sparked by the 5 October 1968 march raised excessive hopes and fears; the state responded with a crackdown and a set of concessions that satisfied neither community and instead of bringing a resolution brought polarisation; militants on both sides became locked into an escalating cycle of violence with each other and with the security forces; and a decade after the Border Campaign had been quelled, the armed struggle broke out again with another IRA.

## EPIPHANY

On 21 December 1968, in a paper that was widely circulated, Gogarty reflected on what lay ahead for the civil rights movement in the year to come. He recognised that the 'brutal and repressive response of an arrogant regime' had brought 'tremendous success', but that it was now 'very doubtful [that] marches ... will achieve much more'. Staying with the same strategy would be 'pushing luck too far', as 'an unfavourable public reaction is not unlikely'. So, yet again, 'a programme of Civil Disobedience' was proposed. Gogarty's plan, by contrast, was written by someone who had obviously studied the 'science of non-violence'. Gogarty made clear that civil disobedience 'must always be adapted to suit the local scene', and that 'the advice of experts' should be taken as to 'just how and when any co-ordinated action ... can be effectively implemented in Northern Ireland'. Taking inspiration from across the Atlantic and from across Irish history, he recommended 'occupation', 'Boycott', 'Disruption of public transport', 'Hunger strike', 'Local elections based on the Universal Adult Franchise', 'Non-payment of rates' – and 'establishing a TV image'. Before any of this could start, however, the 'general public' had to be 'educated in all its aspects ... by lecture, symposium and public meeting'.[123]

The confidence with which Gogarty presented this plan was continuously undercut by a frustrating awareness that he was powerless to implement it. He complained, 'the civil rights movement is not at present contemplating a programme of civil disobedience' and that leading activists were still 'ignorant of the know-how and the potentialities' of non-violence. The movement was 'in great danger of betrayal'.[124] Just over a week later, the leftists marched for four days from Belfast to Derry through the Protestant heartland of Northern Ireland, and were ambushed by loyalists at Burntollet.[125] The *Observer* journalist Mary Holland was in Derry to see the DCAC receive the marchers and address the thousands waiting in Guildhall Square. She heard the moderates 'begging the people to go home, to refrain from violence, and to think of world opinion. The crowd said what they thought of world opinion in no uncertain terms, asked what it had ever done for the poor of Derry, and told their "leaders" that they were too late.'[126] The movement had become an insurrection. The following month, on 18 February 1969, Gogarty sent a letter to a friend in Canada offering 'a brief survey' of 'the revolution' that was soaked in bitterness. 'I went out to get myself another drink & reread what I have just written,' he added at the end, 'it is horrible but I will let it stand.'[127]

NOTES

1. International Civil Rights Conference, 4–5 October 2008, in Derry, Northern Ireland (personal notes).
2. *Derry Journal*, 3 October 2008.
3. Anne Devlin, 'The Long March' in *Ourselves Alone, with A Woman Calling and The Long March* (London: Faber, 1986), p.155.
4. See, for instance, Austin Currie, *All Hell Will Break Loose* (Dublin: O'Brien Press, 2004), and Alvin Jackson, *Ireland 1798–1998* (Oxford: Blackwell, 1999).
5. James Joyce, *Dubliners* (Harmondsworth: Penguin, 2000).
6. Confidential memorandum, undated, Dublin, National Archives Ireland (NAI), S 9361 G.
7. Frank Curran, *Derry: Countdown to Disaster* (Dublin: Gill & Macmillan, 1986), p.14.
8. Brendan Lynn, *Holding the Ground: The Nationalist Party in Northern Ireland, 1945–72* (Aldershot: Ashgate, 1997), pp.26–8, 33, 48, 52 and 61.
9. *Derry Journal*, 8 October 1968; Brendan Lynn, 'Nationalist Politics in Derry 1945–1969' in Gerard O'Brien (ed.), *Derry and Londonderry – History and Society: Interdisciplinary Essays*

*on the History of an Irish County* (Dublin: Geography Publications, 1999), pp.601–24, pp.605 and 606.

10. Eddie McAteer, *Irish Action: New Thoughts on an Old Subject* (Belfast: Athol Books, 1979), p.56.
11. Lynn, *Holding the Ground*, p.130.
12. IRA, 'Proclamation of 12 December 1956', cited in J. Bowyer Bell, *The Secret Army: The IRA, 1916–1979* (Dublin: Poolbeg Press, 1989), p.291.
13. Brian Hanley and Scott Millar, *The Lost Revolution: The Story of the Official IRA and the Workers' Party* (Dublin: Penguin, 2009), p.14.
14. Henry Patterson, *Ireland Since 1939: The Persistence of Conflict* (Dublin: Penguin, 2006), p.136.
15. Henry Patterson, *The Politics of Illusion: A Political History of the IRA* (London: Serif, 1997), p.92.
16. *United Irishman* (March 1962).
17. *Derry Journal*, 25 June 1968.
18. Currie, *All Hell Will Break Loose*, p.99.
19. Richard Rose, *Governing without Consensus: An Irish Perspective* (London: Faber, 1971), pp.457–73.
20. Reinhold Niebuhr, *Moral Man and Immoral Society: A Study in Ethics and Politics* (London: Charles Scribner's Sons, 1932), pp.241–4.
21. Mahatma Gandhi, *Essential Writings* (Oxford: Oxford University Press, 2008), p.314.
22. Niebuhr, *Moral Man and Immoral Society*, p.250.
23. Ibid., pp.252–3.
24. Sean Chabot and Jan Willem Duyvendak, 'Globalization and the Transnational Diffusion Between Social Movements: Reconceptualizing the Dissemination of the Gandhian Repertoire and the "Coming Out" Routine', *Theory and Society*, vol. 31 (2002), pp.697–740, pp.699, 701, 706 and 727–8.
25. Taylor Branch, *Parting the Waters: America in the King Years 1954–63* (London: Simon & Schuster, 1988), p.87.
26. McAteer, *Irish Action*, pp.52–3.
27. Lynn, 'Nationalist Politics in Derry 1945–1969', p.607.
28. Lynn, *Holding the Ground*, p.55.
29. McAteer, *Irish Action*, p.53.
30. Gandhi, *Essential Writings*, p.94.
31. CSJ, 'Northern Ireland – The Plain Truth' (second edition), in Conn McCluskey, *Up Off Their Knees: Commentary on the Civil Rights Movement in Northern Ireland* (Dublin: Conn McCluskey, 1989), p.217.
32. Patterson, *Ireland since 1939*, p.193.
33. Www.news.bbc.co.uk/panorama/hi/front_page/newsid_8454000/8454813.stm, accessed 25 January 2010.
34. *Dungannon Observer*, 18 May 1963.
35. Ibid., 15 June 1963.
36. Marisa Chappell, Jenny Hutchinson, and Brian Ward, '"Dress Modestly, Neatly ... As If You Were Going to Church": Respectability, Class, and Gender in the Montgomery Bus Boycott and the Early Civil Rights Movement' in Peter J. Ling and Sharon Monteith (eds), *Gender in the Civil Rights Movement* (London: Garland, 1999), pp.69–100, pp.72–3 and 88.
37. For a fuller study of the role of gender and class, see Tara Keenan-Thomson, 'From Co-op to Co-opt: Gender and Class in the Early Civil Rights Movement', *The Sixties*, vol. 2 (2009), pp.207–25.
38. *Dungannon Observer*, 31 August 1963.
39. McCluskey, *Up Off Their Knees*, p.13.
40. *Belfast Telegraph*, 4 September 1963.
41. *Tyrone Courier and Dungannon News*, 6 June 1963.
42. Tara Keenan Thomson interview with the McCluskeys, 5 March 2003, Foxrock, Ireland (personal notes).
43. Tara Keenan-Thomson interview with Dinsmore, 25 November 2003, Dungannon (personal notes).
44. Conn McCluskey to Minister of Health and Local Government, 14 December 1964, Belfast, Public Record Office of Northern Ireland (PRONI), D/2993.
45. *Dungannon Observer*, 7 September 1963; *Dungannon Observer*, 21 September 1963.

46. McCluskey, *Up Off Their Knees*, pp.10–12, 16–17 and 129.
47. *Tyrone Courier and Dungannon News*, 23 January 1964.
48. CSJ, 'What the Papers Say', cited in Bob Purdie, *Politics in the Streets: The Origins of the Civil Rights Movement in Northern Ireland* (Belfast: Blackstaff Press, 1990), p.98.
49. Introduction to the Files of the Campaign for Democracy in Ulster, 8 April 1974, PRONI, D/3026/1; Patrick Byrne to Conn and Patricia McCluskey, 13 August 1967, PRONI, D/3026/1.
50. Peter Rose, *How the Troubles Came to Northern Ireland* (Basingstoke: Palgrave, 2000), pp.48 and 89.
51. *Contemporary British History*, Witness Seminar on British Policy in Northern Ireland 1964–1970, 14 January 1992, in London, England.
52. Memorandum to the Central Committee of the Campaign for Democracy in Ulster, Kevin McNamara Papers, cited in Rose, *How the Troubles Came to Northern Ireland*, p.103.
53. Witness Seminar, 14 January 1992.
54. RUC Report on Civil Rights March from Coalisland to Dungannon, 29 August 1968, PRONI, CAB/9B/1205/7.
55. *Disturbances in Northern Ireland: Report of the Commission Appointed by the Governor of Northern Ireland (Cameron Report)* (Belfast: Her Majesty's Stationery Office, 1969), p.21; Graham Gudgin, 'Discrimination in Housing and Employment under the Stormont Administration' in P.Roche and B. Barton (eds), *The Northern Ireland Question: Nationalism, Unionism and Partition* (Aldershot: Ashgate, 1999), pp.97–121, p.100.
56. Brian Dooley, *Black and Green: The Fight for Civil Rights in Northern Ireland and Black America* (London: Pluto Press, 1998), p.47.
57. RUC Report on Civil Rights March from Coalisland to Dungannon; Currie, *All Hell Will Break Loose*, pp.96–8.
58. Northern Irish Civil Rights Association (NICRA), *We Shall Overcome ... The History of the Struggle for Civil Rights in Northern Ireland, 1968–78* (Belfast: NICRA, 1978), p.9.
59. Dooley, *Black and Green*, p.49.
60. *Cameron Report*, pp.21–2; Currie, *All Hell Will Break Loose*, pp.100–1.
61. Introduction to the Frank Gogarty Papers, PRONI, D/3253/1.
62. *Fortnight*, 5 April 1974.
63. *Dungannon Observer*, 3 August 1968.
64. *Irish Democrat* (August 1968).
65. Roy Johnston, *Century of Endeavour: A Biographical and Autobiographical View of the 20th Century in Ireland* (Dublin: Lilliput Press, 2002), p.235; *Irish Democrat* (April 1965).
66. Simon Prince, *Northern Ireland's '68: Civil Rights, Global Revolt and the Origins of the Troubles* (Dublin: Irish Academic Press, 2007), p.47.
67. Joint Memorandum on Citizens' Rights, 1966, PRONI, CAB/4/1347.
68. Memorandum by the Attorney General, 28 October 1966, PRONI, CAB/4/1347.
69. *Tuairisc* (August 1966).
70. *Irish Democrat* (March 1967).
71. *Tuairisc* (August 1966).
72. Johnston, *Century of Endeavour*, pp.217–18.
73. *Irish Democrat* (March 1967); Tony Coughlan, *Draft History of the Connolly Association* (unpublished manuscript).
74. NICRA, *We Shall Overcome*, p.11.
75. Currie, *All Hell Will Break Loose*, p.101.
76. Mike Milotte, *Communism in Modern Ireland: The Pursuit of the Workers' Republic since 1916* (Dublin: Gill & Macmillan, 1984), pp.136 and 164; Patterson, *Ireland since 1939*, pp.10 and 13.
77. Simon Prince interview with Kevin Boyle, November 2006, Chelmsford, Britain (personal notes).
78. Martin Luther King, Jr, 'Behind the Selma March', *Saturday Review*, 3 April 1965.
79. Ibid.
80. RUC Report on Civil Rights March from Coalisland to Dungannon.
81. Andrew M. Manis, *A Fire You Can't Put Out: The Civil Rights Life of Birmingham's Reverend Fred Shuttlesworth* (Birmingham, AL: University of Alabama Press, 1999), p.368.
82. County Inspector David Johnston to J.G. Hill, 7 July 1969, PRONI, HA/32/2/28.
83. Currie, *All Hell Will Break Loose*, p.106.
84. RUC Report on Civil Rights March from Coalisland to Dungannon.
85. Terence O'Neill, *The Autobiography of Terence O'Neill* (London: Faber, 1972), p.102.

86. *Dungannon Observer*, 24 August 1968.
87. Hanley and Millar, *Lost Revolution*, p.103.
88. RUC Report on Civil Rights March from Coalisland to Dungannon.
89. King, 'Behind the Selma March'.
90. Eamonn McCann, *War and an Irish Town* (London: Pluto, 1993), p.91.
91. Fionbarra Ó Dochartaigh, *Ulster's White Negroes: From Civil Rights to Insurrection* (Edinburgh: AK Press, 1994), pp.15 and 19.
92. Margot Gayle Backus, '"Not Quite Philadelphia, Is It?": An Interview with Eamonn McCann', *Éire-Ireland*, vols 3–4 (2001), pp.178–91, p.183.
93. *Derry Journal*, 5 July 1968.
94. King, 'Behind the Selma March'.
95. See Prince, *Northern Ireland's '68*.
96. McCluskey, *Up Off Their Knees*, pp.110–11; McCann, *War and an Irish Town*, pp.96–7.
97. Hanley and Millar, *Lost Revolution*, p.104.
98. *Derry Journal*, 8 October 1968.
99. Northern Ireland Civil Rights Association Parade and Meeting in Londonderry on Saturday 5 October 1968, PRONI, HA/32/2/26; *Derry Journal*, 6 December 1968.
100. *Cameron Report*, p.29; Rex Cathcart, *The Most Contrary Region: The BBC in Northern Ireland, 1924–84* (Belfast: Blackstaff Press, 1984), pp.198–9 and 207–8.
101. *New Left Review* (May–June 1969).
102. Memorandum by the Prime Minister, 14 October 1968, PRONI, CAB/4/1406.
103. King, 'Behind the Selma March'.
104. *Derry Journal*, 25 October 1968.
105. Branch, *Parting the Waters*, pp.752 and 777.
106. Mitchell, 'Peace Groups since the 1930s', *DAWN – An Irish Journal of Nonviolence*, nos. 38–9 (April 1978), pp.32–42, 37.
107. Lorenzo Bosi, 'The Dynamics of Social Movement Development: Northern Ireland's Civil Rights Movement in the 1960s', *Mobilization*, vol. 11 (2006), pp.81–100, p.84.
108. McCann, *War and an Irish Town*, p.113.
109. Eamonn McCann, 'Who's Wrecking Civil Rights?', August 1969, PRONI, HA/32/2/28.
110. Aldon Morris and Naomi Braine, 'Social Movements and Oppositional Consciousness' in Jane Mansbridge and Aldon Morris (eds), *Oppositional Consciousness: The Subjective Roots of Social Protest* (Chicago, IL: Univeristy of Chicago Press, 2001), pp.20–37, p.23.
111. Derry Labour Party and Young Socialists pamphlet, 19 July 1969, PRONI, HA/32/2/28.
112. McCann, 'Who's Wrecking Civil Rights?'
113. *Londonderry Sentinel*, 16 October 1968.
114. Paddy Doherty, *Paddy Bogside* (Dublin: Mercier Press, 2001), p.62.
115. *Londonderry Sentinel*, 16 October 1968.
116. For a fuller discussion, see Gianluca De Fazio, 'Civil Rights Mobilization and Repression in Northern Ireland: A Comparison with the US Deep South', *The Sixties*, vol. 2 (2009), pp.163–85.
117. *Derry Journal*, 28 January 1969.
118. *Derry Journal*, 28 February 1969.
119. Eddie McAteer to Corinne Philpott, 24 March 1969, cited in Enda Staunton, *The Nationalists of Northern Ireland 1918–1973* (Blackrock: Columba Press, 2001), p.260.
120. District Inspector McGimpsey, 'Incidents at Guildhall Square, Londonderry, on the evening of Friday 3rd January 1969', 14 January 1969, PRONI, HA/32/2/26.
121. District Inspector Bill Meharg to J.E. Greeves, 28 January 1969, PRONI, HA/32/2/26, details an assault on a Protestant by five men armed with knives; a court case relating to an incident with the police is covered in the *Derry Journal*, 26 August 1969.
122. *New Left Review* (May–June 1969).
123. Frank Gogarty, 'Towards a Programme of Campaign for 1969', December 1968, Belfast, Linen Hall Library Political Collection, P1063.
124. Ibid.
125. Bowes Egan and Vincent McCormack, *Burntollet* (London: LRS, 1969), pp.26–40; and police report.
126. *Observer*, 5 January 1969.
127. *Defamator*, no. 4, PRONI, D/3219/3; Frank Gogarty to George, 18 February 1969, PRONI, D/3253/1.

# CHAPTER NINE

# The David Thornley Affair: Republicanism and the Irish Labour Party

## SHAUN McDAID

This chapter examines the politics of Dr David Thornley, historian, broadcaster, Irish Labour Party (ILP) TD and Member of the European Parliament (MEP). His career in political office spanned 1969 to 1977. It will discuss Thornley's views on the national question within the wider context of both the ILP's officially stated policy towards Northern Ireland and the views of some of its more prominent members throughout the party's long history. In particular, the extent to which Thornley's views on Northern Ireland diverged from those of his contemporaries within the party, and how far his position on the national question was in abeyance with party policy, will be explored. The attempt to examine Thornley's attitude to the national question will not be limited to his political utterances; his historical writings will also be examined in an attempt to piece together the views of this complex, difficult, but undoubtedly gifted individual.

David Thornley was born in England to Irish parents in July 1935. As a youth, he returned to Ireland and was educated at Sutton, county Dublin, before enrolling at Trinity College Dublin at the age of 16, where he studied history and political science. In 1959 he was awarded a PhD by the same university for his thesis on Isaac Butt and the Home Rule movement. However, it is for his work as a broadcaster with RTÉ that Thornley is perhaps best known and most widely remembered by his contemporaries, having been a presenter and contributor to the popular current affairs programmes, 7 Days and Division.[1] Thornley, like others discussed in this volume, has been chosen because of the controversy surrounding his political ideology. Although he was, during his parliamentary career, a member of the ILP – a party committed to national unity by peaceful means alone – his position on the national question, and in particular his attitude to militant republicanism, remains a source of contention. This is largely due to his appearance on a speaking platform at an illegal demonstration in Dublin organised by Provisional Sinn Féin in 1976, which took place in defiance of a government ban. The events surrounding this occurrence will be of central importance in this chapter. Depending on one's interpretation, Thornley's attitude towards the national question can therefore be viewed as either constitutional or revolutionary, or a mixture of both these contradictory positions. This apparent dichotomy in his political ideology will be addressed in further detail.

Until recently, no single work of academic literature has focused on Thornley's life and politics. However, in 2008 a volume of essays entitled *Unquiet Spirit: Essays in Memory of David Thornley* was published, edited by Thornley's daughter, Yseult.[2] This book contains some of Thornley's collected writings and speeches, and also reminiscences about him by his family, friends and colleagues. While a book about Thornley is both welcome and overdue, the book, by its nature, eschews a more forensic criticism of his political ideology that a standard biography might be expected to provide. That is not to suggest that Thornley's appearance on the Sinn Féin platform was ignored in *Unquiet Spirit*; however, it is fair to suggest that the subject is dealt with in a sympathetic manner. This chapter will provide a more critical account of this incident, which ultimately cost Thornley his political career. The use of archival sources will provide a more detailed account of Thornley's career than has hitherto been available. To begin, Thornley's views on the national question and the ILP's attitudes towards republicanism, particularly during the period 1969–77, will be considered.

### THE IRISH LABOUR PARTY AND THE NATIONAL QUESTION

While both Fine Gael and Fianna Fáil can trace their origins to the Sinn Féin organisation, which was central to the struggle to achieve independence from 1919 to 1921, the ILP has no such heritage. It began life in 1912 as the political wing of a trade union movement, the Irish Trades Union Congress and Labour Party. Its primary objective was to organise and unite the workers of Ireland and to improve their conditions generally.[3] It has never been a Marxist organisation, and it has counted few genuine adherents to that political faith among its ranks throughout its history.

During the 1918 general election, the ILP acceded to a request from Sinn Féin not to field candidates on the grounds that the national question was more important than the socioeconomic problems plaguing Ireland at that time. As a 'reward' for stepping aside, Sinn Féin invited the ILP leaders to draft the socioeconomic policy, or 'Democratic Programme', for the new Irish parliament.[4] In the short term, however, this decision did not hamper the ILP's electoral fortunes. In the 1922 general election the party won 21.4 per cent of the vote – a figure higher than that of the anti-Treatyites – and returned seventeen of its eighteen candidates.[5]

The effects of the civil war on the party were 'more enduring'.[6] Since 1922 the political cleavage in Ireland has been defined by the civil war. This is not necessarily unusual in a European context: the political cleavage in Greece and Spain is similarly defined by civil war. However, in Ireland, the result of this legacy has been to retard the development of a left-right alignment in the state's electoral politics.[7]Consequently, the political culture of the state has tended to be defined by the national question, with a generally conservative consensus on socioeconomic matters becoming apparent. The ILP has also avoided compensating for its lack of economic radicalism by embracing a more republican political ideology. However, it has been contended that the ILP had a more republican outlook at various times in its history.

In 1942 rumours circulated that Peadar O'Donnell, the veteran anti-Treaty republican, and Seán MacBride, the former (short-lived) IRA chief-of-staff, would stand as ILP candidates in the upcoming local elections. Nothing, however, came of these. The party also criticised the government for its stance towards the republican hunger-strikers of the 1940s. However, this criticism essentially focused on the apparent incongruity of de Valera's revolutionary past as compared to his uncompromising attitude to challenges to the state's legitimacy when in power. If indeed the ILP did benefit from republican support, then the benefit proved to be short-lived: the party's vote declined from 15.7 per cent in 1943 to 8.8 per cent in 1944.[8]

Michael Gallagher has argued that by 1957 Labour had become 'the most republican of the three main parties' in Dáil Éireann.[9] Prima facie, the ILP certainly appears to have taken a more republican line during the 1950s, and William Norton, the party leader, called for partition to be ended at its annual conference in 1957. In the same year, Gallagher contends, the future ILP leader Brendan Corish stated that he would be 'prepared to chance' the fact that a potential 32-county government would have to coerce unionists into an acceptance of united Ireland.[10] But, on closer inspection, what Corish actually said was that he would be prepared to chance that 'whatever form of government there is in the 32 counties would be acceptable to the [unionist] minority'.[11] Earlier in the debate, Corish 'violently disagreed' with 'the use of force',[12] stating that those who approved of the IRA should 'think about what it means in terms of human life and human suffering'.[13] This was hardly irredentist in tone and does not suggest that the ILP had a more republican outlook than any other party in Dáil Éireann at the time.

This moderate policy continued after the outbreak of the Troubles in Northern Ireland in 1968. The ILP's Northern Ireland policy was indisputably constitutional in nature. While the party maintained its call for an all-Ireland socialist republic, this was to be voluntary and achieved by 'persuasion, dialogue and communication, not by the bomb and the bullet'.[14] Apart from the tokenistic references to socialism, it differed little from Fianna Fáil's stated Northern Ireland policy as announced by Jack Lynch in Tralee in September 1969,[15] and later at the party's Ard Fhéis in January 1970, which sought the end of partition by peaceful means.[16] The ILP's commitment to a somewhat vague constitutional nationalism was confirmed in 1972 with its endorsement of the Social Democratic Labour Party's (SDLP) *Towards a New Ireland* policy document. Some prominent members of the ILP openly disagreed with the acceptance of the SDLP's policy, but at its 1972 conference violence was emphatically rejected, as were amendments tabled in support of the IRA campaign.[17] Thornley criticised the party for turning its back on the principles of Marxist republicanism as espoused by James Connolly. The hanging of Connolly's portrait at the party conference was considered by Thornley as somewhat disingenuous. He argued that if the party forgot the legacy of Connolly, then it should replace his portrait with 'that of John Dillon'.[18]

As the Troubles in Northern Ireland worsened, the relationship between both the ILP and the SDLP deteriorated, culminating in a refusal by the ILP to support the SDLP's 1975 annual collection, on the basis that prominent members of the northern party had overzealously criticised members of the Parliamentary Labour Party.[19] However, there was no 'greening' of the ILP's official Northern Ireland policy during this period. Thus the Labour Party did not, at any stage of its history, advocate Irish unification by force of arms. In 1983 the veteran TD Kevin Boland somewhat unkindly noted that he only ever knew of two ILP members who were concerned with republican matters and both of them were dead. One was trade union leader Michael Mullen, who had served time for republican offences; the other was David Thornley.[20]

## DAVID THORNLEY: EARLY LIFE AND CAREER

Thornley moved to Ireland as a youth and appears to have been brought up in a republican household; books by Dan Breen and Desmond Ryan provided the young Thornley with a very particular view of the revolutionary period, one he seems to have held until the end of his life.[21] He was also a devout Catholic, and sang tenor at Dublin's Westland Row Church. His love of music was well known. He was particularly fond of the American singer Paul Robeson, a socialist who famously became involved in a Welsh miner's dispute.

While perhaps best known for his role as a television presenter, Thornley began his career as a lecturer in politics at Trinity College Dublin. He was remembered as a good teacher, more approachable than the older Trinity historians, Theo Moody, Leland Lyons and the eccentric R.B. McDowell.[22] His key academic work was his study of Isaac Butt, the progenitor of modern constitutional nationalism; *Isaac Butt and Home Rule* was published in 1964. While Thornley was an advocate of the radical republicanism of James Connolly, his work as a historian does not display any particular republican bias. In academic affairs, he appears to have achieved the admirable feat of empathy with his source material without becoming the servant of any particular ideological dogma.

As a historian, he was not a follower of Irish republican myth, as his work on Butt clearly illustrates. For example, he argued that the 'extent to which the Irish people were immutably committed to separatism [in the nineteenth century] can be grossly exaggerated; a study of the election of 1868 reveals, perhaps, how close Ireland came ... to the acceptance of Liberal unionism'.[23] In this work, he also cautioned that 'there is no more dangerous simplification of our history than to regard the desire of the Irish people for independence as an immutable force, an historic nationhood ... always recognisable as the incorruptible will of the folk to satisfy its group consciousness by the purging from its soil of the invader'.[24]

Butt, Thornley argued, 'awoke the spirit of constitutional nationalism which was to judge him' for not being radical enough in his pursuit of home government for Ireland.[25] Similarly, he contended that Butt's conservative political philosophy, particularly after 1848, was largely 'irrelevant' and resulted in the stagnation of Butt's political career for two decades.[26] The portrayal of Butt is thus of a man often out of step with nationalist Ireland, almost destined to be replaced by Parnell, who was more attuned to contemporary nationalist Irish opinion. However, while Thornley's portrayal of Butt as a man 'destined to miss the nationalist boat' might have some merit, it perhaps overstates the extent to which he was attempting to catch the 'nationalist boat' in the first place. As Roy Foster has noted, Butt 'might equally be seen as someone with a Protestant, even Orange, pedigree who shared in and helped create a sense of Irishness that accepted historic English influence while claiming realistic autonomy, and required no apology for its credentials at all'.[27] Indeed, viewed in this way, Butt could perhaps be classified as a variety of modern Irish unionist.

Thornley's work on Patrick H. Pearse, signatory of the 1916 Proclamation, sought to tackle republican mythology head on. He argued that it was 'not merely difficult but almost blasphemous to discern a human being of flesh and blood' in Pearse. However, for Thornley, 'it is the historian's obligation to make the attempt'. He criticised the hagiographical tone of Louis Le Roux's 1933 biography of Pearse, at that time the only full-length study of the 1916 veteran's life. In this book, Le Roux argued that it would be unsurprising if Pearse was someday canonised, since, in his view, he possessed 'all the qualities which go to the making of a saint'.[28] No such sanctification was attempted by Thornley, who among other things challenged Pearse's reading of history: that the Irish separatist tradition began in 1169 and embraced the supporters of Edward Bruce, Art MacMurrough, Shane O'Neill and just about everyone else who had ever taken up arms in Ireland.[29] For all Thornley's republicanism, he did not attempt to distort the facts of the past in order to enhance Pearse's reputation. As Conor Cruise O'Brien noted, the historian interprets, but there are 'great brute facts that he can't interpret away'.[30] Thornley certainly had enough respect for the discipline of history to avoid such ideologically motivated tampering with the facts.

Despite his devotion to the Catholic faith, Thornley often found himself in disagreement with the Catholic hierarchy regarding its social teaching, in particular the issue of contraception. He became involved in a public debate with the outspoken Dungannon cleric, Father Denis Faul, after the latter's published correspondence in the *Irish Times* denouncing the use of the contraception.[31] Thornley wrote to the same newspaper proclaiming that if he once more had to read 'the pontifications of the celibate Father Denis Faul on the mysterious workings of the male and female genitalia, I confess I shall bring up my breakfast'. He went on to add: 'if Faul or Faulkner, give me Faulkner ... It is the Fauls who cause the Paisleys'.[32] Thornley was not one to impose his brand of religion on others. In 1974 he publicly criticised the Taoiseach, Liam Cosgrave, for voting against his own government's bill on the liberalisation of contraception, arguing that Cosgrave had 'behaved like an idiot' in so doing.[33] It was clearly politically inexpedient to be involved in such debate given, as Noel Browne noted, that the subjects of sex and socialism caused the most anxiety in Ireland.[34]

Thornley was well equipped for such high-profile debate in the national media. He had enjoyed considerable success as a current affairs journalist with RTÉ. His greatest achievement in broadcasting was the influential *7 Days* programme concerning the referendum on the voting system. During the campaign in 1968 by the Fianna Fáil government to amend the constitution to change the voting system from proportional representation (PR-STV) to first-past-the-post, Thornley and his colleague Basil Chubb's analysis showed that such a move would ensure a Fianna Fáil majority in perpetuity, and the referendum was defeated.[35]

Following his election to Dáil Éireann in 1969, Thornley devoted less time to his historical work and more to political activity. Even more time was devoted to politics after his appointment as an MEP in June 1973. He had previously dabbled in politics, having been involved in Noel Browne's electoral campaigns in 1954 and 1957. Browne, described by Conor Cruise O'Brien as 'half mad and dangerous to know', downplayed the role of Thornley in his electoral success.[36] Thornley was also active in the establishment of the left-wing think tank, the '1913 Club', established in 1957, whose members included Owen Dudley Edwards and Aidan Clarke.[37] In Strasbourg, he served on three parliamentary committees: economic and monetary affairs, cultural and youth affairs, and external EEC relations. There is little evidence, however, that he took his role as an MEP all that seriously. He earned one of the quotes of the year from the *Irish Times* in 1975, when he observed: 'when I attend a session of the European Parliament, I don't know what I'm talking about half the time'.[38] The political lifestyle, combined with his increasingly heavy drinking, took an unfortunate toll on Thornley's health. It appears that from 1969 onwards he became more republican in outlook and more attracted to the politics of violence. The outbreak of the Troubles in Northern Ireland provided the impetus for this republicanisation.

## DAVID THORNLEY AND NORTHERN IRELAND

Following the outbreak of violence in Northern Ireland in 1968, it was clear that David Thornley was somewhat out of step with the ILP's Northern policy; a policy that was primarily formulated by Conor Cruise O'Brien, the party's spokesman on foreign affairs since 1969. Both O'Brien and Thornley had been elected to Dáil Éireann at the 1969 election; Thornley topped the poll in Dublin North-West, the first ILP candidate ever to do so.[39] O'Brien's diplomatic experience made him the obvious choice for the foreign affairs spokesman, but it is doubtful that he would have been given the job had it been known how events in Northern Ireland would transpire. O'Brien's open hostility to traditional nationalism was no secret, and he was already on record for describing the Irish constitution as annexationist and irredentist.[40] Both outspoken and opinionated individuals, a rift between O'Brien and Thornley was practically unavoidable. Indeed, following the publication of O'Brien's controversial and retrospectively influential *States of Ireland*, a critique of the traditional nationalist analysis of the 'Irish problem', Thornley was incensed, calling unsuccessfully for O'Brien's expulsion from the ILP.[41]

Thornley's was not the only republican voice in the ILP at the time. His views were mirrored by those of Tipperary TD, Sean Treacy, and controversial Limerick deputy, Stephen Coughlan. The latter, notorious for his right-wing views, had opposed the anti-apartheid campaign against the Springbok rugby team's visit to Limerick, threatening fellow party member and anti-apartheid campaigner Barry Desmond with a kick 'up the transom' if he showed his face in the city.[42] Coughlan was also accused of remarks justifying the 1904 campaign of violence against Jews in Limerick, and had led a campaign against a small number of Maoists who found themselves living in Limerick in 1969.[43] Both Coughlan and Treacy had empathised with Northern Irish Catholics who had resorted to violence against what they saw as the oppressive unionist government in the region.[44] Thornley's views on Northern Ireland were broadly similar, and he was to enunciate them vocally on a number of occasions.

Despite his interest in the plight of Catholics across the border, however, Thornley never actually visited Northern Ireland. Thornley's former student, Rodney Rice, recalls being wrestled by Thornley at a New Year's Eve party, the third victim of Thornley's horseplay on that occasion. Thornley later boasted of having 'taken on the three biggest men in the room'.[45] But physical courage did not extend to making the journey northwards. He had been debating whether or not to go to Belfast in 1970 as part of an ILP investigation group, and is reported to have declared: 'Now I know how Collins felt in 1921.' The forthright Frank Cluskey, clearly unimpressed by this comparison, retorted: 'yes, and if you fucking keep on going like this, you'll fucking know how Michael Collins felt in 1922'.[46]

The Troubles in Northern Ireland provided a sobering corrective to the views of many traditional anti-partitionists. This was particularly true of those who felt that the Republic should attempt to use force to end what was regarded as the British occupation of Northern Ireland. The events of 1969 had shown the extent to which the Irish Defence Forces were incapable of taking any offensive action with a view to ending partition. The presence of British troops on the streets of Belfast and Derry, and events such as the introduction of internment in August 1971, were a source of anger to many traditional republicans, and were a visual sign of the military impotence of the independent Irish state. The behaviour of the British Army in nationalist areas, and the incompetent way in which Operation Demetrius (internment) was handled, had provoked anger on both sides of the border, serving to swell the numbers of the Provisional IRA.[47] The actions of the British Army in Northern Ireland certainly affected Thornley's attitude to the northern state, and increased his sympathy for those who sought to overthrow it.

In December 1971, Thornley gave a full account of his views regarding the national question in a Dáil adjournment debate on Northern Ireland. Stylistically, it ranks as one of the best speeches made in that assembly during the 1970s. It cut to the very core of the national question, and arguably exposed some of the hypocrisy inherent in many Irish nationalists, particularly those in the twenty-six counties. It posed awkward questions about the legitimacy of the independent Irish state and its violent origins, prompting listeners to consider at what point violence is justifiable. Thornley threw into sharp relief how narrow the gulf was which separated the constitutional parties in Dáil Éireann from the revolutionary past that had created the modern state. The portraits of revolutionary leaders that adorned the walls of Dáil Éireann, Thornley stated,

> remind us perpetually of the circumstances in which this House was born, the circumstances of republican pride, the circumstances of violence, circumstances not mandated by the ballot box except to the extent that the 1918 general election may be seen

to have mandated the republican campaign of the Irish Republican Army between 1919 and 1921.

The electorate in 1918, he reminded deputies, 'voted for Sinn Féin', 'not the gunmanship that followed'.[48] This was perhaps another example of Thornley's respect for history and his refusal to allow the events of the past to be distorted for what he saw as hypocritical political ends, even if that meant facing up to uncomfortable or unpalatable truths about the retrospective legitimisation of the southern state's violent republican genealogy.

Thornley's speech also slated the hypocrisy of the constitutional claim on Northern Ireland – a claim in which he firmly believed – while none of the southern political parties were prepared to introduce the kinds of changes to make a state with an explicitly Catholic ethos more attractive to northern Protestants. When unionists such as Ian Paisley 'draw attention to the defects in our social service, in our legal code and our constitution the most the Taoiseach has been able to reply to this is to suggest a meeting of the Churches which might throw up suggestions to change the constitution'. 'If we are going to ask the North to join us in any other circumstances than bombing … them into this part of the country, then we will have to grasp these nettles', to show that the Republic was 'worthy to invite the North to join us.'[49] The speech then turned to the issue of violence in Northern Ireland, and here the lines between an advocacy of constitutional and revolutionary politics became blurred. It could be argued, from the sentiments expressed in this speech, that Thornley effectively justified the paramilitary campaign of the Provisional IRA. The more extreme remarks contained in the speech do not feature in the edited extracts published in *Unquiet Spirit*, but they are worthy of close scrutiny.

Thornley stated that he found bombings which kill innocent bystanders 'disgraceful and disgusting',[50] but argued that 'those who go across the border to carry out attacks upon unionist installations should not be placed in the same category as ordinary criminals … I do not propose that it should be the function of the Gardaí to collect them and hand them over for extradition'. He further stated that Irish soldiers or police should not be used as 'felon setters' for the Northern Ireland prime minister, Brian Faulkner.[51] At this point, it is evident how far Thornley diverged from the constitutional nationalism of the majority of those within his party. He went on to express his empathy for those members of the Northern Ireland minority who resorted to violence, particularly those faced with a lifetime of unemployment and social deprivation. If he found himself in similar circumstances, 'I would feel if someone handed me a gun or a rock that it was the proper thing to fire it.'[52] While of course Thornley's attitude to violence could be considered highly questionable, his highlighting of the connection between social deprivation and the areas worst affected by violence in Northern Ireland was certainly a legitimate point. It is perhaps regrettable that he chose not to pursue this leftist critique further, having instead become increasingly beguiled by the politics of Provisional Sinn Féin, whose lobbyists 'flattered [him] absurdly, while laughing at him behind his back'.[53]

While Thornley's attitude to the tactics of the Provisional IRA was ambivalent, there were others in Dáil Éireann who, Thornley believed, were hypocritical in their attitude to violence. In particular, he referred to the Arms Crisis of 1970, when members of the government attempted to import weapons using public money for use by Northern Irish republicans. It is clear that he did not believe that the then Taoiseach, Jack Lynch, was completely innocent of any involvement in the affair, or was at the very least wilfully ignorant of the plot. He argued that if 'this Dáil conceals a flavour, it is that a smell of death and corruption has hung over it since the events of May 1970'.[54] He went on to say that he would prefer the country to be led by Charles Haughey, 'who I would have thought to be the greatest operator and gangster since time began in this Dáil', because he was 'outsmarted, trapped and placed in a position by the Taoiseach [Lynch]'.[55] This was one of the first occasions where the moral standards of Haughey had been subjected to public scrutiny in the Dáil. Thornley had previously made caustic remarks about Haughey during the Arms Crisis, as he believed his denial of knowledge of the affair to be dishonest and motivated by cynicism and self-interest.[56] In 1972, however, Thornley's own moral standards, particularly his attitude to the Provisional IRA, also came under increasing scrutiny.

### THORNLEY AND THE POLITICS OF PROVISIONAL REPUBLICANISM

If Thornley had highlighted the inherent contradictions concerning attitudes to the legitimacy of republican violence at the heart of the Irish political establishment, then he too shared those ambiguities. Indeed, he seems to have gone further still by providing tacit, and arguably active, support for the Provisional republican movement. He regularly condemned the actions of the Provisional IRA, a movement that, he said, 'no thinking socialist' could support.[57] However, while refusing to explicitly condone the Provisional republican movement's campaign, Thornley appears to have understood its motivations and overtly sympathised with its objectives. One possible reason for his apparently contradictory statements concerning the IRA was that Thornley was simply being careful to avoid being accused of outright support for the Provisionals. However, if Thornley's attitude to the IRA is judged by his actions rather than by his statements, then his condemnation of militant republicanism appears less sincere, as his behaviour after 1972 illustrates.

His sympathy for the perpetrators of violence was, perhaps, symptomatic of his apparent psychological obsession with firearms, which became increasingly evident during this period. Once, during a blood transfusion session, he caused much distress when a large, loaded revolver fell from his pocket as he lay on the couch donating his pint of blood.[58] Thornley carried the weapon for his personal protection, seemingly believing that his life was under threat. It appears that he might, at this stage, have been suffering from paranoia. On one occasion during his tenure at Trinity College, he sat in his office with the curtains drawn and showed the gun to one of his students, claiming that he needed it because someday 'they' were going to come for him.[59] This apparent paranoia might have been influenced by his increasingly unhealthy lifestyle. Politically, he began to display an increasing attraction to the politics of violence and the Provisional Sinn Féin movement.

In May 1972, Thornley had criticised the Offences Against the State bill as an attempt to introduce internment 'through the back door'.[60] While his criticisms may have been valid from a civil liberties perspective, it would appear that the reason for his opposition had more to do with his empathy with those in the Provisional IRA. As that year drew to a close, he visited the Provisional IRA's Seán MacStíofáin at the Mater Hospital in Dublin. The latter had been engaged on a hunger strike at Mountjoy Prison;[61] he suffered no lasting ill effects, leading Noel Browne to suspect that the strike by the 'presently hale and healthy half-English romantic republican' was bogus.[62] This visit to one of the most prominent republican subversives, intent on the destruction of the northern and southern states, was a significant signal that Thornley was no longer an adherent to the ILP's commitment to a peaceful Northern Ireland policy. Four years later, his ambivalence towards the Provisional republican movement cost him his political career.

At Easter 1976, Provisional Sinn Féin had organised a demonstration to commemorate the sixtieth anniversary of the 1916 Rising at the General Post Office in Dublin. Despite the proscription of the demonstration under Section 27 of the Offences Against the State Act, official estimates report that over 8,000 people attended. Those present included Belfast Provisional IRA leader Joe Cahill, the president of Provisional Sinn Féin, Ruairi Ó Bradaigh, and the party's vice-presidents, Máire Drumm and Daithi Ó Conaill.[63] Thornley decided to disobey the government's ban and attend the demonstration; he also chose to sit on the speakers' platform aside the coterie of Provisional republican leaders. Thornley used ambiguous language in an attempt to justify his presence on the platform, claiming that he had attended the demonstration in order to defend the right of freedom of speech and freedom of assembly, not to condone the actions of the Provisional IRA.[64] However, if this was his intention, then it must be questioned why he did not attend the demonstration as an ordinary spectator. Instead he chose to mount the platform and sit beside the leadership of the political wing of the Provisional IRA as they made anti-government speeches. The fact that his presence, side by side with those who wished to destroy the institutions to which Thornley was elected, would be viewed as tacit support for the Provisional IRA, could not have escaped someone of Thornley's powerful intellect. For the Parliamentary Labour Party (PLP), this was one apparent breach of party policy too many. At the PLP meeting on 28 April 1976, it was clear that Thornley would not escape censure for his actions at the Easter demonstrations.

The party leader, Brendan Corish, began the meeting by insisting that Thornley's presence at the illegal demonstration left Labour 'in a particularly vulnerable position when it came to condemning the actions and atrocities of the Provisional IRA. David Thornley's actions were grossly injurious to the interests of the Party and was a violation of his Party pledge.'[65] In response, Thornley gave a brief and somewhat obscure defence of his actions on the day in question. In it, he referred to his commitment to the ILP. He claimed to have stood for the party because of a genuine belief in its principles, despite having been offered 'a safe Fine Gael seat by Gerry Sweetman', the former right-wing minister for finance in the 1954–7 government. He also claimed that he had 'always been loyal to the Party even with decisions with which he did not agree'. He went on to say that he had entered politics at the considerable financial loss of his two salaries (£8,000 and £2,500 from lecturing and broadcasting respectively). He then left the meeting, 'not out of disrespect but [because] if he remained he might be provoked into saying something he would later regret'.

There was general condemnation of his actions from all sides of the party. Jimmy Tully noted that the 'Provisional IRA were as determined to pull down this state as Northern Ireland', and condemned a 'self-professed Marxist' like Thornley associating himself with what he considered to be a fascist organisation. John Horgan claimed to be 'sickened' by Thornley's actions. Thornley's old opponent, Conor Cruise O'Brien, spoke only briefly in support of the motion to withdraw the party whip, on the grounds that if such action were not taken, 'Labour's condemnation of the Provos would be seen as less than total.' Justin Keating claimed that Thornley, far from upholding the right to free speech, was providing encouragement to those who were opposed to that right, and his presence on the Provisional Sinn Féin platform had been 'synical [*sic*] and opportunist'. He further complained that there had always been equivocation about violence in the country and that, up until recently, there was 'no real law against the IRA and too little enforcement of it'. Thornley's colleague at the European Parliament, Liam Kavanagh, indicated that he would no longer serve with Thornley at Strasbourg, adding that Thornley knew that by his attendance at the demonstration he was 'putting his head on the block'. He added that Thornley had told him in advance of his decision to attend, which suggests that he had thought about his decision for some time, and had not merely gone to the demonstration on the spur of the moment.

Some sympathy was expressed for Thornley by the aforementioned Stephen Coughlan and John O'Connell. Both men described Thornley as 'irrational', and O'Connell was concerned that there was so little personal sympathy for Thornley in these circumstances. Michael D. Higgins, while condemning Thornley's actions, advocated that action be taken short of the removal of the party whip; this was supported by Jack Fitzgerald and John O'Connell. Higgins suggested that a reaffirmation of the party pledge by Thornley might be sufficient punishment without resorting to more serious disciplinary action. Higgins has recently argued that Thornley opposed the actions of the Provisional IRA but felt that it should be allowed 'a place in the public space, and in public discourse'.[66] Despite the protestations of those who personally sympathised with Thornley, the motion to remove the party whip from him was passed by twenty-two votes to three.[67] He also faced legal action for his presence at the Easter demonstration, being fined £10 by the Dublin courts.[68] Politically speaking, however, Thornley was not finished yet – despite the efforts of some within the PLP. Thornley himself remarked in December 1975 that many ILP members would be grateful 'if I should ride off into the sunset on a white horse like John Wayne, only slightly shorter and slightly fatter'.[69]

He continued to take an active part in Dáil debates, particularly those with a Northern Ireland or security focus. He was extremely critical of an Emergency Powers Bill debated in the Dáil in September 1976: he referred to Fine Gael's chief whip, John Kelly, whom he 'once described as a "fascist hyena". Now he was afraid that the description had turned out to be correct.' In particular, he opposed a provision in the bill to allow for the detention of a person for up to seven days solely on the word of a Garda of at least the rank of Superintendent. He stated that he 'did not relish the prospect of some diminutive gentleman in sneakers and jeans coming up to me, tapping me on the shoulder, putting me away for seven days and saying "goodbye" without explanation'. He felt this provision was potentially open to abuse, not by uniformed Gardaí for whom Thornley professed the utmost respect, but by 'sloppy, creepy un-uniformed Garda' who frightened him 'extremely'. This bill, he argued, was an opportunistic attempt by the government to exploit security issues during the general election campaign.[70]

Despite outspoken criticisms of the political establishment, the party whip was restored to him in February 1977 after pressure was applied by the Dublin Regional Council of the ILP, no doubt influenced by the prospect of a general election.[71] Despite his return to the party fold, his political career did not last much longer. It seems likely that his association with Provisional Sinn Féin cost him much electoral support in his Dublin North-West constituency. In the 1977 general election, in which the ILP lost three of its seats, Thornley actually lost his deposit, the first Labour TD to do so since 1923.[72] He left the ILP not long afterwards to join the Socialist Labour Party, founded by Noel Browne; according to John Horgan, a 'last act of filial piety'.[73] He passed away in June 1978, the result of heavy drinking, and, according to some observers, undiagnosed diabetes.[74] His health had been declining for some time; in November 1976 he was hospitalised in England during a visit to the UK.[75] His death, at the age of just 42, was undoubtedly a tragic event. Dáil Éireann lost one of its most colourful characters; his family, a young husband and father.

## CONCLUSION

It would appear that despite having individual republicans within its ranks at various stages of its history, the ILP as a party has been opposed to the use of violence to attain Irish unity. Like all the parties in the Irish state, it aspired to the eventual reunification of the island of Ireland under a single parliament in Dublin, while never openly supporting those who used force to attempt to achieve this goal. This is perhaps unsurprising, given that the party did not originate as part of a separatist organisation, unlike the other two main parties in the Irish state. It has never had, unlike elements within Fianna Fáil during the Arms Crisis, any association with militant republicans. Neither was the ILP an overtly socialist party, its origins being in the trade union movement. This begs the question why Thornley chose to join the party in the first instance, although it seems that he respected the leftward turn the party took under the leadership of Brendan Corish, the Wexford TD whose Labourite pedigree was impeccable.

What of Thornley himself, and his attitude to the question of revolutionary politics and those who used violence ostensibly for political ends? As this chapter has shown, it appears that his attitude to the politics of violence evolved over the years. It would seem that during the later 1960s Thornley was at least prepared to accept the ILP policy towards Northern Ireland: that no solution was possible which involved the use of violence. However, as the Troubles in Northern Ireland worsened, and as his health deteriorated due to his increasing recourse to alcohol, his views on the North hardened. His visit to Seán MacStíofáin in 1972 and his appearance with leading members of the Provisional IRA on the speakers' platform at the Easter demonstrations in 1976 clearly demonstrate that he no longer subscribed to the ILP's Northern Ireland policy, and he was intelligent enough to know that this is how his activity would have been perceived both by the public and by his senior party colleagues. Although claiming not to support the tactics employed by the Provisional IRA, his actions told a different story; by these actions he essentially displayed contempt for the democratic institutions of the state and the constitutional politics endorsed by his party. Ultimately, that decision proved to be his political undoing.

On a personal level, Thornley's assessment of Isaac Butt could be applied to himself: he combined 'a love of country with a susceptible emotional nature', and like Butt, 'lacked the supreme self-confidence which enables the Parnells, the O'Connells (at least until 1843), and the de Valeras to ride tigers in the certain knowledge that they will be able to dismount at their own convenience'.[76] However, where Butt eschewed revolutionary politics, Thornley, in his final years, appears to have embraced them, and lost his political career as a result. However, to examine Thornley's career solely through the prism of failure would be an injustice to a man who had done the state some service, not least through his work with Basil Chubb during the referendum on proportional representation. His perceptive historical and political writings have also stood the test of time, and his work on Butt remains required reading for Irish political historians. Similarly, in highlighting the ambiguous attitudes of many in the political establishment to republican violence, he pre-empted a long, often bitter Irish historiographical debate. That he chose to offer his support to the Provisional republican movement ultimately ensured he ended up on the losing side.

NOTES

1. Donald H. Akenson, *Conor: A Biography of Conor Cruise O'Brien*, 2 vols (Montreal: McGill-Queen's University Press, 1994), vol. i, p.343.
2. Yseult Thornley (ed.), *Unquiet Spirit: Essays in Memory of David Thornley* (Dublin: Liberties Press, 2008).
3. Niamh Puirséil, *The Irish Labour Party, 1922–73* (Dublin: University College Dublin Press, 2007), p.6.
4. Ibid., p.8.
5. For more, see Michael Gallagher, 'The Pact General Election of 1922', *Irish Historical Studies*, vol. 22, no. 84 (1979), pp.415–16.
6. Ronan Fanning, *Independent Ireland* (Dublin: Helicon, 1983), p.41.
7. See Shaun McDaid and Kacper Edward Rekawek, 'From Mainstream to Minor and Back: The Irish Labour Party, 1987–1992', *Irish Political Studies*, vol. 25, no. 4 (2010).
8. Brian M. Walker (ed.), *Parliamentary Election Results in Ireland 1918–92: Irish Elections to Parliaments and Parliamentary Assemblies at Westminster, Belfast, Dublin, Strasbourg* (Dublin: Royal Irish Academy, 1992), pp.166–76.
9. Michael Gallagher, *The Irish Labour Party in Transition, 1957–82* (Manchester: Manchester University Press, 1982), p.126.
10. Ibid., p.128.
11. *Dáil Éireann Debates*, vol. 156, col. 367, 30 October 1957. Unionists would, of course, constitute a minority within any 32-county Irish polity.
12. *Dáil Éireann Debates*, vol. 156, col. 366.
13. *Dáil Éireann Debates*, vol. 156, col. 44.
14. *Labour Party Annual Report 1970*, p.30.
15. University College Dublin Archives (UCDA), T.K. Whitaker Papers, P175.
16. UCDA, Fianna Fáil Parliamentary Party Archives, P176/776. It should be noted that the events surrounding the Arms Crisis cast significant doubt over Fianna Fáil's commitment to peace in Northern Ireland in 1970.
17. *Irish Times*, 28 February 1972; Puirséil, *Irish Labour Party*, p.294.
18. *Irish Times*, 28 February 1972.
19. Parliamentary Labour Party (PLP) Minutes, Labour Party Archive (LPA), Dublin, 23 July 1975.
20. Kevin Boland, *Fine Gael: British or Irish?* (Cork: Mercier Press, 1983), p.49.
21. Thornley (ed.), *Unquiet Spirit*, p.10.
22. In conversation with R.F. Foster, 5 April 2009. See also Willie H. Maxwell's reminiscence in Thornley, (ed.), *Unquiet Spirit*, pp.48–50.
23. David Thornley, *Isaac Butt and Home Rule* (London: McGibbon & Kee, 1964), p.10.
24. Ibid., p.15.
25. Ibid., p.387.
26. Ibid., pp.17–19.
27. R.F. Foster, *Paddy and Mr Punch: Connections in Irish and English History* (London: Allen Lane, 1993), pp.26–7.
28. David Thornley, 'Patrick Pearse – The Evolution of a Republican' in F.X. Martin (ed.), *Leaders and Men of the Easter Rising: Dublin 1916* (London: Methuen, 1967), p.151.
29. Ibid.; see also Thornley (ed.), *Unquiet Spirit*, p.233.

30. Quoted in Diarmuid Whelan, *Conor Cruise O'Brien – Violent Notions* (Dublin: Irish Academic Press, 2009), p.109.
31. For an example see *Irish Times*, 4 April 1967.
32. John Horgan, *Labour: The Price of Power* (Dublin: Gill & Macmillan, 1986), p.73.
33. *Irish Independent*, 20 July 1974.
34. Noel Browne, *Against the Tide* (Dublin: Gill & Macmillan, 1986), p.263. For more on the contraception issue, see Brian Girvin, 'Contraception, Moral Panic and Social Change in Ireland, 1969–79', *Irish Political Studies*, vol. 23, no. 4 (2008), pp.555–77.
35. Thornley (ed.), *Unquiet Spirit*, p.12.
36. Ibid., p.11; Conor Cruise O'Brien, *Memoir: My Life and Themes* (London: Profile, 1998), p.323.
37. John Horgan, *Noel Browne: Passionate Outsider* (Dublin: Gill & Macmillan, 2000), p.189.
38. *Irish Times*, 31 December 1975.
39. Gallagher, *Irish Labour Party*, p.98.
40. Ibid., p.140.
41. O'Brien, *Memoir*, p.339.
42. Barry Desmond, *Finally and in Conclusion: A Political Memoir* (Dublin: New Island Press, 2000), p.158; Puirséil, *Irish Labour Party*, p.278.
43. Puirséil, *Irish Labour Party*, pp.278–80.
44. Gallagher, *Irish Labour Party*, p.140.
45. Thornley (ed.), *Unquiet Spirit*, p.60.
46. Akenson, *Conor*, p.343.
47. Alvin Jackson, *Ireland 1798–1998: Politics and War* (Oxford: Blackwell, 1999), p.375; R.F. Foster, *Luck and the Irish: A Brief History of Change, c. 1970–2000* (London: Allen Lane, 2007), p.115.
48. *Dáil Éireann Debates*, vol. 257, col. 2487, 16 December 1971.
49. *Dáil Éireann Debates*, vol. 257, cols 2505–6.
50. *Dáil Éireann Debates*, vol. 257, col. 2499.
51. *Dáil Éireann Debates*, vol. 257, cols 2496–8.
52. *Dáil Éireann Debates*, vol. 257, col. 2505.
53. O'Brien, *Memoir*, p.337.
54. *Dáil Éireann Debates*, vol. 257, col. 2488, 16 December 1971.
55. *Dáil Éireann Debates*, vol. 257, col. 2494.
56. *Dáil Éireann Debates*, vol. 246, col. 806, 8 May 1970.
57. *Irish Times*, 11 September 1971.
58. *Irish Independent*, 8 November 1986.
59. In conversation with R.F. Foster, 5 April 2009.
60. *The Times*, 24 May 1972.
61. *Irish Times*, 4 December 1972; Puirséil, *Irish Labour* Party, p.303.
62. Browne, *Against the Tide*, p.252.
63. *The Times*, 26 April 1976 and 24 June 1976.
64. *Irish Times*, 8 May 1976.
65. PLP Minutes, LPA, 28 April 1976. Subsequent quotations are taken from here unless otherwise stated.
66. Quoted in Thornley (ed.), *Unquiet Spirit*, p.160.
67. PLP Minutes, LPA, 28 April 1976.
68. *Irish Times* 24 June 1976.
69. Ibid., 2 May 1976.
70. *Irish Independent*, 3 September 1976.
71. See *Irish Times*, 5 May 1976 and 6 May 1976.
72. Gallagher, *Irish Labour Party*, p.217.
73. Horgan, *Passionate Outsider*, p.268.
74. Ibid., p.258.
75. *Irish Times*, 12 November 1976.
76. Thornley, *Isaac Butt*, pp.16 and 380.

# CHAPTER TEN

# Sinn Féin's Transition from Abstention to Assembly: The Domestic and International Perspective

## ANDREW SANDERS

One of the most fascinating political transformations to take place over the last thirty years in Ireland has been that of Sinn Féin. From a fringe position, abstaining from the British, Irish and Northern Irish parliaments, it has become the largest nationalist party in Northern Ireland and the second largest party overall. Its electoral growth culminated in the return of five MPs to the Westminster parliament and 126 councillors across Northern Ireland in 2005.[1] Two years previously, the party won 162,758 votes in the Assembly elections, 45,000 more than the previously dominant Social Democratic Labour Party (SDLP).[2] Recent work on Sinn Féin has highlighted the period after 1981 as being particularly important in understanding the movement in its present state.[3] The purpose of this chapter is to examine the process of transition that Sinn Féin underwent: from a policy of total abstention to one of full participation in the political institutions of Ireland. It will show how both internal and external factors contributed to this transition, and will assess how these impacted upon the development of Provisional republican policy. The ending of abstention to the Irish Dáil will be the focus of the early part of this chapter, which will then go on to examine the American dimension to the policy changes within Provisional republicanism, as the increased involvement of prominent United States politicians began to shape republican strategy.

Abstention had been a central tenet of republican policy since the early 1900s. Sinn Féin stood on an abstentionist platform in the 1918 Westminster elections; following the partition of the island in 1920–1, the party abstained from the new Irish institutions north and south. This refusal to recognise the separate parliaments persisted in republican ideology, which recognised the indissoluble authority of the Second Dáil – the underground revolutionary government dating from 1921 – and its jurisdiction over the entire island. In December 1938, seven TDs met with the Irish Republican Army's army council and passed what they believed to be the legitimacy of the Second Dáil to the IRA.

Inherent in this, however, was the refusal to recognise the legitimacy of the existing parliaments in Dublin and Belfast; but abstaining from the houses of parliament on the island of Ireland damaged the political credibility of the movement. The fact that, even in areas where they enjoyed popularity among the constituents, Sinn Féin could not represent these areas in parliament because of their adherence to tradition ultimately served to undermine any political aspirations that republicans had. Although the principle of abstention had strong historical roots, it ran clearly against the pragmatic tendency that had emerged within Provisional republicanism during the 1980s. The success enjoyed in elections during the early years of this decade pushed the movement towards political struggle. Brendan Lynn has noted that the first signs of the abstention debate were from a series of articles appearing in the republican newspaper, *Republican News*, between 1975 and 1977, written by an author using the pen name 'Brownie', widely believed to have been Gerry Adams. One principle this author spoke of was 'active abstentionism', a strategy that would attempt to bridge the gap between all-out abstention and political participation.[4]

The debate on abstention had emerged during the 1960s, prior to the 1969–70 split in the republican movement. Politically minded republicans under Cathal Goulding, citing the relative failure of the 1956–62 Border Campaign, sought to advance the movement. Alongside the moves towards politics, and therefore away from militarism, the lack of defence offered to nationalist communities by the Irish Republican Army during the violence of the summer of 1969 prompted a faction led by republicans Joe Cahill, Seán MacStíofáin and Ruairí Ó Brádaigh to break from the Goulding-led movement and to set up their own grouping, which came to be known as the Provisional IRA and Sinn Féin. The irony of the Provisional faction, later led by Gerry Adams, making this same shift during the 1980s was not lost on Cathal Goulding, who stated that 'we were right too soon, Gerry Adams is right too late and Ruairí Ó Brádaigh will never be fucking right'.[5] For ex-Provisional Anthony McIntyre, however, 'it's a fair enough point. The problem is Goulding wasn't right.'[6] The common theme of the two situations – that the group should cease abstaining from houses of parliament – did create an inevitable comparison. While the Goulding faction was motivated by 'the clear belief ... that abstentionism was a dead policy and it needed to be jettisoned',[7] the justification used by the Adams leadership centred on successes enjoyed in elections that took place during the hunger strike campaign in 1981.

The year 1981 saw elections in both the UK and Ireland, which coincided with the hunger strike campaign. Along with the election of leading hunger-striker and former prison officer commanding Bobby Sands to the Westminster Parliament, fellow hunger-striker Kieran Doherty was elected in Cavan/Monaghan and blanket-man Paddy Agnew was elected in Louth during elections for the twenty-second Dáil. The hunger strike that developed out of the blanket and no-wash protests created controversy across republicanism. Gerry Adams claims to have opposed the hunger strike on moral grounds,[8] even though it served as the incendiary for revolution within Provisional republicanism. Richard O'Rawe has subsequently suggested that the hunger strike became a political tool for the republican leadership, who maintained the strike even after the British government had made what was considered an acceptable offer shortly before the death of the fifth hunger-striker, Joe McDonnell.[9]

Conversely, Sinn Féin's Eoin Ó Broin has argued that if 'republicans really wanted to be honest about it, the focus of republicans was so intensely towards the armed struggle at that point that really republicans weren't even thinking politically beyond the politics of armed struggle'.[10] Implicit in this is the fact that wider republicanism was not qualified, and therefore not in a position, to question its leadership during the early 1980s, allowing the leadership to direct the movement in the relative absence of criticism. The O'Rawe line suggests a cold, cynical dimension to Provisional republican strategy at this time, prepared as it was to make any sacrifice in the name of power. Equally, one should consider that the emotional power of 1981 would have been considerably diluted were it only four men dead instead of ten. Past hunger strike deaths, such as those of Michael Gaughan and Frank Stagg, who died in 1974 and 1976 respectively, had not succeeded in creating the same outrage, even though Gaughan endured harsh treatment during attempts to force-feed him.[11] Neither man died in a Northern Irish prison, Stagg jailed in Yorkshire and

Gaughan on the Isle of Man; the close proximity of the 1981 hunger-strikers to support groups undoubtedly increased publicity.

The H-Blocks/Armagh committee retained the Fermanagh–South Tyrone seat in the by-election following Sands's death through Owen Carron, who had been Sands's election agent. Fermanagh and South Tyrone is one of the more intriguing Northern Irish constituencies; in its previous incarnation as Fermanagh and Tyrone, it had been a Nationalist Party stronghold from the 1920s, with a five-year period of Unionist incumbency between 1924 and 1929 the only exception to this near monopoly. Sinn Féin won the seat in May 1955, but their candidate's victory was overturned by the Northern Ireland High Court in October on the grounds of his conviction and imprisonment for treason. The Unionist Party held the seat until 1970, losing to the Unity Party's Frank McManus; Independent Republican Frank Maguire succeeded him in the October 1974 general election. Following Sands's election, the seat again fell under Sinn Féin control in 1982, when Carron altered his political allegiance.[12] His margin of victory in the August 1981 by-election improved upon Sands's majority, something that can be easily attributed to the emotional atmosphere of the immediate aftermath of Sands's death. That Carron subsequently lost the seat in 1983 by nearly 8,000 votes indicates a change in attitude that can be partially explained by his new allegiance; no longer on the H-Block ticket, Carron now stood for the Provisional republican movement. It has subsequently been alleged that the republican leadership believed Carron would have more success in the by-election if the hunger strike was ongoing on polling day.[13] The considerable turnaround in the 1983 election supports this contention; however, by this stage the republican political juggernaut was in full flow.

The mood within republicanism during 1983 was, on the whole, considerably positive. Although Carron had lost his seat, Gerry Adams had succeeded Gerry Fitt in Belfast West, and Danny Morrison was only narrowly defeated in Mid-Ulster, two seats which have subsequently become Sinn Féin strongholds. The party also achieved its first six-figure vote haul. The benefits of electoral participation were becoming clear, as was the increasingly political nature of republicanism.[14]

## THE AMERICAN DIMENSION

Most commentators are in agreement about the importance of the United States to the Irish republican struggle throughout the 1970s and 1980s.[15] The significance of the funding coming in from the USA cannot be overstated; the *Scotsman* reported in early 1983 that 'about 75 percent of the funds which sustain the violence in Northern Ireland come from private US sources, the US Justice Department have concluded after a 12-year investigation';[16] some reported the income to be over three million dollars by the mid-1980s.[17] Equally, the British Foreign and Commonwealth Office noted that the

> Irish Northern Aid Committee, which claims to be the only authorised fund-raising agency in the United States for the Republican movement, have registered remittances to Ireland of nearly $900,000 in the 3 years to January 1975. It is impossible to say how much of this has been used for the purchase of arms ... A representative of the Irish Northern Aid Committee, when appearing before a Congressional Sub-Committee in February 1972, admitted that his organisation had no control over the funds when transferred to Ireland and at least some of them were almost certainly spent on arms ... The US authorities are conscious of the possible implications of these fund-raising activities and we are in frequent contact with them about this.[18]

With these figures supplemented by considerable weaponry, Michael Flannery – the prominent Irish-American founder of Irish Northern Aid (Noraid), the most important republican support group in the United States – noted that 'there is no doubt that Noraid helped considerably sustaining the Provisionals' war'.[19] Noraid, particularly its newspaper the *Irish People*, provides useful insight into the Irish-American view on Ireland during this period; the propaganda value of this newspaper during the hunger strikes, in particular, is of significant value in enhancing scholarly understanding of the nuances, complexities and shifts in republican policy throughout this period.

Further to what effectively amounted to military aid, the influence of prominent United States politicians helped to put pressure on the British government to accede to nationalist demands. The importance of keeping people such as Senator Edward Kennedy and Speaker Thomas 'Tip' O'Neill closely aligned with John Hume from the mid-1970s onwards, became evident in 1994, when Kennedy's support for a US visa for Sinn Féin leader Gerry Adams enabled the latter to embark on a wildly successful media tour of the east coast. The difficulties that Irish republicans encountered in reconciling the considerably different aspirations of ordinary Irish Americans and those of powerful United States politicians decisively shaped this period of republican history, exacerbated as it was by ongoing political turbulence across the wider movement.

The rhetoric of republicans when dealing with Irish America had always been cautious; Adams, for example, was careful not to alienate Irish-American opinion in the matter of the republican movement's adherence to socialism, arguing that 'the Republican movement has always been socialist in the Irish tradition of radical thinkers. It has never been a Marxist movement.'[20] When the 1981 electoral successes were presented to Irish America, Adams played down the new political direction, claiming that 'our electoral intervention in the South in the aftermath of the hunger strike was more of an effort to hang on to the H-Block nationalist vote than a planned or well thought out policy on the progress possible on electoral politics'.[21] The election of Sands had been a stroke of opportunistic genius; the Provisionals had not developed a coherent electoral strategy by this point. Rather, the Provisionals approached the entire situation pragmatically, 'enjoying the ride'. Adams's rhetoric, however, was calculated to keep the Irish-American support base onside. The romantic vision of Ireland that bonded together many members of Irish-American organisations had to be dealt with delicately. They had celebrated Sands's election as 'a stunning blow to the British establishment in North Ireland',[22] although his election campaign was described as 'heavy with political intrigue and undertones of threatened violence'.[23] While Adams's rhetoric to Irish America in the aftermath of the post-hunger strike elections was careful, the *Irish People* had previously commented on the death of sitting MP Frank Maguire with the observation that Sinn Féin might field an abstentionist candidate in the by-election to replace him, with the possibility of a hunger-striker filling this role.[24] They suggested was that this position might have been acceptable to Irish America in any case.

The prison disputes were also massively significant in terms of Irish-American interest in Ireland and consequently of huge importance for the growth of the republican movement within Ireland itself. The Irish in the United States had raised concerns about the possibility of a hunger strike developing. The Irish Embassy in Washington asked in 1980: 'could any civilised society, any humane government, or any person with even a spark of humanity allow such a thing to happen?'[25] Previous hunger strike deaths, such as that of former Official republican Michael Gaughan, merited significant coverage in the United States.[26] Even before the deaths of ten men in 1981, there was considerable evidence that such an event would attract widespread publicity.

The hunger strikes brought in a great deal of monetary support for the cause, particularly from America.[27] As the prison struggle developed, so did Noraid as an organisation, perhaps understandably given the increased exposure of Irish issues across America at this time.[28] The ability to promote the republican movement at a time when financial solvency was crucial boosted the Provisionals' attempts to shift the republican campaign to two fronts: attracting politically inclined members while maintaining the military struggle. Therefore, fundraising, from any available source, became an increasingly important component of republican strategy.

Widespread American support for the first hunger strike, which began on Monday 27 October 1980, was evidenced by the demonstrations that occurred in eighteen cities across the United States, attracting thousands of protestors.[29] With the onset of the second hunger strike, the prominence of the Irish issue in the United States was underlined. To enhance the struggle across the Atlantic, the plight of the prisoners was emphasised: a cynical attempt to play up to the romantic tendencies of Irish America, perhaps, but a successful one nonetheless. The *Irish People* published a series of letters written by hunger-strikers to Irish America. Laurence McKeown, who was taken off hunger strike by his family after seventy days without food, wrote:

> before more young Irish men lay down their lives for the ideals they hold so dear, I implore you, the American people, to now, today, do something positive to help save them. Or must the cries of the Irish people and their imprisoned children once more go unheard? From an English prison camp on Irish soil, I send this desperate appeal to you.[30]

Alongside McKeown's letter was one from Martin Hurson, who by the time of publication had already died. Given the increasingly fragile condition that the hunger-strikers were in as they neared death,[31] it is unlikely that Hurson wrote this letter himself during his final days; it read, 'I urge you to give active support in America and to let the British know that the hunger strikers and the blanket men do not stand alone in their just struggle.'[32] While McKeown's message was powerful, Hurson's message from beyond the grave overshadowed it considerably, regardless of whether it was written by him or not.[33] Encouragement was also forthcoming from Brendan Hughes, the leader of the first hunger strike in 1980; 'the impression we get, here on the blanket, is that America is England's weak spot ... it is now we must push like never before against the Sassenach and it is now we must demonstrate to him the power of the Irish nation and her exiled children in America'.[34]

These letters served to motivate Irish America, increasing both fundraising opportunities and pressure upon United States politicians to push the British government to accede to the prisoners' demands. The republican leadership's ability to garner political support, particularly among elected representatives of Great Britain's historic ally, gave them considerable political experience in an international context that they would not otherwise have been able to exploit. While Irish America itself had largely maintained an interest in Ireland, it was not until the hunger-strikes placed the issue on a global platform that United States politicians, particularly those of Irish descent, really began to take an interest.

Although admittedly interested in Irish affairs for much of the 1970s, the 'Four Horsemen' of Edward Kennedy, Tip O'Neill, Senator Daniel Moynihan and Governor Hugh Carey had been brought around from their initially hostile approach to a more constitutional opposition to the British presence in Ireland, thanks largely to the influence of John Hume.[35] During the hunger strike, the group wrote to Prime Minister Margaret Thatcher expressing their concern at its continuation: 'One Senior Irish Diplomat describes American Press Coverage of Ulster as "Disastrous." The IRA's American lobby was therefore "stronger than ever".'[36] Their new-found concern, that negative press could boost the Provisional republican movement, was well justified.

While American figures undoubtedly wanted to prevent the deaths of the hunger-strikers, actual support for the prison campaign appears to have been limited to Irish-American organisations, although it is fair to say that support for these organisations increased considerably during this period. It is also important to note that with increased support came increased funding. As indicated above, the political benefits the movement gained during the hunger strike period were matched by the financial gains, which, in addition to contributing to the political campaigns that were now part of republican planning, were used to maintain the military dominance of the Provisional IRA. This was a crucial mechanism to keep the entire movement behind the Adams leadership, as it entered a new stage of electoral participation. It is clear that the constant stream of death provided the republican movement with levels of publicity in the United States to which it would not otherwise have been privy.

Particularly important during this period was Senator Edward Kennedy from Massachusetts. Kennedy had taken an interest in the Irish situation during the early 1970s; addressing a crowd at Trinity

College Dublin, he condemned 'oppression' in Northern Ireland, and later criticised the policy of internment without trial. In October 1971, Kennedy, along with Connecticut Senator Abraham Ribicoff and representative Hugh Carey of New York, called for the withdrawal of British troops from Ulster, famously adding: 'Ulster is becoming Britain's Vietnam.'[37] Representing a state that claims to be one-quarter Irish,[38] it seems obvious that Kennedy would have taken an interest in Northern Ireland; indeed he claimed that 'were I neither Catholic nor of Irish heritage, I would feel compelled to protest against the killing and violence in Northern Ireland'.[39] Despite his heritage, Kennedy's involvement in Northern Ireland had a streak of opportunism to it; in July 1969 his involvement in a fatal car accident at Chappaquiddick, Massachusetts,[40] had brought considerable criticism and during the anti-desegregation protests of the period he was heavily criticised for failing to deal with the perception that white rights were being lost during the civil rights period.[41] The Northern Irish situation offered Kennedy the opportunity both to divert attention from his personal problems and to provide his constituents with evidence that the concerns of Irish people were important to him. One problem, implicit in a retrospective statement from his memoir, was that Kennedy had initially a poor understanding of the Northern Ireland situation:

> My understanding of the situation in Northern Ireland really began to evolve after I met John Hume, a brilliant young member of Parliament from Northern Ireland. We had met briefly in 1972, after I cosponsored a resolution with Abe Ribicoff calling for the withdrawal of the British troops from Northern Ireland and establishing a united Ireland. But it was really in late 1972 that John began the great education of Edward Kennedy about Northern Ireland and established the seeds that grew into a wonderful relationship.[42]

The 'very powerful impression'[43] that Hume made upon Kennedy is identifiable in a statement made on St Patrick's Day 1981 by the Friends of Ireland, an organisation set up by Kennedy and O'Neill in 1981 with a view to promoting a more constitutional line on Ireland within the United States: 'we take satisfaction that American support for the violence has declined ... we urge all Americans to join us in condemning the violence in Northern Ireland, and to forswear any word or deed that fosters further violence.'[44] The Friends of Ireland then wrote to Margaret Thatcher during the hunger strike to 'question a posture of inflexibility that must lead inevitably to more senseless violence and more needless deaths in Northern Ireland'.[45] Clearly, the prevention of violence was a motivation for the Friends of Ireland, but it should be recalled that their nationalist persuasions were not significantly hindered by their increasingly constitutional position. With their most prominent American sponsors falling under the influence of John Hume, Irish nationalists attempting to reach out across the Atlantic would have to follow suit, or risk losing this crucial legitimising support.

The importance of Kennedy in particular is underlined with his role in obtaining a United States visa for Gerry Adams. Kennedy admits that he was persuaded by his sister, Jean Kennedy Smith, then the American Ambassador in Dublin, that

> Adams no longer believed that continuing the armed struggle was the way to achieve the IRA's objective of a united Ireland. He was in fact working to convince the IRA's more aggressive members to end the violence and pursue the political path. Most convincingly, Adams had held a series of conversations with John Hume that led Hume to believe a ceasefire and negotiations could soon be achieved.[46]

Again, the role of Hume was important; the Hume–Adams statements from the previous year,[47] backed up by Hume's discussions with Kennedy following the funeral of Tip O'Neill in January 1994, helped decisively to sway the Massachusetts Senator. He decided that granting Adams's visa could help promote the peace process, a position for which he gained the support of fifty members of Congress.[48] Kennedy continued to observe that 'in August 1994, the IRA called an historic ceasefire, an event that Mr Adams has said would not have transpired had he not been granted the visa'.[49]

### THE END FOR ABSTENTION

Retention of international support was a central issue for the leadership of the Provisionals as they began to consider the political advancement of the movement. Clearly, the hunger strikes had altered the landscape of republicanism; but the ability of republicans to attract support during the subsequent elections had forced a radical rethink of policy. Politics was now viewed as a justifiable and prosperous avenue for republicanism, but one that was impeded by the republican principle of abstention.

Adams noted the weaknesses of the election campaign of the prisoners during the 1981 disputes and highlighted the problem that non-representation on the political stage posed for the candidates.[50] All of this contributed to bring the debate over abstention back to the fore of republican thinking. A motion from 1980 forbidding participation in Northern local elections was changed following Sands's election.

The role of the prison campaign in justifying the shift away from traditionalism was emphasised by Gerry Adams, who noted that 'the most lasting effect of the campaign within the [six] counties was its educational value'.[51] He subsequently cited the October 1982 Assembly elections in which Sinn Féin won five seats with 10 per cent of the vote, as an example of how beneficial political involvement could be to the movement.[52] While this was written in retrospect, the Assembly elections of 1982 serve as a definite starting point for the process that would end republican abstention. In the United States, it was considered that the election would lead to an increase in votes for extremist organisations. The *Sun* newspaper in Baltimore argued that 'the Sands affair is certain to help Protestant extremists in coming local election, and possibly pro-IRA candidates as well'.[53] The results of the 1983 Westminster election do not, however, bear out this prediction: the Ulster Unionist Party was returned as the largest party in Northern Ireland, winning eleven seats.[54]

Certainly, the spirit of political change across Northern Ireland was keenly felt within the republican movement. Adams argued retrospectively that this period offered an opportunity for the movement to develop their politics.[55] Claims that this development came at the cost of the lives of republican volunteers are perhaps superfluous in this context. While one could reasonably criticise the Adams leadership for continuing the hunger strike even after an acceptable offer had been received, republican volunteers had never been reticent to place themselves in mortal danger in the name of the republican struggle. According to the Sutton Index of Deaths, 110 volunteers were killed by the British security forces, some under controversial circumstances. This figure is still considerably lower than the number of its own volunteers that the IRA killed (132).[56]

Certainly, the move was framed positively in Irish America, where it was suggested that this was the most suitable method of furthering the republican struggle, indicating the loyal adherence of many in the United States to the Provisional leadership. The *Irish People* suggested that 'the nomination of Sinn Féin candidates in the twenty-six county general election for the first time in twenty years gives a clear opportunity for another true declaration of Irish nationalism as that made so forcibly last June in the vote for the H-Block candidates ... Sinn Féin – the only Republican party – is complementing and reinforcing the Republican fight in the North'.[57] Despite the triumphant rhetoric, electoral success did not follow: Sinn Féin failed to win a seat, while the political wing of the Official IRA, Sinn Féin – the Workers' Party, picked up three seats. The two anti-H-Block seats, won the previous year, were thus lost by Sinn Féin, with Francis O'Donoghue achieving 529 votes in Cavan and Monaghan and Donnchadha MacRaghnaill only 213 more in Louth.[58]

This relative failure was offset by Sinn Féin's success in the 1982 Northern Ireland Assembly elections, previously mentioned, and the indications were clear that electoral participation was now very much part of the republican agenda. That the Dáil should be considered an acceptable house of government in which Provisional republicans were prepared to sit indicates the considerable development of the Irish Free State and Republic over a period of six decades. The overwhelming majority of people in the south had supported the institutions of the state almost from their inception, and saw no merit in voting for abstentionists, a fact that, alongside the election of Joe Sherlock from the Workers' Party to the Dáil in 1981,[59] convinced republican leaders that real power could be attained with the dropping of abstention. Furthermore, Sinn Féin found itself in a position where its claims of being a 'national' party were somewhat undermined by the heavy northern-focus of the party.[60] Adams's presidential address observed:

> I can understand that some comrades view a change of the abstentionist policy as a betrayal of republican principles. Some of you may feel that a republican organisation making such a change can no longer call itself 'republican'. If there are delegates here who feel like this I would remind you that another republican organisation has already done what you fear we are going to do tomorrow. I would remind you that the Army Authority of Óglaigh na hÉireann, the rank and file volunteers, assembled in the General Army Convention, has democratically made a judgement on this issue and that Óglaigh na hÉireann has remained united in its determination to pursue the armed struggle and is united in its confidence in us and in our ability to pursue the political struggle. There was no walk-out from the IRA by IRA Volunteers.[61]

This was undoubtedly a significant success for Adams, with the support of the republican hard-liners in the IRA considerably more difficult to ensure than that of the political party. It should also be noted that the

IRA had killed thirty-seven people during 1986; over half of all of those to die, a result of the conflict that year. It was very much the case that hard-line republicans still had an outlet for their physical force tendencies.

The abandonment of abstention in 1986 caused a group of such republicans to leave and set up their own organisation, which became known as Republican Sinn Féin. While this group attracted enough support in 1985 to defeat a motion on abstention, sufficient change of opinion had occurred over the course of twelve months to allow for this position to be reversed. Ruairí Ó Brádaigh, who led the break-away faction, compared this to the same debate that had occurred during the 1960s, noting: 'on both occasions ... the conspiracy to push for an end to abstentionism was hatched long before the vote took place'.[62] Whether or not it can be argued that this was a conspiracy or merely sound political leadership is a moot point. Certainly, doubts about the integrity of the republican leadership during this period have been raised in recent years, and, for Ó Brádaigh, the conspiracy had deep historical roots. He, along with colleagues who would join him in Republican Sinn Féin, had been at the helm of the Provisional movement from its very inception and yet had become marginalised during the 1970s. A major reason for this takeover of the movement by the younger northern-based leadership was the PIRA ceasefire from 22 December 1974 to 22 September 1975, which seriously discredited the old leadership of the movement. The lack of support for the ceasefire is evidenced by the continued Provisional IRA violence throughout the period.[63]

The termination of the ceasefire was announced spectacularly with the detonation of eighteen bombs in a single day.[64] Following the appointment of Gerry Adams as joint vice-president of Sinn Féin in 1978, the influence of Ruairí Ó Brádaigh and Dáithí Ó Conaill gradually declined as the old guard were shifted to the sidelines of the party. Their areas of influence were also mainly among older members of the party in the South, while Adams retained the crucial support of the North and particularly the IRA.[65] The 1979 merger of the two republican newspapers, *An Phoblacht* and *Republican News*, also indicates the new, single vision for the organisation, with the northern aspects of the struggle moving decisively to centre stage.

In 1990 Ó Brádaigh reflected upon the 1969–70 and 1986 splits in the movement and claimed that 'the people who formed the Workers' Party were more open about it. They wanted to go down the constitutional road and said so. In 1985, at our Ard Fheis, the whole platform party left the stage when abstentionism was debated. To me, that was dishonest.'[66] Adams noted that the 1986 Ard Fheis was very well attended,[67] adding to conspiracy theories that extra delegates had been shipped in to bolster support for the new leadership's position, in an echo of similar charges of malfeasance in 1969:

> Our electoral intervention has exploded the myth that the republican movement enjoyed no support and it has extended our relationships with our constituents. We can now get certain things done and we have access to the departments of the establishment bureaucracy that are relevant to people's everyday problems and needs.[68]

At the 1986 Ard Fheis, Adams's presidential address focused on the issue of abstentionism and he spoke pointedly on the possibility of a split:

> Many republicans have deep and justifiably strong feelings about abstentionism. I share and understand those feelings. But none of us, regardless of the strength of our views, has the right to present the establishment and our supporters with the opportunity to project internationally the spectacle of yet another republican 'split'.[69]

Whereas in 1969 Joe Cahill had argued, 'the split that took place ... was over the failure of the IRA to defend the people of the North ... abstentionism was used as a vehicle for the split',[70] in 1986 Adams criticised the republican movement for a new deficiency: 'The central issue is not abstentionism. It is merely a problematic, deeply rooted and emotive symptom of the lack of republican politics and the failure of successive generations of republicans to grasp the centrality, the primacy and the fundamental need for republican politics.'[71]

Although he spoke in strong terms regarding the lack of political acumen on the part of republicans, Adams's use of language concerning the move was carefully emotive.[72] The key parallel of the 1969 abstention debate existed, but it is important to note the considerably changed circumstances of a decade and a half of violence and over 2,500 deaths, in addition to the prison disputes. The years in between the two splits had taught Provisional republicans a great deal about their struggle and the need to constantly re-evaluate their strategy. Integral to the success of their strategy was the retention of the support of the republican rank and file, and this was the focus of Adams's rhetoric from this period. As noted above, Adams had succeeded in retaining the support of the IRA as their campaign raged on outside of the political sphere.[73] During the 1970s, with the armed campaign at its height, it would have been far more difficult to push through such a shift towards politics. What could be termed a betrayal of a republican tradition could more easily come to pass in the 1980s with the armed campaign, although still active, not at the same level as the previous decade and with the political fillip of the hunger strike elections still fresh in the minds of republicans.[74] For those of a more military inclination, the fact that they could continue their war unabated was a crucial factor in maintaining military unity at this time.

The Ó Brádaigh faction was not prepared to accept such a massive shift in republican policy. Although many republicans were happy to exchange principle for power, the uncompromising stance of Ó Brádaigh and others stemmed from their strict adherence to the principles for which so many republicans had died in recent years. The tensions between the younger Northern leadership and the older southern-based faction were demonstrated by the fact that when the Ó Brádaigh family were involved in a car crash, only Martin McGuinness visited them in hospital; Gerry Adams and Danny Morrison, pointedly, stayed away.[75]

## THE MILITARY DIMENSION

Lessons from history indicate that the republican armed struggle cannot easily be reconciled with republican political struggle. In 1955, Sinn Féin won two seats at the general election, in Mid-Ulster and Fermanagh and South Tyrone,[76] two victories that were ultimately snatched from the party because of the imprisonment of both MPs for treason-felony. The complicated series of events in Mid-Ulster took almost a full year to be resolved, with an Independent Unionist candidate finally emerging victorious. The pyrrhic successes of 1955 were ultimately undone by the Border Campaign of the following year, which reassociated the movement with violence. In the 1959 election, Sinn Féin failed to replicate their successes of four years previously and their vote fell by almost 100,000.[77] It is certainly unclear whether the historical significance of this fact was ever taken into consideration by Provisional republicans, but nevertheless it does provide a degree of evidence that the political development of Sinn Féin was hampered by the militarism of the IRA. This created significant problems for the Provisional republican leadership, who would have to balance the two tendencies in a manner satisfactory to the republican rank and file.

While the 1986 split was only initially confined to the political party, the fact that the much anticipated military split was postponed until 1994 emphasises the uniquely political aspect of this division. Although Republican Sinn Féin claim that the Continuity IRA share their ideals,[78] the lack of action on the part of this armed faction for a full seven years after Republican Sinn Féin emerged can be attributed to the fact that the Provisional IRA remained the most deadly paramilitary group in Northern Ireland until the ceasefire year of 1994.[79] The continued military activity of the Provisional IRA contented militarists through to the ceasefire, at which point they departed for the Continuity IRA.

With Republican Sinn Féin adhering loyally to the republican principle of abstention, the Provisional IRA maintained their own adherence to the republican principle of physical force against British and loyalist targets, which frequently resulted in the deaths of civilians.[80] Throughout the 1980s the IRA struggle took on new forms: the bombing of the Grand Hotel Brighton during the Conservative Party conference in 1984, which targeted Margaret Thatcher, was one particularly spectacular attack. Although the bomb failed to secure its principal target, five people were killed and several others were seriously injured. It has been argued that the bomb indicated a growing dissatisfaction within Provisional republicanism: 'The Provos have been in disarray and badly demoralised, believing that the electoral successes of their political wing actually helped their rivals for Catholic support, the Social Democratic Labour Party, by encouraging a spate of political initiatives, including the New Ireland Forum, in which the SDLP have played a prominent part.'[81]

A ceasefire during the 1970s had cost Ó Brádaigh the leadership of the movement, and Adams was not about to make the same mistake. Comments from an IRA Army Council member around this time indicate the hard-line approach of the army despite the political gains enjoyed by the political wing: 'As long as British troops are on the streets of Ireland, there will be more bombs in Britain.'[82] Crucially, it was also noted that '[s]ome IRA members are either conservative or apolitical and are deeply suspicious of the socialist inclination of the new leadership. They fear that Sinn Féin, the political wing, may eventually take the route of the old, official IRA ... towards non-violence and socialist politics.'[83]

During a debate between the PIRA and the Communist Party of Ireland in 1987, a Sinn Féin representative argued that 'the suggestion that the armed struggle "cripples Sinn Féin's capacity for radical advance" is ... off the mark. It had no effect whatsoever on our ability to take radical political positions on other subjects.'[84] In a sense this is true: IRA activities did not prevent Sinn Féin from promoting radical policies; however it would be naive to assume that such activities would not affect Sinn Féin's ability to appeal politically to persons opposed to military action. We have already noted how violence had negatively impacted upon the political ambitions of Sinn Féin during the 1950s. But an important feature of the republican mentality is the perceived legitimacy of Provisional IRA violence, regardless of its bloodiness. That the essence of the republican quarrel with Britain was political in nature did not detract from the legitimacy of the military campaign.

Joe Cahill argued that the dissidents who left the party in 1986 should have stayed and fought their corner. This view was echoed in America, where republicans believed that 'it seems inevitable given the patriotism and honorable motives of those who walked out of the Ard Fheis last Sunday, that they will soon return and be welcomed with respect'.[85] Cahill later stated that while he would not have a problem with taking seats in the Irish Dáil, he 'would have a real problem about Westminster or Stormont'.[86] While the traditionalist republican view on abstention would dictate that Leinster House was as important as Westminster or Stormont in maintaining partition, it seems logical that it would be the least objectionable of the three. Independent Ireland had developed considerably since the 1920s, certainly to the point where someone like Joe Cahill, so opposed to changes implemented among republican leaders during the 1960s, could apparently be quite comfortable to recognise the legitimacy of the Dáil twenty-six years later.

For Mitchel McLaughlin of Provisional Sinn Féin, the main problem faced by Republican Sinn Féin was that they were still arguing the same points as they had done during the split of 1969–70, and had failed to provide a satisfactory political analysis of the situation now facing the Republican movement. More significantly, Republican Sinn Féin had failed to adapt to the political developments that had taken place over the course of the sixteen or so years.[87] Workers' Party official Dessie O'Hagan concurs with this, arguing that 'Republican Sinn Féin still thinks this is the 1950s ... or even the 1920s.'[88]

## CONCLUSIONS

The Ard Fheis took place in Dublin on 1–2 November 1986 and centred on the issue of resolution 162: 'this Ard-Fheis drops its abstentionist attitude to Leinster House. Successful Sinn Féin parliamentary candidates in 26-County elections: a. Shall attend Leinster House as directed by the Ard Chomhairle; b. Shall not draw their salaries for personal use.'[89] Gerry Adams justified the debate on the grounds that,

> We are a political organisation and political organisations must, by their very nature, discuss and debate issues which they consider pertinent. We cannot do so properly unless all sides of the argument are articulated, unless all sides are accorded equal respect and consideration and unless all are bound by the democratic wishes of their comrades.[90]

Adams stated confidently that

> There is going to be no split in Sinn Féin on this or any other issue. Some comrades may decide to leave us. Perhaps they have already decided to do so. Some may have decided already if the vote goes against them that they will publicly walk out tomorrow. This is a wrong course of action for anyone to take. It means they want us to accept their vote but that they won't accept ours. If this is so, it is something I deeply regret ... To leave Sinn Féin is to leave the struggle ... The spectre of a 'split' is being raised to panic and intimidate us ... This leadership is not going to be blackmailed by any such speculation.[91]

In his oration following the decision to end abstention to the Dáil, Martin McGuinness offered retrospective criticism of abstention at the same time as reaching out to the dissenters:

> those opposed to this issue know there isn't going to be any split in Sinn Féin, they also know that the ranks of the IRA contain a minority of volunteers who, while opposed to the removal of abstentionism from Leinster House, have committed themselves to stand shoulder to shoulder in unity with their comrades. They will not split, they will not walk away from the armed struggle. They are the real revolutionaries. If you allow yourself to be led out of this hall today, the only place you're going is home. You will be walking away from the struggle. Don't go my friends. We will lead you to the republic.[92]

Although the two Northern leaders were outwardly confident that the movement would not split on the issue, it was clear that such an event was inevitable, particularly after Ruairí Ó Brádaigh opposed Resolution

162. Ó Brádaigh questioned, 'how do you expect to build a democratic socialist republic out of Leinster House? How can serious social change come out of Leinster House? How can the fundamental change in property relations come out of Leinster House? No way can it do that.' He closed stating: 'we have not been wrong for 65 years, we have not been wrong for all those 70 years – we have been right and we should continue to be right'.[93]

Support for the motion to end abstention was strong: 429 of 628 delegates at the Ard Fheis voted in favour of the motion.[94] Ó Brádaigh and his supporters walked out of the Ard Fheis to a prebooked hotel room in which Republican Sinn Féin was founded. Journalist Kevin Toolis, who witnessed the birth of the new movement first hand, is somewhat critical of the new group, and his account of the 1986 Ard Fheis makes interesting reading:

> Later that same evening, Ó Brádaigh, with Ó Conaill in a white trench-coat beside him, and a motley collection of aged southern Republicans gathered in a prebooked hotel on the western outskirts of Dublin and founded a new party, Republican Sinn Féin, to maintain the true faith in an ever tighter vessel. A hastily mimeographed statement with the name of the new party handwritten on to the original typed text was handed round to journalists. There was a mad theatrical air to the proceedings. I was expecting Dáithí Ó Conaill, the archetypal fifties IRA gunman, to produce a Webley revolver from each pocket of his voluminous trench-coat, call the meeting to order and urge his followers to attack a border post that night.[95]

Their claim that they 'stand by the Republic of 1916 and the First All-Ireland Dáil of 1919',[96] was authenticated by the blessing given to them by Tom Maguire, 'the last general officer of the Irish Republican Army of 1921 ... also the last faithful survivor of the Second (All-Ireland) Dáil elected in the same year'.[97] Maguire, who in 1986 was 97 years of age, stated: 'I hereby declare that the Continuity Executive and the Continuity Army Council are the lawful Executive and Army Council respectively of the Irish Republican Army, and that the governmental authority, delegated in the Proclamation of 1938, now resides in the Continuity Army Council, and its lawful successors.'[98] It is worth considering the fact that Maguire was speaking in 1987 and, indeed, had passed away prior to the 'official' announcement of the formation of the Continuity IRA. He was not only aware of the existence of the Continuity Army Council, but also of the name that the organisation adopted. Maguire's reasons for changing his allegiance were simple: 'I do not recognise the legitimacy of any Army Council styling itself the council of the Irish Republican Army which lends support to any person or organisation styling itself Sinn Féin and prepared to enter the partition parliament of Leinster House.'[99]

With the realisation during the early 1980s that the political arena could offer the Adams leadership a stage to further their struggle and that these aspirations were irreconcilable with a military strategy, it became inevitable that they would seek a change as soon as possible. The challenge for the Adams leadership was to manoeuvre the republican movement into a position where this would become apparent to a majority of members. As evidenced by later splits in the movement – with the Continuity IRA emerging in 1994 and a group that came to be known as the Real IRA formed in 1997[100] – the militarist imperative remained strong within Irish republicanism, and Adams had to act carefully to retain the support of the movement during this period. The leadership was able to create this situation through participating, as abstentionist candidates, in elections during the early 1980s and by carefully maintaining the Provisional IRA's campaign, boosted by the acquisition of arms from Libya,[101] with a series of notable strikes at their perceived enemies, such as the bombings at Hyde Park and Regents Park in London in July 1981, the murder of controversial unionist politician the Reverend Robert Bradford in November 1981, and the bombing of the Conservative Party conference in Brighton that nearly killed Margaret Thatcher in 1984.

Although much ground had to be covered between Sinn Féin's decision to end abstention to the Irish Dáil in 1986 and the formation of the Northern Ireland Assembly in 1998, the importance of this period to the realisation of a power-sharing government at Stormont Castle is clear. While in 1998 Sinn Féin was only the fourth largest party in Northern Ireland, the significance of their presence in the Assembly cannot be understated. A movement that had based its policies on a steadfast refusal to participate in any form of government that did not hold a mandate for the entire island of Ireland was now firmly a part of the state apparatus of Northern Ireland. A mere five years later, Sinn Féin had grown to the second largest party in the Assembly and the dominant nationalist partner in government. This could not have been possible had it not been for decisions made during the mid-1980s by the Sinn Féin leadership based upon their belief that the party had to move into the arena of political participation.

This act required careful manipulation of the two main support bases for Irish republicanism: Ireland and the United States of America. These acts have attracted considerable controversy to the republican leadership, particularly with regard the exploitation of the 1981 hunger strike. Aside from this, the cautious approach adopted by the Adams leadership combined an entry into the political arena with the maintenance of military activity. The latter would, over time, be scaled down and finally halted in order to fully legitimise the movement as a constitutional political entity. This two-pronged approach ensured that the split that occurred in 1986 on the issue of abstention did not significantly affect the Provisional republican movement; the careful management of these issues allowed for a relatively smooth passage into the Northern Ireland Assembly a little over a decade later. While the methods used by the republican leadership to facilitate these moves fall under increasing scrutiny, with the forthcoming Brendan Hughes interviews likely to further muddy the waters,[102] the security of Adams's grip on the republican movement is likely to be tested again. Dissatisfaction with the Provisional leadership is evidenced by intensified dissident republican activity throughout 2009,[103] an upward trend that is particularly worrying for prospects of peace in Ireland.

## NOTES

1. For the 2005 Local Government Elections in Northern Ireland, see www.ark.ac.uk/elections/flg05.htm, accessed 5 December 2009.
2. Northern Ireland Elections, Northern Ireland Assembly Elections 2003, www.ark.ac.uk/elections/fa03.htm, accessed 5 December 2009.
3. Martyn Frampton, *The Long March: The Political Strategy of Sinn Féin, 1981–2007* (Basingstoke: Macmillan, 2009).
4. See Brendan Lynn, 'Republicanism and the Abstentionist Tradition, 1970–1998', presented to the Institute of Irish Studies, Queen's University Belfast, May 2001. www.cain.ulst.ac.uk/issues/politics/docs/lynn01.htm, accessed 5 December 2009.
5. Cathal Goulding, speaking in 1990, quoted in the *Observer*, 3 January 1999. Dessie O'Hagan has noted that 'it's a flippant remark and Cathal was a very serious man, admittedly with a wicked sense of humour', suggesting that this is perhaps more apocryphal than some suggest. Dessie O'Hagan, interview with author, Belfast, 10 August 2007.
6. Anthony McIntyre, interview with author, Belfast, 7 September 2005.
7. John Lowry, interview with author, Belfast, 9 August 2007.
8. Gerry Adams, *The Politics of Irish Freedom* (Dingle: Brandon Press, 1986), pp.78–9.
9. Richard O'Rawe, *Blanketmen: An Untold Story of the H-Block Hunger Strike* (Dublin: New Island Books, 2005), pp.184, 190. O'Rawe faced considerable criticism from Provisional republicans at the time his allegations were made. Anthony McIntyre has recently argued that, over time, O'Rawe's position has only been strengthened. See *The Pensive Quill*, 'Victory to the Blanketmen', www.thepensivequill.am/2009/09/victory-to-blanketmen.html, accessed 5 December 2009. Councillor Michael McIvor is among those who has refuted O'Rawe's claims as recently as October 2009; see Cllr McIvor: Sinn Féin 'allowed' no one to die on hunger strike, www.longkesh.info/2009/10/10/cllr-mcivor-sinn-fein-%E2%80%98allowed%E2%80%99-no-one-to-die-on-hunger-strike/
10. Eoin Ó Broin, interview with author, Belfast, 20 May 2005. See also Ó Broin's *Sinn Féin and the Politics of Left Republicanism* (London: Pluto Press, 2009).
11. See Tim Pat Coogan, *The IRA* (London: Harper Collins, 1995), pp.415–18.

12. See www.ark.ac.uk/elections/ for all information on Northern Ireland elections. Here accessed 5 December 2009.
13. O'Rawe, *Blanketmen*, pp.218–19.
14. Richard English, *Armed Struggle: The History of the IRA* (London: Macmillan, 2003), p.203.
15. See, for example English, *Armed Struggle*, p.117; Reginald Byron, *Irish America* (Oxford: Oxford University Press, 1999), pp.257–8; Andrew Wilson, *Irish America and the Ulster Conflict, 1968–1995* (Belfast: Blackstaff Press, 1995).
16. *The Scotsman*, 5 February 1983.
17. Adrian Guelke, 'The United States, Irish Americans and the Northern Ireland Peace Process', *International Affairs*, vol. 2, no. 3 (July 1996), pp.521–36, 524.
18. Statement on International Peace-Keeping Forces in Northern Ireland, in North America and the Northern Ireland Problem, undated. The National Archives, London (TNA), FCO 82/487. On Noraid itself, see Brian Hanley, 'The Politics of Noraid', *Irish Political Studies*, vol. 19, no. 1 (summer 2004), pp.1–17.
19. Quoted in English, *Armed Struggle*, p.117.
20. *Time Magazine*, 19 November 1979.
21. *Irish People*, 26 November 1983.
22. *Irish People*, 18 April 1981.
23. Ibid.
24. *Irish People*, 21 March 1981.
25. Embassy of Ireland, Washington DC, press release, *c.* 1980, Boston College, Burns Library (BCBL).
26. *Irish People*, 15 June 1974.
27. Jack Holland notes that Noraid managed to collect more during three months of the 1981 hunger strike than it had done in most other years; see Jack Holland, *The American Connection: US Guns, Money and Influence in Northern Ireland* (Dublin: Poolbeg Press, 1989), p.57.
28. *Irish People*, 27 January 1979.
29. *Irish People*, 29 November 1980 (labelled as 29 September 1980).
30. *Irish People*, 12 September 1981.
31. See David Beresford, *Ten Men Dead* (London: Grafton, 1987) for further details on the progression of the hunger strike.
32. *Irish People*, 12 September 1981.
33. Were it written by someone else and falsely attributed to Hurson, the cynical exploitation of a dying man would surely have drawn considerable controversy but would fit neatly alongside the O'Rawe argument that the hunger strike was itself being exploited by the republican leadership.
34. *Irish People*, 1 November 1980.
35. See Gerard Murray and Jonathan Tonge, *Sinn Féin and the SDLP: From Alienation to Participation* (Dublin: O'Brien Press, 2005), pp.85–7. Andrew Wilson notes that Hume worked hard to convince the four horsemen to openly condemn Irish republicans, something that was not common among Irish American politicians. Wilson, *Irish America*, p.130.
36. 'British Press Coverage of Today, 15 May 1981, of Prime Minister Thatcher's response to Telegram from Senators Kennedy and Moynihan, Speaker O'Neill and New York Governor Carey', telex communication, 15 May 1981, BCBL.
37. *Time Magazine*, 1 November 1971.
38. See Irish Massachusetts, www.irishmassachusetts.com/, last accessed 5 December 2009.
39. 'Hearings on Northern Ireland, Testimony of Senator Edward Kennedy, House of Representatives Committee on Foreign Affairs, Subcommittee on Europe, 28/2/1972', in 'Attitude of Government and citizens of the United States of America towards Political Situation in Northern Ireland', TNA, FCO 87/102.
40. Kennedy drove his car off a bridge, killing his passenger, Mary Jo Kopechne, before leaving the scene of the accident.
41. See Jeanne Theoharis and Komozi Woodard, *Freedom North: Black Freedom Struggles Outside the South, 1940–1980* (New York: Palgrave Macmillan, 2003), p.140.
42. Edward M. Kennedy, *True Compass* (New York: Twelve, 2009) p.355.
43. Ibid.
44. Friends of Ireland, Joint St Patrick's Day Statement, 1981, BCBL.
45. Letter from O'Neill, Kennedy, Carey and Moynihan to Margaret Thatcher, 6 May 1981, BCBL.
46. Kennedy, *True Compass*, pp.460–1.

47. See Gerard Murray, *John Hume and the SDLP: Impact and Survival in Northern Ireland* (Dublin: Irish Academic Press, 1998), especially chapter 9.
48. *Time Magazine*, 28 August 2009. See also 'Ted Kennedy Providing a Leading Voice for Human Rights and Democracy around the Globe', www.tedkennedy.org/service/item/foreign_policy, accessed 5 December 2009.
49. Kennedy, *True Compass*, p.463. Adams himself spoke of the importance of this event; see 'Senator Teddy Kennedy', www.sinnfein.ie/contents/17239, accessed 5 December 2009. Timothy Lynch has discussed the impact of the Adams visa in 'The Gerry Adams Visa in Anglo-American Relations', *Irish Studies in International Affairs*, vol. 14 (2003), pp.33–44.
50. Adams, *Politics of Irish Freedom*, p.84.
51. Ibid., p.86.
52. See Gerry Adams, *Hope and History: Making Peace in Ireland* (Dingle: Brandon Press, 2003), p.15.
53. *The Sun* (Baltimore), 5 May 1981.
54. Compared to three for the Democratic Unionist Party, two of which (Belfast East and North Antrim, which have been held by Peter Robinson since 1979 and Ian Paisley since 1970 respectively) have been DUP strongholds. See Northern Ireland Elections, Westminster Election 1983, www.ark.ac.uk/elections/fw83.htm, accessed 5 December 2009.
55. Adams, *Hope and History*, p.28.
56. See the Sutton Index of Deaths, www.cain.ulst.ac.uk/cgi-bin/tab3.pl, accessed 5 December 2009.
57. *Irish People*, 13 February 1982.
58. See Elections Ireland, www.electionsireland.org/results/general/23Dáil.cfm and www.electionsireland.org/results/general/24Dáil.cfm, accessed 21 November 2009.
59. Representing Cork East in 1981–2, 1987–92 and 2002–7; see www.electionsireland.org/results/general/22Dáil.cfm, accessed 5 December 2009. The Workers' Party then had two TDs in the twenty-fourth Dáil; see www.electionsireland.org/ results/general/24Dáil.cfm., accessed 5 December 2009.
60. Brian Feeney, *Sinn Féin: A Hundred Turbulent Years* (Dublin: O'Brien Press, 2002), p.325.
61. Extract from Presidential Address by Gerry Adams on the Issue of Abstentionism, Dublin, 1 November 1986, www.cain.ulst.ac.uk/issues/politics/docs/sf/ga011186.htm, accessed 21 November 2009.
62. Ruairí Ó Brádaigh interview, *Irish News*, 29 January 1990.
63. See CAIN: Events: IRA Truce – 9 February 1975 to 23 January 1976, www.cain.ulst.ac.uk/events/truce/chron.htm, accessed 5 December 2009.
64. See Robert White, *Ruairí Ó Brádaigh: The Life and Politics of an Irish Revolutionary* (Bloomington, IN: Indiana University Press, 2006), pp.223–42.
65. This idea is promoted by, among others, Mark Ryan, *War and Peace in Ireland: Britain and the IRA in the New World Order* (London: Pluto Press, 1994), p.68; and David Sharrock and Mark Devenport, *Man of War, Man of Peace? The Unauthorised Biography of Gerry Adams* (London: Macmillan 1997), p.247.
66. Ruairí Ó Brádaigh interview, *Irish News*, 29 January 1990.
67. Adams, *Hope and History*, p.46.
68. Adams, *Politics of Irish Freedom*, p.151.
69. Gerry Adams's Presidential Address from 1986 Sinn Féin Ard Fheis, in Sinn Féin, *The Politics of Revolution: Main Speeches and Debates, 1986 Sinn Féin Ard Fheis* (Dublin: Republican Publications, 1986), p.6.
70. Robert W. White, *Provisional Irish Republicans: An Oral and Interpretative History* (London: Greenwood Press, 1993), p.54.
71. Gerry Adams's Presidential Address from 1986 Sinn Féin Ard Fheis, in Sinn Féin, *Politics of Revolution*, p.10.
72. Adams, *Politics of Irish Freedom*, pp.159–60.
73. W.D. Flackes and Sydney Elliott, *Northern Ireland: A Political Directory 1968–88* (Belfast: Blackstaff Press, 1989), p.413; note that murders by Republicans numbered 42 for year 1985, 41 for year 1986 and 69 for year 1987, although attempted murders fluctuated from 140 to 87 to 176 over the same time period.
74. Patrick Walsh, for one, makes this argument; see *Irish Republicanism and Socialism: The Politics of the Republican Movement, 1905–1994* (Belfast: Athol Press, 1994), p.240.
75. See White, *Ruairí Ó Brádaigh*, p.295.

76. Elections Ireland: The 1955 Northern Ireland General Election, www.electionsireland.org/results/general/ni/1955.cfm, accessed 5 December 2009.
77. See Elections Ireland: 1959 Northern Ireland General Election, www.electionsireland.org/results/general/ni/1959.cfm, accessed 5 December 2009.
78. Geraldine Taylor (Belfast Republican Sinn Féin), interview with author, Belfast, 8 August 2007. The *Sunday Business Post* did not even report the formation of CIRA until 14 January 1996, although evidence of such a group exists from 21 January 1994, when a firing party fired shots over the grave of Tom Maguire.
79. See the Sutton Index of Deaths, www.cain.ulst.ac.uk/cgi-bin/tab3.pl, accessed 5 December 2009.
80. Ibid. Indeed, during the 1980s the IRA killed over 100 civilians, compared to 41 by the UVF and 5 by the UDA.
81. *Observer*, 14 October 1984.
82. *Scotsman*, 5 November 1984.
83. *Guardian*, 18 July 1985.
84. Communist Party, *Open Letter from the Communist Party of Ireland to the Provisional IRA*, June 1987, cited in English, *Armed Struggle*, p.7.
85. *Irish People*, 8 November 1986.
86. Joe Cahill interview, *Irish News*, 30 January 1990.
87. White, *Provisional Irish Republicans*, p.150.
88. Dessie O'Hagan, interview with author, Belfast, 9 August 2007.
89. Text of the motion on abstentionism (Resolution 162) as presented to the Sinn Féin Ard Fheis, Dublin, 2 November 1986, www.cain.ulst.ac.uk/issues/politics/docs/ sf/resolution162.htm, accessed 5 December 2009.
90. Extract from the presidential address of Gerry Adams, then President of Sinn Féin, on the issue of abstentionism (Resolution 162), Sinn Féin Ard Fheis, Dublin, 1 November 1986, www.cain.ulst.ac.uk/issues/politics/docs/sf/ga011186.htm, accessed 5 December 2009.
91. Ibid.
92. Speech by Martin McGuinness, then Vice-President of Sinn Féin, on the issue of abstentionism (Resolution 162), Sinn Féin Ard Fheis, Dublin, 2 November 1986, www.cain.ulst.ac.uk/issues/politics/docs/sf/mmcg021186.htm, accessed 5 December 2009.
93. Speech by Ruairí Ó Brádaigh, former President of Sinn Féin, opposing the motion on abstentionism (Resolution 162), Sinn Féin Ard Fheis, Dublin, 2 November 1986, www.cain.ulst.ac.uk/issues/politics/docs/sf/rob021186.htm, accessed 5 December 2009.
94. See J. Bowyer Bell, *The Secret Army: The IRA* (Dublin: Poolbeg Press, 1999), p.575.
95. Kevin Toolis, *Rebel Hearts: Journeys within the IRA's Soul* (London: Picador, 1995), p.320.
96. *Saoirse* (June 1987).
97. Ruairí Ó Brádaigh, *Dílseacht: The Story of Comdt General Tom Maguire and the Second (All-Ireland) Dáil* (Dublin: Irish Freedom Press, 1997), p.3.
98. Thomas Maguire, speaking on 25 July 1987, quoted in *Saoirse* (February 1996).
99. Thomas Maguire, speaking in 1986, quoted in Ó Brádaigh, *Dílseacht*, pp.48–9.
100. Literature produced by this group suggests that they actually called themselves Óglaigh na hÉireann, but they came to be known as the Real IRA. See *The Sovereign Nation: The Republican Voice* (July–August 2007).
101. Brendan Lynn, 'Republicanism and the Abstentionist Tradition, 1970–1998', presented to the Institute of Irish Studies, Queen's University Belfast, May 2001, www.cain.ulst.ac.uk/issues/politics/docs/lynn01.htm, accessed 5 December 2009.
102. See *Belfast Telegraph*, 9 November 2009.
103. See Independent Monitoring Commission, *Twenty-Second Report of the Independent Monitoring Commission* (London: Her Majesty's Stationery Office, 4 November 2009).

CHAPTER ELEVEN

# Paisley and his Heartland: A Case Study of Political Change

JAMES GREER

In February 2008 the First Minister of Northern Ireland, Ian Paisley, welcomed the Irish Taoiseach, Bertie Ahern, to his North Antrim constituency. In the town of Ballymena, in front of a multitude of cameras, the two men jovially led the ceremonial opening of a luxury leisure complex.[1] The event, with its leading personnel and the high-end service industry it was celebrating, was very much intended to embody the new, agreed Ireland. Happening as it did amidst a whirlwind of landmark political firsts that followed the signing of the St Andrew's Agreement by Paisley's Democratic Unionist Party (DUP), the specific historic resonance of this event was perhaps lost on many; but for the small group of local ex-Paisleyites protesting outside the significance was clear. For them, this ceremony represented a further betrayal, or, as one defector from the DUP stated, 'another confounding act in the growing list of Paisley turnarounds since his Damascus-type conversion to seeing Sinn Féiners and Irish Premiers as long lost friends and allies'.[2] The symbolism of the event was especially dismaying for the protesters since it was taking place in an area many of them had worked hard to make Paisley's heartland. Another long-standing DUP activist emotionally summed up the mood of the demonstrators, commenting: 'I am heartbroken that Dr Paisley has sold out having followed him for forty years.'[3] For many others across the political spectrum, the most recent stage of Paisley's political career, and the motivations that drove these conciliatory actions, remain equally perplexing, especially when they are measured against the apparent intransigence that marked his first fifty years as a public figure. In the lengthy list of Irish public figures who have originated on the radical fringes before journeying towards power and respectability, Paisley remains amongst the most unexpected and contested.

The defections from the local DUP following St Andrews suggested to the *Belfast Newsletter* that the past tense now had to be employed: Ballymena was now Paisley's 'once impenetrable heartland'.[4] The core objective of this chapter is to examine the reality behind the previous 'heartland' status granted to Ballymena Paisleyism, and to explore a number of related questions. What were its roots? How was it constructed? And what does this case tell us about the broader character of Paisleyism and its surprising evolution? The temporal framework of this study focuses attention on the formative events of the early 1960s, through the civil rights crisis, the traumatic early years of the Troubles, and concluding with scrutiny of the pivotal strike by the Ulster Workers' Council (UWC) in 1974.

A local case study of this kind creates a fresh avenue for reaching a more nuanced understanding of the dynamics evident within the fragmenting politics of unionism. In rooting the emerging phenomenon of Paisleyism within one unionist community, the distinct character and early development of this multifaceted movement emerges, as does the importance of local distinctions. This is primarily a study of small-town and rural politics, one which will reveal much of the recent history of an under-researched locality. But more broadly, it acts to counter or question generalisations often made within the scholarly literature that distort the experiences of many communities. Too often this period has been observed from a Belfast perspective. This may be understandable given the concentration of political violence and power within that city, but often the importance of varying local contexts has been lost or obscured.

The Ballymena district is deserving of concentrated study. The area constituted a vital arena in the political development of Northern Ireland, disproportionate to its size and notwithstanding the relative absence of political violence emanating from it. The list of politicians who congregated in the district is both eclectic and significant, and highlights how Ballymena – after years of political hibernation – was often at the centre of Northern Irish political life. Besides Ian Paisley, it includes the then Northern Irish prime minister, Terence O'Neill; the former home affairs minister and Ulster Vanguard leader, William Craig; the high Tory journalist, T.E. Utley; and the leader of the radical civil rights organisation People's Democracy, Michael Farrell. These diverse figures all competed for the electorate's vote during the time frame of this study. This cast list helps to reveal how the area became the scene of many set-piece elections, protests, ideological divisions and power shifts, which had consequences far beyond its electoral boundaries. An analysis of these developments within the heartland of Protestant Ulster provides fresh insights, from the grassroots upwards, into unionism's role in, and response to, the crisis that was engulfing Northern Ireland.

UNWELCOME TERRAIN FOR A YOUNG RADICAL

In his biography of Ian Paisley, Steve Bruce notes, with a hint of comic exaggeration, that by the late 1970s Paisley was winning his North Antrim Westminster seat 'by the sorts of majorities found in the communist states of Eastern Europe'.[5] After narrowly claiming the seat in 1970, taking it from the long-standing Unionist MP, Henry Clark, by a majority of 2,676 votes,[6] the speed with which Paisley stamped his electoral authority on the area was remarkable. Within four years Paisley was defeating his Unionist opponent with a majority of 27,631 votes.[7] Such was the dramatic speed of change in this politically and socially conservative constituency. Thirty-five years after claiming the seat, Paisley retained it in 2005, securing over 54 per cent of the vote.[8] This remarkable electoral longevity has received much comment, but often the picture of one-party dominance acts to obscure the struggles, alliances and compromises inherent in the creation of Paisley's heartland. By placing Paisley within context of the political history of the area, the unlikely nature of his later dominance is thrown into relief. The constituency that soon appeared to be the natural home of Paisleyism was in the early 1960s a long-established closed shop for new political forces, an unwelcome terrain for a young radical political entrepreneur.

Within the North Antrim Westminster constituency, the town of Ballymena has long been the largest population centre, as well as the leading commercial district and the seat of local government for much of the area. Less than thirty miles from Belfast, it can be viewed as the unofficial capital of the constituency. Reflecting the centrality of the town in the DUP's history, the party's ex-representative Clifford Smyth has described Ballymena as 'the DUP's holy city'.[9] Paisley himself was actually born in Armagh (in 1926), but the Baptist ministry of his father brought the family to Ballymena and ensured that the young Paisley grew up in the area and was shaped by its culture. The geographic boundaries of this study are largely defined by the local government jurisdictions of

Ballymena Rural and Urban District Councils, which merged in 1973 to create Ballymena Borough Council. The borough – one of three council areas within the contemporary North Antrim Westminster seat alongside Ballymoney and Moyle – is centred upon Ballymena town, but it includes an expanse of rural county Antrim and numerous smaller villages. The 1971 census recorded that the total population of the district was 50,669: the majority 34,106 belonging to the Rural District Council, with 16,503 resident in the Urban District.[10]

Political analysis of the district prior to the introduction of Direct Rule in 1972 is, however, complicated by the multiplicity of electoral constituencies to the Stormont Parliament that infringed on Ballymena local government territory.[11] The majority of the area was placed in two Stormont constituencies: the Urban Council within the old Mid-Antrim seat, and the bulk of the Rural Council within the Bannside constituency, which later proved so pivotal to the political future of Northern Ireland. The evolving functions and characters of these three layers of governance and representation – local, Stormont and Westminster – were to play a vital role in the political development of Paisleyism.

In order to qualify the assumption that this was always natural Paisley territory, it is necessary to outline the political, social and cultural environment that local Paisleyites faced in 1966. As a small protest movement, Paisleyism faced sustained opposition from across all the major Protestant and unionist institutions within Northern Ireland. Most importantly, as a challenge to the status quo, the movement ran counter to the established power of the Unionist Party. From partition through to the emergence of Paisley, the Unionist Party in the area represented a virtually unopposed political force, with successive Unionist Party nominees inheriting the position of natural leaders of a solidly unionist electorate. A striking example of this power is provided by the Bannside constituency of the Stormont parliament and by the career of Terence O'Neill. The former prime minister of Northern Ireland gained the seat unopposed in 1946, and held it until 1969 without facing an electoral rival.[12] Indeed, from 1929 to 1970 the Unionist Party continuously held the seat, facing an electoral opponent only twice. In the neighbouring Mid-Antrim constituency, Unionist candidates had to fight off challenges from Independent and Progressive Unionist[13] opponents in the first decades of the Northern Irish state, but after the Second World War and until the eruption of the Troubles they were returned unopposed. Therefore Robert Simpson, the Unionist MP for Mid-Antrim from 1953 to 1972, had no experience of campaigning for election until he faced a Northern Ireland Labour Party (NILP) opponent in 1969.

As throughout Northern Ireland, the Protestant alliance that facilitated the Unionist Party's fifty-year near monopoly of power incorporated overwhelming support from across all the major Protestant denominations, and from the Loyal Orders. Furthermore, support was received from across a surprisingly broad slice of the left–right political divide, and from all classes of local Protestant society.[14] Unsurprisingly, such a prolonged, unchallenged period of power opened up familiar avenues of patronage. A significant example is provided by the close relationship, and indeed interchangeable membership, between the Unionist Party, the Ulster Farmers' Union and the Ministry for Agriculture. Economist Alan Greer has noted that 'the creation of a monopolistic consultative relationship between the Ministry and the Union was rooted in overlapping political and rural elites'.[15] Such a structure of consultation and power left a considerable imprint on the lives of many people in the large rural and farming community of the Ballymena district. Agricultural policy was only one instance where many undoubtedly benefited from a direct line to power; but equally, others felt excluded from what were often closed, tightly defined hierarchies of influence. Within the unionist-dominated culture and society of the Ballymena district the local nationalist minority was clearly most at risk from this form of exclusion, but for many Protestants a sense of alienation was also fostered. As a member of a small church, and neither a member of the Loyal Orders nor of the Unionist Party, Paisley was outside the traditional centres of power.[16]

If the recent history of the district was unwelcoming to independent unionist challengers, so too, at first glance, was its political geography. Following O'Neill's rise to the premiership in 1963, the most vocal unionist disquiet at his leadership emerged from the west of Ulster.[17] In the border counties and in Derry City, the demographic balance between nationalism and unionism, combined with the implied logic of civil rights reform on issues such as housing and the electoral franchise, seriously threatened Unionism's control of a number of key local government constituencies. Furthermore, it was in many of these areas where unionists had recent memories of activities by physical force republicanism: the IRA's Border Campaign only having ground to a halt in 1962.

The situation in much of the east of Ulster was clearly different. The census figures for the Ballymena district during the period in question show a consistent 80 per cent Protestant population.[18] This was also an area that had no recent experience of significant republican activity, nor indeed an area where Irish nationalism and the emerging civil rights movement had any coherent institutionalised platform. From this perspective, it is perhaps surprising that a Protestant cleric should go on to make political capital playing upon the ethno-national insecurities of this particular Protestant community. Analysis of the district's demographics does, however, point us towards factors that help to explain Paisley's rise. Most obviously, the size of the local Protestant majority allowed room for non-official Unionist dissent to emerge at a time of national crisis, without the fear that by splitting the vote a nationalist would claim victory. This electoral breathing space opened up room for policy and ideological divisions, which could not be thrashed out as easily among unionists in other areas because of their requirement for a united unionist vote.

The other striking feature of the Ballymena district is its distinct religiosity. This remains an area caricatured as 'the buckle on Ian Paisley's North Antrim Bible belt constituency'.[19] Emerging from this vibrant religious culture is the assumption that clerics are expected to perform leadership roles within the wider community. But what more precisely marks the religious culture in Ballymena is the numerical strength and cultural importance of Presbyterianism. In 1971 Presbyterians made up 54 per cent of the population of the district, a population much larger than the other Protestant churches; the Church of Ireland members numbered 12 per cent and the Methodists only 3 per cent.[20]

The institutional structure of the Presbyterian Church in Ireland facilitates a greater degree of lay participation in church governance and a decentralised democratic decision-making process not evident within the Episcopalian or Catholic traditions.[21] One consequence of this culture, reflected in the history of the area, is the frequent occurrence of congregations challenging and removing the authority of their minister. It is, however, important to qualify any image of Presbyterian egalitarianism. As Ian McBride has noted, social status continued to play a significant role in the internal dynamics of the Presbyterianism, and its 'ecclesiastical democracy' has on occasion led the church to turn in decidedly illiberal theological and political directions.[22] Nonetheless, it remains a central paradox of the district's sociopolitical history that this Dissenting culture flourished in parallel with a political deference towards a Unionist Party that continually put forward aloof, landed-class Episcopalians to represent the area.

BEFORE THE STORM: PAISLEY AND PRE-CIVIL RIGHTS POLITICS

It was a further by-product of the Dissenting culture of the area that provided the launch pad for the man who was to destroy this uneasy sociopolitical détente. The tendency within reformed Protestantism for schism is reflected in the 14 per cent of the Ballymena population that belonged to smaller denominations, such as the Reformed Presbyterians. From the patchwork of smaller break-away churches and independent gospel halls emerged the Free Presbyterian Church in 1951, formed and led for over fifty years by Ian Paisley. It was the gradual growth of a network of Free Presbyterian Churches throughout Northern Ireland that first brought Paisley to the wider public's attention. His compelling style of preaching, laden with personal testimony and societal comment, made him a young star within the orbit of evangelical Protestantism. His direct attacks on the larger Protestant denominations soon elevated Paisley to the status of *bête noire* within the minds of the established forces of Ulster Protestant life.

Whilst acknowledging the important role of Free Presbyterianism within Paisley's politics, it is important not to exaggerate the power of an institution that was, and remains, relatively small. Census figures reveal that in the entire county of Antrim only 1,773 people defined themselves as Free Presbyterian in 1968. At the beginning of the twenty-first century, the Free Presbyterian Church's total membership throughout Northern Ireland has stabilised around the 12,000 mark.[23] These figures reveal that Paisleyism's success is not one of parallel political and religious growth. The majority of Paisley's political supporters have not joined his church, and indeed many reject or largely ignore his theology.

Accepting the limitations in the power of the Free Presbyterian Church enables a proper examination of the impact of Paisley's religious message, and of its interaction with the politics of Northern Ireland prior to the civil rights crisis. From this broader perspective, Paisley's religiosity has played a significant role in his success. The impact of the Free Presbyterian Church is most clearly evident in the ideologically committed activist base it provided. A large section of Paisley's religious base consistently evangelised in support of his political message. Clifford Smyth's recollection of a Paisleyite election campaign in this period highlights the central role played by the Free Presbyterians and the religious revival sentiment that was created: 'campaigning is accompanied by a series of prayer meetings held either in private homes, or in the Ballymena Free Presbyterian Church.

At such meetings God's blessing is called upon the electoral campaign.'[24] Secondly, the church, and its ministry, helped Paisley gain acceptance within the broader evangelical Protestant community, which stretches across all the Protestant denominations, including a large segment of conservative Presbyterians. Paisley's straightforward theology, his charismatic preaching and his awareness of the utility of different media, such as biblical tracts and pamphlets, all assisted in elevating his evangelical reputation outside his church.

The core message behind Paisley's religious message was that Protestantism and scriptural teaching were being diluted by the mainstream churches. According to Paisley, the leadership of these churches had created a 'Protestantism ashamed of its name, apologetic of its past, uncertain of its doctrine, wavering in its policy and ritualistic in its worship'.[25] Driving this process, according to Paisley, was the tentative progress of the ecumenical movement in Northern Ireland, which saw improved relations between the Catholic and Protestant hierarchies. Ecumenists across the denominations tended to favour liberal interpretations of the Bible, which coincided with distinctly liberal viewpoints on societal and political matters.

Paisley gave a public display of his opposition to this ecumenical tendency outside Ballymena Town Hall in 1959, when he led a protest against a sermon given by the prominent English Methodist Donald Soper. During the protest a Bible was thrown at the cerebral Soper, and later, with a similar lack of subtlety, Paisley's colleague, the Revd John Wylie, threw rosary beads at the Methodist during the Belfast leg of his Ulster tour.[26] As Bruce explains, it was Soper's 'left-wing politics' that irked Paisley as much as his ecumenicalism.[27] Within a Northern Irish context, Paisley saw the ecumenical worldview as a threat to the traditional tenets of *both* unionism and Protestantism. Being a sound Protestant was seen as a necessary prerequisite to being a sound unionist. When Paisley's *Protestant Telegraph* denounced the Unionist Party for apparently selecting a Jewish candidate in a Belfast local government election, it proclaimed that 'Mr Smith is not, and cannot be, a Traditional Unionist.'[28]

The power of Paisley's politicised faith was that it tapped straight into the dormant Dissenting suspicion of elites, in both political and religious spheres. Moreover, it did so through a discourse that was for many a familiar and agreeable blend of militant Protestant unionism. As the pages of the *Protestant Telegraph* record, this discourse often included vicious anti-Catholicism, where topics such as the fertility rates of Catholics and lurid allegations about the sex lives of clerics filled the pages.[29] Furthermore, the allegedly increasing dangers presented by Catholicism were clearly linked with the reforming policies of Terence O'Neill. The message of Paisleyism was clear: 'the hoards of Romanism and the compromise of O'Neillism' were a threat to 'our Protestant heritage'.[30] The synthesis of religious and political analyses resulted in a Paisleyite message that was at once advocating a radical departure – rejecting the established institutions in political and religious life – while simultaneously appealing to the community's sense of heritage, cultural identity, insecurity and conservatism.

Paisley's pre-civil rights critique of O'Neill was based upon a mistrust of the prime minister's soundness with regard to the constitution, and a corresponding belief that the new prime minister encouraged a weak security policy towards Irish republicanism. To support these assumptions, Paisley utilised the display of a republican flag – in apparent contravention of the Flags and Emblems Act – outside the office of a Republican candidate for the 1964 West Belfast Westminster election. With the support of the local Unionist candidate, Paisley became the public face of a campaign for the removal of the flag.[31] When grassroots pressure influenced the police to remove the flag, the area erupted into sustained rioting. Paisley later made political capital out of the state's acceptance of large republican demonstrations to commemorate the fiftieth anniversary of the Easter Rising, and out of O'Neill's surprise invitation to Irish Taoiseach Seán Lemass.

The character of O'Neillism encouraged the growing acceptance amongst conservative unionists of Paisley's thesis of elitist betrayal. O'Neill's biography reads almost as a caricature of a remote unionist leader of the old school, with his landed-class heritage, Etonian education, distinguished military career and easy progression into politics. This background, together with his aloof public persona, contrasted starkly with Paisley's rootedness in the community and his communication skills. More significantly – as evidenced by his failure to consult colleagues regarding his invitation to Lemass – O'Neill's premiership displayed an unwillingness to engage with the structures vital to the continuation of unionist unity.[32]

By 1966, the twin approach of political anti-elitism and militant Protestantism that Paisley espoused was having an impact in Ballymena, but he was still very much on the margins of public life. However, Paisley's short imprisonment in that year was to provide him with an avenue towards larger public appeal. An anti-ecumenical march to the general assembly of the Presbyterian Church, led by Paisley, ended in serious violence when the RUC policing the event were attacked by

Catholic youths.[33] Outside the General Assembly, Paisley and his supporters loudly, but peacefully, denounced the Presbyterians. The violence of that day and the alleged provocation by the Paisleyite demonstrators made headlines throughout Britain and Ireland. Despite the lack of evidence that the Paisleyites had directly been engaged in violence, a clamour for Paisley to be prosecuted developed. When indeed Paisley and four other loyalists were charged with a public order offence, they refused to pay the fine and were subsequently imprisoned.

Sympathy for Paisley was widespread, with supportive rallies held throughout Northern Ireland. An application for the use of Ballymena Town Hall was, however, rejected by the local council. Only one councillor supported the Paisleyite application, stating that he saw no reason to restrict free speech. The remaining councillors held the view expressed by James Millar, that the meeting threatened to destroy the peace of the town.[34] The Paisleyite response to this rejection was unsurprisingly strong. Speaking at the rearranged meeting – which eventually took place at a small gospel hall – the Free Presbyterian the Revd James Beggs portrayed the council's decision as sectarian. Beggs' sermon highlighted the anti-establishment pretensions of the movement and how it seamlessly wove together narratives of political and religious betrayal with opposition to local centres of power. He stated that the banning of the meeting from the Town Hall was a 'classic example of O'Neillism. As for James Millar, he runs true to form. He has very close association with the World Council of Churches, because his brother is an Irish Presbyterian Minister and The Presbyterian Assembly would like to grind the Free Presbyterian Church into the ground.'[35] The town hall controversy reveals a central Paisleyite strategy of the time, namely the politicisation of public space and of aspects of public life, which previously had been surprisingly apolitical. Locally, Paisleyites campaigned on issues such as the right to march and the refusal of employers to allow the presence of unionist flags and emblems in the workplace.[36] But the most significant result of this tendency was the introduction of party politics into local government. In May 1967 John McAuley, under the Paisley brand 'Protestant Unionist', became the first Paisleyite elected in Ballymena. In doing so, he became the only councillor who sat under a designated party banner. Many of the established councillors had clear links with and sympathies for the Unionist Party, but they had been elected and sat as Independents, not as Unionist Party councillors. In many regards the election of McAuley signalled the beginning of the end of a period when party politics, and the constitutional issue, had played a relatively minor role in the discourse of local government.

The political geography of the district ensured that only one nationalist representative was elected to the council every term. Throughout this period, and indeed up until 1985, this representative was the Independent nationalist, Paddy Burke.[37] Described by those who served on the council alongside him as a pious Catholic and an unapologetic nationalist, Burke was also one of the most powerful men on the council.[38] Indeed, prior to the reform of local government in 1973, which removed housing powers from councils, Burke was the established chairman of the Housing Committee, which oversaw local authority lettings.[39] Further evidence of the less divisive environment of local government in the 1960s can be seen in the election, with the help of Protestant votes, of John O'Mullan. The current local SDLP representative, P.J. McAvoy, recalls O'Mullan as 'an Independent pro-business, Catholic builder, who built half of the town'.[40]

Emphasising the success and prominence of men such as Burke and O'Mullan is not to argue that prior to the outbreak of the Troubles, Ballymena was somehow an integrated community, miraculously free of the sectarian divisions and impulses that marked much of Northern Irish life. Clearly the area's social conservatism (evident in both nationalist and unionist communities), combined with the cultural and residential segregation of the two traditions, ensured that in many regards the area followed the trend detailed in Rosemary Harris's seminal work on rural Ulster; namely the facilitating of two communities, who shared essentially the same common values, to remain both neighbours and strangers.[41] Nonetheless, the more consensual style of local government reveals how the fault lines of segregation were defined differently in this period, and how arguably they were showing some signs of blurring.

Clifford Davison, an Independent councillor from 1967 to 1977, recalls 'a good working' and 'non-political council'.[42] With the reorganisation of local government in 1973, however, much of the current character of local government in Northern Ireland had emerged, in the shape of competing party blocs providing a localised version of the national party system, greatly reducing the number of Independents on the council. The irony in the Ballymena district, as in the rest of Northern Ireland, was that this process of increased party political competition had occurred in parallel with the drastic reduction in the powers that local government could exercise.[43] Consequently, despite bitterly divisive campaigns, it often was to appear that apart from exercising basic statutory duties, local government had been reduced to the status of arguing over political and religious symbolism. Paisleyism was, of course, well equipped to fight these largely symbolic battles.

## 'O'NEILL OUT!': FROM PROTEST MOVEMENT TO ELECTION

The election of a local Protestant Unionist in 1967 should not be seen as marking the beginning of a dramatic growth in the popularity of Paisley's message. McAuley's narrow election victory was in large part facilitated by the NILP's self-defeating decision to run two candidates.[44] This is reflective of the broader truth that although Paisleyite and wider unionist discontent predated late 1968, it was the social unrest and constitutional uncertainty that emerged from the civil rights crisis that opened a pathway to power for Paisley. The dynamic that emerged was one of successive civil rights demonstrations, followed by what the media proclaimed as Paisleyite counter-protests. In fact, the loyalist protesters – although sympathetic to Paisley – were often not aligned with him. Frequently protests were dominated by right-wing Official Unionists or the Loyal Orders, but the schisms within Official Unionism, combined with the media-friendly clarity that Paisley offered, ensured the creation of the straightforward template: Paisley *versus* the Civil Rights Movement.

The Unionist government, facing pressure from civil rights agitation and London, had its space for political manoeuvre further restricted by the sustained opposition to reform from within its own ranks. Therefore the failure of right-wing opposition to O'Neill to manifest itself more strongly within the local Unionist Party requires further explanation. The primary reason for this failure can be found in the sparse structure of the party locally: top-heavy with local dignitaries, but lacking in grassroots activists. This was, after all, a constituency party lacking in the experience, and consequent internal discipline, gained from fighting competitive elections. Furthermore, as the work of Patterson and Kaufmann has highlighted, the Orange Order, a bulwark against opposition to the party elsewhere, continued to be less important socially and politically in County Antrim than it was in areas where unionists found themselves in the minority.[45]

It is also important to note that many within the local Unionist Party remained loyal to Terence O'Neill. This loyalty was strongest among those in the explicitly liberal wing of the party, who were overrepresented in positions of leadership. Of more significance, however, were the ambiguities of O'Neill's leadership. The gesture politics and contradictions of O'Neill's programme allowed a wide spectrum of local unionists, holding wildly varying perspectives, to perceive that the Unionist Party was still their natural home. Supporting all these factors was the persistence within the Unionist Party of a strong sense of social deference. Repeatedly, unionists who eventually joined either the DUP or Ulster Vanguard recalled their frustration at the staid, hierarchical structures of the Unionist Party. When they campaigned for change within the party, it was often felt that the status of the leadership was sufficient to stifle debate.[46]

The performance of O'Neill and Henry Clark as constituency representatives also provided an open goal for Paisley. O'Neill himself later acknowledged that due to the pressures of the premiership, he had neglected Bannside, and Clark's somewhat sparse attendance at Westminster was repeatedly the focus of Paisley's attacks.[47] Equally, Unionists locally recall Clark not being a visible presence on the ground in North Antrim. When Clark did enter public debate in the local media, it was mostly to advocate the Conservative Party's programme. Representative of the Westminster Unionist parliamentary party's separation from Stormont politics, and the gap between Clark and the requirements of much of his constituency, is this press release from April 1968:

> A future Conservative and Unionist Government will have to be ruthless in its efforts to put the country back on the road to prosperity. Tens of thousands of Civil Servants will have to be axed and all Government spending which does not directly benefit industry will have to be cut.[48]

It is unsurprising that many in a constituency that required serious investment in housing and infrastructure were not encouraged to remain loyal to the Unionist Party brand when this was the short-term vision on offer. As the current North Antrim Ulster Unionist representative Robert Coulter recalls: 'the Unionist government was not seen to be governing for the whole [unionist] population'.[49]

A comparison between the party structure and type of representation offered by the Unionist Party and that of Paisleyism is instructive. Firstly, as already stated, Paisley could rely upon a disciplined, ideologically committed activist base. This base was open to and evangelised for new members. Secondly, from an early stage Paisleyism was an avenue for social mobility within the Protestant community. Many in prominent positions within the Protestant Unionist Party, and the majority of the early representatives of the DUP, were from backgrounds that were believed to inhibit progress within the Unionist Party. Indeed many of these early Paisleyites were ex-Unionist Party members whose political opposition to O'Neillism was enhanced by a sense of being socially excluded from the more rarified circles of the local Unionist Party elite.

The clash between the two political cultures occurred in February 1969 when Ian Paisley opposed the sitting prime minister in elections for the Stormont parliament. Throughout Northern Ireland the divisions within unionism resulted in a complex electoral battle, with the decentralised structure of the Unionist Party and its semi-autonomous local branches producing an array of candidates standing on both pro- and anti-O'Neill tickets. In notable cases, the two wings of the party supported independent unionist candidates who opposed the Official Unionist nominee. Within Bannside, despite substantial concern at the direction of O'Neill's policy, the majority of the local party rallied around the prime minister. Indeed, for the next two years Bannside drew in a multitude of senior Unionists and Orangemen from across Northern Ireland, campaigning to fend off Paisley's challenge.[50] Paisley's campaign strategy was founded upon his critique of the civil rights movement as republicanism in new clothes, and of O'Neill as a weak protector of unionist interests against the demands of the Labour government. But social conditions in the constituency also played a significant role in the campaign. Michael Farrell, the third candidate in the race, clearly recalls his shock at the poor standard of housing and amenities in the area. He was 'absolutely shocked by the poverty of the area. We thought that the Prime Minister's constituency would have been better looked after.'[51]

When the result was announced, the sea change that had occurred in the area was clear for all to see. The prime minister held the seat, but had only defeated Paisley by 1,414 votes. Tellingly, Paisley chose to concentrate on social conditions in his concession speech, noting:

> As I toured around Bannside during my campaign I saw houses with dry toilets and without running water and other houses where water had to be carried from as far away as three miles. In view of matters like this it would not have been very nice for Capt. O'Neill to stand up ... to talk about progressive Ulster and then have to answer his constituents' questions about their own poor conditions.[52]

When asked of his plans for the future, Paisley commented: 'I don't think I will stand again ... My pulpit is my throne and I would not put Parliament on the same level.'[53] However, within fourteen months Paisley was the MP for Bannside, with a majority of 1,202 votes. Having received an inconclusive mandate for reform, and under immense pressure from all sides, O'Neill resigned as prime minster and Unionist Party leader in April 1969. Soon he and the liberal Unionist MP for South Antrim, Richard Ferguson, resigned their seats at Stormont. The subsequent by-elections of 1970 have been described as 'probably the most vital in the history of the Stormont House of Commons'.[54]

Writing about the Bannside Unionist Party's campaign, Graham Walker has declared, '[i]t was perhaps the most convincing expression of the civic and pluralist strand to Unionist ideology in the history of Northern Ireland as a political entity.'[55] The Unionist Party candidate, local doctor Bolton Minford, put forward a secular vision that emphasised the economic benefits of the Union and the need for a shared sense of community with Catholics. Not only was this far removed from the sectarianised rhetoric of Paisley, it was also distinct from the traditional Unionist Party message and noticeably more definitively liberal than the previous ambiguities of O'Neillism. Faced with this new-found pluralist message, and at a time of great political upheaval, many conservative unionists simply preferred the certainties offered by Paisley. Now carrying the political momentum, within months Paisley defeated Henry Clark and gained the Westminster seat, winning by a majority of 2,679 votes.[56] But these victories did not signal the accession of Paisleyism to hegemonic status in the area. Rather, in the coming decade political Paisleyism had to adapt and was forced to form alliances, often as the junior partner, with other local forces.

## PAISLEY THE PARLIAMENTARIAN AND THE FRAGMENTATION OF UNIONISM

Now established as a distinctive voice in both Stormont and Westminster, Paisley's public profile continued to grow. The media-friendly clarity of his message ensured that for many observers, Paisley had already become the voice of Protestant Ulster, regardless of the still limited success of his party. Paisley's elevated status at this time was largely due to the institutional and ideological disarray evident across unionism. The tentative moves towards reform taken by a succession of Unionist leaders, combined with constitutional uncertainty over the intentions of the British government, served to divide Unionist Party branches, Orange Lodges, churches and indeed families throughout Ulster. This sense of communal unease was exasperated by the commencement of the Provisional IRA's widespread bombing campaign in the summer of 1970. Within this quickly evolving, and often traumatic, context, unionism's analysis of the best way forward was fragmented and uncertain. And whilst Paisleyism was free of the internal squabbles over party leadership that characterised the Unionist Party, it, too, could not escape this malaise and struggled to define its agenda.

Integral to the development of Paisley's career was the formation of the DUP in October 1971. Paisley worked together with the Belfast Unionist MPs Desmond Boal and Johnny McQuade to form the new party. This political marriage can be seen as an attempt to ally the largely rural 'Pious Protestants'[57] of the Protestant Unionist Party with the working-class loyalism of Boal and McQuade's constituencies. Paisley himself was closely associated with Belfast – not least through his congregation on the Ravenhill Road and his involvement in the public disturbances previously discussed – but for some of the rural evangelicals who made up his base support, this was at first an awkward marriage. To some, the removal of the word *Protestant* seemed like an acknowledgement of the need 'to dilute the emphasis which the Protestant Unionist Party had placed on religious issues'.[58] However, largely through Paisley's personal standing, the vast majority of Protestant Unionists accepted the new party. Indeed, new party chairman Boal's manifesto, that the DUP would be 'right wing in the sense of being strong on the Constitution, but to the left on social policies',[59] was in some regards an extension of the tone of Paisley's campaigns in Bannside and North Antrim.

The broader disarray within unionism was reflected locally in Ballymena. In the Unionist Party, moderates and supporters of the leadership of Brian Faulkner largely succeeded in maintaining control of the local branch up until 1974, but the party's electoral fortunes continued to decline. Fatally for the long-term future of the Unionist Party, at grassroots level the stream of members defecting to other parties gathered pace. The attempts by O'Neill, Chichester-Clark and Faulkner to hold the broad church that was the Unionist Party together failed, as members on all wings became disillusioned and sought more clearly defined political homes. In Ballymena, this resulted in prominent liberal O'Neillites, such as the Mayor James Millar and Senator Cameron Millar, joining the recently formed Alliance Party.[60] More significantly, on the prevailing right wing of unionism, the emergence of Vanguard, first as a pressure group in February 1972 and then as an independent political party in March 1973, decimated local Unionist Party branches for a generation.

As for the DUP, its own official history defines the early 1970s as a difficult period in the party's development, experiencing low recruitment and uncertainty over the key constitutional issue that divided unionism: whether to advocate devolution, or the deeper integration of Northern Ireland into British political life.[61] Due in large part to this temporary confusion within the DUP and the deep structural problems

of the Unionist Party, it was Ulster Vanguard that became the main political vehicle for hard-line unionist opposition to Faulkner and anger
at the abolition of Stormont in March 1972. This was noticeably the
case even in Paisley's own constituency, where the large loyalist rallies
held to protest against British government policy were under the banner of Vanguard. In addition to these rallies – which regularly attracted
over 2,000 people – industrial action further highlighted the impetus
that Vanguard had right from its formation in the area. In the spring
of 1972 the *Ballymena Observer* dramatically proclaimed that 'industrial, business and social life in Ballymena and the surrounding area
came to a complete standstill … as thousands of workers left the fac-
tories and shops closed in support of the two day strike called by Vanguard'.[62]

How had Vanguard, rather than Paisley, succeeded in claiming this
leadership role organising unionist opposition? The shifting roles and
objectives of Vanguard are complex, as are its links to groupings such as
the Orange Order, Protestant trade unionists and the emerging loyalist
paramilitaries. On its formation, some members saw the movement as
simply a pressure group, aiming to shift the Unionist Party on to safer
Orange waters by uniting conservative unionist opinion, while others
envisaged Vanguard as the vehicle for a radical reformation of unionism.
This later tendency grew in importance until the leadership swiftly
began to explicitly explore proposals such as a federalised United Kingdom or an independent Northern Ireland.[63] Although many were
attracted to these ideas, the short-term success of Vanguard was based
more directly upon the immediate concerns revealed in its policies towards security, and the return of Stormont. In the context of 1972,
the bloodiest year of the Troubles,[64] Vanguard's blunt demands for
tougher action against the Provisionals and for the return of a major-
ity-rule, devolved government appealed to large sections of a unionist
community in a state of collective dislocation, shocked at how quickly
the certainties of pre-1968 Northern Ireland had evaporated.

Just as Vanguard's position on the constitutional future of Northern
Ireland was fluid, and at times ambiguous, so too was its relationship
with loyalist paramilitaries, specifically the Ulster Defence Association
(UDA). Formed in September 1971 as a coalition of the loyalist vigi-
lante groups that had emerged as a result of the communal violence
since 1969, the UDA was most prominent in Belfast, but was a significant force throughout much of Northern Ireland.[65] Importantly, it
remained a legal organisation until 1992, claiming responsibility for
acts of violence under the cover name the Ulster Freedom Fighters

(UFF). The secretive nature of the group, and its loose and ill-defined structure, make definitive proclamations on its strength difficult, but in the early 1970s the UDA is widely believed to have had up to 40,000 members/supporters.[66]

The concentration of its violent activities in locations such as Belfast and mid-Ulster has left the role and character of the UDA in other areas under-researched. What is clear is that the UDA did fulfil a significant function in rural areas and small towns such as Ballymena, often with distinctive local and sociological characteristics. Within Ballymena, the UDA quickly developed a visible presence, marching through the town and marshalling other loyalist rallies.[67] What distinguished the character of the UDA in the district from that of the Belfast UDA is perhaps best encapsulated by the biography of its 'Officer Commanding' during this period, the aforementioned Independent councillor Clifford Davison.[68] Davison has recently decided to publicly acknowledge his role in the UDA, in order to reject allegations that he was involved in any illegal activity.[69] The overlap between respected community roles and militant loyalism evident in Davison's *curriculum vitae* is a window into the competing currents of the period. While a member of the Ballymena UDA, Davison was also a successful architect, on the board-of-governors of a local Catholic grammar school, and deputy mayor of Ballymena. Furthermore, for a short period of time, Davison's membership of the UDA overlapped with his career in the Ulster Defence Regiment. According to Davison, his respected position and middle-class credentials were typical of many of those central to the formation of the UDA in the area.[70] He recalls his main responsibilities as OC as being '[r]ecruiting members, attending rallies, organising no-go areas and assisting the workers' strike'. According to Davison, the local UDA were unarmed during his short period of involvement, and he defined its main function as providing an effective 'show of strength' when the unionist community felt under threat.[71]

Clifford Davison's story is part of a bigger picture of local 'respectable' support, both explicit and implicit, for the UDA. The lack of direct involvement in any violence on the part of the Ballymena UDA in this period distinguishes it from much of the rest of the organisation, but nonetheless local members were part of a larger pan-Northern Irish coalition, which had members in other districts who were, by the end of 1971, beginning a campaign of violence and murder. When the respectable image of the UDA began to disintegrate, it does appear to have rapidly lost members, such as Davison, and the group played a much less public role in the life of the district thereafter. Nonetheless, the visible role of the UDA raises serious questions about the broader relationship between political unionism and militarist loyalism.

In the bloody 1972–3 period, when predictions of an outright civil war were commonplace, the differing responses of Vanguard and the DUP to the emergence of the UDA are telling. A spokesman for the Ballymena branch of Vanguard saw 'the whole concept of Vanguard in straightforward terms: LAW [the Loyalist Association of Workers] would organise the people on the factory floor; Vanguard would organise people on a community basis, and the UDA would, where necessary, offer protection to communities.'[72] This vision of an emergency coalition of unionists – clearly playing upon the historical memory of 1912 – was, however, rejected for the time being by the DUP. Indeed, the DUP was if anything a moderating influence on unionist anger during this vital period. Reflective of this policy was the DUP chairman Desmond Boal's address to a rally in the town, where he criticised Vanguard for its flirtation with the UDA and for 'encouraging loyalists to break the law', stating that 'to oppose the British Army would be folly'.[73] Clearly the DUP's approval of the 1974 Ulster Workers' Council Strike, and its leading role alongside the UDA in the failed 1977 loyalist sequel, dents any attempt by the party to distance itself totally from the charge that it co-operated with paramilitaries.[74] Nonetheless, the DUP chairman Maurice Morrow has a case when he argues that the party provided a safety valve at pivotal moments, directing unionist anger into democratic politics.[75]

Whatever the moral grounding of the DUP's decision to keep a greater distance than many of its political rivals from loyalist paramilitarism, it was part of a broader moderation that surprised many. Most strikingly, Paisley dissented from the majority unionist position and opposed internment without trial. Reflecting on the escalation and broadening of the PIRA's campaign, Paisley told the local press: 'I do not think that internment is the answer. I believe that there is enough law in Northern Ireland to arrest these men and stand them on trial and have them properly dealt with by the courts.'[76] When seeking to explain this perhaps surprising degree of moderation, it is useful to explore the impact of the parliamentary experience on Paisley's outlook. Initially ostracised as a demagogue by other MPs, Paisley quickly adapted his message and tone; from firebrand preacher and street protester to Westminster parliamentarian.

Notably, Paisley gained the trust and support of the former newspaper publishing magnate and sometime confidant to the establishment, Cecil King. Convinced from an early stage that Paisley was 'no fascist thug', King encouraged the Conservative government to begin serious talks with Paisley, and to consider him a man they could do business with.[77] As Ruth Dudley Edwards notes, the actual influence that the eccentric King had within the circles of power was by this stage fast declining, but to 'a new MP who felt lost and despised at Westminster, it was both comforting and heady to be taken seriously and be treated kindly by people of such status and apparent influence'.[78] The political culture of Westminster and access to people Paisley believed to be influential both appear to have played a role in modifying elements of his agenda. This realignment, which King saw as Paisley 'moving over to a more responsible attitude',[79] remains significant. It highlights the fact that as political Paisleyism evolved from a protest movement to an established parliamentary party, it was necessary to adapt and seek acceptance beyond its base; on a local, regional and national stage.

## THE UWC STRIKE

The period from Paisley's election to Westminster to the signing of the Sunningdale Agreement in December 1973 was, therefore, an uncertain time for the DUP. As a new political party attempting to organise on a national level while facing intense political competition, the DUP struggled to define its agenda. Sunningdale, however, was to give the party a renewed focus. Unionist Party leader Brian Faulkner's signature to the Agreement opened up yet more divisions within his own party, with over one-third of the Ulster Unionist Council (UUC) rejecting the principles of the Agreement from the start.[80] When a Single Transferable Vote–PR election to a reformed Stormont was called in June 1973, the picture of local opinion that emerged was complex. The new electoral system – alien to both the electorate and the parties – the long list of eighteen candidates standing for seven seats, and uncertainties over the position of the Unionist Party, all combined to produce a confusing picture. Paisley's performance in topping the poll – comfortably ahead of William Craig, who finished third – was impressive. But also notable was the pro-Agreement Unionist Party's performance, with a candidate securing second place and the largest party share of the vote.[81] The continuing fluidity of the local unionist vote had once again been highlighted.

Intra-Unionist Party dissent only increased as the government white paper evolved into the Sunningdale Agreement. This climaxed with the Faulknerites' resignation from the party three days after the first meeting of the power-sharing executive, following the Ulster Unionist

Council's rejection of the agreement's provision for a Council of Ire-land.[82] From this fresh schism within the Unionist Party, a new electoral coalition of anti-agreement unionists eventually emerged – the United Ulster Unionist Council (UUUC). Established in January 1974, the UUUC was an alliance between the anti-agreement Unionists, Van-guard and the DUP. The three party leaders – Harry West, Craig and Paisley – helped to co-ordinate a joint election strategy for the decisive Westminster election of February 1974. Agreeing that only one UUUC candidate should stand in each constituency, the coalition won eleven of the twelve Northern Irish seats, decimating the pro-agreement Faulknerites and severely damaging the legitimacy of the fragile power-sharing executive.

As the sitting MP, Paisley was selected for the UUUC in North Antrim, and recorded a 27,631 vote majority over the pro-agreement Unionist, the doyen of British conservative journalism, T.E. Utley.[83] The co-ordination of resources that the UUUC provided was signifi-cant in stabilising the DUP. Furthermore, the temporary truce in party competition between anti-Sunningdale unionists, along with Van-guard's earlier decision not to contest the local government elections of 1973, had given the DUP some much needed local breathing space.

The long-term prospects for a power-sharing agreement based upon the communal consent of both nationalism and unionism looked bleak. The overall results of the February elections pointed towards the col-lapse in unionist confidence in the Sunningdale Agreement. However, while West, Craig and Paisley pondered over how to politically kill off the Agreement, other forces within loyalism instigated more immedi-ate and effective plans. The newly formed UWC's plans for mass in-dustrial action originated from the workers at Northern Ireland's main power plant, Ballylumford, near Larne. This skilled workforce was soon allied with the loyalist paramilitaries.[84] Wary that the politicians might hamper the strike, the trade unionists and paramilitaries only informed Paisley, West and Craig of the definitive plans to wind down Ballylumford's production one day before the strike began.[85] Hesi-tantly at first, the three leaders agreed to support the plans.

The UWC strike in the Ballymena district is reflective of both the strike's wider character and the balance of political power within the UWC. Both locally and nationally, when the strike commenced it was largely co-ordinated by Vanguard and the UDA.[86] Whilst a small number of DUP members featured on organising committees,[87] it remains the case that the most prominent example of unionist collective action of recent times did not feature any significant involvement from the local

MP, Ian Paisley. Unsure of the strike's chances of success and ostracised by much of the UWC executive – who felt closer to Craig – Paisley's minor role in the fourteen days of the strike was reflected in his decision to attend a funeral in Canada during the pivotal days of the stoppage.

The strike's success in bringing down the Sunningdale executive was greeted with a mass rally in Ballymena, where the returning Paisley addressed the crowd alongside a jubilant Craig.[88] In the immediate aftermath, it was uncertain which of the two men would go on to play the bigger political role, but much of the smart money was on Craig. The irony of the UWC's legacy, however, was that those integral to its success – the paramilitaries, loyalist trade unionists and Craig's Vanguard – gained little political capital. Those paramilitaries temporarily inspired to enter electoral politics – most notably the UVF – were met with indifference by the electorate. Within a year of the strike, Harry Murray, the pivotal shop steward at Ballylumford, failed to get elected as a councillor in North Down after going through a dramatic political rethink and standing as an Alliance candidate.[89] After a solid performance in the Convention elections of 1975, Vanguard party unity was shattered by Craig's advocacy of voluntary power-sharing with the SDLP. Believing that other unionists would support his moves, Craig was in fact denounced by Paisley and subsequently by the majority of Vanguard's representatives on the Convention. His career would never recover.

In contrast, Paisley recovered from his marginalisation by the UWC, successfully defeating the rival forces in his constituency. After the flurry of constitutional experiments that characterised the early 1970s, the post-UWC climate was shaped by political deadlock and a series of electoral pacts that reduced intra-unionist party competition. The result was a period of relative stability within unionism.[90] This sterile climate enhanced the standing of Paisley, and enabled his political strategy to stabilise around the core message of opposing any perceived weaknesses emanating from within unionism towards the forces of Irish nationalism. Following the template of 'O'Neill must go', this remained Paisley's most successful mode of operation.

Within the boundaries of these zero-sum politics, Paisley's personal standing increased, even surviving the debacle of the DUP-instigated loyalist strike of 1977. This continued popularity was given clear expression in the first election to the European Parliament in 1979, when Paisley topped the poll with over 170,668 votes, humiliating the two Ulster Unionist candidates.[91] His now unchallenged status as the leading bulwark against Official Unionist 'treachery and betrayal'[92] ensured his position within North Antrim and gave him a huge following throughout Northern Ireland. However, although the DUP had some notable successes expanding its vote throughout the 1980s and 1990s,[93] the party's standing failed to approach that of their leader. The DUP remained mainly a supporting player within unionism. It was to take the Belfast Agreement, its intractable implementation process and its legacy of disarray within the UUP, in order for the DUP to become the leading unionist party. When established at the top table, Paisley displayed a pragmatism and an appetite for power that many, but not all, had failed to see within the young cleric who had transfixed local and national politics in the 1960s.

## CONCLUSION

Analysis of the development of unionist politics in the Ballymena area reveals the multiplicity of factors that shaped the career of Ian Paisley. By placing the movement in the localised context of 1960s Ballymena, the substantial barriers that Paisley first had to overcome in order to gain power become clear. He broke the mould of unionist politics by operating outside the traditional avenues of power: the Orange Order, the Unionist Party and the main Protestant denominations. In doing so, Paisleyism acted both as an agent of social mobility and a force that would play a leading role in the dismantling of unionist unity.

The development of Paisleyism in this period is characterised by the parallel operation of gradual expansion, with institutional and political malleability. Through this process the movement was able to grow from a fringe protest group to become the established political force in the area in less than a decade. This development was shaped within the differing spheres of the church, street protest, local government, Stormont and Westminster. Of special importance to Paisleyism's evolution were the strategic alliances it formed with other forces. Analysis of these alliances, and the wider political life of the Ballymena district, highlights that Paisleyism was at no stage in this period a hegemonic force; indeed, at various stages its future looked uncertain. That Paisley was to strengthen his influence on the district, seeing off rivals such as the Ulster Unionist Party and Vanguard along the way, is further testimony to the influence of evolving ideologies, temporary alliances and the luck intrinsic in the particular interaction between local and national conditions. An understanding of the fluidity of the political context that gave birth to the DUP helps to explain the undoubted shifts in political outlook and discourse it has employed throughout its history. This journey has taken Paisley from greeting Seán Lemass with a barrage of snowballs, to greeting Bertie Ahern with a warm embrace; from the stark anti-Catholicism of the *Protestant Telegraph* to a desire 'to be part of the wonderful healing in this province today'.[94]

NOTES

I would like to thank all the interviewees for their time and assistance.

1. BBC Online, www.news.bbc.co.uk/1/hi/northern_ireland/7221270.stm, accessed 20 October 2009.
2. *Ballymena Times*, 4 February 2008. Quote from ex-DUP member Councillor Samuel Gaston.
3. *Newsletter*, 1 February 2008. Quote from Ruby Gillespie, former long-standing DUP member and friend of the Paisley family.
4. Ibid. By February 2008 six councillors had left the DUP in protest over St Andrews, eventually resulting in an Ulster Unionist becoming mayor. Most defectors were to join ex-DUP Member of the European Parliament Jim Allister's new party, Traditional Unionist Voice.
5. Steve Bruce, *Paisley: Religion and Politics in Northern Ireland* (Oxford: Oxford University Press, 2007), p.118.
6. ARK Northern Ireland Elections, www.ark.ac.uk/elections/dna.html, accessed 20 October 2009.
7. Ibid.
8. Ibid.
9. Clifford Smyth, *Paisley: Voice of Protestant Ulster* (Edinburgh: Scottish Academic Press, 1987), p.106.
10. Northern Ireland General Register Office, *Census of Population, 1971: County Reports* (Belfast: Her Majesty's Stationery Office, 1973).
11. Stormont boundaries taken from www.election.demon.co.uk/stormont/boundaries.html, accessed 24 October 2009. Outskirts of Ballymena Rural District Council fell within the boundaries of the Antrim and Larne Stormont constituencies.
12. ARK Northern Ireland Elections, www.ark.ac.uk/elections/dna.html, accessed 20 October 2009.
13. For an authoritative account of the Independent Unionist tradition, see Colin Reid, 'Protestant Challenges to the "Protestant State": Ulster Unionism and Independent Unionism in Northern Ireland, 1921–39', *Twentieth-Century British History*, vol. 19, no. 4 (2008), pp.419-45.
14. See Graham Walker, *A History of the Ulster Unionist Party* (Manchester: Manchester University Press, 2004).
15. Alan Greer, *Rural Politics in Northern Ireland* (Aldershot: Avebury, 1996), p.2.
16. The specific circumstances surrounding Paisley's decision to leave the Orange Order are unclear, but Smyth suggests he did so in 1962 due to a dispute with a Presbyterian minister in the Order. Smyth, *Paisley*, p.10. Paisley retained links with the much smaller Independent Orange Order.
17. See Henry Patterson and Eric Kaufmann, *Unionism and Orangeism in Northern Ireland since 1945: The Decline of the Loyal Family* (Manchester: Manchester University Press, 2007), pp.63–88; James Greer, 'Unionist Politics and the Suffocation of O'Neillism' in Olivier Coquelin, Patrick Galliou and Thierry Robin (eds), *Political Ideology in Ireland* (Newcastle upon Tyne: Cambridge Scholars Publishing, 2009).
18. Northern Ireland General Register Office, *Census of Population, 1971: County Reports* (Belfast: Her Majesty's Stationery Office, 1973).
19. *Guardian*, 17 February 2001.
20. Northern Ireland General Register Office, *Census of Population, 1971*.
21. See Peter Brooke, *Ulster Presbyterianism: The Historical Perspective, 1610–1970* (Dublin: Gill & Macmillan, 1987).
22. Ian McBride, *Scripture Politic: Ulster Presbyterians and Irish Radicalism in the Late Eighteenth Century* (Oxford: Oxford University Press, 1998), p.92.

23. Myrtle Hill, *The Time of the End: Millenarian Beliefs in Ulster* (Belfast: Belfast Society, 2001), p.51.
24. Clifford Smyth, 'The DUP as a Politico-Religious Organisation', *Irish Political Studies*, vol. 1, no. 1 (1986), p.35.
25. Ian Paisley, *This We Shall Maintain* (Belfast: the author, 1968).
26. *Ballymena Observer*, 7 August 1959.
27. Bruce, *Paisley*, pp.76–7.
28. *Protestant Telegraph*, 24 September 1966.
29. *Protestant Telegraph*, 16 November 1968.
30. *Protestant Telegraph*, 13 May 1967.
31. Bruce, *Paisley*, p.79.
32. For a detailed examination of O'Neill's style of government, see Marc Mulholland, *Northern Ireland at the Crossroads* (Basingstoke: Macmillan, 2000).
33. Bruce, *Paisley*, pp.83–9.
34. *Ballymena Observer*, 4 August 1966.
35. *Ballymena Observer*, 11 August 1966.
36. *Protestant Telegraph*, 7 January 1967
37. Interview with P.J. McAvoy, 30 August 2008. SDLP Ballymena Councillor.
38. Interview with Roy Gillespie, 20 August 2008. Ballymena DUP Councillor, 1973–2007. Traditional Unionist Voice Councillor 2007–present.
39. *Ballymena Observer*, 1 June 1967.
40. Interview with P.J. McAvoy, 30 August 2008.
41. Rosemary Harris, *Prejudice and Tolerance in Rural Ulster: A Study of Neighbours and Strangers in a Border Community* (Manchester: Manchester University Press, 1972), pp.125–31.
42. Interview with Clifford Davison, 23 January 2009.
43. See Derek Birrell, 'Local Government Councillors in Northern Ireland', *Studies in Public Policy*, no. 83 (Strathclyde: University of Strathclyde Press,1981).
44. *Ballymena Observer*, 25 May 1967.
45. Eric Kaufmann, *The Orange Order: A Contemporary Northern Ireland History* (Oxford: Oxford University Press, 2007), p.5; Patterson and Kaufmann, *Unionism and Orangeism in Northern Ireland since 1945*, pp.17–62.
46. Interview with Lyle Cubbitt, 28 August 2008. Former Ballymena Unionist Party member; later prominent in Vanguard and the Traditional Unionist Voice.
47. *Protestant Telegraph*, 25 April 1970.
48. *Ballymena Observer*, 11 April 1968.
49. Interview with Robert Coulter, 9 August 2008. Ulster Unionist Member of the Legislative Assembly (MLA) for North Antrim.
50. Graham Walker, 'The Ulster Unionist Party and the Bannside By-Election 1970', *Irish Political Studies*, vol. 19, no. 1 (summer 2004), pp.59–73.
51. Interview with Michael Farrell, 6 February 2009.
52. *Ballymena Observer*, 27 February 1969.
53. Ibid.
54. W.D. Faulkes, *Northern Ireland: A Political Directory* (London: BBC Publications, 1983), p.264.
55. Walker, 'Bannside By-Election', p.62.
56. ARK, 'North Antrim Elections 1950–70', www.ark.ac.uk/elections/dna.htm, accessed 28 November 2009.
57. Steve Bruce, *God Save Ulster!* (Oxford: Clarendon Press, 1986), p.64.
58. Smyth, *Paisley*, p.30.
59. CAIN, 'Abstracts on Organisations', www.cain.ulst.ac.uk/othelem/organ/dorgan.htm, accessed 30 November 2009.
60. *Ballymena Observer*, 19 April 1973.
61. David Calvert, *A Decade of the DUP* (Belfast: Crown Publications, 1981), pp.6–7; see also Bruce, *Paisley*, pp.102–3.
62. *Ballymena Observer*, 30 March 1972.
63. See Ulster Vanguard, *Community of the British Isles* (Belfast: Vanguard Publications, 1973); and *Ulster a Nation* (Belfast: Vanguard Publications, 1972).
64. See Malachi O'Doherty, *The Telling Year: Belfast, 1972* (Dublin: Gill & Macmillan, 2007).
65. See Ian Wood, *Crimes of Loyalty: A History of the UDA* (Edinburgh: Edinburgh University Press, 2006).

66. Henry McDonald, *UDA: Inside the Heart of Loyalist Terror* (Harmondsworth: Penguin, 2004), p.5 suggests that the figure for UDA 'supporters' was 40,000. A similar figure is given by Gordon Gillespie in 'Loyalist Politics and the Ulster Workers Council Strike of 1974' (unpublished doctoral thesis, Queens University Belfast, 1994), p.8. CAIN, 'Abstracts on Organisations' states that 'At its peak in the mid-1970s, the UDA could organise 30,000 members on the streets of Belfast.' See www.cain.ulst.ac.uk/othelem/organ/uorgan.htm, accessed 20 January 2010.

67. *Ballymena Observer*, 15 June 1972.

68. Interview with Clifford Davison, 23 January 2009.

69. *Irish News*, 15 May 2006.

70. Interview with Clifford Davison, 23 January 2009.

71. Ibid.

72. Ballymena Vanguard policy statement. See James McKibbon, 'Ulster Vanguard: A Sociological Profile' (unpublished doctoral thesis, Queens University Belfast, 1996), p.103.

73. *Ballymena Observer*, 23 March 1972.

74. For differing analyses of the relationship between Paisleyism and violence, see Bruce, *Paisley*, pp.209–45; Margaret O'Callaghan and Catherine O'Donnell, 'The Northern Ireland Government, the Paisleyite Movement and Ulster Unionism in 1966', *Irish Political Studies*, vol. 21, no. 12 (2006), pp.203–22.

75. Interview with Baron Maurice Morrow, 6 February 2009. DUP Chairman and MLA for Fermanagh and South Tyrone.

76. *Ballymena Observer*, 18 February 1971.

77. Cecil King, *The Cecil King Diary, 1970–1974* (London: Jonathan Cape, 1975), p.138.

78. Ruth Dudley Edwards, *Newspapermen: Hugh Cudlipp, Cecil Harmsworth King and the Glory Days of Fleet Street* (London: Pimlico, 2004), p.401. Dudley Edwards portrays Provisional IRA leaders Joe Cahill and Dáithí Ó Conaill as having a similar 'naïve' trust in the Kings' influence, pp.401–4.

79. King, *Cecil King Diary*, p.110.

80. Patterson and Kaufmann, *Unionism and Orangeism in Northern Ireland since 1945*, p.158.

81. ARK, 'North Antrim Elections 1973–82', www.ark.ac.uk/elections/dna.htm, accessed 30 November 2009.

82. Patterson and Kaufmann, *Unionism and Orangeism in Northern Ireland since 1945*, p.165.

83. ARK, 'North Antrim Elections 1973–82', www.ark.ac.uk/elections/dna.htm, accessed 30 November 2009.

84. For full details on the strike, see Gillespie, 'Loyalist Politics and the Ulster Workers Council Strike'; Robert Fisk, *The Point of No Return: The Strike Which Broke the British in Ulster* (London: Andre Deutsch, 1975).

85. Fisk, *Point of No Return*, p.48.

86. Interview with David Burnside, 27 March 2008. Former Ulster Unionist MLA for South Antrim and Vanguard press officer, 1974–7. Interview with Clifford Davison, 23 January 2009. Interview with Lyle Cubbit, 28 August 2008.

87. Interview with UWC Ballymena committee member, 20 August 2008. Interviewee requested to remain anonymous.

88. *Ballymena Guardian*, 6 June 1974.

89. Gordon Gillespie, 'The Legacy of the UWC Strike', paper given at 'Between the Strikes: Northern Ireland, 1974–81', symposium held at Queens University Belfast, 7 November 2009.

90. Walker, *History of the Ulster Unionist Party*, pp.221–8.

91. ARK, 'European Elections', www.ark.ac.uk/elections/fe79.htm, accessed 20 January 2010.

92. *Independent*, 27 February 1999. Paisley's description of David Trimble's leadership of the Ulster Unionist Party, www.independent.co.uk/arts-entertainment/the-man-of-peace-known-as-the-reverend-ian-paisley-1073372.html, accessed 20 January 2010.

93. By 1983 the party had consolidated three Westminster seats; Paisley being joined by Peter Robinson in East Belfast and Rev. William McCrea in Mid-Ulster.

94. *Guardian*, 8 May 2007, Ian Paisley at the reopening of the Stormont Assembly, 8 May 2007, www.guardian.co.uk/uk/2007/may/08/northernireland.northernireland, accessed 1 December 2009.

# Index